Homeowners and Neighborhood Reinvestment

HOMEOWNERS AND NEIGHBORHOOD REINVESTMENT

George C. Galster

Duke Press Policy Studies

Duke University Press

Durham and London 1987

© 1987 Duke University Press
All rights reserved
Printed in the United States of America
on acid-free paper ∞
Library of Congress Cataloging-in-Publication Data
Galster, George C., 1948–
Homeowners and neighborhood reinvestment.
(Duke Press policy studies)
Bibliography: p.
Includes index.
1. Dwellings—Valuation. 2. Dwellings—Maintenance
and repair—Economic aspects. 3. Home ownership.
4. Neighborhood. I. Title. II. Series.
HD1377.G34 1987 307.3'36 87-13448
ISBN 0-8223-0725-1

Contents

Tables and Figures

FIGURES

Acknowledgments

Many people deserve copious thanks for their contributions to this book. It is unfortunate that words are so limited in their ability to express gratitude. Let what follows only be suggestive, therefore.

A dozen undergraduate students performed the most crucial (but not thankless) task for this research: personally interviewing homeowners and coding their responses. The Wooster interviewers were: Terry Barclay, Paul Benson, Julie Dickson, Marilyn Duker, Nancy Homans, Marti Keiser, and Rob Stetson. The Minneapolis interviewers were: Susan Dahlgren, Susan Graf, Andrea Hanson, Laura Kasdorf, and Lori Moline. The energy that they lavished on their task was remarkable. The worth of the findings reported in this book is due fundamentally to their careful treatment of raw data.

The College of Wooster provided lavish amounts of support over an extended period. Its Research Leave program supplied invaluable resources of time and the opportunity to interact with new colleagues. Its Faculty Development program provided financial assistance for conducting the Minneapolis interviews. And its usual provision of computer and clerical assistance made the analysis and write-up feasible. Finally, the ongoing personal encouragement received from administration officers supplied critical psychological stimuli. It is through such multifaceted generosity that the College of Wooster clearly demonstrates its commitment to the professional enrichment of its faculty.

The clerical assistance in developing this complicated manuscript was immense. Many thanks are due: Linda Farmer, Sally Fetzer, Jennifer Fowler, Mimi Moore, Jean Shunk, and Charlotte Wahl. Their work was unstintingly accurate, professional, and pleasantly transmitted.

Several friends epitomized what it means to be a professional colleague. Professors William Apgar and John Kain of Harvard University and Robyn Phillips of the University of California at San Diego shared numerous useful conversations with me during the formative stages of several ideas that later became formalized in this book. Professors Marcus Pohlmann of Rhodes College and Phillip Clay of MIT provided helpful comments on particular chapters. Professors David Varady of Cincinnati University and John Yinger of Syracuse University each read an early draft of the entire manuscript. They supplied voluminous, detailed, useful suggestions on all aspects of the work's analysis and presentation. I am in my colleagues' debt for their commitment of time and creativity. The book has been strengthened considerably through their inputs.

But one colleague and friend must be singled out. My interest in home-owners, housing upkeep, and neighborhood change was first piqued in 1975 by my College of Wooster sociologist colleague, Garry Hesser. Together we designed and conducted the homeowner survey in Wooster that same year. In subsequent years we had innumerable discussions about conceptual and empirical issues surrounding the topic. Those resulted in several coauthored journal articles in the areas of residential satisfaction and home upkeep behavior, which proved to be prototypes for the investigations presented in this book. When Professor Hesser moved to Augsburg College in Minneapolis he replicated the homeowner survey there, and was kind enough to share these data and other details of Minneapolis housing policies with me. Over the years he has provided unflagging support for this research by both words and actions. Indeed, he was the one who taught a narrowly trained economist the importance of interdisciplinary analysis and in particular the crucial roles that sociological aspects of the neighborhood play. In a very fundamental sense this book could not have been written without Garry Hesser.

The final acknowledgment is reserved for my ever-present, ever-supportive foundation: my family. They tolerated many summers and evenings with a frequently absent, distracted, and frustrated husband and father as a result of the research. I am amazed by their grace and forbearance. To Patricia, Geoffrey, and Joshua go my deepest thanks.

George C. Galster
July 1986

1 Introduction

Neighborhoods, Reinvestment Policy, and the Homeowner

The vast majority of Americans reside in homes but *live* in neighborhoods. The demographic, socioeconomic, and physical characteristics of the areas immediately surrounding peoples' dwellings clearly are crucial determinants of the well-being of all but the most reclusive residents. And what happens to these characteristics over time is never certain. Many neighborhoods retain their essential character for generations. Others seem to deteriorate, either gradually as blight nibbles away at a once-healthy environment, or suddenly as some traumatic event such as racial transition or a distasteful nonresidential land use impinges upon them. Still others, after languishing for years in a decayed state, are miraculously rejuvenated as a new set of residents move in and renovate the homes.

Because the neighborhood is so crucial to the quality of urban life, the questions raised by these complicated patterns of stability, decline, and rebirth capture the attention of citizens, analysts, and policymakers alike. Is neighborhood decay inevitable as the resident population ages? To what degree is home reinvestment dependent upon owners' financial wherewithal? Is the level of maintenance of property tied to the race of the owner? Do older structures inexorably decay and therefore erode the neighborhood environment? Are housing reinvestments always discouraged in deteriorated neighborhoods? What role, if any, do social norms and interrelationships in the neighborhood play in encouraging home upkeep? How does the presence of nonresidential land use in the area affect investment decisions? Do residents have to be satisfied with their neighborhood before they are willing to reinvest? To what extent do the actions of one homeowner influence the behavior of others nearby? Does a rapid turnover of ownership lead to decay? What role do owners' expectations have in shaping their investment choices? What happens if ownership passes from owner-occupant to absentee owners?

How these questions are answered will crucially shape the sorts of public policies that are developed to ensure an adequate level of neighborhood reinvestment. For example, if elderly homeowners were found to be particularly prone to undermaintain their dwellings, special upkeep assistance might be designed for them, or they might be encouraged to move into different, more easily maintained quarters. If the willingness to reinvest were present, but the financial capability to do so were absent, the public sector might institute a program of home repair grants. If willingness to reinvest were absent due to pessimism about neighborhood trends, policies to boost confidence through investments in new sidewalks, lighting, and plantings in the area might be suggested. If rapid racial transition were proved deleterious to housing upkeep, strategies to promote gradual, widely dispersed integration would be indicated.

Whether for lofty purposes (protecting the commonweal from the vagaries of the unfettered market) or more prosaic ones (preserving the property tax base), there is no doubt of the consistent interest shown by public policymakers at all levels of government in spurring neighborhood reinvestment. What is less consistent are the answers to the above questions implicit in the spectrum of programs that have been promulgated over the years (see Strickland and Judd 1982). At the federal level we have witnessed such initiatives as Model Cities, the Community Development Act, the Community Reinvestment Act, and housing rehabilitation programs like Section 8 and Homesteading. At the local level, efforts embodying such diverse components as housing and zoning regulations, public infrastructure improvements, subsidized grants and loans for home repairs, and incentives for homeownership have been observed.

Have these policies proved to be an effective use of public resources? Clearly, an answer can be found only after a careful analysis of their impact on the preeminent group of investors in neighborhood housing: owner-occupants of single-family homes—the "homeowners." Indeed, at the aggregate level, the magnitude of the actions that homeowners regularly undertake to maintain, upgrade, or downgrade the quality of their homes commends them as the largest single group of housing producers in the nation. In recent years homeowners have spent over $30 billion annually on maintenance, repairs, and improvements, or almost $700 per dwelling. This represents about two-thirds of all such expenditures on the existing stock of residential dwellings, and about three-fourths of the annual value of new construction of single-family homes. Thus, in large measure the future of our housing stock, and, by implication, of most of our urban neighborhoods, rests with the homeowners.

It is the fundamental premise of this book that we must understand the behaviors of homeowners regarding the upkeep of their dwellings if we are to comprehend the origins of neighborhood change and to develop appropriate public policy responses to such dynamics. Will homeowners in a given neighborhood maintain their dwellings at constant quality and choose to remain in them for extended periods? If so, a neighborhood will tend to remain stable both in terms of physical quality and of household composition. Will homeowners upgrade their dwellings, thus enhancing the physical environment as well as local property values, and perhaps encourage thereby the displacement of less well-off renter households in the neighborhood? Or will homeowners allow their homes to deteriorate, hastening their occupancy by lower-income homeowners or even conversion to absentee-owned rental dwellings?

The decision by homeowners to maintain or alter the quality of their homes (hereafter called "upkeep") is a complex one indeed. Even though the home typically represents a significant financial asset for the homeowner, the homeowner's household derives current use from living in the shelter over and above its eventual market value. Furthermore, the decision to sell the asset is typically connected with moving the household to a different dwelling. Thus, the housing upkeep calculus involves an amalgam of investment, consumption, and expected mobility considerations by the homeowner.

The individual home is an important item of consumption, both in terms of the portion of the household budget devoted to it, and as a complement to a wide array of other economic and social activities undertaken by homeowners. But the consumption of housing is unique because the satisfaction or sense of well-being gained from it does not depend solely on the quantitative and qualitative characteristics of the individual occupied structure and the parcel on which it is located. In addition, the neighborhood in which the house is located plays a vital role in determining the consumption (as well as asset) value of the dwelling. However, unlike features of the individual structure and parcel, neighborhood characteristics are largely beyond the control of the individual homeowner. Two distinct dimensions of the neighborhood can be identified that may impinge on the use value and asset value of the dwelling. The *physical-demographic* dimension consists of such things as the condition of neighboring structures, quality of local public services, air pollution levels, and the characteristics of neighboring households like socioeconomic status, age, family composition, and race. The *social-interactive* dimension refers to the nature and intensity of social interrelationships between the homeowner and the neighbors.

To add even more to the complexity, the social-interactive dimension may play a role beyond influencing a homeowner's enjoyment from the home. Both directly and indirectly, the social neighborhood can influence the homeowner's upkeep decision. Directly, a strong sense of neighborhood social cohesion can encourage homeowners to maintain or upgrade their property, and can discourage them from falling below neighborhood norms for minimal housing quality. Indirectly, homeowners' values, perceptions, and expectations, which form the basis of their up-keep calculus, may be altered by the social-interactive dimension of neigh-borhood; "confidence" may be instilled where neighbors identify closely with one another and the collective interest.

Finally, the vulnerability of housing to neighborhood effects, coupled with its extreme structural durability, means that current upkeep deci-sions are based heavily on expectations about the future that typically are held with some uncertainty. Estimates must be made as to if, how, and when the neighborhood will change, and whether plans for duration of tenure in the area should be revised. How the market will eventually evaluate any contemplated modifications to the dwelling must also be ascertained.

In sum, to comprehend adequately the upkeep activities by home-owners it is necessary to develop theoretical and empirical models that take account of the complexities flowing from the special nature of owner-occupied housing: the dual role played by the homeowner as housing consumer and investor, the significance of perception and expectation, and the influences of the physical, demographic and social-interactive dimensions of the neighborhood. In the face of this complexity, previous scholarly analyses have unfortunately suffered from a case of disciplinary myopia. The analyses of economists have attempted to specify rigorous theoretical models of homeowners' upkeep behavior, but have assumed away crucial aspects, like joint consumption-investment considerations, expectations, and neighborhood social-interactive characteristics, in order to facilitate mathematical manipulation (see Dildine and Massey 1974, Mendelsohn 1977, Ingram and Oron, 1977). Analyses with a sociological or community-organizing focus have stressed the importance of social relationships, but have provided neither a clear behavioral model through which such relationships may work nor any compelling empirical evidence of their independent influence on upkeep; (see Ahlbrandt and Cun-ningham 1979, Clay 1979, Taub, Taylor, and Dunham 1984). Urban planners have focused on housing upkeep in the broader context of neigh-borhood change, but have placed great weight on factors like confidence, without making clear the implicit behavioral assumptions, and have sup-ported their claims only with casual empiricism (see Public Affairs Coun-seling 1975; Goetze 1976, 1979; Downs 1981).

Given these piecemeal approaches, it is not surprising that conventional analyses about homeowners and neighborhood reinvestment are rife with claims that seem plausible on the surface. For example: lower-income owners are more likely to let their houses visibly decay; home upkeep is purely a matter of economics; long-term residents are good for upkeep because they are "committed to the area"; owners always invest more

when they foresee property values rising, and vice versa; satisfied homeowners will invest more in their homes; nonresidential land uses nearby
discourage upkeep; public subsidies for home improvements áre wasteful
because they merely substitute for private funds that would have been
invested in the absence of subsidies. Unfortunately, none of these state-
ments is correct.

This book represents an attempt to bridge the fragmented set of earlier
investigations and provide a comprehensive, multidisciplinary treatment
of homeowners' housing upkeep behavior. It explores the possibility of
influencing this behavior through public policies, always taking into account the larger context of neighborhood change. In the process the fallacies embodied in the aforementioned "conventional wisdoms" are revealed.

More specifically, the approach considers five sets of characteristics that
underpin homeowners' behavior: 1) dwelling, 2) owner, 3) physical-demographic neighborhood, 4) social-interactive neighborhood, 5) public policy. These characteristics shape home upkeep decisions both directly and
indirectly. They do so first by influencing homeowners' evaluations of
their dwellings and their neighborhoods, and their expectations about
future changes in the area. All these subjective attributes contribute to the
formulation of homeowners' mobility plans—expectations about how long
they will continue to reside in the neighborhood. In addition, expectations
about neighborhood and mobility ultimately affect housing investment.
The book explains each of the causal linkages theoretically and then estimates their parameters empirically, using multiple regression analyses of
data collected from two urban housing markets.

Guideposts for the Reader

Although this book is intended to be of interest to a wide spectrum of
analysts, researchers, and policymakers, not all of its chapters may be
appropriate for every reader. The following is intended to provide
guideposts for those who may wish to focus on sections in which they have
particular expertise or interest.

The book is divided into three main sections. The first, consisting of
chapters 2 and 3, involves theoretical analyses of homeowners' housing
upkeep behavior. Chapter 2 provides the overall conceptual framework
that underpins all subsequent chapters. It is written in nontechnical terms
and should be accessible to all readers. A rigorous theoretical model of
upkeep behavior is specified in chapter 3. Of special note is this model's
incorporation of neighborhood social interaction into the economic upkeep calculus, and its ability to predict different sorts of strategic interac-

tions between homeowners based on their preferences and the circumstances in which they find themselves. Indeed, this model supplies a rationale for several empirical observations noted in later chapters that are inexplicable by conventional theories. Chapter 3 is highly technical, however, and should be omitted by readers unfamiliar with formal microeconomics.

The book's second section (chapters 4 through 10) presents empirical analyses designed to quantify the relationships posited and provide a test of the general theoretical framework. Data come from replicated homeowner surveys conducted in 1975 in Wooster, Ohio, and in 1980 in Minneapolis, Minnesota. These data bases and the sampling and interviewing procedures employed are described in chapter 4. Readers uninterested in such details may skip this chapter. An empirical investigation into the various aspects of the neighborhood is conducted in chapter 5. Factor analysis is used to discern common dimensions represented in an extensive series of variables proxying for numerous physical-demographic and social-interactive characteristics of the neighborhood. Different spatial scales of neighborhoods are also considered, ranging from adjacent dwellings, to blocks, to several square blocks, to census tracts. The results yield a rich, intuitively pleasing array of distinct neighborhood components that are employed as explanatory variables in subsequent models. Other independent variables that proxy for characteristics of the homeowner, the occupied dwelling, and public policies to encourage home upkeep are defined here as well. Those concerned about how neighborhood may be defined operationally should find chapter 5 of special interest. Others may simply refer to the glossary of variables found in the appendix.

Chapters 6 through 8 develop both theoretically and empirically three subcomponents of the conceptual model of home upkeep behavior: residential satisfaction, neighborhood expectations, and homeowner mobility plans. These three aspects of homeowners have frequently been investigated in their own rights (over and above their ultimate effect upon home upkeep), and will also be viewed in a similar light in these chapters. That is, each chapter contains an in-depth theoretical exploration into a given subcomponent, a review of previous empirical work on the subject, and a multiple regression analysis employing both data bases. Readers concerned only about how these three factors influence upkeep behavior may proceed directly to chapter 9.

The primary concern of the book, home upkeep activity, is empirically investigated in chapter 9. The multiple regression model employs as independent variables characteristics of the homeowner, the dwelling, both physical-demographic and social-interactive neighborhood dimensions, and (for the Minneapolis sample) public subsidies for home upkeep. The intervening variables are the three subcomponents noted above: homeowner's evaluations, expectations, and mobility plans. Three alternative dependent variables are employed as measures of upkeep: the probability of choosing an upkeep strategy involving the expenditure of funds, the amount of expenditure once such a strategy has been chosen, and the probability of pursuing a strategy resulting in exterior home defects. As with chapters 6 through 8, chapter 9 presumes a familiarity with multiple regression models.

Chapter 10 provides a compendium of the empirical results gleaned from part 2, and is thus recommended for readers unfamiliar with or uninterested in the details of the regression models. This chapter also demonstrates how these results can be used to predict changes in the aggregate home upkeep levels in a neighborhood, given alterations in that area's physical-demographic and/or social-interactive character. Of special interest is the application of the model results to understanding the consequences of neighborhood succession, racial transition, and gentrification.

Perhaps the most dramatic findings in this regard are those involving variables that have never been employed previously in empirical analyses of home upkeep. The degree to which the individual homeowner "identifies" with the neighborhood and the degree to which all homeowners in the neighborhood are socially "cohesive" prove to interact synergistically in affecting upkeep investments. Homeowners' expectations about qualitative changes in the neighborhood also powerfully affect upkeep strategies in ways that tend to reinforce the changes foreseen, thereby creating "self-fulfilling prophecies." On the other hand, in lower-valued neighborhoods, homeowners' expectations about property value changes stimulate behaviors that tend to countervene the expected change, e.g., inflationary expectations result in deferred upkeep, and vice versa. Thus the type of expectation and the context in which it is held both matter.

The third section of the book (chapters 11 through 13) is concerned explicitly with public policy and neighborhood reinvestment by homeowners. Chapter 11 argues that public intervention in the arena of home upkeep can be justified in principle on both efficiency and equity grounds. In light of the evidence summarized in chapter 10, it assesses whether specific programs are in fact both efficient and equitable. Focuses are on public efforts to augment neighborhood reinvestment via such instruments as infrastructure investments, housing and zoning regulations, neighborhood social organizations, anti-redlining efforts, racial stabilization policies, and media campaigns to "bolster neighborhood confidence."

Chapter 12 focuses on a particular policy tool that has been employed extensively in Minneapolis (and elsewhere) to abet home upkeep activity of moderate-income homeowners: subsidized loans and grants. Benefit-cost analyses are conducted for both policies, and the results are used to formulate guidelines for an optimal rehabilitation grant and loan program that could serve as the foundation for neighborhood policy. Readers involved in formulating, administering, or evaluating similar types of policies should find this chapter of special interest.

In chapter 13 the analysis shifts from a consideration of variations across homeowners to one of cross-tenure differences in the home upkeep behavior of owner-occupiers versus absentee owners. Drawing upon analyses in part 2, theoretical arguments for the comparative superiority of homeowners' upkeep efforts are made, and empirical tests provide conclusive support. The policy implication drawn is that home investment and neighborhood maintenance may be substantially encouraged by actions that expand opportunities for homeownership, especially among lower-income households. Chapter 13 thus should be read by those concerned with the social benefits derived from homeownership, and with policies designed to stimulate it.

The final chapter summarizes the main findings of the work and makes suggestions for future research. It then places the observed individual behaviors, along with aggregate outcomes for a given neighborhood and mutual outcomes for an entire metropolitan system of neighborhoods, into a single conceptual framework. It argues that effective policies for neighborhood development must be designed with such a holistic, systemic view in mind. The central implication is that the cornerstone of neighborhood reinvestment policy should be a people-oriented strategy of rehabilitation and homeownership subsidies, not a place-oriented strategy of infrastructure or other locationally specific investments.

Although much of the analysis carries a clear "economics" flavor, it synthesizes the theoretical and empirical work of a variety of disciplines—particularly sociology, geography, social-psychology, and urban planning. Indeed, a clear message of this book is that the richness of the subject cannot be fully comprehended without a cross-disciplinary perspective. It is the attempt to formulate rigorously and estimate empirically just such a cross-disciplinary model that distinguishes this work. It is hoped that this model can provide a wide variety of readers with significant new insights into a behavior that is crucial to the residential quality of life for most Americans, and that such insights will lead to the development of more effective public policies.

I Theoretical Analyses

2 Neighborhoods, Homeowners, and Housing Upkeep: A Framework for Analysis

Establishing the Context: The Nature of Housing

Housing is a unique commodity. It has at least four attributes that distinguish it from other goods: extreme durability, imperfect malleability, susceptibility to neighborhood effects, and locational fixity. In concert these four idiosyncrasies shape the particularly complex and intriguing human behavior to be analyzed in this book: actions that maintain or alter the quality of residential structures.

It is only the fact that houses are *extremely durable* that raises the concern over their owners' upkeep behaviors in the first place. Maintenance is not a crucial issue for items that are entirely consumed over a short period. But residential structures can continue to provide (in varying proportions) for indefinite periods such consumable "goods" as shelter, protection, and status. Indeed, even with unexceptional levels of care, houses typically have longer useful lives than any of their individual human owners.

This durability means that a home is valuable both because it directly provides the aforementioned consumable attributes, and also because it likely can be sold to another owner for a nontrivial sum. Thus, the owner not only must assess how well the home meets the individual occupying household's needs, but also how its features are evaluated by a more impersonal marketplace. In short, a house is not only a home but an asset. And it is an asset whose value (to both occupant and market) can be affected considerably by the upkeep investment decisions undertaken by its owner. But, again given durability, these are not once-and-for-all decisions. Maintenance and repairs must typically be conducted at frequent, if sporadic, intervals if they are to have the desired effect of countering the natural trends in structural depreciation due to wear and tear and weathering.

Decisions to alter the structure beyond mere repairs are complicated by the second idiosyncrasy of housing: its *imperfect malleability*. Once built of particular materials on a certain parcel of land with given architectural and mechanical features, a dwelling cannot be easily molded into any alternative configuration that may be desired by an owner. Many potential modifications are totally ruled out by technological infeasibility, others by the excessive financial investment they would entail. Thus, to a large degree, the configuration of a house when it was originally constructed influences the various manifestations into which it can be transformed in the future. The same is true of subsequent additions and alterations made after initial construction: once made, they are not easily undone; they become part of the dwelling's idiosyncratic potentialities and constraints.

This lack of perfect malleability of investments embodied in the physical dwelling means that expectations are relevant. An owner must assess both the current value of a contemplated structural alteration and its future value as well, because the modification will transfigure the dwelling for an extended period.

What's more, imperfect malleability means that what an owner can do to modify the dwelling in response to altered household needs or economic means is limited. Often the limitation is severe enough that the optimal dwelling package desired can more feasibly be obtained by switching to a different structure entirely. This implies that decisions to modify a given house are inextricably bound up with decisions to sell it and move to an alternative one.

The worth of a dwelling, both to its current occupants and to a potential buyer is not, however, determined solely by the physical attributes of the individual structure and the lot on which it is located. Rather, its value is highly susceptible to *neighborhood effects*. These neighborhood effects, sometimes called "externalities" or "spillovers," refer to actions taken by other, proximate individuals or institutions that affect the perceived usefulness or market value of a given dwelling. These effects assume a physical-demographic character. Physical neighborhood effects include such things as an adjacent property owner's failing to maintain the premises, an increase in noise or air pollution, or the introduction of a noncompatible land use nearby. Demographic neighborhood effects occur when there is a change in, for instance, the age, race, or economic-status composition of neighboring households. There is abundant empirical evidence that homeowners perceive such physical-demographic characteristics of their neighborhoods as prime determinants of both their own residential satisfaction (see chapter 6) and their property's market value (Kain and Quigley 1970, 1975; Leven et al. 1976; Galster 1982). Indeed, Birch et al. (1979, 39–40) have found that 71 percent of the homeowners surveyed chose neighborhood over house when confronted with the hypothetical question, "Suppose you found two places that cost the same and the difference was that one was in a neighborhood more to your liking and the other was more what you wanted as housing—which do you think you would finally choose?"

The fact that one individual's well-being is significantly affected by the rather unpredictable behavior of neighboring others raises the possibility of "strategic behavior." It also focuses attention on the role played by a given owner's expectations about behaviors of others and suggests a rationale for developing means by which an individual can better predict and even influence the behavior of neighbors. This search for a possible vehicle by which neighborhood externalities may be "internalized" introduces another dimension of the neighborhood: social interaction and psychological dynamics among neighbors. If a modicum of collective control can be created through social pressures and local norms, the susceptibility of housing to neighborhood effects becomes less onerous.

Finally, most housing is for all practical purposes *fixed* in its *location*.[1] This intensifies the importance of the aforementioned neighborhood effects, for a dwelling cannot easily be transported to a more desirable neighborhood if its original one becomes unsatisfactory. Rather, the household leaves the dwelling, thereby vacating it for another, in-moving household with possibly different preferences, perceptions, or purchasing power. Until demolished, a dwelling thus becomes an enduring physical attribute of an urban space.

Locational fixity also allows for the public sector to influence the attractiveness of a given dwelling. The tax and public service package provided by the political jurisdiction in which the dwelling is located will influence its livability and market value. And public incentives to repair and improve property can be made without fear that the benefits of these efforts may be "exported" to other jurisdictions.

In sum, the nature of the housing commodity specifies the elements of a framework for analyzing behavior related to it. Any theory that attempts to provide a comprehensive analysis of homeowners' housing upkeep behavior must take into account these elements. The following section of this chapter systematically examines these elements and specifies a schematic delineating how they affect an individual homeowner's upkeep decision. The last section expands the analysis to demonstrate how the homeowner's decisions about an individual home influence the neighborhood as a whole, and how neighborhood conditions, in turn, feed back upon subsequent individual behaviors.

Elements of the Homeowner's Housing Upkeep Decision

The framework to be employed in this book for understanding the homeowner's housing upkeep decision is represented diagrammatically in figure 2.1. In figure 2.1 sets of characteristics, attitudes, expectations, and be-

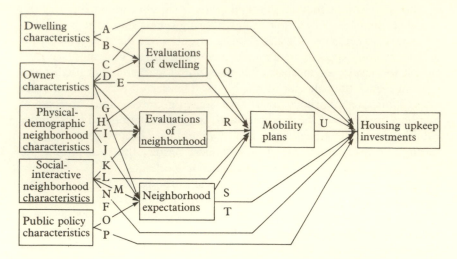

Figure 2.1 Elements of the Homeowner's Housing Upkeep Decision

haviors (all eventually to be specified as empirical variables) are denoted as rectangles, and presumed causal linkages between them are shown as arrows or "paths."

At a given period of observation, the characteristics of the individual, the dwelling, the neighborhood, and any relevant public policies are considered as predetermined (or exogenous). Given all these characteristics, the observer would predict particular evaluations of the current dwelling and neighborhood, and expectations about the future of the neighborhood to be manifested by the homeowner. Given these exogenous characteristics and the evaluations and expectations, the homeowner should evidence certain plans for either remaining in the current location or for moving. All these elements in concert should determine what types of housing upkeep investments are being manifested.

Put differently, the model posits several distinct sets of objective characteristics of the individual and the context as determining several subjective attributes. Together these objective, predetermined elements and subjective, "intervening" elements determine housing upkeep behavior. The causal impacts of objective individual and contextual characteristics upon upkeep may be direct and/or indirect; that is, mediated to greater or lesser degree by the intervening subjective elements.[2]

Consider now in more detail what these various elements are composed of and how they may be interrelated in the context of behavioral assumptions about homeowners. The discussion here will be introductory, suggestive, and nontechnical; a more rigorous mathematical treatment follows in the next chapter.

Overview of Homeowner Behavior

At heart the model posits rational, optimizing decision making on the part of homeowners. That is, homeowners are presumed to maintain or alter their homes in such a way that their perceived well-being is maximized, balancing both immediate and future considerations. (Alternative specifications of homeowner motivations are reviewed at the beginning of chapter 3.) At a given moment the upkeep choices faced by homeowners are threefold: whether to improve the quality of the structure, maintain quality at the current level, or allow quality to decline (either by passive under-maintaining or by active partitioning of the dwelling into one or more rental units). The decision involves both "consumption" and "investment" dimensions for the typical homeowner. First, maintaining or improving structural quality may be seen as increasing "utility" or well-being gained from consuming (i.e., living in) the dwelling, but it requires a sacrifice of income that could be spent otherwise. Reducing housing quality, on the other hand, sacrifices such housing-related utility but allows for greater nonhousing consumption, especially if the generation of added income accompanies the quality decline. Such could be the case if an erstwhile single-family dwelling were subdivided to produce one or more rental properties. A second consideration likely for most homeowners is the wealth effect of such housing investment activity. If utility is placed on the value of the durable housing package as an asset beyond its current value as a consumer good, the calculus of the housing upkeep decision is altered. In other words, spending money on one's home can be considered an investment, because it increases the eventual sales price of the home, and thus the future consumption possibilities of the homeowner.

The homeowner's decision is also related to time. The choice of housing versus nonhousing expenditures cannot be fully understood in the context of a single moment. Because housing is a durable good, spending on it at a given time produces a useful flow of housing-related consumption services as well as an augmented asset value for several periods after this initial time. The degree to which a given housing investment provides continuing consumption and asset benefits in the future depends on the rate of structural depreciation, the homeowner's rate of time preference, and changes in neighborhood conditions. The homeowner's decision thus not only involves choosing the optimal mix of housing and nonhousing expenditures in a given period, but also the optimal pattern of spending in one period versus another.

The intertemporal nature of the housing upkeep decision focuses attention on the central role played by the homeowner's expectations. Expectations about the future costs for housing improvements, the rate of structural depreciation, the interest rate for borrowed funds (i.e., the opportunity cost of nonhousing savings), conditions in the surrounding neighborhood, and the rate of housing-price inflation all affect the perceived utility gained from expenditures on housing, by changing the consumption value of the dwelling being occupied and/or the asset value of the home when it is eventually sold.

Implicit in this discussion of the intertemporal nature of housing upkeep decisions is the decision about mobility. Obviously, a homeowner can adjust the amount of housing consumed by moving to a different dwelling, typically in conjunction with selling the previous home. The well-being gained from pursuing an optimal upkeep strategy on the current dwelling thus must be constantly contrasted with that which can be gained from moving to another dwelling, possibly in a different neighborhood.

Once expectations and mobility plans have been formulated, the homeowner makes an optimal choice of housing versus nonhousing expenditures over the tenure in the dwelling, within the set of constraints formed by both financial limitations of the owner and technological limitations of the structure. The former limitations consist of initial wealth, expected household income flows, and institutionally imposed borrowing constraints. The latter consist of the various architectural and mechanical idiosyncrasies of the physical structure that render alternative dwelling-modification schemes more or less feasible in terms of incremental housing value versus modification cost.

Exogenous Objective Influences

There are five distinct sets of exogenous, objective characteristics that establish the parameters of the homeowner's upkeep-choice problem. The discussion here is meant to be suggestive, not exhaustive; more comprehensive analyses follow in subsequent chapters.

Characteristics of the homeowner directly influence the type of home upkeep strategy chosen and the expenditures allocated to its pursuit (path C from "Owner Characteristics" to "Housing Upkeep Investments" in figure 2.1). The homeowner's preferences for housing and the homeowner's discretionary income are two such characteristics. Those with housing intensive preferences (e.g., homeowners with growing families) gain more relative enjoyment from allocating their income to maintaining or improving their residential environment than from allocating it to other forms of expenditure. And those with higher incomes have an enhanced ability and willingness to spend more both on housing upkeep and on nonhousing consumption, regardless of their relative preferences, assuming housing is a normal good. These two types of homeowners are expected to invest more in housing upkeep, all else equal.

Other homeowner characteristics specify the costs of potential home upkeep strategies. Households containing numerous skilled, able-bodied teenagers or adults likely perceive home maintenance and repair costs as relatively low, because they have an abundance of cheap, efficient labor. Elderly, infirm homeowners, on the other hand, may need to rely on professional contract labor for such upkeep tasks, thereby raising their perceived costs and reducing the attractiveness of upkeep.

Homeowner characteristics may also have indirect impacts upon their upkeep behavior insofar as they influence their evaluations, expectations, and mobility plans (paths D-Q-U, E-U, F-R-U, G-T-S-U from "Owner Characteristics" to "Housing Upkeep Investments" via intervening elements in figure 2.1). Those with higher aspirations or higher self-assessed "needs" would tend to be more critical in evaluating any given occupied dwelling or neighborhood. Just the opposite would be likely for those with fewer alternative residential options: low-income, minority, or female homeowners. Expectations are formed depending on the nature of the information one acquires, and the methods and extent of data acquisition varies by education, income, age, and family status. Finally, whatever their current evaluations and expectations of their residential environment, certain homeowners are likely to formulate distinct mobility plans (path E). Elderly homeowners who have resided many years in their current dwelling may, e.g., perceive high physical and psychic costs of moving, and hence will plan on remaining where they are indefinitely. Young, high-income homeowners with no children and few social attachments to their present location may, on the other hand, formulate plans involving a considerably shorter tenure in the current dwelling, regardless of contextual circumstances.

Characteristics of the dwelling also must be considered as independent contributors to the observed housing upkeep behaviors (path A). Older structures usually deteriorate at a faster rate, thus presenting the homeowner with more frequently needed repairs. Older structures also may be more likely candidates for either upward or downward conversions. Dwellings with particular structural features render certain structural modifications extremely expensive; e.g., those with sagging foundations are unlikely to support the addition of a second-story dormer and those with exposed wiring may not permit the installation of modern appliances or heating and cooling systems. A small lot may preclude the addition of a detached garage or a swimming pool. Larger homes on bigger parcels necessitate larger absolute expenditures to maintain constant quality.

The dwelling also provides the physical context in which the homeowner's subjective evaluation of its adequacy is made. Certain dwelling characteristics may result in any type of occupying household registering dissatisfaction; e.g., extremely small, aged homes that lack certain basic plumbing, heating, or electrical systems. Such dwelling features may indirectly affect the upkeep efforts exerted by altering the homeowner's dwelling satisfaction and resulting mobility plans (paths B-Q-U).

The physical-demographic character of the neighborhood in which a given dwelling is located powerfully influences the type of homeowner upkeep strategies. The value of the dwelling, both as a consumable good in the eyes of the current owner and as an asset as evaluated by the market, is not determined merely by the features of the individual dwelling and the lot on which it is located. This means that the homeowner's perceived payoffs from incremental upkeep investments will depend on the current (as well as future) physical-demographic conditions of the surrounding neighborhood, in conjunction with the homeowner's own preferences and those of the market as a whole (path H). If, for instance, the individual and the rest of the market positively value the socioeconomic status of nearby households, a dwelling in a neighborhood made up of upper-income professionals will be valued more highly (in both consumption and investment aspects) than an identical dwelling in an area of lower-status households. Analogous differentials would be predicted for identical homes in neighborhoods that differ in such things as: racial, ethnic, age, and family-status composition, environmental amenities, local public-service and infrastructure quality, land-use patterns and aggregate housing stock conditions.

But these physical-demographic attributes of the neighborhood not only influence observed upkeep behavior directly, they also provide clues to the homeowner of prospective changes in the milieu (path J). A modest degree of racial integration may fan white homeowners' fears of racial "tipping." The presence of nonresidential land uses may signal a vulnerability of the area to further such encroachments. A crumbling public infrastructure may suggest that the city has written off the area. And the first indicators of reduced property upkeep by other nearby owners may point to the incipient in-migration of lower-income households. All such expectations affect the housing upkeep behavior of the given homeowner.

In addition, the physical-demographic character of the neighborhood can indirectly affect upkeep through altered homeowner evaluations of the adequacy of the residential environment. This in turn can lead to revisions in mobility plans (paths I-R-U). For example, a homeowner may have thought when purchasing the current home that it was "a perfect place for raising my family." But unforeseen trends in the neighborhood in subsequent years may convince this homeowner to move much sooner than contemplated originally.

Finally, the physical-demographic features of the neighborhood can affect homeowners' upkeep activity by influencing the willingness of financial institutions to lend them funds for such. There is a long-standing record of allegations by community groups in lower-income and racially mixed neighborhoods that lending institutions have denied mortgages and home improvement loan applications to their areas on the basis of neighborhood-characteristic criteria that are discriminatory—a process known as "redlining."[3] Analogous claims have been made against home insurers (Advisory Committee 1979). Indeed, such allegations were instrumental in promulgating the legislative responses of the Home Mortgage Disclosure Act and the Community Reinvestment Act in the late 1970s. Whether such institutional practices are illegally discriminatory or rather are based on sound financial principles has been the subject of intense debate, and the empirical evidence is mixed (Listokin and Casey 1980; King 1980; Black and Schweitzer 1980; Schafer and Ladd 1980; Ryker, Pol, and Guy 1984). Nevertheless, it is undeniable that financial institutions assess the collateral of the potential loan (i.e., the home's value) partly on the basis of the surrounding neighborhood's characteristics. Property located in areas having abandoned homes, high poverty rates, and secularly declining home values rationally may be judged as high risk. Homeowners in a neighborhood with such physical-demographic characteristics may, therefore, find it impossible or excessively expensive to obtain financing for major home improvements, in spite of their wishes.

The neighborhood is, however, more than simply a place having particular physical features where particular types of autonomous individuals reside and into which financial resources flow. It is also an arena in which social interaction typically occurs: friendships are made, communal intercourse is carried out, conformity to collective norms is encouraged, and solidarity sentiments are formulated.[4] The key distinguishing feature of owner-occupants as opposed to absentee owners is that the former are directly subject to this social dimension of the neighborhood in which they invest; the latter are not. This means that collectively those in the neighborhood have at least a potential for influencing the upkeep behavior of homeowners residing there.[5] (It is this crucial distinction between owner-occupants and absentee owners that is responsible for much of the observed differences in their upkeep actions, as will be explained in chapter 13.)

Such collective influences can be exerted both blatantly and subtly (path N). Individual behavior that imposes negative externalities on neighbors (e.g., undermaintaining property) may be blatantly greeted with angry phone calls, public scorn, alienated friends, and ostracism from the group. Conversely, upkeep behavior that generates positive externalities may be accompanied by a host of positive social reinforcements. In a more subtle sense, individual homeowners may find over time that they inculcate the values of neighbors, internalize their neighbors' norms, and ultimately identify with their neighbors' interests. These solidarity sentiments encourage individual behaviors that are simultaneously self-serving and group-serving.

The social-interactive dimension of neighborhood may also have two indirect impacts. First, it may reassure each individual owner that all the other homeowners in the neighborhood are likely responding to the same social pressures to maintain dwelling quality. Thus, homeowners in a neighborhood with a great deal of social cohesion may be more likely to be optimistic in their expectations (and in the market's evaluation) of the neighborhood's physical quality and property value projections (paths M-T). Second, it may alter homeowners' expected longevity of tenure. Homeowners who are more attached to their neighborhood by strong familial or friendship ties are less inclined to rupture these connections by moving out of the neighborhood (paths L-U).

Finally, the exogenous influences of public policies may impinge on the homeowner's upkeep calculus. Local governments may, for instance, directly subsidize housing repairs and improvements by providing grants or low-interest loans for this purpose (path P). Or they may enter into association with quasi-public organizations such as Neighborhood Housing Services so as to augment the flow of capital from private financial institutions into particular neighborhoods. More indirectly, the actions of the public sector can greatly influence the expectations held by homeowners in an area and, thereby, their subsequent upkeep activities (q.v. paths O-T). These actions may be substantive or symbolic. Examples of the former include improving neighborhood public parks, streets, lighting, or schools, encouraging the formation of local neighborhood organizations, or rezoning the area to permit or prohibit nonresidential land uses. Illustrations of the latter include the formation of a mayor's neighborhood advisory board with appointees from all neighborhoods, the designation of an official neighborhood X pride week, or the erection of signs proclaiming the boundaries, name, and history of each neighborhood. (These policies will be evaluated more fully in chapters 11 and 12.)

Intervening Subjective Influences

The aforementioned objective characteristics of homeowners, dwellings, neighborhoods, and public policies can affect the observed housing upkeep behavior of homeowners in myriad direct ways as suggested above. But in addition these characteristics determine a variety of subjective evaluations, expectations, and plans held by homeowners, and these features may also contribute to this behavior (paths Q, R, S, T, U in figure

2.1). Indeed, the degree to which these intervening subjective factors serve as conduits for the objective exogenous factors is a key empirical issue to be investigated here.

Homeowners' evaluations of their current dwelling and neighborhood in conjunction determine their sensed level of "residential satisfaction." It is this perception of the adequacy of the residential environment, and not its objective quality in an absolute sense, that is the key predictor of whether a homeowner will continue to reside in the current location or plan to move shortly (paths Q, R). Expectations of future changes in the neighborhood can also alter these mobility plans (path S). For example, homeowners who predict that an "inferior" socioeconomic group will soon begin moving into the neighborhood may decide to move out quickly, so as to avoid both substantial capital losses on their home sales and the personal exposure of their families to such "undesirables." (A detailed model and empirical investigation into the determinants of residential satisfaction will be developed in chapter 6.)

As will be explained more fully in chapter 7, mobility plans are formulated on the basis of personal characteristics, social attachments, evaluations, and expectations. These mobility plans provide a further variable that can help to explain housing upkeep investments (q.v. path U), although not always in an unambiguously predictable way. Compared to those who plan to stay in their dwelling for a considerable period, homeowners who plan to move in the near future would be less concerned about the long-run consequences of current upkeep activities. That is, they would not be present to reap much of the stream of enhanced housing consumption provided by current upkeep, and hence would be less likely to undertake sizable amounts of such. This is especially true if structural modifications to suit the idiosyncratic tastes of the present owner are contemplated. The incipient mover may, however, be likely to undertake cosmetic repairs that enhance the perceived quality of the dwelling by a potential buyer, assuming the seller places weight on the equity value of the home. At the other extreme, if homeowners hold the expectation that they will remain in their dwellings "forever," this seemingly negates any potential asset-enhancing motives for upkeep, unless they place high value on bequests. Part of the perceived value of housing upkeep expenditures is thereby eroded by such an extremely long-run mobility plan. In sum, the relationship between length of expected tenure and housing upkeep likely will depend on the relative weights the homeowner assigns to the consumption versus asset aspects of housing investments, and should be nonlinear.

But all the subjective dimensions of the homeowner are not channeled entirely through mobility plans as their means for influencing upkeep. Quite apart from mobility plans, homeowners' expectations about what

other investors in the neighborhood are likely to do in the future undoubtedly play a vital role in determining levels of upkeep investments (path T).
(The determinants of these expectations will be explored in chapter 8.)
Clearly, the payoffs that one homeowner can expect to reap from investing
(or not investing) in housing upkeep are influenced by the aggregate
amount of housing upkeep undertaken by nearby property owners. Unfortunately for the given homeowner, the actions of other investors cannot be
predicted with certainty. The context for strategic behavior is thus
established.

But what kind of strategies do homeowners employ against their neighbors? The long-standing conventional view has been to posit "minimax"
motives in a classic game-theory framework. From this perspective, homeowners in an uncertain situation try to choose a personal upkeep strategy
so that even if neighboring owners adopt the worst-case option the given
homeowner's loss will be minimized. In practical terms such a strategy
means one of undermaintaining or refraining from unnecessary repairs
and improvements, because any other strategy leaves one vulnerable to
neighbors who do undermaintain. Of course, if all individuals in an area
engage in such a behavior the overall quality of the neighborhood eventually declines, uncertainties intensify, and the strategies result in a self-
fulfilling prophecy (Downs 1981, 16–19). The type of strategic context in
which actions that appear rational to each individual decisionmaker lead to
counterproductive group outcomes has been termed "the prisoners' dilemma" (Rapoport and Chammah 1965), and the inefficient housing upkeep investment patterns that it generates have been thoroughly
investigated.[6]

There is, however, a more recent, contrasting view of strategic behavior: the "threshold model."[7] Though similar to the earlier perspective in
positing that homeowners are motivated by personal financial gain that
can be influenced by the uncertain collective behavior of others nearby,
the threshold model suggests that the individual's optimal upkeep strategy
varies across individuals, and, more importantly, according to the behavior of others. Although the precise relationship differs according to individual characteristics that determine risk aversion, homeowners are presumed to be more disposed to invest in their dwellings when they see other
owners in the neighborhood doing so. The individual's "threshold point"
is that proportion of neighbors investing that will trigger a given individual to invest as well. Depending on the composition of owners in a
neighborhood (i.e., the distribution of their threshold points) the "prisoner's dilemma" may be possible, but only as a special case. In contexts
with high degrees of mutual reassurance (i.e., low threshold points for all)
aggregate upgrading becomes probable when some exogenous factor encourages one individual to upgrade.[8]

The precise form that strategic behavior between homeowners takes in a particular neighborhood is thus an unresolved issue. Yet these interdependent expectations for upkeep investments are undoubtedly significant, and a major goal of both the theoretical and empirical investigations reported here is to shed additional light on the matter. Specifically, a theoretical model will be developed in chapter 3 that allows a prediction not only of the aforementioned sorts of gaming behaviors, but of others as well. The model is based on the homeowner's preferences for both consumption and asset aspects of the home, the initial quality in the neighborhood, and whether the homeowner's expectations involve qualitative changes in the neighborhood or merely property price changes. In overview, it assumes that all homeowners place value on the consumption aspect of the home, and view the quality of the neighborhood as an important contributor to livability. As a result the perceived consumption value of upkeep will be directly related to optimism about changes in neighborhood quality. But it further assumes that the weight placed on the asset aspect grows immensely when homeowners perceive that they can expect a much smaller capital gain from selling the home now than they thought would be forthcoming when they purchased it. If the homeowner resides in a neighborhood where there is a discrepancy between currently expected capital gain and originally expected capital gain, unconventional responses can be predicted. Optimism about property inflation may make homeowners confident that they can attain their capital goals easily, even with little upkeep effort. Pessimism about property inflation may lead them to intensify their upkeep efforts, so as to salvage some minimal gain. In higher-quality neighborhoods, however, homeowners may feel confident that minimal capital gain expectations will be met, regardless of short-run vagaries of the housing market. As a result, their upkeep behavior may be little affected by their property value expectations. Suffice it to note here that empirical estimates shown in chapter 9 will provide strong supporting evidence for these hypotheses.

From Individual to Group and Back Again:
Individual Behavior and Neighborhood Change

The theoretical and empirical framework for the analysis in this book focuses on the behavior of individual homeowners in the context of their urban neighborhoods. As suggested in figure 2.1, for the purposes of this cross-sectional analysis the physical-demographic and social-interactive dimensions of a given individual's environment are taken as predetermined for that moment. One must realize, of course, that in a broader, intertemporal framework, individual behavior and aggregate neighborhood out-

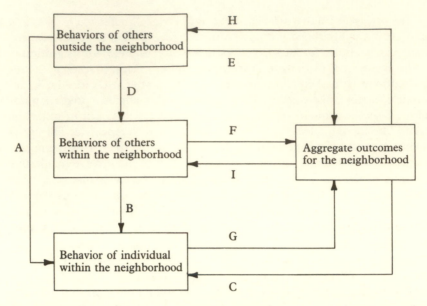

Figure 2.2   Individual Behaviors and Neighborhood Outcomes: Patterns of Circular Causation

comes are related via mutually causal connections. In other words, individual actions in one period affect overall neighborhood characteristics in the next period, which in turn affect subsequent individual behaviors.

The point is illustrated schematically in figure 2.2. Three sets of behavioral agents may be considered as affecting what transpires in a given neighborhood. One consists of agents of institutions and governmental agencies whose policies can affect the flow of resources from their institutions into the given area. Another consists of a particular homeowner whose behavior is being focused upon. The third consists of all other property owners in the given neighborhood, whether absentee-owners or owner-occupants.

At any particular moment a given individual homeowner assesses the current and expected future behaviors of the other two sets of aforementioned agents (paths A, B in figure 2.2) and the current and expected future aggregate conditions in the neighborhood (path C in figure 2.2). In light of these assessments and the personal characteristics of this individual, a housing upkeep investment behavior (and perhaps a mobility behavior as well) is decided upon in ways described in the previous section (path G). Concurrent with this individual homeowner's behavior, other property owners in the neighborhood are also making upkeep and mobility decisions (path F). And mortgage lenders, retail developers, and public-policymakers are also making decisions that will affect the flow of resources into the given neighborhood (path E). This welter of individual behavioral decisions will determine in aggregate what characteristics the given neighborhood will exhibit in subsequent periods (paths E, F, G in figure 2.2). But if these aggregate characteristics actually change in ways that confound the original expectations held by the three sets of agents, further modifications of their behaviors will be generated (paths H, I, C in figure 2.2). Of course, such modifications of individual behaviors may, in turn, alter again the aggregate outcomes for the neighborhood, and the process of circular causation continues.

Consider an illustration of this process. If, for instance, in a particular neighborhood a given homeowner decides for one reason or another to postpone repairs, several other owners independently decide to do the same, and public infrastructure is allowed to decay due to fiscal exigencies, the overall physical conditions in the area will clearly deteriorate over time. This visible decay may, in turn, lead to further adjustment in individual homeowners' upkeep strategies, and may induce some to move out of the area. As the aggregate level of housing prices falls, vacancies are likely to be filled by households of lower socioeconomic status and home-ownership rates may fall. What were once cohesive social-interactive neighborhood networks become fragmented as more residents move out to be replaced by "different" newcomers. In this way not only the physical but also the demographic and social-interactive character of the neighborhood may change. These changes can signal financial institutions that it is now prudent to reduce the flows of mortgage and home improvement loans into the area. Changes in these policies and in the overall character of the neighborhood signal property owners that further adjustments in their housing upkeep behavior are mandated. And thus the neighborhood cumulatively declines.[9]

Of course, whenever one deals with such a social process entailing mutual causation the starting point for the analysis is arbitrary. Nevertheless, a focus on understanding endogenous individual behaviors has strong intuitive appeal, since the neighborhood outcomes are merely the mathematical aggregations of such. It is this focus that guides the present analysis: those who wish to understand neighborhood dynamics must first understand the behavior of individual agents who contribute to producing aggregate dynamics.[10] A primary goal of this book is to contribute to our understanding of neighborhood change through the analysis of individual homeowners' housing upkeep behavior.

The first step in such an analysis is the specification of a rigorous model of homeowner housing upkeep behavior from which may be derived testable hypotheses. To this task the next chapter is devoted.

3 A Model of Housing Upkeep Behavior by Homeowners

It has been conventional in economics to model homeowners' upkeep behavior formally, using the assumption that owner-occupants attempt to maximize the present value of the profits or net returns from investment that they implicitly pay themselves for the privilege of consuming the housing services embodied in their dwelling. The models of Winger (1973), Dildine and Massey (1974), Asmus and Iglarsh (1975), Ozanne and Struyk (1976), and Segal (1980) are representative of this approach. From this perspective, homeowner upkeep behavior becomes indistinguishable from that of investment-motivated landlords or housing contractors. Yet there have been numerous assertions and anecdotal observations that homeowners' upkeep decisions are likely made according to different criteria than those used by purely profit-maximizing landlords; see Grigsby (1963), Smith (1970), Taggart (1970), Peterson et al. (1973). One such different criterion was analyzed in the previous chapter: homeowners may be influenced by neighborhood social interrelationships in a way that absentee landlords are not. All this suggests that a model grounded in consumption theory that embodies the multiple dimensions of neighborhood be developed. Valuable initial steps in this direction have been taken by Sweeney (1974), Mendelsohn (1977), Galster (1981), Kau and Keenan (1981), and Shear and Carpenter (1982), who have specified homeowner upkeep models based on "utility-maximizing" behavior and also attempt to integrate considerations of housing capital gain.[1]

The formal model presented in this chapter follows in the spirit of this latter work. But it extends it by integrating neoclassical economic consumption theory, production theory, and theory of the social-interactive neighborhood developed in the previous chapter. The model is composed of two central elements. The first is the intertemporal "utility function" of the owner-occupant household, the arguments of which are shaped by, among other things, current and expected future physical-demographic dimensions and social-interactive dimensions of the neighborhood. The other is a set of "transformation functions" that embody both the budgetary and the technological constraints involved in obtaining various housing quality packages via modifications of the homeowner's original package. These modifications may take one of four forms of "upkeep strategy": zero maintenance, positive maintenance, upward conversion, or downward conversion.

Several unique contributions are provided by the model:

1. Behavioral impacts of current and expected neighborhood characteristics such as physical condition, demographic composition, housing price levels, and the homeowner's social relationships with neighbors are explicitly modeled.
2. A unified framework is developed within which both homeowners' ongoing housing maintenance and also major upward and downward alterations of housing quality can be understood.
3. Differentiated constraints determined by the type of housing upkeep strategy being considered are specified that embody both budgetary and technological dimensions peculiar to the specific house and homeowner in question.
4. A variety of endogenous interactions are provided for in the model, thus elucidating both the possibilities for and processes of cumulative, mutually reinforcing changes in neighborhood quality.
5. Several types of strategic interactions between homeowners are elucidated and are shown to depend on the nature and parameters of homeowners' utility functions and on the initial quality of their neighborhood.

The chapter first outlines the pure theoretical model, specifying the basic elements of a homeowner's intertemporal utility function, the home's transformation functions, and the homeowner's resulting choice of optimal housing upkeep strategy and expenditure. The richness of the model is then demonstrated by using it to generate expected alterations in upkeep strategy stemming from changes in selected parameters that reflect realistic scenarios. This serves as the rigorous theoretical foundation for the empirical model presented in chapter 9. Readers not thoroughly familiar with microeconomic analysis are encouraged to skip this chapter; it is highly technical.

The Theoretical Model

Because much of the theory is presented in symbolic terms, a glossary of symbols is presented in table 3.1 for convenience. The reader uncomfortable with mathematical modeling is urged to skip the equations, but to

Table 3.1   Glossary of Symbols Used in chapter 3

$\bar{A}_t$	Units of intentional alterations in the structural stock of housing capital during period t (not due to normal structural depreciation)
$\bar{A}_{UCt}, \bar{A}_{DCt}$	Minimum housing structure capital stock alterations associated with upward and downward conversions, respectively
C_t	Operating costs of home during period t, including utilities and taxes, but excluding maintenance or conversions
d	Rate of structural depreciation of housing structure capital stock
E_t	Housing equity or wealth at end of period t
$f(\ )$	Function showing utility associated with consuming H, Z, N, S, W, E
$g(\ )$	Function showing transformation of maintenance inputs into structural capital stock alterations
$j(\ )$	Function showing contribution to flow of housing services from structural stock
$k(\ )$	Function showing transformation of erstwhile owner-occupied stock into new units of dwelling capital stock for rent
$w(\ )$	Function showing utility gained from value of wealth
H_t	Flow of housing services emanating from housing package during period t, created jointly by structural stock and neighborhood
$\bar{H}_0$	Structural stock of housing at time of purchase
$\tilde{H}_t$	Structural stock of housing occupied by homeowner at end of period t
$\dot{H}_t$	Structural stock of housing occupied by renter(s) in owner-occupied dwelling, if any
L^*	Number of periods for repayment of home mortgage
L	Per period $ payment of principal and interest on mortgage
L'_t	Per period $ payment of principal on mortgage during period t
M	Unit of housing maintenance consisting of a bundle of labor time and materials
N	Index of neighborhood quality embodying physical-demographic dimensions
P_{Zt}	Price per unit of a composite commodity of nonhousing goods in period t
$P_{\tilde{H}t}$	Sales price (capital value) per unit of housing stock in dwelling occupied by owner

Table 3.1   *(Continued)*

$\tilde{P}_{\tilde{H}t}$	Sales price (capital value) per unit of housing stock in portion of dwelling occupied by renter (if any) in period t
P_{Mt}	Price per unit of maintenance inputs in period t
P_{Kt}	Price per unit of upward conversion inputs in period t
$P_{\tilde{R}}$	Net rental price per unit of housing stock in rental portion of dwelling, if any, per period
$P_{\tilde{A}t}$	Price per unit of housing structural stock alteration during period t; varies according to upkeep strategy undertaken
r	Real rate of interest, assumed equal to rate of homeowner time preference
S	Index of social-interaction or cohesion between homeowner and neighborhood
t, T, n, tt	Various subscripts indicating time period
U	Index of ordinal utility or well-being of homeowner
V_t	Market value of entire housing package (structure, lot, neighborhood) at period t
W_t	Nonhousing net wealth held by homeowner at end of period t
X_t	Total dollar expenditure allocated to period t (including changes in wealth)
Y_t	After-tax income of homeowner during period t
Z_t	Units of a composite commodity representing nonhousing goods consumed in period t

gain an intuitive sense of the elements of the model, which can usefully be applied in the graphic exposition of figure 3.1 below.

Intertemporal Utility Function

The homeowner's index of utility is assumed to depend on the consumption of units of four "commodities" in each of $0, 1, \ldots, t, \ldots, T$ periods, as well as on the asset value of wealth at the end of the Tth period. The four commodities consumed during each period are: 1. a "composite bundle of goods" (Z), representing all nonhousing consumption expenditures; 2. "housing services" (H) flowing from the occupied dwelling; 3. a set of physical-demographic attributes of the neighborhood (N) in which the dwelling is located; and 4. a set of social-interactive attributes (S) associated with the neighborhood in which the dwelling is located. The wealth is made up of nonhousing wealth (W) plus the home equity held by the homeowner (E). Symbolically:

$$U = U\,(Z_1, Z_2, \ldots, Z_T, H_1, H_2, \ldots, H_T, N_1\, N_2 \ldots, \tag{3.1}$$
$$N_T, S_1\, S_2, \ldots, S_T, W_T + E_T)$$

It is more specifically assumed that utility is additive in its current consumption and wealth components,[2] and that both H and Z consumption must exceed certain minimal quantities:

$$U = \sum_{t=0}^{T} f(Z_t, H_t, N_t, S_t)(1 + r)^{-t} + w(W_T + E_T)(1 + r)^{-T} \tag{3.2}$$

$$s.t.: H_t > \hat{H}_t,\, Z_t > \hat{Z}_t$$

where r is the rate of time preference, which for simplicity is assumed equal to the real interest rate. The terms of (3.2) are described in more detail below.

For simplicity, all nonhousing goods are collapsed into an arbitrary bundle or market-basket. This composite good (Z) can be measured in units, and be purchased during period t at a per unit price of P_{Zt}. It is assumed that there are lower limits on the amount of Z that can be consumed, imposed by biological necessity and/or social norms, $\hat{Z}_t$.[3]

The housing services (H_t) concept can be described as a unit of housing-related attributes that flows from the housing package (i.e., structure plus yard) and is consumed by the occupant during period t. This flow of housing services is assumed here to emanate solely from the stock of housing structure and land parcel $(\bar{H}_t)$.[4] Symbolically:

$$H_t = j(\bar{H}_t) \tag{3.3}$$

A higher-quality housing package would embody a large stock $\bar{H}$ and hence a higher flow of H. (Note: symbols with a line over them will always denote stocks.) This notion of housing services is conventional in the housing economics literature (see Olsen 1969, Moorhouse 1972, Dildine and Massey 1974, Sweeney 1974, De Leeuw and Struyk 1975, Ozanne and Struyk 1976, Ingram and Oron 1977, Chinloy 1980, and Muth 1982). The homeowner buys an initial housing stock (and associated initial housing service flow) at the time of home purchase. After that point, changes in such H_t consumption can only be had by moving to a dwelling embodying a different $\bar{H}$, or by adding or subtracting $\bar{H}$ from the present dwelling. And different types of the latter modification behavior will have different "prices," as explained below. Finally, it is assumed that the consumption of H_t cannot fall below some minimal level, $\hat{H}_t$.

The vector of neighborhood characteristics N_t consumed represents the various aspects of the physical-demographic dimension discussed in the previous chapter: things such as socioeconomic status or race of neighbors, environmental amenities, condition of neighborhood properties, and public service quality, as perceived by the given homeowner. N_t is consumed jointly with H_t, by the fact of the homeowner's choosing to occupy a particular dwelling in a particular neighborhood. Unlike H_t, however, N_t is not directly under the control of the homeowner, nor is it separately priced by the market. Rather, the capital price per unit of the neighborhood's housing stock ($P_{\bar{H}t}$) is directly related to the degree of net positive amenity associated with N_t, as perceived by the market as a whole.[5]

At this point it is unnecessary to define more specifically how f embodies N. One possibility is to assume that the f utility function is multiplicative between H_t and N_t, that is, that the marginal utility gained from consuming extra amounts of housing services will depend on neighborhood condition, at least to some extent. It is not unreasonable to posit that the enjoyment gained from lavishly landscaping, enclosing a porch, or adding a swimming pool depends upon such neighborhood conditions as litter, noise, and street crime. With such an assumption, changes in N_t are seen as affecting a homeowner's marginal utility from modifying the structure both via its direct consumption value and via its indirect impact on eventual market value of the home. The alternative assumption is that N is additive with H in f; i.e., that N provides a lump-sum amount of well-being but does not affect the relative attractiveness of directly consuming H instead of Z after a home has been chosen. With this assumption N can affect utility only via long-term impacts on E_T via $P_{\bar{H}T}$. As will be demonstrated in the applications section below, these alternative assumptions generate potent implications concerning strategic interactions among homeowners.

The S argument in the utility function is the formal representation of the influences of the social-interactive neighborhood presented in the previous chapter. S_t may be thought of as an index showing the degree to which the homeowner is living in a cohesive neighborhood during period t and thus is subject to the social-psychological incentives associated with such a residential context. As in the case of N, S is viewed as influencing the marginal utility associated with changes in H due to intentional alterations in structural stock $\bar{H}$. For instance, the marginal utility associated with undermaintaining one's home and buying more Z instead would likely be lower, *ceteris paribus*, if it violated the norms of one's neighbors about what constitutes a minimally acceptable housing standard and therefore led to the imposition of social sanctions upon that individual. Unlike the case of N, however, S cannot be priced in advance by the market, because social interaction is so idiosyncratic.[6] Thus, the influence of S occurs in (3.2) via f and not w.

Finally, wealth is viewed as contributing to a homeowner's sense of well-being; its relative weight specified by the w function. The wealth accumulated by the end of period T may be of value in its own right as an indicator of achieved status distinct from ongoing (H, Z) consumption levels. Of course, the primary benefit from wealth is to finance one's consumption in periods subsequent to T at levels higher than would otherwise be permitted by concurrent income during those periods. Thus, homeowners may value enhanced market value (equity) in their homes (E_t) since opportunities for buying an even better home are thereby expanded in the future. The weight given to wealth accumulation by the w function likely varies across homeowners. For example, those who value financial security and low indebtedness would place relatively high value on wealth; those who are elderly and who care little for bequests would be the contrary. Of course, it should be noted that W may be negative during certain periods should the homeowner choose to become a net debtor.

Of even more potential importance in the model are the assumptions that could be made about whether weight assigned E_T by the w function depends on the relationship of E_T to some previously specified target level of home equity. As will be demonstrated in the applications section below, some particularly intriguing theoretical possibilities for strategic interactions between homeowners arise if one assumes that the marginal utility gained from increments to home equity via upkeep investments is positive, only so long as the E_T remains below a threshold-equity level that is held as a reference point by the homeowner. It is reasonable to posit that based on their personal experiences, aspirations, and expectations, homeowners psychologically specify at the time of home purchase some minimally acceptable level of home equity that they will attain by the time of home sale. One such simple specification might be to set this threshold equity as at least as great as the initial equity at time of purchase; no one wants to lose money on a house. Having established such a threshold, homeowners may achieve it actively by making investments in the structural capital of the home, or passively if prices per unit of structural capital appreciate in the neighborhood. In either event, once it is predicted that, in its present state, the eventual E_T of the home will exceed the threshold, the perceived marginal utility from home investments should drop dramatically.

Now that its arguments are defined, the utility function as a whole can be discussed. Equation (3.2) implicitly expresses the homeowner's expectations held during period zero about the well-being that directly will be forthcoming from consuming various amounts of (H_t, Z_t) and that indirectly will be forthcoming from holding nonhousing wealth W_T and a home equity asset of eventual market value E_T. The time period 0 to T is defined as the "planning horizon" over which a given homeowner has formulated expectations and desires to make an optimizing decision. The planning horizon can be interpreted as the duration the homeowner expects to remain in the present dwelling, and may vary from homeowner to homeowner.[7] Without loss of generality, it is assumed that the homeowner's present dwelling was purchased at the beginning of period zero and is expected to be sold at the end of period T. The homeowner's behavior is thus modeled over the period between purchase and sale of a given dwelling. The homeowner's problem is to choose the optimal combination of (H_t, Z_t) during the period (given N_t, S_t), the choice of H_t being accomplished by choosing an appropriate $\bar{H}_t$ via a particular upkeep strategy.

The first term in equation (3.2) represents the utility gained directly from the flow of H_t emanating from the housing package held during period t, in conjunction with that gained from associated levels of Z_t, N_t, S_t. The f function need not necessarily assign the same relative weights to these four arguments in all periods. Such weights undoubtedly vary according to changes in life-cycle stage and socioeconomic status. The parameter r in (3.2) represents the homeowner's "rate of time preference," the rate at which a given amount of future consumption must be adjusted to make it commensurate with the same amount of consumption undertaken in the present. If, for example, a homeowner would gain only 95 percent as much utility from a dollar of consumption one year hence as would be gained from a dollar spent today, the annual rate of time preference would be 5 percent.[8]

The second term in (3.2) is the future utility gained by the financial opportunities generated by the sale of the housing asset at the end of period T, plus any other accumulated wealth.[9] As in the case of ongoing future consumption, this wealth is put in present value terms by discounting with the real interest rate, r.[10]

The stock of housing structural capital held during a period t, $\bar{H}_t$, is a key component implicit in both terms of (3.2). In the first term, $\bar{H}_t$ affects the flow of H_t according to (3.3). In the second term, $\bar{H}_t$ will affect the ultimate asset value of the home E_T by the degree to which it has appreciated or depreciated by the time of sale. This latter aspect is explained below.

The amount of housing structure stock held during a period is the depreciated amount of the original stock purchased at $t = 0$, $\bar{H}_0$, plus the depreciated amount of any intentional alterations in that stock, $\bar{A}$, made in periods since the purchase date. These alterations in the stock are, of course, the result of various maintenance, upgrading, downgrading strategies that might have been chosen by the homeowner, and are distinct from stock changes due to normal depreciation. More formally, the housing structure stock owned and occupied by the homeowner during period t may be expressed:

$$\bar{H}_t = \sum_{n=0}^{t} \bar{A}_n(1-d)^{t-n} + \bar{H}_0(1-d)^t \tag{3.4}$$

where d is the rate of structural stock depreciation via weathering, wear and tear, etc. It is likely that d varies by neighborhood conditions, regional location, and structure type and age; d is not under the influence of the homeowner.

If a given structure is occupied by a single household during a given planning horizon, the stock shown in (3.4) is the only one relevant for market evaluations. If, however, a given homeowner chooses a downgrading strategy at some point, and the dwelling is subdivided into one or more "new" units that are, in turn, rented out, the housing stock becomes the sum of that now occupied by the resident homeowner $(\bar{H}_T)$ and that occupied by renter households $(\tilde{H}_T)$. In such a case of downgrading or subdividing a dwelling during period t, $\bar{A}_t$ is negative and equal to $\bar{H}_t - \bar{H}_{t-1}$. The correspondence between $\bar{A}_t$ and $\tilde{H}_t$ is not assumed one-for-one, however, as will be explained below. It is likely that the market price (i.e., capitalized value) per unit of these two types of stocks will differ when the dwelling is sold in T. The full market (sales) value of the dwelling can thus be expressed:

$$V_T = P_{\bar{H}T}\bar{H}_T + b\tilde{P}_{\bar{H}T}\tilde{H}_T, \qquad b \begin{cases} = 1 \text{ if dwelling downgraded} \\ = 0 \text{ otherwise} \end{cases} \tag{3.5}$$

where $\tilde{P}_{\bar{H}T}$ is the price per unit housing capital rented from the dwelling. For simplicity it is assumed that both $P_{\bar{H}T}$ and $\tilde{P}_{\bar{H}T}$ depend identically on market perceptions of N_T and that d is invariant over $(\bar{H}_T, \tilde{H}_T)$ compositions.

Intertemporal Constraints

There are two types of constraints upon the homeowner's choice of optimal housing upkeep. One is financial; the other is technological. Both of these types are explained below, then the two are synthesized into the notion of a transformation function.

FINANCIAL CONSTRAINTS   Over the course of the planning horizon the homeowner expects a stream of after-tax income $Y_1, Y_2, \ldots, Y_T$. This stream typically forms a distinctive life-cycle pattern: comparatively low incomes during early years in the labor force, rising rapidly during the middle working years, continuing to rise at a somewhat slower rate until retirement, thereafter a discontinuous drop to a relatively stable, retirement level. If this pattern of expected income does not correspond well to the desired flow of consumption, a better correspondence can be obtained by borrowing or lending. A normal pattern is for one to borrow heavily during early life-cycle stages, to work off debts and accumulate savings during middle stages, and to live off wealth during last stages.

For the typical household the preponderance of debt arises from the decision to own instead of rent a dwelling. This work is not concerned with the modeling of this tenure choice (see Artle and Varaiya 1978; Brueggeman and Peiser 1979; Johnson 1981; and Rothenberg 1981). It is here assumed that, for whatever reasons, a household has chosen at the beginning of period zero to become the owner-occupant of a particular dwelling embodying $\bar{H}_0$ units of housing structural capital. The purchase price of the home was: $V_0 = P_{\bar{H}0}\bar{H}_0 = P_{H0}l^m(\bar{H}_0)j^m(N_0^m)$, with initial downpayment E_0.

Although variable interest–rate mortgages are currently becoming more popular, it is assumed here for simplicity that the household has borrowed (if at all) a principal $V_0 - E_0$ using a traditional, fixed-rate mortgage that was assumed at $t = 0$. The mortgage is to be repaid in L^* equal installments of $\$ L$, each with a per-period repayment of principal equal to $\$ L'_t$. The homeowner's home equity at the end of t is thus the difference between the home's current value and outstanding mortgage principal:

$$E_t = V_t - (V_0 - E_0 - \sum_{n=0}^{t} L'_n) \tag{3.6}$$

Finally, it is assumed that after the home purchase the household has some holdings of wealth (or debt) other than that associated with housing, W_0. Similarly, by the end of the planning horizon (time T) the household plans on having W_T in nonhousing related wealth (or debt).[11]

The expected future stream of after-tax income may, itself, be affected by alterations in the stock of structural capital embodied in the dwelling, $\bar{A}_t$. Certain types of improvements to insulation and heating systems were, for example, deductible from federal income taxes prior to 1987. States also often allow homeowners to deduct expenses for certain structural improvements from their taxable income. On the other hand, structural additions may trigger property value reassessments and, therefore, higher property taxes subsequently.

The final budgetary consideration deals with the necessary operating costs of the home, which consist primarily of property taxes, insurance, and utility bills. For the purposes of the present model these components are combined into a single term for each period t: C_t. Home operating costs may be considered a function of the current capital stock of housing. For example, a structure embodying larger amounts of capital may require more energy to heat or cool to some acceptable temperature, will have higher insurance premiums levied on it, and will be assessed at a higher value. Major structural upgrading also would normally result in higher insurance premiums and property tax assessments. It is conceivable, however, that certain repairs and improvements could reduce utility costs, such as when insulation is added or an inefficient heating system is replaced. In any event, insofar as upkeep activities in a given period alter the expected stream of operating expenses in future periods, an additional budgetary dimension is added to the calculus of homeowner's choice.

TECHNOLOGICAL CONSTRAINTS   Except for moving, the purchase of additional housing services (H) can be accomplished only by the alteration of the current stock ($\bar{H}$) by some amount $\bar{A}$. Again, assuming a planning horizon defined as that over which the homeowner will not move, these alterations can be accomplished in one of four ways. During a given period t each is mutually exclusive; across periods they can coexist in all combinations. Each of the alternatives embodies a different set of technological possibilities:

1. *Positive maintenance:* an expenditure that attempts to preserve or marginally improve the qualitative aspects of the structure and parcel by offsetting depreciation. Examples include interior or exterior painting, replastering and wallpapering, repairing the structure or mechanical systems, mowing the lawn, etc.[12]
2. *Upward conversion:* an expenditure to make major additions or improvements to the structure or parcel. Examples include upgrading the heating, cooling, plumbing, or electrical systems; adding a room, garage, porch, pool; etc.
3. *Downward conversion:* an expenditure to transform the single-family dwelling into two or more distinct, new packages that can be rented and thereby provide additional income to the homeowner. In making such a decision the homeowner becomes an owner-occupant in a multiple-unit structure. Such downward conversions usually take the form of partitioning the dwelling, perhaps adding extra kitchen and bath facilities, a separate entrance, etc. The use of the term "downward" is not intended as pejorative; merely that the $\bar{H}$ consumed by the owner-occupant is intentionally reduced.
4. *Zero maintenance:* a strategy of withholding any expenditures on the dwelling (other than insurance, utilities, and taxes) and instead spending all disposable income on Z or possibly adding to W. Such passive

undermaintenance does nothing to offset the depreciation of the structural capital embodied in the dwelling.

Each of these four alternative housing upkeep strategies involve idiosyncratic constraints. These constraints combine both technological and input price considerations, and are discussed separately in the following sections.

Positive maintenance. Consider the positive-maintenance strategy in more detail. When positive maintenance is undertaken during period t, increments in the number of units of housing capital stock ($\bar{A}_t$) occur through the purchase of homogeneous units of maintenance activity (M_t), each priced at P_{Mt} per unit.[13] The ability to transform units of M_t into $\bar{A}_t$ via maintenance is given by the technological relationship:

$$\bar{A}_t \text{ via maintenance} = g(M_t) \tag{3.7}$$

Where $\bar{A}_t = 0$ when $M_t = 0$; $0 < d\bar{A} / dM < 1$;
$d^2\bar{A} / dM^2 < 1$

The price per unit of maintenance activity (P_{Mt}) can vary across homeowners depending on their evaluation of leisure time forgone if they do the work themselves or on the price of professional labor if the work is contracted out.[14]

The g function embodies the technological constraints in positive maintenance and is primarily determined by aspects of the structural capital stock: size, condition, architecture, construction material type, and age. It is also influenced by the skill and physical attributes of the individuals performing the maintenance; i.e., the conversion of a given amount of paint or construction materials into $\bar{A}_t$ depends on the productivity of the worker.[15] The assumption of diminishing returns from M is reasonable, because the housing structure is far from a perfectly malleable form of capital.[16] Given the basic structural package, added amounts of maintenance expenditures will produce successively smaller increments in $\bar{A}$ past some point. Marginal returns will reach zero at a point; e.g., when the dwelling has been freshly painted and no further cosmetic improvements will result from additional coats of paint.

Given these technological considerations, the effective price per unit of $\bar{A}$ obtained by maintenance can be expressed:

$$P_{\bar{A}t} \text{ via maintenance} = P_{Mt} / (dg / dM) \tag{3.8}$$

Note how the constraint implied by (3.8) differs from a conventional budgetary constraint in utility-maximization problems. The latter would be shown graphically as a linear constraint connecting the two commodity axes ($\bar{A}_t, Z_t$), with slope equaling the commodity price ratio and prices being independent of quantities purchased. Here, however, the constraint is expressed as a nonlinear function (concave to the origin), because the price of $\bar{A}_t$ is an increasing function of the amount of $\bar{A}_t$ purchased, q.v. denominator in (3.8). This nonlinear constraint, which shows the feasible (both financial and technological) combinations of $(\bar{A}_t, Z_t)$ for a given period under a positive maintenance strategy, is called the "maintenance transformation function." This and all other transformation functions implicitly embody an optimal intertemporal expenditure pattern, as they take as given the total expenditure X_t that will be allocated to the particular period: $Y_t - L_t - C_t - \Delta(W_t + E_t)$, where $\Delta(W_t + E_t)$ is the change in the amount of nonhousing plus housing wealth held by the homeowner.

Upward conversion. Unlike positive maintenance, the option of upward conversion does not likely: (a) involve significant diminishing returns from productive inputs; and (b) depend on the starting level of housing stock. Major upgrading is assumed to involve additions of perfectly malleable housing structural capital $\tilde{H}_t$ that can be purchased at a constant per unit price of inputs P_{Kt}. Note that P_K is not the same as P_H; the latter evaluates the structural capital in the market context of N, not merely on an input cost basis like the former. Although there are no diminishing returns here, it is likely that, due to the "lumpy" nature of upward conversion, there exists some minimum amount of stock alteration that must accompany even the most modest upward conversion. Let this minimum change be defined as $\bar{A}_{UCt}$. Thus, the price of alterations via upward conversion is expressed:

$$P_{\bar{A}t} \text{ via upward conversion} = P_{Kt} \qquad (3.9)$$

The upward-conversion transformation function is thus defined as the feasible combinations of $(\bar{A}_t, Z_t)$ attainable in period t with an upward conversion upkeep strategy. Because no diminishing returns are specified, the function would appear graphically as a linear constraint between the $\bar{A}_t$ axis and the Z_t corresponding to $\bar{A}_{UCt}$.[17]

Downward conversion. Instead of buying units of maintenance or structural capital to add to the existing stock of housing, the option of downward conversion entails the separation of capital from some portion of the dwelling previously occupied by the homeowner and its subsequent rental on the market to one or more other households. (When the newly created dwelling unit is rent-free, e.g., in the case of a "granny flat," the "rent" would need to be defined in terms of utility gained by the owner.) The technological capability of transforming structural housing stock $(\bar{A}_t)$ into homogeneous units of structural stock suitable for renting $(\tilde{H}_t)$ via downward conversion is given by:

$$\bar{A}_t \text{ via downward conversion} = k(\tilde{H}_t) \qquad (3.10)$$

where $\bar{A} = 0$ when $\tilde{H} = 0$; $d\bar{A} / d\tilde{H} < 0$; $d^2A / d\tilde{H}^2 < -1$

The specification of diminishing returns again seems mandated. Clearly, the most minimal means of downward conversion would be to rent an unused room, and allow the tenant to share certain facilities with the homeowner. Progressively more complicated partitioning and subdividing would become increasingly constrained by the structural features of the dwelling. The specific form of k would be determined by such attributes of the dwelling as the existence of an unused, reasonably isolated bedroom, multiple bathrooms or stairways, layout of rooms, etc., as well as the specific mode of conversion anticipated.

The market contract rent per unit of the $\tilde{H}$ bundle created through downward conversion would be influenced by the associated marketwide perception of the given neighborhood. From this flow of new income the homeowner must subtract the amortized costs per unit of $\tilde{H}$ for the labor and materials used for the downward conversion as well as the incremental per-period managerial, tax, and operating costs involved in the landlord function. Let this net rent (profit) per period per unit of housing capital from the rental unit(s) be $P_{\tilde{R}}$. Now $P_{\tilde{R}}$ will continue to flow beyond period t from the undepreciated $\tilde{H}$ remaining, and must be appropriately time-discounted. Thus, the price per unit of $\tilde{A}$ converted downward becomes:

$$P_{\tilde{A}t} \text{ via downward conversion} = \sum_{n=t}^{T} [P_{\tilde{R}t} / (dk / d\tilde{R})] (1-d)^{n-t}(1+r)^{-n}$$

(3.11)

The above technological and budgetary relationships for downward conversion may be augmented by two added constraints in certain circumstances. First, if the dwelling in question is located in a jurisdiction with rigidly enforced zoning constraints or housing codes, a new lower bound on the magnitude of certain types of downward conversion may be imposed. Second, there is likely some minimal amount of $\tilde{A}_t$ that must be sacrificed if any downward conversion is anticipated, given the lumpy nature of conversion. Let this minimal amount be defined as $\tilde{A}_{DCt}$, with an associated initial minimum net rental income of $P_{\tilde{R}t}[k^{-1}(\tilde{A}_{DCt})]$.

Zero maintenance. Investing nothing in the dwelling to either increase or decrease its units of structural capital differs fundamentally from the above three strategies because there are no financial or technological constraints involved. There may be, however, legal proscriptions against this strategy if pursuing such for a given period would result in the dwelling's violating local housing codes. This is the "default strategy"; what necessarily occurs if none of the others are undertaken.

Optimal Housing Upkeep

In this multiperiod formulation, the problem of the homeowner is to choose not only the optimal combination of (H_t, Z_t) for any given period, but also the optimal amount of consumption in one period relative to another over the planning horizon, such that intertemporal utility is maximized. The homeowner does so by choosing an optimal intertemporal pattern of spending associated with altering the stock of housing capital; i.e., by choosing to pursue a particular upkeep strategy (or mix of strategies) as described above. The choice here is further complicated because housing has both consumption and asset dimensions; i.e., the consumption of housing services is possible only through the holding of a durable, valuable asset. The present value of the homeowner's expenditures during the period zero to T is constrained by the present value of the expected available income stream during the planning horizon and by the maximum allowable indebtedness (or conversely, minimum desired wealth accumulation) embodied in the W_T term.[18]

FORMAL OPTIMIZATION PROBLEM   Expressed more formally, the homeowner's problem in period $t = x$ is to:

$$\text{MAX } U = \sum_{t=x}^{T} f(H_t, N_t, S_t, Z_t)(1+r)^{-(t-x)} + w(W_T+E_T)(1+r)^{-(T-x)}$$

(3.12)

s.t.:

$$\sum_{t=x}^{T} (P_{Zt}Z_t + P_{\bar{A}t}\bar{A}_t + C_t)(1+r)^{-(t-x)} + \sum_{t=x}^{L^*} L(1+r)^{-(t-x)}$$

$$+ (W_T+E_T)(1+r)^{-(T-x)} - P_{\bar{H}T} \sum_{t=x}^{T} \bar{A}_t(1-d)^{T-t}(1+r)^{-(T-x)}$$

(3.13)

$$+ (P_{\bar{H}T}-\check{P}_{\bar{H}T}) \sum_{tt=0}^{T} k^{-1}(\bar{A}_{tt})(1-d)^{T-tt}$$

$$= \sum_{t=x}^{T} Y_t(1+r)^{-(t-x)} + W_x + E_x$$

Where the current home was purchased in period $t = 0$, $L^* = T$ if $L^* > T$, and tt denotes the period of a downward conversion, if ever.

Equation (3.12) is merely the utility function (3.2) restated to allow the decision period $t = x$ to differ from the time when the home was purchased, $t = 0$. The first two terms in constraint (3.13) denote the out-of-pocket expenditures on nonhousing and housing consumption, including mortgage payments, if any. The third term gives the discounted present value of end-of-period wealth. The last two items on the left-hand side provide the accounting adjustments denoting that expenditure on $\bar{A}_t$ simultaneously alters E_t.[19] The right-hand side of (3.13) shows flows of income during the period plus the initial wealth endowment.

The homeowner is assumed to have knowledge or expectations about the intertemporal levels of: physical-demographic neighborhood quality $(N_0, \ldots, N_T)$, neighborhood social-interactive cohesion $(S_0, \ldots, S_T)$, prices of nonhousing consumption $(P_{Z0}, \ldots, P_{ZT})$, prices of alterations in the housing stock via various strategies $(P_{\bar{A}0}, \ldots, P_{\bar{A}T})$, after-tax income stream $(Y_0, \ldots Y_T)$, the rate of housing depreciation (d), and the real rate of interest (r). In addition, the homeowner is assumed to have expectations about how the market will evaluate the physical-demographic neighborhood and how it will price housing capital $(P_{\bar{H}T}$ and $\tilde{P}_{\bar{H}T})$ when the dwelling is sold at the end of period T. Thus, the homeowner's choice of optimal H_t stream becomes one of choosing the optimal $\bar{A}_t$ pattern (and hence Z_t).

Substituting from (3.3), (3.4), (3.5) and (3.6), the objective function (3.12) can be expressed:

$$\text{MAX} \sum_{t=x}^{T} f(j[\sum_{n=0}^{t} \bar{A}_n(1-d)^{t-n} + \bar{H}_0(1-d)^t], N_t, S_t, Z_t)(1+r)^{-(t-x)}$$

(3.14)

$$+ w[W_T + P_{\bar{H}T} [\sum_{n=0}^{T} \bar{A}_n(1-d)^{T-n} + \bar{H}_0(1-d)^T] - (P_{\bar{H}T} - \tilde{P}_{\bar{H}T})$$

$$\sum_{tt=0}^{T} k^{-1}(\bar{A}_{tt})(1-d)^{T-tt} - (V_0 - E_0 - \sum_{n=0}^{T} L'_n)] (1+r)^{-(T-x)}$$

Forming a Lagrangian from (3.14) and (3.13), differentiating with respect to $\bar{A}_t$, Z_t and the Lagrangian multiplier, and setting each derivative equal to zero, the first-order conditions for a maximum are obtained. These may be expressed as familiar marginal utility ratios—equal to price ratios:

$$\frac{U_{Zt}}{U_{\bar{A}t}} = \frac{P_{Zt}}{[P_{\bar{A}t} + \sum_{n=t+1}^{T} (dC_n / d\bar{A}_t - dY_n / d\bar{A}_t)] (1+r)^{-(n-t-1)}}$$

(3.15a)

$$\frac{U_{\bar{A}t}}{U_{\bar{A}t*}} = \frac{[P_{\bar{A}t} + \sum_{n=t+1}^{T} (dC_n / d\bar{A}_t - dY_n / d\bar{A}_t)] (1+r)^{-(n-t-1)}}{[P_{\bar{A}t*} + \sum_{n=t*+1}^{T} (dC_n / d\bar{A}_{t*} - dY_n / d\bar{A}_{t*})] (1+r)^{-(n-t*-1)}}$$

$$(3.15b)$$

$$\frac{U_{Zt}}{U_{Zt*}} = \frac{P_{Zt} (1+r)^{-t}}{P_{Zt*} (1+r)^{-t*}} \tag{3.15c}$$

Where:

$$U_{Zt} = f_{Zt} (1+r)^{-(t-x)} \text{ and} \tag{3.16}$$

$$U_{\bar{A}t} = \sum_{n=t}^{T} f_{Ht} j_{\bar{A}t} (1-d)^{T-n} (1+r)^{-(n-x)} + w_{\bar{A}t} P (1-d)^{T-t} (1+r)^{-(T-x)}$$

$$(3.17)$$

and $P = P_{\bar{H}T}$ if $\bar{A}_t$ is maintenance or upward conversion; $P = (P_{\bar{H}T} - \bar{P}_{\bar{H}T})k_{\bar{A}t}^{-1}$ if $\bar{A}_t$ is downward conversion; $P_{\bar{A}t}$ is given by (3.8), (3.9) or (3.11) as relevant; $f_{\bar{H}t}$, $j_{\bar{A}t}$, $w_{\bar{A}t}$, f_{Zt}, are partial derivatives of the function with respect to the subscripted argument, and U is marginal utility.[20] Recall that $j_{\bar{A}t}$ is a function of S and, possibly N as well.

Two qualifications must be made concerning the first-order conditions (3.15 a, b, c). First, they hold exactly only in noncorner solutions; i.e., for optima occurring when some nonzero level of housing alterations $\bar{A}_t$ are undertaken. It is possible that the utility-maximizing combination of $(\bar{A}_t, Z_t)$ in some period t may be $\bar{A}_t = 0$. In other words, the marginal utility from the first dollar spent on housing alterations during t may be less than the marginal utility gained from the last dollar of expenditure allotted to the period when spent on Z. In such cases the clear optimal choice is the zero-maintenance strategy. Second, the conditions show the optimum only for a given upkeep strategy during t involving nonzero $\bar{A}_t$; i.e., for the particular price $P_{\bar{A}t}$ chosen. If one is considering pursuing a single type of upkeep behavior during the period until T, the intertemporal vector of $P_{\bar{A}}$ as defined by the relevant equation (3.8), (3.9) or (3.11) is employed in (3.15 a, b, c). A more realistic, though complicated, possibility is that an overall strategy during the period t to T may consist of combinations of particular upkeep behaviors; e.g., upgrading during t followed by positive maintenance thereafter, or zero maintenance from t to $t + 5$, downgrading in $t + 6$, and positive maintenance thereafter. With such strategies the intertemporal vector of prices is defined at each t by the appropriate behavior being contemplated at that moment.

Needless to say, there are a large number of permutations of such combined-upkeep strategies that may be seriously considered by a given homeowner. The model simply posits that whatever their number or variety, a homeowner comparatively evaluates the expected utility derived from each of the alternative strategies, assuming that each strategy has been designed so that during each t the first-order conditions are fulfilled (i.e., the "local optimum" has been reached). That strategy yielding the highest total utility level (i.e., the "global optimum") will be selected.[21] Implicit in this choice will be an optimal amount (and direction) of structural capital alteration $\bar{A}_t$ during each period from t to T. And given that the particular strategy selected to accomplish this change requires certain quantities of inputs having certain prices, an optimal housing expenditure during each period will be chosen simultaneously. It is assumed that the homeowner makes this decision once and for all during the planning horizon, unless new information is acquired about expected future parameter values that warrants a reformulation of strategy before T.

INTERPRETATION OF FIRST-ORDER CONDITIONS   Each of the above first-order conditions has an intuitively appealing interpretation. Equation (3.15c) says that the homeowner should consume nonhousing items in such intertemporal combinations that their comparative (expected) price ratio equals their marginal utility ratio. If P_Z is expected to be constant over time, (3.15c) says that this optimal combination involves equating the marginal utility ratio to the compounded rate of time preference (or discount rate) between the two periods under consideration: t to t^*.

A similar interpretation can be given to (3.15b), although both sides of the equation are more complex. The price here is defined not only in terms of direct expenses incurred in altering housing capital in a particular way $(P_{\bar{A}t})$ but also in terms of indirect changes in future operating costs and after-tax incomes induced by these alterations. Thus, (3.15b) suggests that the real price of a particular home modification relative to another will be lower, the greater the reductions in operating costs and tax burdens ensuing from it. It follows that more of this modification should be undertaken relative to the other, *ceteris paribus*. As seen in (3.17), the marginal utility ratio embodies components of both direct consumption utility (from added housing services provided via $\bar{A}_t$) and indirect utility (from added housing wealth via $\bar{A}_t$). If both numerator and denominator on the right-hand side of (3.15b) are viewed as approximately equal by the homeowner, (3.15b) reduces to an expression that says that the pattern of housing stock alterations should be such that the extra utility gained from a further marginal alteration in one period t equals that lost from the requisite sacrifice in another period t^*, with each period's utility appropriately adjusted for structural capital depreciation and interest rates (i.e., opportunity costs of capital).

Equation (3.15a) is the intertemporal analog of the two-good, one-period optimum. The expression yields the conventional rule of equating marginal utility ratios to the price ratios to get the optimal combination of $(\bar{A}_t, Z_t)$, in a given period t. Because the durability and asset value of housing are explicitly modeled, (3.15a) differs from the conventional analysis insofar as an added unit of housing capital provides utility in both a different manner and degree. Not only is utility gained during the period in which the housing capital is purchased, but housing services continue to flow from it into the future, albeit at a lower, depreciated level, q.v. the first term in (3.17). Utility is further gained insofar as the added housing capital is not completely depreciated at the eventual time of sale, thus providing equity E_T, q.v. the second term in (3.17).

GRAPHIC INTERPRETATION OF OPTIMUM   The homeowner's problem of choosing the optimal combination of $(\bar{A}_t, Z_t)$ may be usefully portrayed graphically, as in figure 3.1, if one makes the simplifying assumption of a single-period planning horizon.

The marginal rates of substitution between $\bar{A}_t$ and Z_t implicit in the f and w utility functions (3.2) are shown by indifference curves $U_I - U_{VIII}$. Tradeoffs between alterations in the housing structural stock by positive maintenance or upward conversion and nonhousing goods are shown by representative indifference curves $U_I - U_{IV}$. Sacrifices in Z are compensated for with increments in both the current and future consumption value of the housing stock and in its expected future asset value. These indifference curves asymptotically approach $\hat{Z}$, the minimum acceptable nonhousing consumption, but can intersect the Z_t axis because zero alterations ($\bar{A}_t = 0$) does not imply that the current stock of housing ($\bar{H}_t$) is zero. At point F the combination $(0, Z_{tF})$ corresponds to the consumption of the flow of housing services (H_{tF}) emanating from stock $j(H_{t-1}[1-d])$ according to equations (3.3) and (3.4) In other words, F represents the Z_t that could be consumed out of current resources if a zero maintenance strategy were adopted during t: X_t / P_z. Note that the marginal rate of substitution between $\bar{A}_t$ and Z_t (i.e., the slope of the indifference curves, $U_{\bar{A}t} / U_{Zt}$, as given by (3.15a), (3.16), (3.17)) can be defined only after the homeowner's characteristics and the several parameters have been specified: d, N_t, S_t, $P_{\bar{H}t}$, $\hat{P}_{\bar{H}T}$, r and $\bar{H}_{t-1}$.[22]

Indifference curves relevant to the housing upkeep strategy of downward conversion are shown as $U_V - U_{VIII}$. These curves should not be

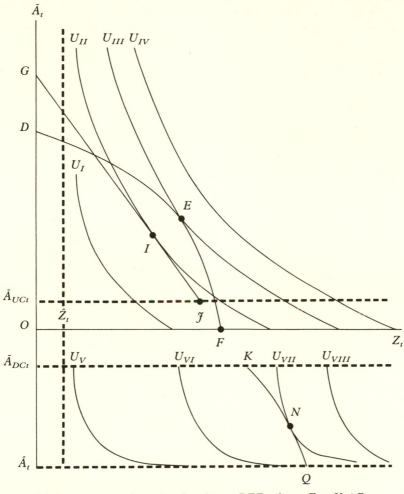

Maintenance transformation function = DEF, where: $F = X_t / P_{Zt}$
Upward conversion transformation function = $GI\mathcal{J}$, where:
$\mathcal{J} = (X_t - P_{kt}\bar{A}_{UCt}) / P_{Zt}$
Downward conversion transformation function = KNQ, where:
$K = (X_t + P_{\dot{R}t}\bar{A}_{DCt}) / P_{Zt}$ and $X_t = Y_t - L_t - C_t - \Delta(W_t + E_t)$

Figure 3.1   Representative Indifference Curves and Transformation Functions
for a Given Period

viewed as extensions of curves $U_I - U_{IV}$ because the nature of $\bar{A}_t$, Z_t tradeoffs are qualitatively different here. As far as direct-consumption utility goes, the marginal rate of substitution for $\bar{A}_t$ slightly above zero is likely quite different from that for $\bar{A}_t$ slightly below zero. As far as asset value goes, a sacrifice of $\bar{A}_t$ for consumption purposes by the homeowner via downward conversion does not necessarily imply a concomitant sacrifice in asset value, because the rented portion of the dwelling is still available for sale. Indifference curves $U_V - U_{VIII}$ approach $\hat{A}_t$ asymptotically, as $\hat{A}_t$ is the alteration associated with the homeowner's being left with a housing package delivering the minimum $\hat{H}_t$ flow of housing services for personal use.

The three transformation functions for positive maintenance, upward conversion, and downward conversion are shown by DEF, GIJ, and KNQ, respectively. They can be exactly specified only after the attributes of the homeowner, of the dwelling, and the values of P_{Mt}, P_{KT}, $P_{\bar{R}t}$, d, and r have been given.[23] The concave curvature of positive maintenance and downward conversion transformation functions reflect the presumed diminishing returns in g and k functions, respectively. The terminal points F, J, K of the functions indicate the maximum amount of Z_t that could be purchased in conjunction with the first marginal increment in $\bar{A}_t$ possible with the respective upkeep strategy. Note that minimum feasible investments via conversion are shown as $\bar{A}_{UCt}$ and $\bar{A}_{DCt}$. Because the slopes of these transformation functions (the right-hand side of equation (3.15a)) embody both technological and input price constraints, the slopes can be termed "marginal rate of transformation."

In the context of figure 3.1, the first-order condition expressed in (3.15a) can be viewed as finding the combinations of $(\bar{A}_t, Z_t)$ where each transformation function is tangent to an indifference curve; i.e., where the marginal rates of substitution and transformation are equal. In figure 3.1, these points are E for positive maintenance, I for upward conversion, and N for downward conversion. The homeowner then compares the total level of utility associated with each of these three points (plus the point F, the zero maintenance strategy where $\bar{A}_t = 0$) and chooses the strategy yielding the highest utility. As drawn in figure 3.1, $U_E > U_I > U_F$ but $U_E \lesssim ?U_N$. Note that the relative slopes of the maintenance and upward conversion transformation functions need not be as shown in figure 3.1; it may sometimes be the case that $U_I > U_E$, or $U_F > U_I$, etc., depending on the particular homeowner, dwelling, input prices, depreciation rates, market rents, and interest charges. The central point of intuition to be conveyed by figure 3.1 is that parameter changes will alter the slopes of one or more transformation functions and/or slopes of indifference curves, thereby producing new optimal upkeep strategy choices.

Implications and Applications of the Model

Now that the basic framework of the model has been presented, it can be employed to predict how housing upkeep behavior should change in response to changes in key parameters or variables. Testable predictions thus derived from the model (summarized in table 3.2) will provide the foundation for the empirical analysis in forthcoming chapters. Before turning to specific applications, some introductory comments about how parameter changes affect the model in general are in order.

*Overview: Changing Slopes of Indifference Curves
and Transformation Functions, Income and Substitution
Effects, and Discontinuities*

Certain parameter changes affect the marginal valuations that the homeowner's utility function give to $\bar{A}$ and Z, as shown by the left-hand side of equation (3.15a) in conjunction with (3.16) and (3.17). In the context of figure 3.1, such changes can be seen as altering the marginal rate of substitution (i.e., slope) of the family of indifference curves. Any factor that reduces the marginal rate of substitution (i.e., creates more housing-intensive preferences) can be unambiguously predicted to lead to a reduced likelihood of the homeowner choosing either a zero-maintenance or downward-conversion strategy, relative to the other two. And, assuming $G > D$ in figure 3.1, it also would increase the likelihood of a homeowner choosing an upward conversion instead of a positive maintenance strategy. In such case, however, it will likely be a corner solution. Regardless of whether such an alteration in strategy occurs, however, the new optimum will be associated with greater $\bar{A}_t$ and upkeep expenditures (or smaller $\bar{A}_t$ sacrifices in the case of downward conversion).

Other parameter changes affect the relative prices of $\bar{A}$ and Z, as shown by the right-hand side of equation (3.15a), where $P_{\bar{A}t}$ is given by equations (3.8), (3.9), and (3.11), as appropriate. In figure 3.1 such changes can be seen as altering the marginal rate of transformation of Z into $\bar{A}$; i.e., the slope of the particular transformation function for which the parameter is relevant. Unlike the previous case of altered marginal rates of substitution, however, altered marginal rates of transformation produce more ambiguous effects, depending on the relative magnitudes of "income and substitution effects."[24]

Suppose one is considering a change that reduces the ability to make transformations between $\bar{A}_t$ and Z_t; i.e., a change that raises absolutely the effective price of one or the other good. Because the higher price means the "real income" or purchasing power of the homeowner has been re-

Table 3.2   Summary of Predicted Effects of Selected Parameter Changes on Housing Upkeep

Change	Amount of H	Amount of $\bar{A}_t$	Expenditure on $\bar{A}_t$	Choice of upkeep strategy
Higher-Income Homeowner	Higher	Higher	Higher	Downward conversion less likely
Middle-Age vs. Younger or Elderly Homeowner	Higher	Higher	?	Downward conversion less likely, upward conversion more likely
Longer Length of Tenure	?	?	?	?
Older Structure	Lower	?	?	Upward and downward conversion more likely
Wooden Structure	Lower	?	?	?
Larger Structure and Parcel	Higher	?	?	Downward conversion more likely
Lower N Price (market perception)	?	?	?	Zero maintenance more likely, downward conversion less likely
Lower N Quality (owner perception)	Lower?	Lower?	Lower?	Upward conversion and positive maintenance less likely
Lower S	Lower	Lower	Lower	Upward conversion and maintenance less likely
Higher Interest Rates	Lower	Lower	Lower	None
Higher P_Z	Lower?	Lower?	Lower?	?
Higher P_M, P_K, Lower $P_{\bar{R}}$	Lower	Lower	Higher?	The given strategy with higher price less likely
Higher $\bar{P}_{\bar{H}T}$, $P_{\bar{H}T}$	Higher	Higher	Higher	?

Note: ? indicates ambiguous prediction

duced, the income effect predicts that the optimal consumption of both goods should be somewhat less than before the price increase. The substitution effect, on the other hand, predicts that the optimizing homeowner should also modify the composition of the consumption bundle such that relatively less of the now higher-priced good is consumed. Both effects predict that the optimal amount consumed of the good with the risen price should be less, although the change in the total amount spent on it cannot be predicted since the price per unit is now higher. The effects work in opposing directions for the good with the constant price. It is thus impossible to predict with certainty how the optimal quantity (or total expenditure) of this good will change, given a rise in the price of the other. Since $\bar{A}_t$ and Z_t are "normal" goods, we would usually expect the income effects to predominate, however.

As the slopes of indifference curves and/or transformation functions change as a result of parameter changes, the local optima (tangencies between a given transformation function and indifference curve) will be altered in a continuous fashion unless, of course, they reach the extreme points of the given transformation functions (i.e., "corner solutions"). The global optimum (local optimum with highest utility level) may, however, shift discontinuously from one transformation function to another with such parameter changes because the given parameter may affect only one such function. Thus, parameter changes can alter the probabilities that a homeowner will pursue one type of upkeep strategy over another, as well as the degree to which $\bar{A}_t$ occurs given the choice of a particular strategy. Both aspects will be investigated empirically in chapter 9.

These general analytical processes aid in the following examination of the implications of selected parameter and variable changes in the model.

Characteristics of Homeowners

Consider first the likely effects of income differences among homeowners. One might expect that those who have higher incomes will view the home as a prime visible symbol of their status attainment, and that their preferences for housing services (f_H) will be stronger. This augments the expected utility gain from an increment in $\bar{A}_t$ (q.v. first term in (3.17)), and lowers the marginal rate of substitution (i.e., flattens the indifference-curve slope) between $\bar{A}_t$ and Z_t.

The predictions are much more complicated in the case of transformation functions. On the one hand, if higher-income homeowners implicitly value their time at a higher wage, they will perceive the price of any upkeep strategy involving such personal time commitment as higher. In terms of figure 3.1, this effect pivots all transformation functions around their abscissa intercepts (J, F, K) so as to reduce the marginal rate of transformation. This increases the probability that a zero-maintenance strategy is chosen. Of course, such an effect ceases when the opportunity cost of the homeowner's time surpasses that of contract laborers who could be hired to perform the given upkeep activity. On the other hand, a diametrically opposite effect can be predicted. Those with higher income streams likely gain more tax savings from qualifying housing improvements ($dY_t / d\bar{A}_t$ is larger), hence the effective price of $\bar{A}_t$ is lower for particular positive-maintenance or upward-conversion strategies. Graphically, these two transformation functions pivot around F and $\mathcal{J}$ such that D and G are higher, respectively, thereby increasing at any point the associated marginal rate of transformation. The opposite is true for downward conversion. Any earnings from rental properties are taxed more heavily at the margin for higher-income homeowners, hence the price of downgrading is higher. In graphic terms, the downward conversion transformation function in figure 3.1 pivots clockwise around K.

There is another reason why positive $\bar{A}_t$ strategies are more likely to dominate downgrading for higher-income homeowners. When the desirability of augmenting Z by sacrificing housing services is perceived, higher-income homeowners are likely to respond by selling their current dwelling and moving into one embodying a smaller amount of housing capital. Lower-income homeowners may, however, have fewer choices to move into less-expensive accommodations while remaining owner-occupants. They are thus more likely to convert their dwellings into multi-family structures.

Finally, of course, higher income is associated with lower financial constraints. Graphically, this is shown in figure 3.1 as a parallel shift of all transformation functions out away from the origin,[25] with a larger resultant optimum in both $\bar{A}_t$ and Z_t, given their presumed normal-good status.

All the foregoing allows one to predict that higher-income homeowners usually have higher consumption levels of both $\bar{A}_t$ and Z_t, greater expenditures on $\bar{A}_t$, and a lower likelihood of adopting downward-conversion strategies. This is, of course, a conventional prediction. It is theoretically possible, however, that those who value their time highly will opt for zero-maintenance strategies. This is the first of numerous instances to be cited herein where the theory supports the conventional wisdom, but with the caveat that the result is based on assumed ranges of parameter values that define the homeowners, houses, and context of the behavior. This prediction and those following are conveniently summarized in table 3.2.

The life-cycle stage of the homeowner is also likely to affect housing upkeep. Marriage is likely to cause an increase in the relative weight given to housing consumption; i.e., f_{Ht} becomes greater. A decrease in marginal rates of substitution is likely to continue through child-rearing stages. The perception of the need for interior space and bathrooms may be most acute during the homeowner's middle age, when children are adolescents. The corresponding changes in marginal rates of substitution point to the increased likelihood that upward conversion would be the global-optimum upkeep strategy. But elderly homeowners whose children have left the home often evidence weakened preferences for housing. This, coupled with their relatively shorter planning horizons, would lead one to predict a reversal of the housing consumption trend established during earlier life-cycle stages. Furthermore, the decreased space needs of the elderly may make the sacrifices in housing stock required by downward conversion seem trivial, thus increasing the probability of such a strategy.

These alterations, which are due to preference-related dimensions of life cycle, are abetted by changes in the prices of upkeep strategies. Middle-aged homeowners likely perceive a lower effective price for maintenance activities (and also for upgrading, if the work is done by the homeowner) than do younger or older homeowners. Middle-aged homeowners have more experience and efficiency with home repairs than younger ones, and they have fewer physical restrictions than older ones. This lower $P_{\bar{A}t}$ increases the marginal rate of transformation, i.e., pivots their positive maintenance (and possibly, upward conversion) transformation function clockwise around point F in figure 3.1. Note that this effect, though resulting in greater optimal $\bar{A}_t$, typically results in lower expenditure on $\bar{A}_t$, since the dominant income effect leads to greater consumption of (and expenditure on) Z_t. It is hard to predict whether the elderly perceive higher or lower prices of housing upkeep, compared to young homeowners. On the one hand, the elderly likely have more physical impairments and thus a greater reliance on expensive contract labor. On the other hand, retirees may place little opportunity cost on their time.

The combined effects of life-cycle stage thus yield the conventional prediction of a curvilinear relationship between amounts of housing upkeep, $\bar{A}_t$, and life-cycle stage: growing $\bar{A}_t$ through child-rearing stages, peaking when children are adolescents, tapering off thereafter. In parallel with this relationship is the predicted pattern of increased relative probability of positive maintenance or upward conversion strategies, followed by a decrease in this probability as children leave to form separate households, and perhaps, the homeowner's spouse dies. The pattern of expenditure on $\bar{A}_t$ is less predictable, depending on whether the presumed income effects of the altered marginal rates of transformation dominate the pure substitution effects of the altered marginal rates of substitution.

The final homeowner characteristic to be examined is expected length of residence in the dwelling. The theoretical consequences of lengthening the period from t to T will vary, depending on the relative f and w components of (3.2). On the one hand, homeowners who expect to remain in their current dwellings a longer period of the time should perceive a greater consumption utility gain from any $\bar{A}_t$ (i.e., more terms are added in the Σ f_{Ht} component of (3.17)), because the homeowner will be able to enjoy the benefits of the $\bar{A}_t$ for a longer future time. On the other hand, a larger period before expected home sale means that any current alterations will be more depreciated and that the increments to E_t must be time discounted more heavily, q.v. the effect of a larger T in the $w_{\bar{A}t}$ component of (3.17). For homeowners for whom the consumption aspect of housing predominates over the investment aspect, the predicted effect of higher T would be a reduction in the marginal rate of substitution. This would lead not only to greater $\bar{A}_t$ consumption and expenditures, but to an increased likelihood of upward conversion. Upward conversions are likely tailored to the idiosyncratic preferences of the particular homeowner. But with a longer planning horizon, homeowners with such preferences can better afford to downplay even pessimistic expectations about eventual market evaluations of such improvements because they're more likely to get their money's worth out of upward conversion through pure consumption benefits alone. But this pattern of investments increasing with expected longevity should cease at some future point when all investments made currently will be completely depreciated. And a final complication is that those who plan to remain in their home until death will likely place no weight whatever on the investment component of utility ($w_{\bar{A}t}$ is zero in (3.17)). Thus, even if two homeowners have the same T but one views this time as the end of his/her life, that person should manifest lower upkeep levels, *ceteris paribus*.

Note, finally, how the conventionally predicted direct correlation between upkeep activity and expected length of residence appears only as a special case in the model. There have been no previous attempts to disentangle empirically the countervailing effects of expected length of tenure, but such is done in chapter 9.

Characteristics of Dwellings

Independently of the characteristics of homeowners, features of the occupied dwelling are likely to influence housing upkeep behavior through their impacts upon the amount of structural capital depreciation incurred during each period. Consider first the general role of depreciation in the model, then how specific dwelling characteristics may relate to depreciation.

Structural capital depreciation creates three distinct consequences. First, it reduces the ordinate (but not the abscissa) of the starting point (o in figure 3.1) from which subsequent alternative transformations may be made. This reduction is equivalent to a loss in housing services consumed, even though the ability to consume Z is unaffected. This in itself does not alter either marginal rates of substitution or transformation, but the prior mix of H_t, and Z_t is rendered suboptimal. Thus, assuming both $\bar{A}_t$ and Z_t are normal goods, one would predict that the optimizing adjustment to this would be to increase $\bar{A}_t$ and decrease Z_t.

Second, greater amounts of depreciation during future periods unambiguously should increase marginal rates of substitution. Because less of any given $\bar{A}_t$ invested will remain over future periods, the future utility gained from both consumption and asset dimensions of $\bar{A}_t$ should be lower, as shown in (3.15a) and (3.17). This consequence should lead to increases in the likelihood of a zero-maintenance strategy, and to lower amounts (and expenditures) of $\bar{A}_t$ if a positive-upkeep strategy is still chosen.

Third, greater depreciation can be expected to alter the shape of the positive-maintenance transformation function. If more aspects of the house need repair, there obviously will be a greater $\bar{A}_t$ investment possible before any diminishing returns set in. This means that for a more sizable range of possible $\bar{A}_t$ values, the marginal rate of transformation for the positive-maintenance transformation function will be effectively constant, the value being determined by the price per unit maintenance, P_M, and the constant returns portion of maintenance function g. The effect of this is to increase the optimal $\bar{A}_t$, and enhance the probability that a positive-maintenance strategy will be selected. Note that this third argument does not apply to transformation possibilities for upward or downward conversion. In fact, it may be that serious structural deterioration may greatly inhibit certain types of upgrading, such as additions.

The differing consequences of these three effects of depreciation can be viewed with the aid of figure 3.2. It portrays a hypothetical homeowner in two alternative scenarios (both assuming one-period optimization). The first is a low-depreciation scenario, wherein the zero level of structural stock alterations during the period is given by $\bar{A}_T$. The relevant positive-maintenance transformation function is TM, and the indifference curve tangent to TM is U_1. The optimal maintenance in this low-depreciation scenario is thus shown by point X, indicating an amount of alterations equal to $X - \bar{A}_T$. Contrast this to the high-depreciation scenario. The initial stock of structural capital available during the period as a base for possible alterations is comparatively lower; let $\bar{A}_S$ represent this point of zero alterations. The first effect noted above is illustrated by the tangency between an indifference curve from the same family of functions as U_1—call it U_3—and a maintenance transformation function parallel to TM but shifted down so it began at S—call it SP. If this were the only effect, the new optimal maintenance would be shown by W, with $W - \bar{A}_S$ amount of alterations. The second effect noted above is shown as a change in the indifference mapping. Suppose the relevant mapping is now represented

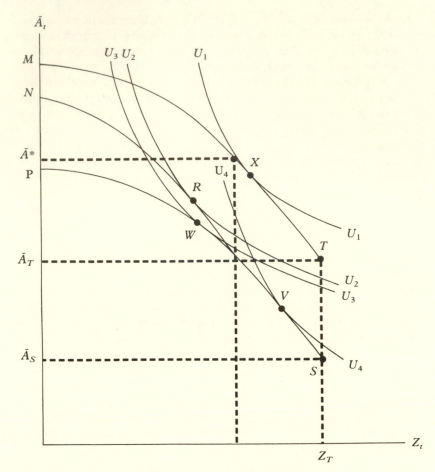

Figure 3.2   Alternative Effects of Structural Depreciation

by indifference curve U_4, in which case the optimum would be at V, and alterations would be $V - \bar{A}_s$. The third effect noted above alters the new maintenance transformation function SP such that, like TM, diminishing returns set in only past $\bar{A}*$; this new function is SN. In the absence of any changes in marginal rates of substitution (represented by U_2), this would mean an optimum at R, with $R - \bar{A}_S$ alteration. Given U_4, such a modified transformation as drawn would create no added impact (i.e., optimum at V).

The net effect of these three components can be seen as a comparison of the low-depreciation optimum X to high-depreciation alternative optima. If the higher marginal rate of substitution dominates (optimum equals V), greater depreciation will be associated with lower expenditures on upkeep (and an increased probability of zero maintenance). The opposite will be the case if the other two effects in conjunction dominate (optimum equals W or R). But notice that regardless of which effect predominates, the level of housing structural capital falls on balance faster with greater depreciation, even in spite of corresponding upkeep efforts. In other words, none of the alternative optima in the high-depreciation scenario (R, W, or V) succeeds in bringing the dwelling up to as high a level of structural capital at the end of the period as that associated with optimum X in the low-depreciation case.

Given this general discussion of depreciation, the influences of specific structural attributes can be more easily outlined. Older structures and those of wood clapboard construction probably evidence a higher rate of depreciation (d) (Chinloy 1980) and thus lose a larger portion of structural capital, $\bar{H}_t (1 - d)$ each period. As such they are subject to the countervailing effects of greater depreciation upon positive maintenance behavior discussed above. But there is added consideration for older structures. Insofar as older homes may possess structural or equipment features that are obsolescent, upward conversions (and, to a smaller degree, maintenance) should result in comparatively larger reductions in dwelling operating costs. That is $\Sigma \, dC \, / \, dA_t$ should significantly reduce the effective price of upward conversions in the right-hand–side denominator of (3.15a), thus increasing the marginal rate of transformation (pivoting GJ clockwise around J in figure 3.1). If older structures are also associated with an architecture conducive to the creation of multiple units within the dwelling (multi-story, many smaller rooms on a closed floorplan, etc.), the technical capabilities for downward conversion increase. In other words, the k function in (3.10) may exhibit improved returns of $\bar{H}_t$ from downward conversion, and the transformation function KQ would pivot counterclockwise around K in figure 3.1. In summary, one can't predict with certainty how $\bar{A}_t$ amounts and expenditures of positive-maintenance behavior will vary with structural age or with wood-sided construction. It is likely, however, that either upward conversion, or downward conversion is a relatively more probable optimal strategy for an older dwelling than is positive maintenance. Such a prediction is not forthcoming from more heuristic conventional theoretical treatments.

The size of the dwelling and the lot on which it is located can be expected to be directly related to a greater amount (not rate) of depreciation. For any given depreciation rate d, the higher initial embodiment of structural capital implicit in larger dwellings means that the absolute amount of capital lost each period is greater. In addition, the possibility of converting a structure into one containing rental units is enhanced when the structure is larger, because there are more likely to be spare rooms and plumbing facilities that are currently underutilized by the owner and are easily convertible to rental use. A larger lot may permit certain downward conversions that otherwise may be prohibited on the basis of density-zoning restrictions. Thus, once again, there is no unambiguous prediction that can be derived from the model about the relationship of structure and parcel size, and consumption and expenditure levels of $\bar{A}_t$. One can predict, however, that downward conversion becomes an increasingly more likely global-optimum strategy for larger housing packages.

Interest Rates and Prices

An alteration in a homeowner's expectations about future interest rates (r) yields straightforward predictions from the model. An expectation of a higher interest rate (or discount rate) tends, of course, to lead the homeowner to defer consumption to future periods (q.v. equations (3.15b) and (3.15c)). It also alters the composition of the consumption bundle in any given period away from $\bar{A}_t$ by increasing the marginal rate of substitution, i.e., decreasing the $w_{\bar{A}t}$ term in (3.17). Thus, the model generates the conventional prediction that higher interest rates will inhibit investments in the existing owner-occupied housing stock.

If prices of nonhousing goods (P_Z) were expected to rise in the future relative to prices of various $\bar{A}_t$ options, one would predict a shift of consumption away from Z. Graphically, such expectations are shown in figure 3.1 by a clockwise pivoting of FD around D and $G\mathcal{J}$ around G, and a shift to the left of K and a similar pivoting around K. These changes would create both income and substitution effects for $\bar{A}_t$. If normally the income effect would predominate, one should witness lower optimal $\bar{A}_t$ expenditures and consumption.

Conversely, if the prices of maintenance (P_M) or upward conversion (P_K) inputs are expected to rise in the future, or the price of rental units ($P_{\bar{R}}$) is expected to fall (all relative to P_Z), alterations opposite those described in the previous paragraph occur for maintenance and upward conversion. Transformation function DF pivots clockwise around F; $G\mathcal{J}$ shifts $\mathcal{J}$ to the left, and G pivots downward. The same qualitative changes are shown in the downward conversion transformation function KQ as above, but in this case these changes are due to lower $P_{\bar{R}}$ instead of higher P_Z.

Unlike the above price changes that affected the marginal rates of transformation, altered expectations about the future sales value of the owned housing stock ($P_{\bar{H}T}$, $\tilde{P}_{\bar{H}T}$) affect the marginal rate of substitution (assuming that $w > 0$ in the utility function). More optimistic expectations about sales value increase the second term in (3.17), and should thus lead unambiguously to greater consumption of and expenditures on $\bar{A}_t$. Only if $\tilde{P}_{\bar{H}T}$

expectations vary greatly from those about $P_{\bar{H}T}$ would we expect any significant change in the relative probability of downward conversion versus the other upkeep strategies.

Neighborhood Physical-Demographic Characteristics and Property Values

A primary contribution of the foregoing model is that it explicitly integrates neighborhood considerations into the homeowner's upkeep calculus. Here the physical-demographic dimension of the neighborhood and the market's valuation of this dimension will be considered. At the outset it should be recalled that regardless of an individual homeowner's personal evaluation of the surrounding neighborhood, the homeowner may perceive that the market as a whole evaluates (and therefore prices) the neighborhood differently.[26] The former will affect a homeowner's utility via the consumption component f; the latter via the wealth component w. Because each generates different effects in the model, they will be considered separately.

The homeowner's own evaluations of present quality and expectations about future physical-demographic quality of the neighborhood do not alter the transformation functions in the model and, thus, do not alter the relative probabilities of one upkeep strategy being chosen versus another. These personal evaluations can affect, however, the marginal rates of substitution, but if and only if N is a multiplicative function of H_t in f, i.e., if f_{Ht} in (3.17) is a function of N. In this case, more pessimistic current or future evaluations of neighborhood quality serve to reduce the marginal-utility gain in the future stream of housing services flowing from the structural capital added by $\bar{A}_t$; i.e., the first term in (3.17) is lower because f_{Ht} is reduced by the decrement in N. This increase in the marginal rate of transformation reduces the probabilities of either upward conversion or positive maintenance being selected as the optimal strategy.

In sum, one would normally predict that a homeowner's negative evaluation of and pessimistic expectations about the physical-demographic neighborhood should be negatively correlated with amounts of and expenditures on $\bar{A}_t$. But the degree to which this is the case depends upon the particular form and parameter values of a given homeowner's utility function; in particular, whether f_{Ht} is a function of N_t (and, if so, the weight given N). In the extreme case where N_t is an additive element to the utility gained from consuming H_t, intertemporal or cross-sectional variations in N will have no effect on upkeep behavior whatsoever.

The homeowner's expectations of how the market will evaluate the neighborhood (and hence will price structural capital) can be complex, depending on how these expectations affect the homeowner's perception of the relationship between E_T and the threshold home-equity level. Three distinct possibilities must be considered.

The simplest case is when both before and after an altered expectation, E_T is given a positive weight in the utility function. This is equivalent to assuming no equity threshold. In such a case the homeowner perceives that a previously static market evaluation of the neighborhood (or, equivalently, the overall metropolitan housing price level) has now changed to one of decline, which reduces the incremental asset value of any $\bar{A}_t$. The $w_{\bar{A}_t}$ term in (3.17) is now lower, because $P_{\dot{H}T}$ is now lower. This increase in the marginal rate of substitution should yield lower optimal levels of $\bar{A}_t$ consumption and expenditure, and enhance the possibility of a zero-maintenance strategy vis-à-vis any of the other three alternatives. Just the opposite is true if unforeseen property value appreciation is expected. In such a case there is an inverse relationship between pessimism about future property values and upkeep activity.

The second case is when E_T is consistently perceived to have exceeded the threshold equity level (perhaps due to fortuitous circumstances in the past), regardless of new expectations. This is equivalent to the case where w never assigns value to E_T. Where homeowners are confident they will get their money out, no matter what, alterations in their expectations will be unrelated to upkeep activity. So long as E_T remains above the threshold, there will be no marginal utility gained from $\bar{A}_t$ via the w component in any event of altered $P_{\dot{H}T}$.

The final case is where a prior relationship between E_T and the threshold equity level is reversed as a result of new expectations about neighborhood property values. For instance, suppose originally complacent homeowners perceive their E_T above threshold, but suddenly become more pessimistic so that E_T falls below it. In this circumstance w assigns new weight to $\bar{A}_t$, and an added incentive to upkeep will ensue as the marginal rate of substitution is suddenly augmented. Conversely, homeowners with E_T below threshold may come to perceive that due to predicted inflation in neighborhood values, they'll exceed the threshold much sooner than they originally planned. Such will lead to a reduced marginal rate of substitution as the w component begins to assign zero marginal value to $\bar{A}_t$. Thus, in this third case, pessimism is directly related to upkeep activity.

In sum, homeowners' expectations about future property values in the neighborhood will yield radically different changes in marginal rates of substitution, depending on the precise assumptions made about the wealth component of their utility functions, and their current assessment of achieved versus threshold levels of home equity. Changes in marginal rates of transformation are more predictable, and should be affected only in the case of downward conversion. Because the expected flow of rentals from potential newly created units depends on the market evaluation of neighborhood quality, any such lower evaluations reduce the expected returns from downward conversion by reducing $P_{\bar{R}}$. As this transformation function shifts K to the left (see figure 3.1) and clockwise around this new K, it reduces the probability of downward conversion being chosen as the global-optimum strategy.

Neighborhood Social Interaction and Cohesion

The effect of an alteration in a homeowner's perceptions about the current or future social cohesion of the neighborhood (or, equivalently, a comparison involving otherwise-identical homeowners with differing S vectors) can be viewed in terms of altered marginal rates of substitution (assuming j_{Ht} is a function of S). If there is strong social interaction between a homeowner and the neighbors, the chances for collectively induced behavioral modifications are enhanced via the application of social sanctions or rewards. In such a cohesive neighborhood context the individual not only receives utility directly from the consumption of $\bar{A}_t$ (possibly through both improved housing service flows and asset values), but also indirectly from the social-psychological feedback from the neighbors. Thus, the utility gained from a high $\bar{A}_t$ can be increased by the compliments and enhanced prestige accorded the homeowner by neighbors. Conversely, strategies involving little $\bar{A}_t$ may carry with them a utility disincentive: the potential of eroded personal reputation and alienation from neighbors.

In terms of figure 3.1, these social-interactive effects can be seen as reducing the slope of the indifference curve mapping $U_I - U_{IV}$. This, in turn, leads to the prediction of a reduced probability of selecting a zero-maintenance strategy, and of an increased amount of $\bar{A}_t$ expenditure when either a positive-maintenance or upward-conversion strategy is selected. If, in addition, there are especially virulent neighborhood social sanctions against the conversion of single-family to multiple-unit structures, the marginal rates of substitution relevant for downward conversion will fall; i.e., indifference curves $U_V - U_{VIII}$ will flatten. This will reduce the likelihood that downward conversion is selected as a global-optimum strategy.

Strategic Interaction among Homeowners

As noted in chapter 2, there are conflicting theories about what type of strategic gaming interactions among homeowners occur in urban neighborhoods. This section shows how the model provides insights into how various types of strategic behaviors follow from the specification of the utility function of homeowners and of initial neighborhood conditions.

But first, consider how the basic terminology of strategic behaviors can be usefully redefined and understood in the context of the present model. A "threshold" for generating responses of homeowners to a neighborhood improvement can be seen as an initial situation where most homeowners are following a behavior that is a corner solution, e.g., a zero-maintenance strategy. In such a case, initial decreases in the marginal rate of substitution may be insufficient to erase the corner solution. Only when such decreases exceed a particular threshold value will an optimum occur that involves a positive-maintenance behavior. Thus, with any specification of the utility function (3.1) such that marginal utility of $\bar{A}_t$ is somehow affected by N, the model demonstrates possible "free-rider" behavior, i.e., a situation where changes in marginal rates of substitution between $\bar{A}$ and Z via new N are insufficient to alter upkeep behavior of the individual. But an even wider variety of strategic behaviors are possible that do not depend on the initial presence of a corner solution; but rather on the utility-function specification.

Consider four alternative behavioral types. An "asymmetric free-rider" is a homeowner who does not increase the level of upkeep behavior when improvements in the physical-demographic character and/or property values of the neighborhood occur or are expected. A "symmetric free-rider" is one who does not alter upkeep behavior regardless of actual or anticipated changes in the neighborhood in either direction. A "crowd-follower" responds to any changes in the neighborhood in such a way that the actions reinforce those aggregate changes. Finally, a "trend-bucker" intensifies upkeep behavior as a counterresponse to declines in the neighborhood. Which type of behavior is forthcoming will depend on the magnitude and direction of marginal rate of substitution changes that result from changes in the homeowner's evaluation of neighborhood quality and/or in the expected market prices of housing in the neighborhood. And these changes, in turn, will depend on the utility-function specification.

To clarify, take first the specification of the physical-demographic character of the neighborhood N in the f component of the utility function. If the marginal utility of $\bar{A}_t$ is independent of N, changes in N will not lead the homeowner to alter upkeep behavior; i.e., the homeowner will be a symmetric free-rider (ignoring the wealth component of utility for the moment). If N does affect marginal consumption utility of $\bar{A}_t$, the relationship of N and $\bar{A}_t$ will be direct, i.e., the homeowner will be a crowd-follower. Thus, the theory clearly suggests that no individual strategic behaviors that tend to offset aggregate changes in physical-demographic neighborhood quality can be forthcoming through the consumption component of homeowner utility.

Such is not the case, however, when considering the wealth component of utility. The three possible perceptions of the relationship between E_T and the threshold home-equity level are again crucial here. If E_T is given a positive weight in the utility function regardless of expectations (equivalently, there is no equity threshold), pessimism about neighborhood property values (independent of neighborhood quality) will be inversely related to upkeep activity. In other words, crowd-following actions will be forthcoming. If E_T is given no weight (either because w is always zero or because E_T exceeds the threshold), revised property-value expectations will produce no alterations in $\bar{A}_t$; symmetric free-riders result.

But if the new property-value expectations serve to alter the perceived relationship between achieved and threshold equity levels (and hence the weight assigned to $\bar{A}_t$ by w changes dramatically), the other two behaviors are forthcoming. If a prior complacency that E_T will exceed threshold is replaced by a new pessimism, upkeep will be intensified and trend-bucker behavior will be manifested. If a prior worry about E_T reaching threshold is replaced by a newfound optimism about local property value inflation (again, independent of qualitative neighborhood changes), upkeep will be reduced, and asymmetric free-rider behavior will result.

Thus, the model predicts that four distinct sorts of strategic behaviors may be forthcoming, depending on how one specifies the wealth component of the utility function. Two behaviors are indistinguishable from those produced via the consumption component of the utility function, but two are unique possibilities. To put this differently, the model suggests that strategic behavior resulting from changes in the qualitative evaluation of the physical-demographic neighborhood is relatively limited compared to the options that may arise over changes in the monetary (market) evaluation of the neighborhood, independent of its direct consumption value. This, in turn, suggests that empirical models that intend to elucidate such strategic interactions (such as that estimated in chapter 9) must consider qualitative and monetary neighborhood expectations separately.

Another relevant issue is how the initial neighborhood conditions may be important in generating particular behaviors. First, in neighborhoods of low physical-demographic quality it is more likely that initially many homeowners are at a corner-solution strategy of zero maintenance. This means that regardless of preferences and subsequent changes in marginal rates of substitution due to altered expectations, asymmetric free-rider behavior is more likely. Second, in such neighborhoods, typical homeowners may have very modest expectations about property-value appreciation when they first buy. If this is true, the initial E_0, achieved E_T, and threshold equities may be approximately equal. This means that any new expectations are likely to render a different comparative relationship between achieved and threshold equities, resulting in subsequent asymmetric free-rider or trend-bucker behavior, depending on the degree of optimism or pessimism, respectively.

The social-interactive dimension of the neighborhood also plays a role. Even if f_{Ht} is not related to N, so long as it is related to S social cohesion can affect strategic behavior. For example, if most homeowners in a cohesive neighborhood adopt a higher level of housing investments, they may through social pressures induce some homeowners who otherwise might be free-riders to increase their $\bar{A}_t$ expenditures. Similarly, social cohesion may be seen as reducing thresholds for moving away from a prior corner solution by augmenting any reductions in marginal rates of substitution forthcoming by improvements in N.

The model thus clearly explains why no single pattern of homeowner strategic interaction has been observed (Taub, Taylor, and Dunham 1984, ch. 6): this interaction depends on the aggregate nature of the preferences of homeowners in the neighborhood and on the initial physical-demographic and social conditions in the neighborhood. Specifically, the model suggests that free-rider behavior is less likely the greater the increase in marginal utility via enhanced consumption and/or wealth accumulation opportunities resulting from improvements in N or $P_{\bar{H}T}$. As for the context, it indicates that for any given set of homeowners, free-rider behavior is less likely the higher the initial level of N and $P_{\bar{H}T}$; or the greater the improvement in N; or the greater the improvement in $P_{\bar{H}T}$, so long as it does not result in exceeding threshold equity; and the greater the degree of social cohesion. Thus, like the threshold model, the present model suggests that no single strategic behavior will result in all circumstances. Unlike the threshold model, however, it does not derive such a conclusion from variations in homeowners' degree of risk aversion. Another nuance: the present model uniquely suggests a theoretical possibility of trend-bucking behavior, where homeowners in declining areas intensify their upkeep efforts.

*Interaction Effects among Parameters: Cumulative
Causation and Neighborhood Change Revisited*

The previous discussion of model predictions has been couched in *ceteris paribus* terms. In real neighborhoods, however, it is likely that several of the above hypothetical parameter changes would endogenously generate changes in other parameters.[27] Of most interest are those interactions occurring through the medium of neighborhood.

Consider some exogenously induced change in the demographic character of a given homeowner's neighborhood. If the homeowner immediately translates this change as a decrease in current and/or expected future neighborhood quality, the upkeep response will be based on this changed perception, subject of course to strategic interactions. The change may even reduce the homeowner's expected length of tenure in the dwelling, depending on the characteristics of the individual homeowner.

A given individual homeowner may not, at first, react to such changes in neighborhood demographics at all. But should the population changes involve significant alterations in the purchasing power, preferences, or expectations of the average homeowner in the neighborhood, the aggregate neighborhood upkeep strategy may be altered, with associated changes in the quality of many homes in the area. Our given homeowner thus will likely perceive these changes in N eventually, and respond accordingly. In addition, the hypothetical change considered might produce a dissolution of any previous neighborhood cohesion. Thus, homeowners who might previously have been subjected to strong pressures to maintain or improve their dwelling may now not have such an added social stimulant to their expenditure on housing. Finally, new aggregate homeowner characteristics could well lead to different types of strategic interaction.

Of course, the interaction between parameters need not be initiated from an exogenous impact upon the neighborhood; it can start with a change in a given homeowner. An individual homeowner may move into a different life-cycle stage or may have an alteration in income. The homeowner's expectations about future prices or interest rates may change, or the homeowner's social attachment to neighbors might wax or wane as a result of idiosyncratic personal reasons. Any and all of these changes will likely alter the manner and degree to which housing quality is maintained by the individual. Any such alterations will, in turn, affect other neighborhood homeowners' perceptions of neighborhood quality and their subsequent upkeep behavior, as described in the previous paragraph. These aforementioned endogenous linkups between parameters represent the formal theoretical mechanism of cumulative causation discussed in chapter 2. In sum, the model presented here offers a rich framework within which the fragility of neighborhood stability and the idiosyncratic, self-reinforcing dynamics of neighborhood change can be deciphered.

Summary

This chapter presents a formal model of the decision made by homeowners about what upkeep behavior to pursue during the time that they own their current dwellings. The problem is formulated as one of intertemporal maximization of utility, where the utility derived from alterations in the housing stock potentially comes both from the consumption of the altered future stream of housing services and from the future asset value of the

altered stock. Constraints to utility maximization take the form of transformation functions that embody both the financial and the technological
capacities for transformations between the consumption of nonhousing
goods and purchasing alterations in the housing stock. Financial considerations include not only market prices for direct expenditures, but also
indirect effects on future home operating costs and on the homeowner's
tax liabilities.

The local-optimum combination of housing versus nonhousing expenditures for a given period is shown to correspond to the familiar rule of
equating marginal rates of substitution and transformation for each of
three alternative upkeep strategies: positive maintenance, upward conversion, and downward conversion. Alternative intertemporal sequences of
upkeep behaviors also must obey these first-order conditions. Comparisons of the total discounted present values of utility associated with
each of those alternative upkeep strategy sequences and with the zero
housing-alteration option yield the global-optimum strategy.

In the model, optimal upkeep behavior is potentially affected by the
physical-demographic and social-interactive neighborhood contexts via
the utility-function specification. If the marginal utility of additional consumable or salable housing services is a function of neighborhood attributes, the willingness of the homeowner to augment this flow by alterations in structural capital will depend on current and expected future
neighborhood qualitative conditions and property values. But the model
clearly shows how variation in the behavioral responses to neighborhood
change can occur due to differences in the weight homeowners place on
asset value considerations, in the degree to which neighborhood affects the
value of incremental housing services, and on the initial level of neighborhood quality. The social relationships between the homeowner and
neighbors (the social-interactive neighborhood described in the previous
chapter) is formally modeled as a parameter altering the marginal utility
that homeowners associate with alterations in their housing stock. In this
way a clear mechanism by which neighborhood cohesion can affect individual home upkeep behavior is established theoretically.

This specification also elucidates the origin of strategic interactions
among homeowners. The nature of these interactions depends on utility-
function specification and neighborhood context. The special case of the
free-rider problem is shown to be more likely the less a homeowner's
marginal utility from home upkeep is affected by neighborhood conditions, the lower the initial level of neighborhood quality and expected
future property values, and the lower the degree of neighborhood social
cohesion.

Finally, testable predictions are drawn from the model by exploring the
implications of various individual parameter changes. The predictions are

summarized in table 3.2. Although many predictions are conventional, others give rise to outcomes that confound the conventional wisdom, depending on the parameters of the particular homeowners and neighborhood under consideration. In the context of the entire model, it is shown how certain parameter changes can endogenously alter others, thereby setting in motion a process of cumulative changes in neighborhood quality. The formal model and the predictions it generates form the foundation for the empirical analyses of forthcoming chapters.

II   Empirical Analyses

4 Data Base and Sampling Methodology

Chapters 2 and 3 presented a theoretical framework for understanding the nature and significance of homeowners' housing upkeep investments; the next six chapters focus on the specification and estimation of an empirical model based on this framework. This chapter describes the two urban data bases employed in the empirical analyses and the procedures used for obtaining these data. The subsequent six chapters explicate components of the path model presented at the end of chapter 2. Chapter 5 considers in more detail the empirical features of these two samples, and gives the definitions for all the independent variables in the model. These variables are categorized into objective characteristics of: sampled homeowners, their dwellings, the physical, demographic, and social-interactive neighborhoods in which they live, and various public policies impinging upon them that could affect their housing investments. Chapters 6, 7, and 8, respectively, describe and estimate the equations explaining the three intervening variables in the path model: homeowners' residential evaluations, neighborhood expectations, and expected length of tenure. Finally, chapter 9 gives the specification of the variables of ultimate concern to the analysis: those measuring homeowners' housing upkeep behavior. Results of empirical estimates for upkeep equations that employ both independent and intervening variables are given. Chapter 10 provides a concise summary of the main results of chapters 6 through 9, and discusses their importance for predicting neighborhood reinvestment levels.

Overview of Wooster and Minneapolis

One distinctive feature of the empirical analysis is that it is replicated in two quite different housing market contexts. One context is Wooster, Ohio, a municipality of almost 20 thousand population located fifty-five miles south of Cleveland. It is the county seat and main commercial and retail center of Wayne County, a trade area with 90 thousand residents. Wooster has an unusually diversified economic base of light industrial and post-secondary educational institutions. As such, Wooster is anything but a "bedroom suburb"; it represents a relatively autonomous small city.[1]

According to 1975 statistics (the year when data to be analyzed were collected), 97 percent of Wooster's households are white, with disproportionate numbers of female-headed (31 percent) or elderly-headed (25 percent) households. Household heads are unusually prosperous and well-educated, especially by small-town standards. Median income is $11,627 (1975 $), with only 6 percent earning less than $5,000. One-fourth held college degrees.

Wooster's housing stock is made up of a wide variety of structural vintages. Numerous well-maintained homes from the mid-1800s era are scattered throughout the market area. And because Wooster has had a continued slow population growth (about 2 percent per decade) and rising real incomes, there are also significant proportions of new homes (over one-fourth after 1960), both at the luxury end of the market and at "tract" quality levels. About two-thirds of the structures are single-family dwellings and are owner-occupied. Relatively few are substandard (e.g., only 1 percent lack complete plumbing or heating), and there are no areas of such consistently poor-quality dwellings in Wooster that they fairly could be labelled slums. The generally high quality of the stock is also indicated by the robust $27,000 median for single-family property values in the city.[2]

Minneapolis, by contrast, is a medium-sized central city of 371 thousand located in a SMSA of over 2 million population. (For more details about Minneapolis, see Minneapolis, City of [1981].)[3] Unlike many other major midwestern cities, Minneapolis has not been heavily dominated by smokestack industries; its economic base rests on technical and professional services and light industry. This is reflected in the 1980 occupational distribution of the city's workforce: 26 percent in managerial or professional, and 35 percent in technical or sales positions.

Although the two cities obviously differ in scale, Minneapolis's household composition is in many ways similar to Wooster's. Both have about 25 percent elderly households, 25 percent college-graduate households, and over 90 percent white households. The last figure is exceptionally high for Minneapolis, in comparison to comparably sized central cities.[4] Minneapolis does, however, possess a relatively larger share (16 percent) of very low-income (i.e., under $5,000) households than Wooster.

As would be expected in a mature central city circumscribed by newer, suburban municipalities, Minneapolis's housing stock has a smaller proportion of post-1960 dwellings (18 percent) than does Wooster's. The share of owner-occupied dwellings is also smaller (49 percent). But, as in Wooster, Minneapolis's population size and purchasing power have stayed relatively stable, its housing stock is in relatively good physical condition, and housing commands substantial prices in the marketplace: a mean of $52,600 for owner-occupied units in 1980.

In summary, the two contexts for empirical investigations share several important similarities. Though distinct in scale, housing stock composition, and metropolitan context, both Minneapolis and Wooster housing markets were, at the time of the study, comparatively stable, high quality, and moderately priced. Neither market was characterized by boom or bust conditions, nor by noteworthy dynamics of racial tipping or slum incursion at the neighborhood level. The overall characteristics of the household demanders were remarkably similar in the two markets. (There were, of course, further distinctions that could be made about the owner-occupants sampled in each city and about the dwellings and neighborhoods they inhabit, but such discussions are postponed until chapter 5, when particular variables are specified.)

Thus, the above similarities should permit one to ascertain more clearly whether homeowners' behaviors in such a generally stable, prosperous housing market context are consistent between a small city and a large city. As implied in chapter 3 (and explicated fully in forthcoming chapters), one reason to suspect they may not be consistent is the potentially distinctive nature and role of neighborhood social interaction and cohesiveness in the two settings. And, of special importance, there is another clear difference between the Wooster and Minneapolis housing markets: the former was characterized in 1975 by laissez faire; the latter in 1980 by a variety of innovative, large-scale public programs designed to improve neighborhoods and augment homeowners' upkeep efforts. The details of these programs will be presented in chapter 5 in the context of variable specification. The comparative empirical analysis involving Wooster and Minneapolis provides, therefore, a unique opportunity to explore particular sorts of important cross-sectional behavioral variations without adding undue amounts of extraneous contextual difference.

Interviewing and Sampling Procedures

The strategy for training interviewers, the sampling procedure, and part of the questionnaire design were developed by Professor Garry W. Hesser, Director of Metro-Urban Studies at Augsburg College in Minneapolis, and former Chairperson of Urban Studies at the College of Wooster. Professor Hesser and I collaborated on the 1975 Wooster survey, pursuant to a consulting contract with the City of Wooster Planning Department. The 1980 Minneapolis survey was conducted solely by Professor Hesser, who was kind enough to share his data with me for the purposes of this research.

Interviewing

Seven interviewers for the Wooster study and four for Minneapolis were selected according to criteria common to survey-research operations: the ability to relate to and with respondents; tact, demeanor, and ability to understand the nature of the project; objectivity and minimized influence on the answers to the questions; etc. All interviewers were academically trained in the social sciences, with specific training in research methodology.

Each interviewer was provided with a three-hundred–page manual on interviewing.[5] The manual, compiled by Professor Hesser, emphasized both the skills and ethics of interviewing. Prior to the actual interviewing, Professor Hesser conducted training sessions and pre-test interviewing to emphasize and facilitate the interviewing process and tactics.

Official city and college identification was provided to each interviewer. Respondents, though urged to cooperate, were always given the option to refuse either the entire interview or particular questions that they deemed too personal, private, etc. For example, thirty-one persons in the Wooster sample could not or would not answer the "total income" question (3.1 percent).

The interviewers' contacts were made during the period between 10 July and 10 September 1975 in Wooster, and between 1 July and 1 October 1980 in Minneapolis. Interviews took place in the evenings and weekends, as well as during what might be considered working hours during the week, and averaged about forty-five minutes in length.[6]

At the conclusion of each interview, each respondent was thanked and given a note with telephone numbers where further information and comments could be sought and/or given. The interviewers were instructed never to provide information, opinions, or suggestions to the respondents. Instead, the telephone numbers were provided in order that the citizens could secure reliable and direct access to persons who could answer their questions or assist them.

Sampling

The sampling strategy in both cities was that of systematic selection. Household units[7] were selected from a complete and current population listing through applying a selection interval.[8] This procedure was used because of its administrative simplicity.

The sampling units were selected according to the generally accepted criteria associated with a stratified sampling approach. Because of the critical nature of geographic distribution, each city was divided into sub-areas, and subsamples were drawn from each area. Because these areas were not equal in size, a second sampling strategy was utilized: unequal probabilities of selection. Warwick and Lininger define this as when "sampling units are chosen by a procedure giving some elements a higher or lower chance of selection than others" (1975, 103).

The details and rationale are discussed in conjunction with the sampling strategy utilized for each city. For now, let it suffice to state that the varying sizes of each of the subareas necessitated a stratification of the population and the selection of subsamples from each geographic area that produced an adequate number of observations for separate analysis of each subarea in question.[9]

In addition to administrative simplicity, this sampling strategy reduced the costs of sampling and interviewing, and contributed to easier field supervision.[10] The strategy was adapted to the special needs and circumstances of each city.

WOOSTER   In an attempt to describe areas having relatively homogeneous populations and houses, the City of Wooster Planning Staff delineated twenty-six "study areas," defined by natural and human-made boundaries. These areas were used as the operational definition of "neighborhood" for the Wooster study.[11]

A complete list of all residential units was compiled for each study area with the assistance of the most current city directory. The list was then updated by means of the building permits issued and demolished units recorded since the directory's publication.

For each of the twenty-six lists a systematic random sample was selected consisting of 15 percent of the units, with care to equal or exceed HUD and/or census sampling procedures, both in quantity and quality. Additional units were selected randomly for each study area for purposes of substitution resulting from refusals. The resulting sample of 1,061 contained 54 vacant units for which no substitution was made.

The addresses of the systematically selected units were compiled into twenty-six area lists. Seven interviewers were trained and assigned to specific areas of the city. Letters from the mayor were sent to each residence approximately one week before the interviewer made her/his first visit to the household. Interviewers wrote additional notes in the lower left-hand corners of the letters to introduce themselves. The effort resulted in an acceptance rate of 92.7 percent. Analysis showed no significant biases resulting from refusals.

MINNEAPOLIS   The sampling framework used in Minneapolis was a multistage approach to simple random sampling.[12] This process enabled the sampling to proceed without the complete list of households that it was feasible to obtain in the smaller city.

All 5,079 blocks[13] in the city were identified, assuring that every household had a known chance of being selected in the sample. Three subsamples were designated using the records of the city of Minneapolis, especially those of the Minneapolis Community Development Agency:

Group I: Blocks within tracts that were currently or previously the recipients of public funds for Urban Renewal or Community Development Block Grants (CDBG) ($N = 1,961$ blocks). Thirty blocks were drawn from this list using systematic sampling.[14]

Group II: Blocks within areas deemed eligible by the existing income and housing condition criteria, but that had never been targeted as Urban Renewal areas or CDBG neighborhood strategy areas; i.e., had never received public funds as a neighborhood area ($N = 507$ blocks). Twenty blocks were selected using systematic sampling.[15]

Group III: Blocks within areas that were never eligible for Urban Renewal or designated as neighborhood strategy areas; i.e., had never received public-housing or neighborhood-rehabilitation funds or been eligible under the guidelines developed by the city ($N = 2,611$ blocks). Thirty-two blocks were chosen.[16]

The total number of primary sampling units (PSUs) was eighty-two, a large enough sample to minimize the sampling error often created by choosing sample cases in groups rather than independently.[17]

Eight owner-occupied households were selected from each block. Sampling rules were clearly established for the interviewers. Starting with the southwest corner of the block, interviewers proceeded counterclockwise from house to house interviewing either the male or female head of the household in owner-occupied housing.[18]

In addition to careful specification of the procedures, including the clear designation of the head of household (or spouse), the interviewers varied their interviewing times to include evenings and weekends for at least half of the blocks to ensure a balance of age, sex, employment status, and so forth.

The resulting sample balanced the convenience and economy of a multistage sample with the care and precision of interviewer training, the large number of PSUs and carefully predetermined rules for the selection of respondents. The result was a stratified sample of households clustered in neighborhood units allowing for analysis of micro-neighborhoods and a control for public funding expenditures targeted at the entire neighborhood.

5 Characteristics of Sampled Owners, Dwellings, Neighborhoods, and Policies

As a first step in making the conceptual model presented in chapter 2 operational, a large number of variables are specified that are viewed as independent (i.e., exogenous or predetermined). These independent variables may be conveniently grouped into the categories previously employed in the path model (figure 2.1): homeowner characteristics, dwelling characteristics, neighborhood characteristics, and public policies. Each is considered in turn below. (For the reader's convenience a glossary of variable names and definitions is provided in the appendix.) Because each set of independent variables is modeled as affecting numerous intervening and dependent variables, discussion of specific predictions for causal relationships is postponed until later chapters.

Another major goal of this chapter is to analyze how the various functional and geographic dimensions of the urban neighborhood may be appropriately measured. Specifically, factor analyses are employed to discern whether the physical, demographic, and social-interactive characteristics of the neighborhood prove to be distinct empirically, and whether blockface and census-tract features are separable in practice. These analyses provide the foundation for the specification of the neighborhood variables to be used in the statistical analyses described in chapters 6 through 9.

Readers wishing to avoid the details of variable specification can easily skip this chapter, and merely refer to the glossary when considering variables in subsequent chapters.

Homeowners' Characteristics

Two distinct dimensions of sampled homeowners are considered here: socioeconomic status and demographic status. Socioeconomic status is measured first by the years of educational attainment in the household (EDUCATION), defined as the higher of the male household head's or spouse's education, or the highest education in a multiple-head household, or the education of a single household head. Implicit in this specification is the assumption that the educational aspect of status is better captured by the highest level of education present in the household, whether it is possessed by a male head or not.

Second, socioeconomic status is measured by household normal discretionary income (INCOME).[1] Although gross household income is employed conventionally, in the context of housing investment it is more desirable to employ a measure that captures the uncommitted purchasing power that households have at their discretion. Thus, from total household income is subtracted the annual payments on the home mortgage, if any.[2] Ideally, one also would like to obtain the long-run, permanent income of the household, because this is a better predictor of consumer expenditure on durable goods than short-run, transitory income. Unfortunately, for present purposes data were available only on household income for the calendar year prior to the survey year. But there was additional information on whether the respondent evaluated this income as "normal," or "above" or "below" normal for a five-year period, and this was used to adjust the reported income appropriately (see glossary for details).[3]

Several variables are used to measure demographic characteristics of the homeowner. Three categories of households are distinguished: married, male-headed households; not married, female-headed households; not married, male-headed, or multiple, unrelated adult–headed households.[4] The former two categories are denoted by dummy variables (MARRIED, FEMALE, respectively), rendering the latter category as the reference class to which coefficients of the dummy variables are compared. The size of the household is measured by the total number of year-round residents in the dwelling, both related and unrelated to the household head (OCCUPANTS). If the race of the household head is black, it is denoted by a dummy variable (BLACK). Subsamples of other racial minorities are too small to permit separate categorization. Finally, a key demographic characteristic is the stage in the family life cycle in which the household finds itself. A conventional breakdown of these life-cycle stages is utilized here:

Stage 1: Head under age forty-five, no children in home (head either married or not)

Stage 2: Youngest child in household under age five (head either married or not, of any age)

Stage 3: Youngest child in household age five to fourteen (head either married or not, of any age)

Stage 4: Youngest child in household over age fourteen (head either married or not, of any age)

Stage 5: Head over age forty-five, no children in home (head either married or not)

Because there is no *a priori* basis for supposing these categories to represent an ordinal or an interval scale, four dummy variables denoting the last four life-cycle stages above are specified (STAGE2, . . . , STAGE5), and the first stage is the reference category.

A final set of household characteristics relates to previous residential and mobility experience. If the given homeowner did not live in a single-family detached home while she or he was a child or immediately prior to the current home, the dummy variables EARLYHOME and PRIORHOME take the value one, respectively. The number of housing moves the homeowner has made in the previous five years is measured by the variable NUM-MOVES. The number of years the homeowner has resided in the current single-family dwelling is measured by LONGEVITY.

The reader should recall that another household characteristic is being controlled for implicitly through restricting the sample analyzed to homeowners who have not moved into their present dwelling within the calendar year of the survey. These recent in-movers may presumably have engaged in housing upkeep behaviors that are atypical of their ongoing activities. New occupants may make immediate cosmetic alterations of the unit according to their tastes. On the other hand, the demands of moving may mean that they have little time or energy for housing upkeep. They probably have less first-hand information about the neighborhood, and their perceptions and expectations are likely different from those they would hold after a longer tenure.

Homeowners' Dwelling Characteristics

As noted in chapter 4, the samples of homeowners employed in the empirical analysis were restricted to those residing in permanent, single-family detached structures. This was done so as to standardize as much as possible for both homeowner behavioral motivations and for building-upkeep payoffs. In other words, owner-occupants in duplexes or multiple-unit structures likely possess a different amalgam of housing consumption versus investment motives than the traditional homeowner. And owner-occupied single-family units that are mobile homes, row- or townhouses, or condominium apartments undoubtedly possess quite different technological "transformation functions" (in the language of chapter 3) for converting upkeep investments into improved housing quality.

But in addition to this implicit control there are several other explicit variables employed to control for various features of the dwelling that are likely to affect the occupying homeowner's evaluation of the structure and investment in it. These variables measure various aspects of the age, structural features, and size of the dwelling.

Differences in dwelling age typically imply differences in architectural style, construction technology, type and efficiency of mechanical systems (plumbing, heating, and wiring), and the time over which the structure has been subject to normal wear and tear, weathering, etc. Because these differences are not likely to be well modelled as a monotonic function, building age is measured instead by a set of categories representing distinct vintages of homes. Specifically, if the dwelling was built during the 1960–69 era, a dummy variable, BUILT60–69, is assigned the value one; zero otherwise. Similarly, if it was built from 1940–59, 1920–39 or before 1920, the dummy variables BUILT40–59, BUILT20–39 and BUILTPRE-20, respectively, are assigned the value one. Given this specification, the coefficients of these four structural vintage variables should be interpreted as the difference between the given vintage and that of a house built after 1969.

Although some structural features are measured implicitly by the vintage variables, others are measured explicitly by the following four variables. If the dwelling has an enclosed garage,[5] the dummy variable GARAGE takes the value one, zero otherwise. If the dwelling has whole-house air conditioning,[6] the dummy variable AIRCOND takes the value one, zero otherwise. If the dominant type of exterior construction consists of wood clapboard siding,[7] the dummy variable WOOD takes the value one, zero otherwise. Finally, the absence of a central heating system is measured by the dummy variable NOHEAT.

The quantitative aspects of the dwelling package are measured by three variables. ROOMS measures the number of finished rooms of all kinds in the dwelling (excluding bathrooms).[8] BATHRMS measures the number of bathrooms (including fractional) in the dwelling.[9] YARD measures the street frontage (in feet) of the yard on which the dwelling is located.[10] The relationship of these quantitative aspects of the dwelling to the size of the occupying household is measured by the given dwelling variable divided by the number of full-time residents (OCCUPANTS): the variables ROOM/OCC, BATH/OCC and YARD/OCC, respectively.

Neighborhood Characteristics

A major contribution of this work consists of its explicit theoretical and empirical integration of various dimensions of the urban neighborhood into an analysis of homeowners' housing investments. Here it is thus of prime importance to discuss in detail how the concept of neighborhood can be made empirically operational. Two conceptual questions must be confronted at the outset: What is the appropriate geographic scale for the urban neighborhood as it relates to homeowners' investments? Are there distinct dimensions of this space that are separable along physical, demographic, and social-interactive aspects? Analyses of the Wooster and Minneapolis data provide some interesting and useful answers to these questions. These analyses follow in this section.

The Geographic Concept of Neighborhood

Clearly, if the geographic neighborhood is to be made operational in a way that provides explanatory power for homeowners' behaviors, it must correspond to the neighborhood as perceived by homeowners' themselves (Lynch 1960; Keller 1968, 97–102; Hunter 1974, ch.2; Downs 1981, ch.2; Galster 1986). Fortunately, two studies provide guidance here. In his study of Chicago neighborhoods, Suttles (1972, ch.3) provided the valuable insight that the perceptual, social, and spatial aspects of neighborhood are intrinsically interrelated, and that varied degrees of importance and particular social functions are associated with different spatial levels of neighborhood. The most elemental spatial unit was viewed by residents as the "block face," the area defined by where children were allowed to play without supervision. The second level was labelled the "defended neighborhood," the smallest area possessing a corporate identity as defined by mutual opposition to another area. The third level, the "community of limited liability," typically consisted of an administrative district in which individuals' social participation was selective and voluntary. The highest geographic level of neighborhood, the "expanded community of limited liability," was viewed as an entire sector of a city.

Birch et al. (1979:35–37) surveyed homeowners in several large cities to reveal their perceptions of spatial levels of neighborhood. These perceptions of neighborhood, which closely correspond to Suttles's hierarchy, were: (1) a one-block radius around the homeowner's dwelling, (2) an area over which there were relatively homogeneous housing values and populations where one felt "socioeconomic brotherhood," or, if this second level could not be defined because of excessive heterogeneity, (3) an area defined by neighborhood names, school district boundaries, or major transportation arteries, and (4) entire suburbs, townships, and submetropolitan regions.

In the present study a variety of variables are used to provide several measures of the two lowest spatial levels defined above. Both respondent-specified and researcher-specified geographic definitions of neighborhood are employed. Homeowners were allowed to use their own implicit concept of neighborhood when responding to questions about "expected changes in your neighborhood," "future neighborhood property values," "the neighborhood as a good place to live," and their "expected tenure in the neighborhood." But the interviewer sometimes explicitly imposed a spatial context on respondents, as when respondents were asked about their familiarity with and social interaction with the "half-dozen or so families who live closest to you." Data were also aggregated at the block-face level and census-tract level in Minneapolis, and at the block-face level and at the planning-area level in Wooster. (These geographic levels are described more fully in chapter 4; suffice it to recall here that a Wooster planning area is approximately one-fourth of a Minneapolis tract in both area and population.

The Physical Characteristics of Neighborhood

For simplicity in previous chapters no distinction was made between the physical aspects of the neighborhood and the demographic aspects of the neighborhood's residents. Clearly, there is no conceptual reason why these two aspects must be combined into a single dimension. This chapter begins by treating them as distinct, and then tests empirically whether such a distinction is justified.

Four variables describing the physical character of the space around sampled homeowners in Wooster are employed: three at the planning-area level and one at the block-face level. The variable DILAP measures the proportion of all dwellings in the planning area having one or more of the following exterior defects: broken or boarded-up windows; badly peeling paint; broken steps, railings, or siding; sagging or holed roof, or roof with many missing shingles; sagging, settling, or cracked foundation.[11] AVEVALUE gives the mean property value for specified owner-occupied units in the planning area.[12] This is thought to proxy for a host of unspecified qualitative and quantitative features of dwellings in the neighborhood. DENSITY measures the number of households per acre of residential land use in the planning area. Finally, a dummy variable, NONRESID, denotes where the interviewer assessed that the block face had nonresidential land uses present.

A comparable set of variables proxies for the physical characteristics of neighborhood in Minneapolis include three at the block-face and one at the census-tract level. DILAP denotes the proportion of owner-occupied dwellings on the block face with one or more of the aforementioned exterior defects.[13] AVEVALUE is the mean value of specified owner-occupied units on the block face as assessed by respondent owner-occupants. NONRESID is defined as in Wooster. At the tract level, AVEV gives the median value of specified owner-occupied dwellings, and COMHSHLD the proportion of commercial land uses.[14]

The Demographic Characteristics of Neighborhood

The demographic character of planning areas in Wooster is measured by four variables.[15] The percentage of all households that were black is measured by PERBLACK. The mean household income (in 1974) of all households in the area is measured by MNINCOME, PEROWNER gives the percentage of dwellings in the area that are owner-occupied. And STABLE is the percentage of households in the area (both tenures) that have resided in their current dwellings ten years or more.

In Minneapolis three variables at the block-face and four at the census-tract level proxy for demographic characteristics. On the block face, PERBLACK, MNINCOME, and STABLE are defined analogously as in Wooster, except that only owner-occupants are considered. At the tract level, three similar variables are employed—PBLACK, AVEINC, PERSTA—that are defined as those above, respectively, except that the tract variables measure race, income, and length of residence for all households.[16] In addition, the percentage of all dwellings specified owner-occupied in the census tract is defined as POWNER.

The Social-Interactive Characteristics of Neighborhood

An identical set of eight variables proxying for social-interactive characteristics of the neighborhood is employed in both Wooster and Minneapolis. This set is designed so as to provide a variety of measures of both behavioral and attitudinal aspects of how the homeowner and the neighborhood interrelate socially.

The behavioral component may be viewed in terms of the frequency and intensity of interneighbor contacts and activities. In this vein two variables are specified. KNOWNAME measures the number of adults in the half dozen households living nearest the respondent who are known by name by the respondent: 4 if "all"; 3 if "nearly all"; 2 if "half"; 1 if "just a few"; 0 if "none." CHATWITH measures the respondent's assessment of "how often s/he talked with the half-dozen households living closest." In Wooster the response options are coded: 6 if every day; 5 if several times a week; 4 if once a week; 3 if two to three times a month; 2 if once a month; 1 if a few times a year or rarely; 0 if never.

In the Minneapolis survey the question was asked with the added proviso, "weather permitting, during a typical week." The response options are coded: 7 if every day; 6 if six times a week; 5 if five times a week; 4 if four times a week; 3 if three times a week; 2 if twice a week; 1 if once a week; .25 if once a month; 0 if never.

The first variable employed to measure the attitudinal component of the social-interactive neighborhood involves whether the respondent "would give out any information if a bill collector came around asking about a neighbor." The response codes are: 1 if "definitely would not"; 2 if "probably would not"; 3 if "probably would"; 4 if "definitely would." This variable is intended to capture an aspect of the respondent's loyalty to his/her neighbors. Five other variables are based on respondents' assessments of other residents in their neighborhoods, as measured on five-category scales. The variable names assigned to these assessments and the extrema on each scale are: FRIENDLY: 1 if "unfriendly people," . . . , 5 if "friendly people"; HELPFUL: 1 if "unhelpful neighbors," . . . , 5 if "helpful neighbors"; SIMILAR: 1 "people different from me," . . . , 5 if "people similar to me"; ACTIVITY: 1 if "people stress family privacy," . . . , 5 if "people stress activities with neighbors"; COMMON: 1 if "people having nothing in common" . . . , 5 if "people have much in common."

Together these six variables should provide an indicator of the respondent's sentiments of solidarity with neighbors and neighborhood. Although there are no identical items asked in national surveys, a 1978 HUD study did receive responses to certain analogous items that suggest the Wooster and Minneapolis distributions of responses to the above items are typical.[17]

Factor Analyses of Neighborhood Variables

It has been argued theoretically in previous sections that the urban neighborhood can be understood at distinct spatial levels and that there are distinct descriptive and functional dimensions at each spatial level. Testing whether these conceptual distinctions have any empirical content is the purpose of this section.

Before describing these tests, the reader may usefully refer to table 5.1, which presents a summary of the various geographic specifications of neighborhood employed, and the different disaggregated variables that attempt to capture the physical, demographic, and social-interactive characteristics at each spatial level. Recall that each variable is intended to proxy for the individual respondent homeowner's perception of a certain facet of the neighborhood.

Factor Analyses of All Neighborhood Variables

It has become conventional in urban empirical research to employ factor analysis when dealing with large numbers of variables measuring related aspects of the same phenomenon. See, for comparison, the works of Kain and Quigley (1970), Leven et al. (1976), Ahlbrandt and Cunningham

Table 5.1   Summary of Geographic Specifications of Neighborhood for Physical, Demographic, and Social-Interactive Variables

	Wooster	Minneapolis
1. Area: Nearest Half-Dozen Households		
Physical:	none	none
Demographic:	none	none
Social-Interactive:	KNOWNAME	KNOWNAME
	CHATWITH	CHATWITH
	BILLINFO	BILLINFO
2. Area: Block Face		
Physical:	NONRESID	NONRESID
		DILAP
		AVEVALUE
		PERBLACK
Demographic:	none	PERBLACK
		STABLE
		MNINCOME
Social-Interactive:	none	none
3. Area: Planning Area		
Physical:	DILAP	—
	AVEVALUE	
	DENSITY	
Demographic:	PERBLACK	—
	STABLE	
	MNINCOME	
	PEROWNER	
Social-Interactive:	none	—
4. Area: Census Tract		
Physical:	—	AVEV
		COMHSHLD
Demographic:	—	PBLACK
		PERSTA
		AVEINC
		POWNER
Social-Interactive:	—	none
5. Area: Assessed by Respondent		
Physical:	none	none
Demographic:	none	none
Social-Interactive:	FRIENDLY	FRIENDLY
	COMMON	COMMON
	ACTIVITY	ACTIVITY
	HELPFUL	HELPFUL
	SIMILAR	SIMILAR

Note: for definitions of variables, see text or glossary

(1979), and Krumm (1980), which employ the technique to discern common patterns among numerous variables measuring neighborhood characteristics. Following in the same vein, for both individual samples a principal-components (factor) analysis was conducted for the specified disaggregated neighborhood-related variables summarized in table 5.1.[18]

Suffice it to note here that there was remarkable similarity between the two analyses[19] in the degree to which the individual social-interactive variables loaded predominantly on two factors for which neither physical nor demographic variables had large loadings. Together these two factors explained 25 percent of the variance in Wooster and 29 percent of the variance in Minneapolis. This strongly supports the hypothesis that these social-interactive variables do indeed capture a distinct empirical dimension of neighborhoods as perceived by individual homeowners, although this result may also have been the product of the distinct (small) geographic scale implicit in these variables.

Conversely, in both samples demographic and physical characteristics loaded heavily on the same factors, suggesting that these two sets of neighborhood characteristics may not identify distinct dimensions of the environment. These findings provide support for the theoretical model of homeowners' housing investments in chapters 2 and 3, in which the physical and demographic aspects of neighborhood were treated as indistinguishable but very distinct from the social-interactive dimension.

Given these initial results, further principal component analyses were undertaken that considered the sets of physical-demographic and social-interactive variables separately, in order to ascertain more subtle forms of interaction within each subset of variables.

Factor Analysis of Physical-Demographic Neighborhood Variables

Analysis of the variables describing the physical-demographic dimensions of neighborhood generated three factors in Wooster and five factors in Minneapolis that had eigenvalues greater than one. Together these factors captured 73.7 percent and 80.4 percent of the variance in the respective variable sets.

These results again confirm the earlier conclusion that the factors show no distinct divisions between neighborhood physical and demographic variables. The results do, however, suggest that distinctions can be made between different spatial levels of variables. In the Minneapolis case one factor consists entirely of variables describing census-tract characteristics, if one considers only variables with factor loadings greater than .40. Two others (STABLE and NONRESID) each load almost exclusively on one block-face variable. Although two factors load heavily on both block-face and

Table 5.2 Specification of Neighborhood Physical-Demographic Indexes

Index name	Component variables and weights*
Wooster sample	
AREAQUAL	$= -.281$ (DILAP $- 3.52$) / $5.56 + .229$(MNINCOME $- 14,505$) / $5352 + .284$ (AVEVALUE $- 29,948$) / $9739 - .143$(DENSITY $- 13.9$) / $7.36 + (3.68)$
RACECOMP	$= 1.0$(PERBLACK $- 2.69$) / $3.69 + (1.74)$
TENURE	$= .414$(PEROWNER $- 67.31$) / $17.5 + .613$(STABLE $- 54.6$) / $12.4 + (3.41)$
Minneapolis sample	
TRACTQUAL	$= .032$(AVEV $- 51,947$) / $13,639 + .321$(PERSTA $- 36.6$) / $13.2 + .270$(AVEINC $- 16,221$) / $2,651 + .338$(POWNER $- 64.1$) / $22.9 - .251$(COMHSHLD $- 6.45$) / $4.18 + (3.99)$
BLOCKQUAL	$= .414$(AVEVALUE $- 63,214$) / $24,126 + .388$(MNINCOME $- 25,271$) / $13,879 - .057$(DILAP $- 15.6$) / $17.7 + (2.20)$
RACECOMP	$= .507$(PBLACK $- 6.50$) / $15.6 + .525$(PERBLACK $- 9.62$) / $2.14 + (3.58)$
TENURE	$= 1.00$(STABLE $- 63.0$) / $20.1 + (3.32)$

	Mean		Standard Deviation	
	Wooster	Minneapolis	Wooster	Minneapolis
AREAQUAL	3.71	—	.765	—
TRACTQUAL	—	4.13	—	.958
BLOCKQUAL	—	2.22	—	.788
RACECOMP				
Whites only	1.68	2.03	1.02	3.56
Blacks only	.039	1.57	.315	5.19
TENURE	3.45	3.36	.851	.726

*Coefficients are factor scores generated by principal components analysis; all variables have mean subtracted and then are divided by standard deviation, and then have constant added so that minimum = 1

tract variables, this occurs for only two sets of analogous block-tract variables: average property values (AVEVALUE/AVEV) and percentage black households (PERBLACK/PBLACK). Thus, with the exception of property values and racial composition, it appears that there are distinct patterns of characteristic variation embodied in the block-face versus the census-tract geographic levels of neighborhood in Minneapolis. A similar conclusion is reached in the Wooster sample. One factor loaded almost exclusively on NONRESID, the only block-face variable in the Wooster data; the other two loaded on planning-area variables.

At this point one must confront the inevitable dilemma involved in using previous factor-analysis results in specifying more aggregated variables for subsequent regression analyses. If one collapses all individual variables into an index corresponding to each factor, one captures the maximum amount of variation in the data, but at the sacrifice of heuristic interpretability of the index variable. In addition, distinctions among various geographic levels of variables are blurred, as are potential differences in relationships among individual component variables of the indexes and other (dependent) variables. On the other hand, if one does not use the information provided by the factor analyses, one must grapple with an unwieldy number of individual variables, and the chances of multi-collinearity grow.

A compromise position between these two extremes is taken in the present analysis, which stresses the specification of indexes that, though informed by the factor analyses, emphasizes interpretability and distillation of separate variable groups having particular theoretical interest. More specifically, results from both samples suggest that four indexes capture the key variations in the physical demographic dimension of neighborhood: quality, race, tenure, and nonresidential land use.

The quality index is composed primarily of variables describing the physical condition and mean values of neighboring properties and the mean incomes of neighboring households. This aspect is implicit in one factor in Wooster involving variables measured at the planning-area level, one factor in Minneapolis involving variables at the census-tract level, and another factor in Minneapolis involving variables at the block-face level. Using the factor-score coefficients obtained from the analysis, and after normalizing the variables, these three quality indexes are defined as in table 5.2: AREAQUAL, TRACTQUAL, BLOCKQUAL, respectively. The coefficient signs of each constituent variable correspond to *a priori* presumptions about how homeowners evaluate neighborhood quality; e.g., mean incomes get a positive weight in the indexes but dwellings with exterior problems get a negative weight.

The race index provides a straightforward measure of the black racial composition of the neighborhood. This racial aspect appeared as a distinct factor in the Minneapolis sample, but did not in Wooster. But because there is long-standing scholarly interest and debate over the effects of racial integration on (white) homeowner behavior (see e.g., Downs 1981, ch.7), race is specified as a distinct variable (RACECOMP) in both samples. See table 5.2 for details.

The tenure aspect of neighborhoods is specified to include the proportions of owner-occupied and over ten-year residency households in Wooster planning areas, and the latter proportion only in Minneapolis block faces.[20] This TENURE variable follows from factor 2 in Wooster and factor 4 in Minneapolis. See table 5.2 for details.

The "nonresidential land use" aspect is modelled simply as the above-specified dummy variable NONRESID. In both samples the factor analyses suggested that the interviewer's perception of nonresidential land uses on the block face represented a distinct dimension of neighborhood data variation. And once again, because there is considerable interest in the issue of how housing investments, encroaching nonresidential land uses, and zoning interrelate, there is further justification for specifying a distinct variable. Because this aspect consists only of a single dummy variable in both samples, the variable is not normalized to mean zero and standard deviation one, as are the aforementioned component variables in indexes.

*Factor Analyses of Social-Interactive
Neighborhood Variables*

As in the case of the physical-demographic neighborhood variables, a separate principal components analysis is conducted for the eight variables measuring the individual homeowner's social interactions within the neighborhood.[21] In both samples the results are similar. In each, two significant factors were produced, accounting for 51.2 percent and 54.3 percent of the variance in Wooster and Minneapolis, respectively. In each, the first factor loaded most heavily on the five attitudinal aspects of the social-interactive neighborhood: HELPFUL, SIMILAR, FRIENDLY, COMMON, ACTIVITY. And the second factor loaded most heavily on the two behavioral aspects—KNOWNAME and CHATWITH—and on the loyalty aspect, BILL-INFO.

The results thus support the theoretical position that there are separable attitudinal and behavioral aspects to the social-interactive dimension of neighborhood, and that those aspects display highly consistent patterns of variation across diverse samples. The signs of the factor loadings are also consistent with *a priori* expectations, with the exception of that for BILLIN-FO. If, indeed, BILLINFO represented a measure of loyalty to neighbors, one would have predicted that it would load negatively on the two factors, given the variable's coding. What the results suggest instead is that the

Table 5.3   Specification of Neighborhood Social-Interactive Indexes

Index name	Component variables and weights*
Wooster sample	
IDENTIFY	=.178(HELPFUL − 4.32) / .92 + .396(SIMILAR − 3.72) / 1.13 +.160(FRIENDLY − 4.37) / .850 + .483(COMMON − 3.35) / 1.08 +.257(ACTIVITY − 2.51) / 1.23 + (4.05)
INTEGRATE	=.501(KNOWNAME − 3.09) / 1.08 = .458(CHATWITH − 4.67) / 1.42 +.321 (BILLINFO − 1.58) / .735 + (4.31)
Minneapolis sample	
IDENTIFY	=.245(HELPFUL − 4.00) / 1.09 + .207(SIMILAR − 3.26) / 1.25 + .244(FRIENDLY − 4.31) / .879 + .222(COMMON − 3.08) / 1.11 + .193(ACTIVITY − 2.42) / 1.18 + (3.63)
INTEGRATE	= + .280(KNOWNAME − 2.63) / 1.26 + .253(CHATWITH − 4.18) / 2.76 + .867 (BILLINFO − 1.65) / .817 + (2.56)

*coefficients are factor scores generated by principal components analysis; all variables have mean subtracted and then are divided by standard deviation, and then have constant added so that minimum = 1

responses to the BILLINFO question are more a reflection of whether the respondents know anything about their neighbors, rather than their sense of solidarity with them.

Consistent with the use of the factor analyses for specifying the physical-demographic neighborhood indexes above, here the two factors can be readily employed to define two straightforward variables measuring the individual homeowner's social-interactive neighborhood. The first consists of an index made up of the five aforementioned attitudinal variables related to the respondent's identification with neighbors and neighborhood (IDENTIFY) with index weights based on factor score coefficients of the first factor (see table 5.3 for details). The second consists of an index of the three aforementioned variables measuring the degree of familiarity and interaction with neighbors; i.e., the integration of the respondent into the neighborhood: INTEGRATE. The index weights are based on the factor-score coefficients produced by the second factor (see table 5.3). Together these IDENTIFY and INTEGRATE variables serve as empirical proxies for the homeowner's attachment to the neighborhood.

But as argued in chapter 2, it is not only the degree of individual attachment to the neighborhood that influences housing investment. It is also the aggregate degree of neighborhood cohesion that can influence the strength of the pressures on the individual homeowner to conform to neighborhood housing norms. And, as will be explored more fully in later chapters, it is likely that both the degree of individual attachment and of aggregate cohesion interact in complicated ways.

The strategy employed to proxy for this neighborhood level of cohesion is simply to aggregate the individual homeowner's scores for the IDENTIFY and INTEGRATE variables and calculate their means for the various geographic areas.[22] In Wooster this aggregation is conducted at the planning-area level; in Minneapolis at the block-face level. These neighborhood mean values for homeowners' identification and integration define the variables NIDENTIFY and NINTEGRATE, respectively.

Public Policies

At the time of the Wooster housing survey in 1975 there had not yet been any governmental programs active in the city that had attempted to assist homeowners' housing investments or to stabilize neighborhoods.[23] Wooster thus represented an example of a *laissez faire* housing market.

In contrast, by 1980 the city of Minneapolis had been engaged for a decade in a variety of homeowner assistance and neighborhood stabilization programs. Minneapolis had been an active participant in the federal Urban Renewal program, and by the termination of the program in 1977 had spent a total of $167.7 million on such projects across twenty-one designated areas (Ojile 1977). HUD-sponsored programs like Public Housing and Section 8 were also widely utilized.

The inception of the Community Development Block Grant Program (CDBG) in 1975 brought with it a variety of new programmatic emphases. Three types of CDBG-sponsored programs were undertaken. Neighborhood Physical Development projects focused on the acquisition, rehabilitation, demolition and sale of substandard properties and on a grant and loan program for structural repairs. Facility Rehabilitation projects aimed at building modern urban infrastructure. Public Service projects were administered through nonprofit agencies in an attempt to extend the array of quality services available to neighborhood residents. Between 1975 and 1980, over $35 million was spent on these initiatives. Although initially spread over a larger area, by 1979 the CDBG programs were concentrated in nineteen neighborhood strategy areas (NSAs).[24] At the time of the 1980 survey, these NSAs were receiving on average $228 per capita from CDBG.

In addition to the aforementioned federal housing programs, Minneapolis began developing a variety of state- and local-funded programs designed to encourage homeownership, energy conservation, and the repair and improvement of both rental and ownership properties. Well over a dozen such policies were in operation at the time of the survey.[25] Of particular interest to this study are the half-dozen grant and loan programs designed to stimulate the repair and rehabilitation of owner-occupied dwellings. These programs will be discussed in much more detail in chapter 12, but their general outline may be sketched here. Overall the subsidies are targeted on the repair of code violations in homes, regardless of where a given homeowner lives in the city. Most programs have an income eligibility ceiling of $18,000 to $19,250. Grants typically are for a maximum of $6,000; loans for a maximum of $12,000 to $15,000. Interest rates for loans are adjustable according to income; some programs defer repayments until time of home resale. By the end of 1980, Minneapolis had provided $18 million in grants and $59.5 million in loans under the auspices of these programs.

In the context of our particular survey of Minneapolis homeowners, the impacts of governmental assistance on housing upkeep behavior potentially could be both direct and indirect. The direct impact would be if the sampled homeowner had personally received any of the aforementioned subsidized grants as loans to assist in property maintenance or improvements. This impact is measured by four variables: GRANT?, LOAN? are dummy variables denoting whether the homeowner has received such grants and/or low-interest loans, respectively, for property maintenance and improvements during the previous five years; and GRANTS$ and LOAN$ take the dollar value of such public assistance. For a summary of the dollar amounts received by sampled homeowners under these programs, see table 5.4. Of the sampled Minneapolis homeowners, 7.4 percent received home-improvement grants, with an average grant of $3,959; 9.0 percent received loans, with an average loan of $13,409.

An indirect impact that could ensue as a result of subsidized improvements is that proximate homeowners who receive no subsidies might perceive such improvements as augmenting both the quality of life in the neighborhood and their own property values. These perceptions, in turn, could stimulate further home-upkeep efforts on their parts. Whether this scenario is empirically supported will be discussed in chapters 9, 11, and 12.

Another indirect impact could arise through the improving homeowners' confidence in the future of the neighborhood, thereby eliciting further unsubsidized private housing investments. If, for example, homeowners perceive that the government is actively attempting to stabilize or support their neighborhood through CDBG infrastructure improvements, housing renovation grants and loans, etc., they may be more likely to invest even if they personally do not receive grants or loans. In fact, some analysts have seen such building of neighborhood confidence as the *sine qua non* of eliciting housing investments (Goetze 1976).

Table 5.4   Characteristics of Minneapolis Policies for Housing Improvements

Neighborhood Types
  Homeowners by Area:
    1. Not qualify for aid   17.6%
    2. Qualify for but yet not received aid   33.9%
    3. Qualify and has received aid   48.5%

Individual Homeowners
  Grant?   7.4%
  Loan?   9.0%

Dollars Received (Last Five Years)

	Grants		*Loans*
0	92.6%	0	91.0%
$1–100	0.2	$1–1,000	0.2
101–500	0.4	1,001–3,000	1.5
500–1,000	0.7	3,001–5,000	1.7
1,001–2,000	0.9	5,001–9,000	1.0
2,001–4,000	0.9	9,001–10,000	1.3
4,001–5,000	1.6	10,001–13,000	0.9
5,001–6,000	2.3	13,001–15,000	1.1
8,300	0.2	15,001–19,000	0.0
		19,001–22,000	0.4
		22,001–26,000	0.0
		26,001–28,000	0.4
Mean	$ 293	Mean	$ 2,682
Std. Dev.	$3,959	Std. Dev.	$13,409

Average Annual $ Received
during Last Five Years:

	Grant $	Loan $
All Homeowners	$ 95	$ 332
Aid Recipients Only	$1,260	$3,611

As explained in chapter 4, Minneapolis homeowners were sampled in three areas that were distinguished by just such a variation in governmental housing programmatic commitment. One sampled area did not qualify for any areal public aid for property investments; i.e., it was neither eligible for Urban Renewal nor CDBG. (Individual owners could, however, get aid if they were personally eligible.) The second area qualified for CDBG, but had not recieved any such aid by 1980. The third area had received either Urban Renewal and/or CDBG funds by the time of the survey. To measure the different investment behaviors possible in these three areas, two dummy variables are specified. NOTQUALIFY takes the value one if the sampled homeowner lives in an area that did not qualify for the above aid programs. QUALIFY takes the value one if the sampled homeowner lives in an area that qualified for CDBG but had not yet received such aid; zero otherwise. Table 5.4 indicates that 17.6 percent of the sample falls into the NOTQUALIFY category; 33.9 percent in the QUALIFY category. The reference category to which the coefficients of the above two variables are to be compared are homeowners in areas that have received Urban Renewal or CDBG funds.

Summary and Conclusions

This chapter defines a robust set of independent variables that will be employed in subsequent analyses of residential satisfaction, neighborhood expectations, mobility plans, and home-upkeep behavior. Attributes of sampled homeowners, their dwellings, their neighborhoods, and of any impinging public policies are described by these variables more comprehensively than in any previous research.

Of particular note is the investigation into how the various functional and geographic aspects of neighborhood can be appropriately measured. Factor analyses reveal startlingly similar findings in both samples:

– Most physical and demographic attributes of a given geographic area are so highly correlated that they justifiably can be collapsed into a single quality index of "physical conditions–socioeconomic status." The presence of nonresidential land uses on the block proves to be a separate factor. In addition, neighborhood racial composition and the tenure characteristics of others in the neighborhood are separated from the above quality index for both empirical and conceptual reasons. Also noteworthy is the fact that neighborhood quality is separable on at least two spatial levels: block face and census tract.

– The variables describing neighborhood social-interactive attributes of the homeowner load onto two distinct factors that are separable from the physical-demographic elements above. One factor is made up of variables describing the individual's degree of collective solidarity sentiments or neighborhood identification; the other, the degree of interpersonal interaction or social integration. These individual factors are aggregated over homeowners in the entire area to obtain two measures of neighborhood cohesion that correspond closely to ideal theoretical constructs.

– Of course, determining that the concept of neighborhood has empirically distinguishable features both in terms of physical-demographic versus social-interactive characters and in terms of small- versus larger-scale geographic areas is one thing. To ascertain whether these separate features provide any power in explaining homeowners' residential satisfaction, expectations, mobility plans, or home-upkeep behavior is another matter. The next four chapters devote themselves to this task.

6 Homeowners' Residential Satisfaction

The previous chapter identifies and defines numerous exogenous variables that describe the characteristics of homeowners and the residential context in which they find themselves. This chapter investigates theoretically and empirically the evaluative linkages between these two sets of variables—homeowners' satisfaction with their residential environment. A conceptual framework is developed, previous research is reviewed, and an empirical model is specified and empirically estimated. The goal is to ascertain which objective characteristics of the homeowner, dwelling, physical-demographic neighborhood, and social-interactive neighborhood provide predictive power for homeowners' residential evaluations, for it is these subjective aspects that likely affect mobility plans and, ultimately, housing investment.

More specifically, the conceptual framework models the degree of housing satisfaction as a psychological measure of the perceived gap between a respondent's residential needs and aspirations and the reality of the current residential context. The need/aspiration level established as a benchmark for evaluation of the status quo is viewed as a function of the homeowner's prior residential experiences, perceived status, sensed personal efficacy, life-cycle stage, and potential for mobility—elements embodying both absolute and socially relative comparisons. The degree to which homeowners will tolerate a gap between benchmark and actual residential situations is also seen as variable, depending on their family status and psychological state. Thus it is unlikely that all homeowners will manifest equal degrees of satisfaction from the same residential environment. The empirical upshot: the specification of the model must allow for such cross-household variations in how contexts are translated into evaluations. Failure to do so renders most previous work vulnerable to aggregation bias.

This implication shapes the empirical models of satisfaction developed below. Satisfaction with the dwelling is modeled as a function of household and dwelling characteristics, and satisfaction with the neighborhood as a function of household and neighborhood characteristics. In order to assess the degree of cross-homeowner variation described above, regression models for both satisfaction measures are estimated for subsamples of various homeowner types. For particular groups evidencing different translations of residential contexts into satisfaction, interaction variables are specified that permit distinct coefficients to be estimated for the given contextual feature for each group. Ordinary least squares (OLS) estimates of such synthesized models are then estimated over the entire sample. Next, these synthesized models are reestimated using PROBIT techniques in order to assess the sensitivity of results to the statistical technique employed. Finally, results that are consistent for both OLS and PROBIT techniques are discussed quantitatively, because they will form the subsequent paths in the formation of mobility plans and, ultimately, of home-upkeep behaviors. The reader less interested in the details of the various steps in the above empirical procedure may turn directly to the chapter summary.

A Conceptual Framework for Residential Satisfaction

The preeminent social indicator employed by housing analysts during the last decade to measure residents' evaluation of their environment has been the concept of residential satisfaction.[1] This psychological construct of satisfaction rests on the following conceptual foundation. Individuals may be seen as cognitively constructing a reference condition for each facet of their residential situations. The quantity or quality of the given facet implied by the reference point will depend on the individual's self-assessed needs and aspirations, as well as on social norms (see Morris 1976; Michelson 1976; Galster and Hesser 1981). If the current situation is perceived to be in proximate congruence with (or superior to) the reference situation, a psychological state of satisfaction should be manifested. If, on the other hand, the current situation falls short of the reference situation by more than a threshold deficiency, two alternatives are possible. A homeowner may attempt to reconcile the incongruence by adaptation: redefining needs, reducing aspirations, and/or altering the evaluation of the current situation, thereby producing a modicum of satisfaction.

The other alternative is that a homeowner cannot adapt to the current residential context, in which case dissatisfaction should be manifested. Such an individual, over time, would likely attempt to reduce dissatisfaction by altering conditions in the present dwelling or by moving to another, more congruent residential situation (Foote et al. 1960; Seek 1983). Of course, either attempt may be more or less feasible for different household types in different contexts. The ability to alter features of the current dwelling may, for instance, be severely constrained by the low income or

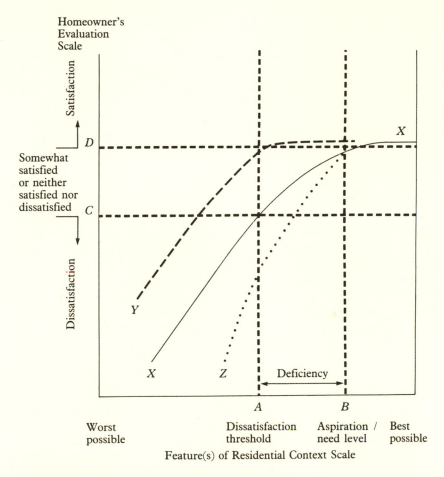

Figure 6.1   Representative Satisfaction with Residential Context Functions

physical limitations of the homeowner, or by the structural capabilities of the dwelling itself. And as shall be discussed in greater detail in chapter 8, numerous economic, social, and informational constraints operate on the mobility decision.

The foregoing conceptual discussion is illustrated visually in figure 6.1. The horizontal axis represents a cardinal or ordinal scale measuring a particular objective attribute residential context (e.g., number of rooms, structural defects, public services in neighborhood). This scale ranges from the worst- to best-possible amounts of the given attribute that can be conceived of by the homeowner. Whether these perceived extrema exist in reality, are more moderate than reality, or are attainable by the homeowner are all irrelevant issues: it is only the respondent's perceptions that matter. Point B is that level of the given attribute that the respondent assesses as the need/aspiration level. Point A is that level of the attribute falling below B by the maximum tolerable deficiency; it thus represents the dissatisfaction threshold. The vertical axis measures the homeowner's ordinal evaluation of the given residential context. If the homeowner has reached or exceeded aspiration/need level B, satisfaction should be expressed. Conversely, if the homeowner has not acquired the threshold A amount, dissatisfaction should be expressed. Intermediate contexts between A and B should elicit qualified or indeterminate degrees of satisfaction or dissatisfaction.

The particular relationship between satisfaction and the features of the residential context is likely to be a curvilinear one. Consider initially the satisfaction function represented by locus of points X–X in figure 6.1. Progressively worse levels of the given attribute below threshold A should elicit progressively greater degrees of dissatisfaction; i.e., conceptually and empirically there appears to be no lower bound for human discontentment. Progressively better residential contexts between A and B should elicit progressively more positive sentiments as aspiration/need level B becomes more proximate. But after the situation has exceeded level B there would seem to be no conceptual reason for predicting concomitant increases in expressed satisfaction. Put differently, once a homeowner has obtained the aspired for or needed degree of an attribute, he or she is as satisfied as possible. Further increases in an attribute might make the person happier, but this is not the construct under consideration.

Another way to support a curvilinear satisfaction function is through neoclassical microeconomic theory. In this framework a fundamental principle is the Law of Diminishing Marginal Utility: increases in the number of a particular item consumed within a given period lead to progressively smaller increments in the consumer's sensed well-being. If satisfaction is interpreted as the consumer's sensed well-being, then a curvilinear satisfaction function follows from the above law, and point B is interpretable as that quantity at which the consumer becomes satiated.

Of course, if one consistently exceeds the aspiration/need level established earlier, this level might be subsequently revised upward: the phenomenon of rising expectations. If this were a universal phenomenon in the housing market we would never observe residents along points of the function to the right of point (B, D). Whether this hypothetical possibility is often the case becomes an empirical matter.

This does raise the question, however, of the way in which aspirations or needs are established by different individuals. Though it is beyond the scope of the present study to delve in depth into the psychological origins of felt needs and aspirations, some comments are appropriate in the con-

text of the empirical modeling of satisfaction. Housing aspirations undoubtedly are influenced by a person's prior residential experiences, perceived status, sense of personal efficacy, and potential for upward mobility. Needs, though thorny to disentangle conceptually from aspirations
(see Galster 1980), are more a function of family size, demographic composition, and life-style stage (see Foote et al. 1960; Michelson 1976). But
whatever the differences between the factors that establish aspirations and
those that establish needs, there is a crucial common thread: the aspira-
tion/need level of a household is not set absolutely by reference to household characteristics alone, but also by a socially-relative comparison. In
other words, aspirations/needs are conditioned significantly by one's reference groups and by what one perceives as feasible in the current housing-market context. Thus, even though the satisfaction function is partly a
reflection of an absolute evaluation of the current residential environment,
it is primarily a reflection of a relative evaluation of it compared to that
consumed by reference groups and what might feasibly be consumed by
the given household. This relativistic nature of the satisfaction function
will be of crucial importance in specifying a model of mobility plans in
chapter 8.

The degree to which a deficiency in some facet of the residential context
will be tolerated by a homeowner is also likely to be variable across household types. For instance, having only one bathroom instead of the
"needed" two is unlikely to elicit as much dissatisfaction from a childless
couple as from a couple with two teenage children. The psychological state
of the homeowner may also be relevant. Marcuse (1971), for example, has
argued that those who are fatalistic or alienated will be less likely to express
dissatisfaction over some deficiency.[2]

The upshot of the foregoing is that the shape of the satisfaction and
residential-context relationship is likely to vary substantially across different households. Compared to our representative homeowner with satisfaction function $X-X$, one with equal aspirations/needs but less tolerance for
deficiencies might demonstrate a function like $X-Z$ in figure 6.1. One
having equal tolerance but lower aspirations/needs might be represented
by $X-Y$. The empirical implication of all this is that aggregation across
various household types may lead to serious bias in estimating satisfaction
and residential-context relationships.

Previous Research on Residential Satisfaction

The earliest empirical research into the correlates of residential satisfaction
employed bivariate cross-tabular techniques (for a review, see Galster
1980). More reliable results have been obtained from the more recent

studies that have employed more sophisticated multiple-regression techniques. Only this latter growth will be considered here; specifically those by: Lansing, Marans, and Zehner (1970); Speare (1974); Speare, Goldstein, and Frey (1974): Morris, Crull, and Winter (1976); Ahlbrandt and Cunningham (1979); Galster and Hesser (1981); and Varady (1975, 1982a, 1983).

These studies share a common conceptual and empirical assumption that residential satisfaction can be modeled as a linear function of two sets of factors: one describing characteristics of the respondent household, and the other describing objective features of the residential environment. In addition, virtually all model a set of respondent subjective evaluations of particular aspects of the residential context as intervening variables between the aforementioned objective features and the overall satisfaction measure. Various dependent variables are utilized: satisfaction with dwelling; satisfaction with neighborhood; satisfaction with a composite index of dwelling, neighborhood, and public services.

A summary of the variables that have proved to be statistically significant correlates of these various measures of residential satisfaction is presented in table 6.1. The signs associated with each variable indicate the correlation. From these studies a number of generalizations may be drawn. Regarding characteristics of households: income, age, occupation, and (sometimes) education are associated with more residential satisfaction; duration of tenure, minority or female heads, married/with more children are associated with less. Regarding objective characteristics of dwelling context: adequate amounts of interior and exterior space are associated with more satisfaction; dwelling age and mechanical or structural defects are associated with less. Regarding objective characteristics of neighborhood: greater social cohesion and interaction is associated with more satisfaction; the presence of low-quality dwellings is associated with less. Regarding subjective evaluations of particular contextual features: perceptions of well-maintained dwellings, good public services, friendliness and homogeneity of neighbors, and rising property values are associated with more satisfaction; crime and other neighborhood problems are associated with less.

The veracity of these generalizations must be challenged, however, because none of the empirical specifications are appropriate, given the conceptual framework outlined above. First, none of the specifications of objective features of the residential context allow for a curvilinear relationship with satisfaction. In terms of figure 6.1, if one fits a linear functional form to a scatter of points generated by a curvilinear satisfaction function, one obtains a biased estimate of the relationship, which will tend to reduce its apparent statistical significance.

Second, most of the aforementioned studies do not disaggregate their

Table 6.1   Summary of Research Findings on Predictors of Residential
Satisfaction

	Objective Household Characteristics	Objective Contextual Characteristics	Intervening Subjective Evaluations
Dwelling Satisfaction	+Income: 3,8 +Education: 3,4,8 +Age: 3,5,8 −Duration of tenure: 3 −Black: 4,5,8 −Single Male: 4 −Married: 5 −Female Head: 4	+Number of Bathrooms: 5 +Yard size: 5 +Mechanical systems: 5 −Structural defects: 5 −Dwelling Age: 3,4,8 −Crowding: 4,8,2	+Neighborhood satisfaction: 2,5 −Neighborhood problems: 3,4,8 −Housing problems: 3,4
Neighborhood Satisfaction	+Income: 6,2,8 +Occupation: 6 −Education: 2 −Black: 5,8 −# Kids: 5	+% Black (for blacks): 5 +Social participation: 1,5,7 +Suburban residence: 8 −Dilapidated structures: 5	+Housing upkeep: 6,5,7 +Homogeneity: 6,5 +Friendliness: 6,5 +Outdoor Space: 6 +Dwelling satisfaction: 5,7,8 +Public service: 5,7 +Rising Property values: 7 −Crime: 5
Composite Residential Satisfaction	+Age: 1 −Duration of tenure: 1	−Crowding: 1	

Note: signs indicate correlation between given variables
1. Speare (1974)*
2. Morris, Crull, Winter (1976)*
3. Varady (1982a); non-elderly
4. Varady (1982a); elderly
5. Galster, Hesser (1981)*
6. Lansing, Marans, Zehner (1970)
7. Ahlbrandt, Cunningham (1979)
8. Varady (1983)
*Results for combined owners and renters; all others for owners only

estimations into household groups that would be expected on *a priori* grounds to possess differently shaped satisfaction functions. In fact, the three studies that do attempt disaggregation (Varady 1975, 1982a; Galster and Hesser, 1981) do find significant differences between subsample results. These findings are never, however, carried to their logical conclusion: the overall specification must reflect these differences or else be subject to serious aggregation bias.

Specification of an Empirical Model of Residential Satisfaction

The theoretical discussion and critique of previous research provide guidelines for the specification of an empirical model of satisfaction to be employed here.

Dependent Variables of Residential Satisfaction

Two separate dimensions of residential satisfaction are specified: one dealing with the dwelling and the other with the neighborhood. This distinction is made first because there is a unique set of objective contextual variables that likely correlates with each measure, and second because it allows for more disaggregation and specificity in estimating the satisfaction function.

Both these variables are made operational in a conventional manner. The dwelling satisfaction variable (HOUSESAT) consists of a summary index measuring ten individual responses to particular satisfaction items related to the dwelling.[3] The exact question was, "Could you indicate if you are currently satisfied, dissatisfied, or neither satisfied nor dissatisfied about these features of your home: (a) plumbing? (b) kitchen facilities? (c) heating equipment? (d) interior condition? (e) exterior condition? (f) modernity? (g) floor space/size? (h) yard space? (i) number of bathrooms? (j) privacy?" Each item response is coded: 0 if dissatisfied, 1 if neither, 2 if satisfied. HOUSESAT is the sum of these item scores, and thus ranges from 0 to 20.

The neighborhood satisfaction variable (NEIGHSAT) is defined by responses to the question, "How would you describe your neighborhood as a place to live?"[4] Response options consisted of checking one of five boxes, with the extrema labelled: "Very Poor Place to Live" (coded 1) and "Very Good Place to Live" (coded 5).[5]

Frequency distributions for both variables indicate that the largest proportions of both samples register the highest satisfaction scores. In Wooster and Minneapolis 46 percent and 43 percent, respectively, indicate satisfaction with all ten items included in HOUSESAT, and 68 percent and 51 percent, respectively, give the highest marks to NEIGHSAT. Although high, these percentages are comparable to those obtained in a national 1978 poll that asked similar questions (HUD 1978, items 5.A, 5.H).[6] This gives confidence that the range of residential satisfaction measures obtained in the Wooster and Minneapolis samples is typical of homeowners in comparably sized communities in the United States.

Independent Variables of Homeowner Characteristics

Variables measuring homeowner characteristics should attempt to control for three things. First, particular households will express more or less residential satisfaction in general, due to differences in their aspirations, tolerance levels, and psychological state. Second, differences in the shape of the satisfaction function for particular residential attributes (described above) can be attributed to variations in household preferences, needs and/or aspirations for these attributes. Third, there will be differences in the likelihood of observed households already having adjusted to a prior state of dissatisfaction through alterations in their dwelling or moving.

The first aspirational aspect is modeled with a series of variables measuring the household's education, income, marital status, family life-cycle stage, and prior housing experiences. As defined in chapter 5, the variables are EDUCATION, INCOME, MARRIED, FEMALE, STAGE1, STAGE2, STAGE3, STAGE4, PRIORHOME and EARLYHOME, respectively. *A priori*, one would expect income, education, and married status to be associated with higher aspirations, so that these variables should all be inversely related to satisfaction. Similarly, aspirations likely rise and then fall as one moves through successive stages of the life cycle, rendering those in earlier stages less satisfied than those in later stages. And those who have not lived in single-family homes either immediately prior to their current residence or when they were growing up should be more likely to be satisfied with their current occupation of such a preferred dwelling.

The general psychological state of the respondent is measured with an index of alienation (ALIENATED). This index is made up of a composite score derived from responses to standard questions about whether: "anything is worthwhile anymore," "children should be brought into the world," "public officials care about average person," "people care about others" (see glossary for details). As suggested by Marcuse (1971), greater alienation could be associated with "fatalistic resignation"; i.e., lower aspirations, higher tolerance for threshold differentials, and hence higher satisfaction. But it is even more likely that ALIENATED captures the respondent's general sense of pessimism and outlook on life, in which case it should be inversely related to satisfaction.

The second aspect of satisfaction functional-form differentials is here considered as varying across groups specified by education, income, marital status, and stage in family life cycle. As explained above, however, these variations are not appropriately modeled by merely adding demographic control variables to a linear regression predicting satisfaction. Rather, the specification must allow for the relationships between satisfaction and each particular objective characteristic of the residential environment to vary within each of the aforementioned household groups.

One possible method for accomplishing this would be to interact each homeowner characteristic with each residential context characteristic, although such a method would multiply independent variables to an unwieldy number. An alternative would be to stratify the sample into groups according to the aforementioned demographic criteria and run a separate satisfaction regression on contextual features for each group. Given the ultimate goal of the research to develop a unified model of homeowner housing investment, however, pursuing a stratification approach in each model component would greatly detract from the comprehensibility of the overall results.

In light of these considerations a "synthetic" strategy is chosen. Satisfaction functions (both dwelling and neighborhood) are estimated separately for each of the following homeowner groups:

Education: More than twelve years; twelve years or less
Income: Above average; below average ("average" defined as $15,000 in
    Wooster, $25,000 in Minneapolis)
Marital status: Married; not married and female headed; not married and
    male/multiple-headed households
Life-cycle stage: Stages 1, 2, 3, 4, 5

See chapter 5 or glossary for details.

If there proves to be a significant difference between the coefficients of a given residential characteristic for a particular group versus the aggregate, that group and characteristic combination alone will be interacted to form a distinct variable in a subsequent regression for the entire sample. In this fashion the final regression will indicate the general patterns of the satisfaction–residential characteristic relationship, while permitting any significant deviations from these general patterns for particular homeowner groups.

The third aspect that needs to be captured by household variables is the likelihood that adjustments to earlier unsatisfactory situations had already been made when the survey was taken. Those with higher incomes would, e.g., be financially more able to alter the current dwelling to better fit needs or to bear the search, transactions, and moving expenses associated with changing dwellings. Thus, in this context INCOME should be directly related to satisfaction, counteracting the earlier relationship posited when INCOME proxied for aspirations. Those who perceive greater constraints on their housing opportunities due to discrimination would be less likely to have adjusted to unsatisfactory conditions. This would mean that households headed by a BLACK or a FEMALE should be less satisfied, *ceteris paribus*. Finally, years of duration of residence in the present dwelling (LONGEVITY) provides a direct measure of how recently there has been a locational adjustment. Earlier research by Clark and Huff (1977) has suggested that the LONGEVITY and HOUSESAT relationship is curvilinear: familiarity and attachment to the residential context grow over time but annoying aspects become progressively less tolerable, the latter eventually dominating. To test this, both LONGEVITY and its squared value are included as separate variables.[7]

The final homeowner characteristic employed is the degree of social interaction with neighbors, as assessed by the respondent and measured by IDENTIFY and INTEGRATE. These indexes were derived and explained more fully in chapter 4. Suffice it to note here that IDENTIFY measures the homeowner's solidarity sentiments with nearby neighbors and INTEGRATE measures the homeowner's familiarity and frequency of contact with them. Both variables are expected to be positively correlated with neighborhood satisfaction. To test for nonlinearities in the satisfaction function, the squared values of both variables are also included in the model, with expectations of negative coefficients.[8]

Independent Variables of Dwelling Characteristics

Absolute measures of the several quantitative aspects of the dwelling (rooms, bathrooms, and lot size) do not likely have a relationship with dwelling satisfaction because they alone do not capture the household's demands for space. Some relative measure of dwelling space vis-à-vis the total number in the household would be preferable (see, e.g., Morris, 1976; Morris, Crull, and Winter, 1976). Here the method chosen was to divide the number of rooms, number of bathrooms, and lot frontage by the number of full-time occupants in the home (OCCUPANTS), thereby creating three new variables: ROOM/OCC, BATH/OCC, and YARD/OCC, respectively.

These three measures of the dwelling's relative size adequacy can be scaled in a manner corresponding to the theory propounded earlier and expressed in figure 6.1. To test for the posited curvilinear relationship, not only these three variables but their squared values are also entered as additional variables: $(ROOM/OCC)^2$, $(BATH/OCC)^2$, $(YARD/OCC)^2$, respectively. If the aforementioned theory works, one would expect each of the ROOM/OCC, BATH/OCC, and YARD/OCC coefficients to be positive, but the coefficients of their respective squared term to be negative.

The other qualitative dwelling characteristics necessarily are measured by dichotomous (dummy) variables, however, thus rendering a more simplified version of the satisfaction function in figure 6.1: a two-segment step-function. These variables include those denoting vintage of structure (BUILTPRE-20, BUILT20–39, BUILT40–59, BUILT60–69), presence of garage (GARAGE) or air conditioning (AIRCOND), wood clapboard siding construction (WOOD), or lack of central heat (NOHEAT). The coefficient of each indicates whether there is a significant difference in the dwelling-satisfaction levels expressed by homeowners having the given feature and those who did not. Though the predicted signs of most of these coefficients are intuitively obvious, those for the structure vintage dummies are not. Because these dummies proxy for a host of unspecified structural attributes besides mere age, such as style, design, and quality of materials and workmanship, it is difficult to predict their relationships to overall dwelling satisfaction. Past evidence leads one to expect, however, a net inverse relationship.[9]

Independent Variables of Neighborhood Characteristics

The various indexes of the physical-demographic and social-interactive dimensions of neighborhood described in chapter 5 provide the basic variables for predicting homeowners' satisfaction with their neighborhoods. As in the case of the continuous dwelling feature variables above, each neighborhood index and its squared value are included as separate variables. Thus, the physical- and socioeconomic-status quality indexes (AREAQUAL in Wooster, and TRACTQUAL and BLOCKQUAL in Minneapolis) should be positively correlated with NEIGHSAT, but their squared terms should all be negatively correlated. Similar expectations hold for the stability of tenure index (TENURE).

The only modification to the straightforward application of the neighborhood indexes described in chapter 5 comes in the case of the black racial composition variable (RACECOMP). In all the aforementioned indexes there is reason to believe that homeowners of all types would perceive the trait in question as being either positive or negative. But there is strong evidence that most white homeowners are averse to neighborhoods with higher percentages of black residents, and that black homeowners prefer neighborhoods with approximately equal racial proportions (see HUD 1978; Galster 1982). Thus, two separate racial composition indexes are employed: RACECOMPB takes the value of RACECOMP only when the respondent homeowner is black and zero otherwise; RACECOMPW takes the value of RACECOMP only when the respondent homeowner is white and zero otherwise. Given this specification and the aforementioned indepen-evidence on preferences for neighborhood racial composition, it is pre-dicted that RACECOMPB will be positively correlated with NEIGHSAT, with the opposite for RACECOMPW.[10] As with the other variables, the squared values of the RACECOMPW variable are also included, but the low number of black observations in both samples precludes such with the RACECOMPB variable.

Finally, in both samples the two aggregate indexes of neighborhood social interaction (and their squared values) are included. One would expect that both the level of social identification in the neighborhood (NIDENTIFY) and of social integration (NINTEGRATE) will be positively cor-related with the individual's NEIGHSAT, but at a diminishing rate.

Summary of Specification for Residential Satisfaction Model

The previous discussion is summarized symbolically in the specification below. The predicted sign of each variable's coefficient is noted. (See glossary or text for symbol definition.)[11]

$$HOUSESAT = C - EDUCATION \pm? INCOME - MARRIED \qquad (6.1)$$
$$+ FEMALE + BLACK - STAGE2 - STAGE3 - STAGE4 - STAGE5$$
$$+ LONGEVITY - LONGEVITY^2 - ALIENATED + PRIORHOME$$
$$+ EARLYHOME + ROOM/OCC - (ROOM/OCC)^2 + BATH/OCC$$
$$- (BATH/OCC)^2 + YARD/OCC - (YARD/OCC)^2 + GARAGE$$
$$+ AIRCOND - WOOD - NOHEAT \pm? BUILTPRE-20$$
$$\pm? BUILT20-39 \pm? BUILT40-59 \pm? BUILT 60-69 \pm? [Z] + e$$

$$NEIGHSAT = C - EDUCATION \pm? INCOME - MARRIED + FEMALE \qquad (6.2)$$
$$+ BLACK - STAGE2 - STAGE3 - STAGE4 - STAGE5$$
$$+ LONGEVITY - (LONGEVITY)^2 - ALIENATED$$
$$+ (AREA- TRACT- BLOCK-)QUAL - (AREA- TRACT- BLOCK-)QUAL^2$$
$$+ TENURE - TENURE^2 + IDENTIFY - IDENTIFY^2 + INTEGRATE$$
$$- INTEGRATE^2 + NIDENTIFY - NIDENTIFY^2 + NINTEGRATE$$
$$- NINTEGRATE^2 + RACECOMPB - RACECOMPB^2$$
$$- RACECOMPW + RACECOMPW^2 \pm? [Z] + e$$

Where C is a constant, e is a random error term with the usual assumed properties, and $[Z]$ is an unspecified vector of homeowner characteristics and residential-context characteristics interaction variables to be deter-mined in preliminary runs over stratified samples, as outlined in the next section. The sign before each variable indicates predicted coefficient sign, if any.

Empirical Results for the Satisfaction Models

Tests for Aggregation Bias

The housing and neighborhood satisfaction indexes first are regressed on the independent variables as specified in equations (6.1) and (6.2) for each of the twelve household strata noted above. The goal here is to ascertain in which strata there are distinctive relationships between satisfaction and a given dimension of the residential environment that presumably reflect interstrata differences in housing needs, aspirations, and deficiency tolerances. On the whole the results indicate several important differences across household groupings—more so with HOUSESAT than with NEIGHSAT. The most noteworthy, which involves the housing satisfaction relationships with rooms and bathrooms, are discussed below.[12]

Consider first the results for the room-per-occupant variable in the Minneapolis sample. In the lower-income, female-headed, and life-cycle stages 2, 3, and 5 Minneapolis strata, the coefficients of ROOM/OCC and (ROOM/OCC)^2 variables are significantly positive and negative, respectively. This means that, as predicted in the above theory, the relationship between dwelling satisfaction and rooms per occupant is nonlinear, and that marginal improvements in ROOM/OCC are associated with progressively smaller increments in satisfaction.

A fuller picture of this function can be gained by examining table 6.2. Table 6.2 presents descriptive statistics for HOUSESAT and ROOM/OCC for the various Minneapolis strata where the latter variable's coefficients are statistically significant, and the values of those coefficients. It also shows three calculated values of ROOM/OCC (denoted A, B, C) where the marginal change in HOUSESAT associated with a marginal change in ROOM/OCC is 5 percent, 1 percent, and 0 percent of the mean HOUSESAT value for the given stratum, respectively.[13] Finally, table 6.2 gives the elasticity of the satisfaction function: the percentage change in HOUSESAT associated with a 1 percent change in ROOM/OCC, calculated at the means of both variables for each stratum.

Each of these functions is qualitatively similar to the general case portrayed earlier in figure 6.1. For each stratum, the value of ROOM/OCC where housing satisfaction is maximized (table 6.2, value C) is somewhat smaller than two standard deviations above the ROOM/OCC mean. What this signifies is that for the majority of the observations in each of these strata, increasing rooms per occupant is associated with greater dwelling satisfaction, but at a decreasing rate. And for some (those consuming large amounts of space) the relationship between ROOM/OCC and HOUSESAT is inverse. For those with younger families (stage 2) these marginal increases in satisfaction cease only when the room-per-person ratio exceeds 2.38. For the $0–25,000 income group and female-headed households (and the

Table 6.2 Estimates of the Relationship between HOUSESAT and ROOM/OCC for Various Homeowner Strata

Minneapolis Stratum	HOUSESAT Mean	ROOM/OCC		
		Mean=u	Std. Dev.	$u+2$(Std. Dev.)
Income $0–25,000	17.4	2.54	1.52	5.58
Female Heads	17.9	3.94	2.07	8.08
Stage2	15.7	1.58	.55	2.68
Full Sample	17.4	2.43	1.36	5.15

Coefficients		ROOM/OCC Values*			
ROOM/OCC	(ROOM/OCC)^2	A	B	C	Elasticity**
.923^c	−.105^b	.25	3.57	4.39	.057
1.37^a	−.158^a	1.51	3.77	4.33	.028
6.51^b	−1.37^b	2.09	2.32	2.38	.219
.701^c	−.076^c	−1.11	3.47	4.61	.046

Note: maximum value of ROOM/OCC in entire sample = 10 (1 case); 8 (5 cases)
$a, b, c,$ = coefficient statistically significant at 1%, 5%, 10% levels, respectively (one-tailed test)
*values A, B, C of ROOM/OCC where partial derivative of HOUSESAT with respect to ROOM/OCC = 5%, 1%, 0% of stratum mean of HOUSESAT, respectively
**% change in HOUSESAT associated with 1% change in ROOM/OCC, estimated at mean of HOUSESAT and at mean ROOM/OCC

Minneapolis sample as a whole) such increments in satisfaction continue until the room-per-person ratio reaches approximately 4.5. This clearly suggests that there is diminishing marginal utility from extra interior space, and that some households consume enough of such space to become satiated.

Of course, satiation undoubtedly occurs well after one becomes satisfied. And the estimated function in itself provides no guide as to where the aspiration or need level (corresponding to point B in figure 6.1) occurs. It is reasonable to posit, however, that this point is proxied for by that ROOM/OCC value where its change is associated with only a 1 percent change in HOUSESAT. These points are presented in column B in table 6.2. For lower-income and female-headed households (and the full Minneapolis sample) these values fall in the 3.5–3.8 rooms-per-occupant range, and for stage 2 the value is about 2.3. In comparison to current mean ROOM/OCC values, the above values typically represent increases of

41 percent–47 percent. And for female-headed Minneapolis homeowners the aspiration/need level is slightly below the stratum mean. This is undoubtedly because 61 percent of such heads are in life-cycle stage 5 and occupy residences that were more appropriate for the larger households they had during earlier stages.

The consumer-theoretical approach to housing satisfaction is further supported by the elasticity calculations (see far-right column of table 6.2). The clear pattern is that the higher the mean ROOM/OCC currently consumed by a stratum, the lower the elasticity. What this means is that those who have obtained higher consumption levels get smaller increments in their dwelling satisfaction with subsequent improvements in such consumption than those who currently consume less. This is unmistakable evidence of the Law of Diminishing Marginal Utility at work.

The estimated relationship between dwelling satisfaction and bathrooms per occupant also supports the theory. In both Wooster and Minneapolis samples BATH/OCC and (BATH/OCC)^2 coefficients are significantly positive and negative, respectively, in four homeowner strata. Analogous to the case involving ROOM/OCC, the relationships between dwelling satisfaction and bathrooms per occupant demonstrate maxima (column C, table 6.3) or satiation levels that are usually slightly less than two standard deviations above the mean value of BATH/OCC for the stratum in question. This is also the case for the assumed aspiration/need level of BATH/OCC (column B, table 6.3), that value associated with a 1 percent marginal effect upon HOUSESAT. With one exception,[14] all strata in both samples have an aspiration/need level of bathrooms per occupant from 45–80 percent more than they currently consume. And highly educated Minneapolis homeowners aspire to a BATH/OCC ratio almost 200 percent higher than they currently consume on average.

There is remarkable cross-sample comparability in the relationship between dwelling satisfaction and bathrooms per occupant. As seen in columns B and C in table 6.3, the Wooster and Minneapolis married, stage 2, and stage 4 strata have virtually identical maxima and aspiration/need levels of BATH/OCC. Each of these values correspond to *a priori* notions about the relative bathroom needs of these three strata. And in both samples the elasticity of satisfaction changes associated with BATH/OCC changes is inversely related to the level of BATH/OCC currently being consumed across strata, again meeting expectations of diminishing marginal utility. In both samples, those homeowners with young children (stage 2) demonstrate the lowest current consumption but highest elasticity.

As for stratified regressions on neighborhood satisfaction, in relatively few strata does the relationship between NEIGHSAT and characteristics such as nonresidential land use, tenure, race, and aggregate social interaction prove to be statistically significant.[15] Coefficients for variables proxying

Table 6.3 Estimates of the Relationship between HOUSESAT and BATH/OCC for Various Homeowner Strata

	HOUSESAT Mean	BATH/OCC		
		Mean=u	Std. Dev.	$u+2$(Std. Dev.)
Wooster Stratum				
Income $0–15,000	17.5	.710	.444	1.60
Married	17.5	.537	.277	1.09
Stage2	15.5	.189	.753	1.695
Stage4	18.2	.490	.192	.874
Minneapolis Stratum				
Education 13+ years	17.2	.605	.396	1.40
Married	17.3	.510	.247	1.00
Stage2	15.7	.362	.168	.698
Stage4	17.6	.440	.285	1.01
Full Sample	17.4	.608	.391	1.39

Coefficients		BATH/OCC Values*			
BATH/OCC	(BATH/OCC)^2	A	B	C	Elasticity**
5.33[b]	−2.26[b]	0.79	1.14	1.18	.086
8.10[a]	−4.50[a]	0.79	0.88	0.90	.100
29.1[a]	−25.6[b]	0.54	0.56	0.57	.239
17.6[b]	−12.3[b]	0.64	0.71	0.72	.149
3.69[b]	−.982[c]	1.01	1.79	1.88	.088
8.31[b]	−4.60[b]	0.52	0.89	0.91	.104
17.9[b]	−13.5[c]	0.60	0.65	0.67	.186
12.5[c]	−9.20[c]	0.59	0.67	0.68	.110
2.56[b]	(−.560)	(0.73)	(2.13)	(2.29)	.066

Note: maximum values of BATH/OCC in Wooster sample = 4.5 (1 case), 2.0 or greater (16 cases); in Minneapolis = 3.0 (1 case), 2.0 or greater (10 cases)

a, b, c = coefficient statistically significant at 1%, 5%, 10% levels, respectively (one-tailed test)

*values A, B, C of BATH/OCC where partial derivative of HOUSESAT with respect to BATH/OCC = 10%, 1%, 0% of stratum mean of HOUSESAT, respectively

**% change in HOUSESAT associated with 1% change in BATH/OCC, estimated at mean of HOUSESAT and at mean BATH/OCC

for a neighborhood's physical and demographic quality and aggregate social identification are, however, consistently significant for virtually all strata, with comparable signs and coefficient magnitudes. Thus it appears that the housing satisfaction model (6.1) is more prone to severe aggregation bias than is the neighborhood satisfaction model (6.2).

This conclusion is further supported by the next step in the test, which was designed to ascertain which of the aforementioned cross-strata differences in coefficients are statistically significant enough to warrant their inclusion in the final model with a special interaction variable; i.e., Z in equations (6.1) and (6.2). The strategy involves first examining the results and grouping strata according to similarities in coefficient signs, magnitudes, and levels of significance. Second, each of these groupings is specified as a dummy variable and multiplied times the given dwelling or neighborhood characteristic variable. These new interactive variables are then added to the regression and their coefficients estimated via ordinary least squares (OLS) over the entire sample, as shown in (6.1) and (6.2). In such a specification, the net coefficient of the characteristic for a given strata grouping is the sum of the coefficients of this grouping's interactive variable and the original characteristic variable. If the direction and/or magnitude of the relationship between a given satisfaction and residential characteristic substantially differs between the given strata grouping and the sample as a whole, the coefficient of the given interactive variable will be significantly different from zero. In this fashion one avoids numerous unwieldy stratified regressions yet provides the means to avoid the major aggregation biases.

OLS estimates indicate that relatively few of these strata groupings demonstrate such statistically significant differences, and most of them occur for HOUSESAT. Only those residential characteristic–strata grouping interaction variables that proved statistically significant in preliminary OLS estimations are retained in this synthesized model, and subjected to the specification bias tests described in the next section.[16]

Tests for Specification Bias

The use of OLS as an estimating technique is premised on two strong assumptions. First, the dependent variables HOUSESAT and NEIGHSAT provide interval measures of residential satisfaction; i.e., that a homeowner scoring, e.g., 4 on NEIGHSAT is actually four times more satisfied than one scoring only 1. Second, satisfaction is a linear function of all the explanatory variables.[17]

In order to assess whether these implicit assumptions may generate biased results, an alternative model is specified.[18] If the model is framed in probabilistic terms, one could imagine that there exists some theoretical interval-level index of satisfaction S, which is a continuous, normally distributed random variable. Unfortunately, one does not have direct observations of S; one only observes homeowners responding in a limited number of N ordinal categories related to their general range of satisfaction as implicitly measured by S. One can assume, however, that there are $N - 1$ cutoff points in S (call them $[S^*_i]$) that specify when individuals will respond in each of N observed categories. If one also assumes that such $[S^*_i]$ are normally distributed random variables, the probability that S falls into a particular response range ij (P_{ij}) can be computed from the cumulative normal probability function. Within each given range ij, S is assumed to be a linear function of the relevant independent variables specified above in (6.1) and (6.2).[19] Under these assumptions it is appropriate to use a PROBIT model for empirical estimations.[20]

Such a PROBIT model of satisfaction was specified and its parameters estimated using maximum-likelihood techniques.[21] Patterns of coefficient statistical significance produced by OLS and PROBIT techniques are then compared to ascertain which relationships persisted between both.[22] The goal is to indicate with more confidence those characteristics of dwellings, neighborhoods, and homeowners that consistently have statistically significant correlations with measures of residential satisfaction, regardless of functional form of the estimating equation. The basic criterion used to ascertain such variables is to include those that are statistically significant (judged by either one- or two-tailed tests as appropriate) in the linear OLS model, and in the PROBIT model as well. In addition, variables are included if in the linear model they have coefficients bigger than their standard errors (and of the predicted sign), and are statistically significant at the 5 percent level or better in the PROBIT model.[23]

Results for Corroborated Models

The variables to be included in these final, corroborated models of dwelling and neighborhood satisfaction based on the above tests for bias are summarized in tables 6.4, 6.5, and 6.6. These tables give standardized (beta) coefficients for the corroborated satisfaction-model variables so that the magnitudes of their different relationships are directly comparable. The beta coefficients shown are those estimated by the linear model (and corroborated by PROBIT). Here and in later chapters the corroborated linear-model parameters are employed, both because they are more easily interpretable and because they facilitate the computation of both direct and indirect causal connections (i.e., "path coefficients") in the larger model. It is these coefficients that form the basis of the remarks that follow.

Table 6.4   Beta Coefficients* of Homeowner Characteristics in Corroborated
Residential Satisfaction Model

| | Dependent variable | | | |
| | HOUSESAT | | NEIGHSAT | |
Independent variable	Wooster	Minneapolis	Wooster	Minneapolis
EDUCATION	—	.07	—	X
INCOME	—	—	—	—
MARRIED	—	—	−.19	—
FEMALE	—	−.12	X	−.10
BLACK	—	−.16	—	X
STAGE2	.17	.13	—	—
STAGE3	.27	.22	—	.13
STAGE4	.26	.17	—	.10
STAGE5	.42	.29	—	.22
PRIORHOME	—	—	NA	NA
EARLYHOME	—	−.06	NA	NA
LONGEVITY	—	.22	—	—
IDENTIFY**	NA	NA	.27	.32
INTEGRATE	NA	NA	—	X
ALIENATED	−.07	—	−.07	—

*using linear model's beta coefficients only when corroborated by PROBIT model
**using both linear and squared terms where appropriate; evaluated at means
NA = not applicable; variable not used in given model
— = coefficient not statistically significant in linear model or PROBIT model
X = coefficient not corroborated by PROBIT model; significant in linear model

DWELLING SATISFACTION   Independent of the features of the residential
context, there are numerous characteristics of the homeowner that prove
to be significant correlates of dwelling satisfaction across the entire sample
(see table 6.4). These findings mean that certain homeowner types evidence higher or lower levels of satisfaction regardless of the dwelling
situation in which they find themselves. This suggests that such households have higher aspirations/needs for dwelling features in general and/or
less tolerance for deficiencies between actual and needed levels.

Stage in family life cycle is the most consistent predictor of dwelling
satisfaction in both samples. As predicted by theory, the level of HOUSESAT
rises monotonically from early through late stages. Compared to identically situated homeowners in stage 1, those in stage 5 are 14 percent and 11

percent more satisfied with their dwelling in Wooster and Minneapolis, respectively. (These and all future percentage estimates are computed using the mean of the dependent variable as base.) By contrast, the comparable figures for those in stage 2 versus stage 1 are only 8 percent and 6 percent, respectively.

No other homeowner characteristics prove statistically significant consistently in both samples. Conforming to expectations are the significant negative coefficients for black- and female-headed households in Minneapolis. They indicate that compared to white homeowners, blacks are 10 percent less satisfied, and compared to single-male or multiple-headed households headed by females are 6 percent less satisfied.[24] The period of tenure in the current dwelling shows the predicted curvilinear relationship, but only LONGEVITY in the Minneapolis sample is even modestly significant. Those with a more alienated outlook have lower dwelling satisfaction in Wooster; compared to those who are least alienated, those who are most alienated are 6 percent less satisfied.

Contrary to expectations, previous residency in non–single-family dwellings is not associated with higher satisfaction with the current (single-family) dwelling. In fact, both EARLYHOME and PRIORHOME have modestly significant negative coefficients in the Minneapolis sample. Also surprising is that differences in marital status, education, or income show no significant relationship with HOUSESAT, *ceteris paribus*. This confounds conventional expectations that couples and those of higher socioeconomic status generally have higher perceived aspirations/needs for dwelling attributes.

As for dwelling characteristics (see table 6.5), features describing the age and size of the structure are evaluated relatively consistently by sampled households. Residence in a home built prior to 1939 generally elicits a 4–7 percent lower dwelling satisfaction rating in Wooster; in Minneapolis the comparable range is 9–10 percent lower. In the Minneapolis sample both rooms per occupant and especially bathrooms per occupant are positively associated with dwelling satisfaction (but at a diminishing rate),[25] though in neither case so strongly as the structural-age variables. Also surprisingly, given the disaggregated analysis above, none of the attempts to specify interactive variables for ROOM/OCC or BATH/OCC revealed any statistically significant distinctions worth adding to the aggregate model.

Only for certain qualitative features of the dwelling does any interactive variable prove statistically significant (see table 6.5). The Minneapolis female–stage 3–stage 4 group demonstrates a much weaker aversion to dwellings built in 1940–59 than the entire sample (a net beta coefficient of −.09 versus −.19, respectively). The Wooster stage 2 group has, on the other hand, lower satisfaction when living in 1960–69 vintage dwellings,

Table 6.5   Beta Coefficients* of Dwelling Characteristics in Corroborated
Residential Satisfaction Model

	Dependent variable HOUSESAT	
Independent variable	Wooster	Minneapolis
YARD/OCC	—	—
ROOM/OCC**	—	.04
BATH/OCC**	—	.16
BUILTPRE-20	—	−.23
BUILT20–39	−.18	−.23
BUILT40–59		
Total	−.16	−.19
FEMALE, STAGE3,4	NA	−.09
BUILT60–69		
Total	—	—
STAGE2	−.08	NA
NOHEAT	—	—
AIRCOND		
Total	—	—
FEMALE, STAGE4	NA	.13
GARAGE		
Total	.09	—
STAGE2	−.05	NA
WOOD		
Total	—	—
STAGE3	−.13	NA

*using linear model's beta coefficients only when corroborated by PROBIT model
**using both linear and squared terms where appropriate; evaluated at means
NA = not applicable; variable not used in given model
— = coefficient not statistically significant in linear model or PROBIT model

whereas other households are indifferent. The Minneapolis female–stage 4 group has the only significant (positive) coefficient for the presence of central air-conditioning. The Wooster stage 2 group has a significant negative net coefficient for the presence of a garage, in contrast to the rest of the sample. Finally, the Wooster stage 3 stratum evidences the only significant (negative) coefficient for residence in a wood clapboard structure. Thus, even though interacting dwelling characteristics with homeowner strata groupings does not always produce significant results, it does so often enough to improve the robustness of the dwelling satisfaction model.

NEIGHBORHOOD SATISFACTION   The coefficients for homeowner characteristics presented in table 6.4 can frequently explain variations in neighborhood satisfaction independent of the residential context. There is little similarity in the patterns of statistically significant coefficients across the two samples, however. Only in the case of neighborhood social identification are coefficients of the same variable statistically significant in both samples.

The predicted pattern of steadily higher levels of neighborhood satisfaction associated with older life-cycle stages is borne out in the Minneapolis sample, but is inexplicably absent in the Wooster sample. Compared to a Minneapolis homeowner in stage 1, one in stage 5 is 10 percent more satisfied with the neighborhood, as computed at the mean. As expected from the theory, homeowners who are either married or more alienated are less satisfied, but only in the Wooster sample.

In neither sample does the coefficient of income or race prove statistically significant, contrary to other researchers' findings (Lansing, Marans, and Zehner 1970; Morris, Crull, and Winter 1976; Varady 1983). However, these studies employed few, if any, control variables for either the physical-demographic or social-interactive dimensions of the neighborhood. Thus, income and/or race may have served as unwitting proxies for these excluded variables.

Of most interest are the results for the index measuring the individual homeowner's identification with neighbors. In both samples the coefficient IDENTIFY is positive, but the coefficient of its squared value is negative. That is, neighborhood is positively correlated with an individual's sense of identification with neighbors, but the relationship becomes weaker at higher levels of identification. The magnitude of this relationship is such that a homeowner having a mean value of IDENTIFY would have at least 25 percent higher NEIGHSAT in both samples, compared to one who only had the minimum IDENTIFY score. This evidence provides further support for the aforementioned theory that suggests that diminishing marginal utility properties should be embedded in empirical models of residential satisfaction. And it also implies that the homeowner's identifica-

Table 6.6   Beta Coefficients* of Neighborhood Characteristics in Corroborated Residential Satisfaction Model

Independent variable	Dependent variable NEIGHSAT	
	Wooster	Minneapolis
AREAQUAL	.11	NA
BLOCKQUAL	NA	.12
TRACTQUAL	NA	.17
NONRESID		
Total	−.07	−.22
EDUCATION(LOW),STAGE1	NA	.02
TENURE		
Total	—	.17
MARRIED	NA	−.19
RACECOMPW**	.01	−.08
RACECOMPB	—	—
NIDENTIFY**	.25	—
NINTEGRATE	—	—

*using linear model's beta coefficients only when corroborated by PROBIT model
**using both linear and squared terms where appropriate; evaluated at means
NA = not applicable; variable not used in given model
— = coefficient not statistically significant in linear model or PROBIT model

tion with neighbors is a crucial determinant of neighborhood satisfaction, independent of other features of the context.

In the final model only two interactive variables have statistically significant coefficients (see table 6.6), but both indicate benefits from disaggregation. The first such variable is the Minneapolis lower education–stage 1 group interacted with the nonresidential land-use dummy. For this grouping the presence of nonresidential land use on the block face is associated with a 15 percent higher level of neighborhood satisfaction, whereas for the rest of the sample it is associated with a 38 percent lower level of satisfaction. This suggests for this group that the value of convenience or stimulation associated with nearby nonresidential land uses outweighs any concomitant increase in traffic, noise, pollution or ugliness—attributes that annoy the majority.

The second such variable interacts married homeowners with the proportion of homeowners on the block face residing there ten or more years. Compared to those homeowners without such long tenure on the block face, those with mean percentage have 13 percent more neighborhood satisfaction in the sample as a whole. For married Minneapolis home-owners, however, there is virtually no net association.

With the two aforementioned exceptions, it is clear that both physical-demographic and social-interactive dimensions of the neighborhood are evaluated comparably by all types of homeowners. Table 6.6 indicates that the aggregate social-identification dimension of neighborhood cohesion is associated with the greatest variation in neighborhood satisfaction in Wooster. Those living in cohesive Wooster areas (i.e., having above-aver-age identification scores) are over one-third more satisfied, *ceteris paribus*. In comparison, those living on Minneapolis block faces with above-aver-age identification scores are only 3–6 percent more satisfied (and the coefficients are only modestly statistically significant). Both samples also show the curvilinear relationship between neighborhood satisfaction and the aggregate level of identification, though more strongly so in Wooster. In neither sample is the aggregate level of social integration (nor its square) statistically significant. Together these findings suggest that homeowners are more satisfied in areas where people share favorable sentiments about their neighbors, but do not necessarily know them well or interact often. That the evidence is stronger in a small town is consistent with the notion that remnants of a *gemeinschaft* or villagelike milieu can intensify the value one places on cohesion.

In Minneapolis the indexes of physical and socioeconomic quality demonstrate roughly comparable, large magnitudes of association with NEIGHSAT. The individual variations in neighborhood satisfaction between the minima and maxima of BLOCKQUAL and TRACTQUAL are 22 percent and 19 percent, respectively. But approximately the same variation can be obtained by comparing observations that simultaneously have the minima for both with those that have the mean for both: 17 percent. By comparison, the associated variations for AREAQUAL in Wooster are 6–10 percent from the mean to maximum. Thus, it is clear that various geographic scales of neighborhood—at least as large as census tracts—have a strong influence on most homeowners' assessments of their neighborhoods as places to live.

Based on the parameters estimated to relate NEIGHSAT with RACECOMPW in Minneapolis, whites living in neighborhoods having the mean proportion of blacks are 30 percent less satisfied than those in all-white areas. Whites living in areas with the highest black concentrations are, on the other hand, only 6.5 percent less satisfied than their counterparts in all-white areas. This may, however, indicate not a white desire for substantially black areas, but rather differences in prior adjustments to unsatisfactory situations via mobility. That is, whites surveyed in slightly integrated areas may dislike this aspect of the environment, but not so much as to trigger a move (yet). On the other hand, whites extremely averse to black neighbors have moved out of substantially black areas long before the survey, leaving behind those whites who are either indifferent or resigned to their residential contexts. In Wooster the variations in neighborhood satisfaction associated with variations in racial composition are virtually nil, as would be expected considering Wooster's lower black proportion.

Summary and Conclusions

One may infer from the model of residential satisfaction developed in this chapter that the relationship between a perceived gap between need-ed/aspired to situation and actual situation will be nonlinear due to the Law of Diminishing Marginal Utility, and variable across homeowner types based on differences in their dissatisfaction thresholds and in their need/aspiration levels. The empirical estimates of the model in both Wooster and Minneapolis samples support both inferences. Indeed several dwelling and neighborhood characteristics demonstrate a nonlinear rela-tionship with satisfaction, and several homeowner strata appear to trans-late similar residential contexts into quite different degrees of residential satisfaction. More specifically:

– The only homeowner characteristic that consistently proves related to either measure of residential satisfaction, regardless of the residential con-text, is life-cycle stage. Typically, those in progressively later stages are more satisfied, suggesting reductions in their need/aspiration levels and/or increases in their tolerance for deficiencies between such levels and actual ones. Coefficient magnitudes for these variables indicate that they are as important as determinants of satisfaction as the features of the residential context themselves.

– The adequacy of interior space and plumbing facilities (measured by rooms per person and bathrooms per person, respectively) are directly related to dwelling satisfaction, but to a progressively smaller degree as the quantity of these features increases, as would be predicted based on the Law of Diminishing Marginal Utility. Also as predicted, these rela-tionships vary by homeowner type. For instance, those with young fami-lies cease gaining marginal satisfaction when the rooms per person exceed 2.4; the comparable figure for female heads is 4.5. Similarly, households with teenagers gain more satisfaction from increments in the bathroom-per-person ratios than households with small children only.

– Age of the home generally is strongly (negatively) correlated with dwelling satisfaction, with pre-1960 vintage homes eliciting lower degrees of satisfaction. Certain homeowner types, however, proved less satisfied in newer dwellings.

– Indexes of the physical and socioeconomic status of the neighborhood proved to be strong predictors of neighborhood satisfaction across virtually all types of homeowners, regardless of the different geographic scales of neighborhood employed in the index. Apparently a fairly large spatial area is evaluated when assessing the quality of the neighborhood.

– The presence of nonresidential land uses on the block face is typically associated with a lower degree of neighborhood satisfaction, but for younger and low-education homeowners the results are the opposite.

– For white Minneapolis homeowners, residence in a more racially integrated area is associated with less neighborhood satisfaction than residence in an all-white area. The precise relationship differs between the samples, due to the comparatively restricted range of racial composition in Wooster.

– Both the individual and the aggregate degree of neighborhood social identification (i.e., sensed helpfulness, friendliness, commonality of neighbors) prove to be a crucial determinant of neighborhood satisfaction. In Wooster such neighborhood cohesion, as defined by aggregate identification scores, has by far the greatest impact of any neighborhood characteristic; in Minneapolis the effect appears not to be as strong. In neither sample does neighborhood cohesion, as defined in terms of interpersonal familiarity and interaction, have nearly as much impact as that defined by more generalized social sentiments.

7 Homeowners' Expectations of Neighborhood Changes

The previous chapter deals theoretically and empirically with how home-owners evaluate their current perceived residential circumstances. Here we consider their expectations for the prospects of their present neighborhood in the future. As before, a conceptual framework is first developed, and then an empirical model is specified and estimated.

The conceptual framework draws from the social-psychological theory of information acquisition and belief formation. This theory suggests that similar objective data will not necessarily be translated into similar expectations by all homeowners or in all contexts. Interpersonal variations occur in both the amount and type of information search conducted and in the assessment of whether new information is valid and important enough to warrant alteration of prior beliefs. Interneighborhood variations occur because of differing social-interactive networks that affect the amount of information acquired and how it is evaluated. The variations suggest the stratified sample estimating procedures that will be followed below.

Two distinct types of expectations are modeled: changes in neighborhood quality and in property values. Models stratified by homeowner type are first estimated in order to access the degree to which objective characteristics of neighborhoods explain expectations across homeowners, controlling for social-interactive neighborhood contexts and public-policy effects. Results of these models then are used to specify particular interaction variables identifying the relationships between idiosyncratic home-owner types and neighborhood condition. These interaction variables are, in turn, added to the general model, which is then estimated over the entire sample. Both ordinary least squares (OLS) and PROBIT techniques are employed to assess the stability of parameter estimates, and final quantitative conclusions are made based on the results corroborated by both methods.

Readers less interested in conceptual issues and details of model estimation may turn directly to the chapter summary.

Conceptual Framework

An "expectation" is a particular relation between a given object and some of its future attributes, as perceived by an individual. The "object" and the "attribute" may be a person, place, thing, or event. For instance, in the expectation: "There will be no minority households living on my block during the next year or two," "block" is the object and "no minority households" is the attribute. In this chapter some facet of neighborhood will be the object and a variety of possible neighborhood characteristics will be considered as attributes. Expectations are thus particular sorts of beliefs; i.e., beliefs about future relations between objects and attributes. And as beliefs, expectations are shaped by the environmental context, the informational content conveyed about this context to the individual, and the individual perceiver.

To understand this claim more fully, we must delve into the nature of human belief formation. The discussion is based on the seminal formulation of Fishbein and Azjen (1975). Belief presumes perception, and perception presumes that some sort of sensory stimuli about objects and their attributes (i.e., "data") have been generated by the environment. This generation of data may be both external and internal to the individual. The primary external data of concern here are changes in the physical, demographic or social-interactive character of the neighborhood. The primary internal data are changes in the household's family status or purchasing power.

Although internal data are always acquired passively via firsthand experience, external data are acquired differently both in regard to means and medium.

External data may be acquired passively, when, for example, you happen to notice on your way to work that several houses on the block are getting a new coat of paint, or a neighbor casually mentions in a conversation that people on either side of her are moving out. Alternatively, external data may be acquired actively as a result of intentional housing-market search. You might, for example, consult with a realtor, attend a city planning commission meeting, or question neighbors about your residential environment. Typically, active search is undertaken when an individual judges the reduction in uncertainty gained by the expected information to offset the costs of the search.

Regardless of whether external data are acquired actively or passively, three alternative media of data transmission are possible. The first is through direct experience and observation, such as a personal "windshield survey" of the neighborhood. The second is through indirect logical inferences, such as a belief that the neighborhood is integrating stemming from the observation of more racial diversity among the customers of the local supermarket. The third is through communication with other observers either personally (e.g., conversations, letters) or impersonally (e.g., newspaper, television, radio, posters).

Variations across Individuals

The particulars of how and whether a given datum will be perceived and whether this perception will be translated into alterations in expectations depend crucially on the individual perceiver. Peoples' passive acquisition of external data can differ qualitatively and quantitatively depending on a host of personal traits. Whether, e.g., commuting to work or taking shopping trips will provide the opportunity to acquire data directly depends on peoples' attentiveness and perceptiveness. Whether they passively gain secondhand data through personal communication varies according to their gregariousness; acquisition through the print media varies according to their functional literacy.

Analogously, whether a search is undertaken and how active it will be differ across individuals. Those who have more tolerance for uncertainty, who expect less valuable data to be unearthed by active search, and/or who perceive a high psychological, out-of-pocket, or time cost from active search will be less likely to search, *ceteris paribus*. Similar differences also influence how extensively one searches once a search is actively initiated. Once initiated, the method of active search likely differs depending on one's income, self-confidence, education, etc.

And, of course, because different media do not necessarily convey the same or even complementary messages, interpersonal differences in the amount and type of data acquisition likely translate into interpersonal differences in the data that cognitively register. Put more simply, a given event in the neighborhood may not be perceived similarly, or even perceived at all, by all residents. And even if a given datum is perceived identically by two individuals, it need not result in identical expectations. Identical expectations will result only if it is judged valid and salient by both equally. The perceived validity of a new perception is determined by a combination of the discrepancy between the incoming message and the prior belief held by the individual, and a set of facilitating factors that describe the characteristics of the data, its source, and its receiver.

If the new datum merely supports a preexisting belief held by the individual receiver it is, of course, judged to be valid. The greater the divergence between the new message and prior belief, however, the greater the likelihood that the new message will be disregarded as nonsense. But this relationship is mediated by facilitating factors. Characteristics of the data may be more or less acceptable depending on their logic, the order in which they are conveyed, and the type of emotion appealed to (e.g., affirmation versus fear). If the data are communicated interpersonally, the source's perceived expertise, trustworthiness, likeability, and/or status may come into play. In addition, the receiver's intelligence, credulity, and self-esteem may affect its acceptance (see Fishbein and Ajzen 1975, ch. 11).

Finally, whether valid data alter expectations depends on the salience of the information in shaping the given attribute. If one attaches much significance to the given datum as a key determinant of the attribute in question, then the relationship between the overall expectation and perceived changes in the given datum will be strong. For example, if a homeowner believes that the type of car owned by a neighbor is the key measure of the neighbor's status, a perceived alteration in auto brand will be salient in shaping expectations concerning neighborhood status. Others would be virtually indifferent to such data if their implicit indicator of status was neighbors' property-upkeep behavior.

Variations across Social-Interactive Contexts

A final complicating factor is that all the aforementioned interpersonal variations in data acquisition and evaluation have as a parameter the social-interactive context in which they occur. If individuals interact frequently with neighbors, they are more likely to acquire passively new data about changes in their environment. Similarly, active searches may be encouraged if there are a host of neighborhood organizations and voluntary associations that can be readily tapped for information. If people identify strongly with their neighbors, they are more likely to view data that neighbors transmit interpersonally as valid. Finally, because interpersonally transmitted messages are often flavored by the biases of the sender, those who receive a preponderance of their data through their neighbors may be socialized into holding the same beliefs about salient indicators as others in the neighborhood. What all this means is that people in more socially interactive and socially integrated neighborhoods are more likely to perceive new external data about their environment and to evaluate it consistently in connection to forming expectations.

Previous Research on Expectations

Assertions of the crucial importance of understanding residents' neighborhood expectations are numerous in the literature: Ahlbrandt and Brophy (1975, ch.1), Kain and Quigley (1975, ch.1), Goetze (1976), Public Affairs Counseling (1975), Leven, et al. (1976, ch.3). Unfortunately, analyses of how such expectations are formed are scarce.

Goetze (1979, esp. ch.1, 2, 4, 7) has provided some impressionistic case-study evidence of particular revitalizing Boston neighborhoods. Although Goetze provides neither a clear theoretical framework nor statistical evidence, he argues that the accelerating complexity of the urban scene has raised uncertainty about neighborhood change and has given increasing power to those who possess more information. Because the organs of media narrow the view on neighborhoods to the perceptions held by only a few "influentials," they intensify the interpretability (if not veracity) of the message. This in turn, according to Goetze, makes these media messages the most pervasive shapers of household and investor expectations. Government policy has only encouraged this trend through capricious interventions, which frequently heighten uncertainty.

In a related study of the same neighborhoods, Hollister et al. (1978) conducted interviews with residents in order to uncover a variety of beliefs about the past, current, and future conditions of the neighborhoods. Based on these responses, overall "neighborhood confidence scores" are derived for each area and then contrasted to overall population profiles of each area. Unfortunately, their conclusions are totally undermined by two methodological pitfalls (see Varady 1984b). First, the confidence measure gives equal weight to attitudes about past, present, and future neighborhood conditions. Many of Hollister's respondents had positive perceptions of the former two conditions, but pessimistic expectations about the future. Second, correlating aggregate confidence scores with aggregate demographic characteristics illustrates the "ecological fallacy": generalization from groups to individuals results in error.

Varady and Rose (1983) and Varady (1984a; 1984b; 1986, ch.6) provide the only rigorous multivariate statistical investigations of the correlates of neighborhood expectations. They employ a sample of households selected from forty Urban Homesteading Demonstration neighborhoods. As expected, households' negative subjective evaluations of the current neighborhood situation were the strongest predictors of increased pessimism, particularly perceptions of the neighborhood as a poor place for children, as having various environmental problems, as having low property upkeep by neighbors, and as characterized by low income and racial change. Beyond these subjective variables, no added objective indicator of either neighborhood or respondent dwelling is significantly related to expectations. Three types of respondents provided answers inversely related to pessimism: unskilled workers, blacks, and those with greater social interaction with neighbors. As important as this seminal investigation is, shortcomings remain. Most important, the dependent variable is not a purely expectational one, but rather is an amalgam of responses involving both future expectations and current evaluations of neighborhood, which are subsequently collapsed into a three-item "pessimism" scale. This renders interpretability of the above results difficult. In addition, no attempt is made to identify the objective household and neighborhood correlates of the subjective variables that prove to have so much explanatory power. Without such we can gain less insight into the conditions that spawn the specific evaluations. Further, the results are based solely on homesteading neighborhoods, and thus may not be generalizable. Finally, both the interpersonal and interneighborhood variations in how data are transformed into expectations discussed above suggest a stratified regression approach, which is not employed (except for race).

In sum, virtually no reliable empirical work has been done in the field of neighborhood expectations. The following sections attempt to remedy, at least partially, this shortcoming.

Specification of an Empirical Model of Neighborhood Expectations

Dependent Variables: Qualitative and Property-Value Expectations

Two variables are employed here to measure homeowners' expectations regarding distinct aspects of their residential environment, which the theory of chapter 3 suggests have different effects. The first, NEIGHEXP, is designed to measure the degree to which respondents are optimistic or pessimistic about near-term qualitative changes in the neighborhood. It is derived from a sequence of survey questions:

1. Do you anticipate any changes in this neighborhood within the next one to two years?
2. If so, what kind?
3. Are these changes good, bad, or neither?

Responses to these questions were coded in such a way that higher values of NEIGHEXP indicate decreasing optimism / increasing pessimism: 1 if foresee changes that are good on the whole; 2 if foresee no changes, or both good and bad changes that cancel out; 3 if foresee changes that are bad on the whole. In sum, NEIGHEXP can be viewed as a measure of homeowner pessimism regarding near-term qualitative changes in the neighborhood.[1]

The second dependent variable specified here attempts to measure a more specific homeowner belief about future changes in neighborhood property values: VALUEEXP. The variable is derived from the responses to the question: "What do you expect to happen to property values in your neighborhood in the next five years?" In Wooster only three response options were given: 1 if rise; 2 if stay same; 3 if fall. In Minneapolis a wider range of expectation responses was provided for: 1 if rise a great deal; 2 if rise somewhat; 3 if stay same; 4 if fall somewhat; 5 if fall a great deal. These numerical codes form the VALUEEXP variable; it thus has higher values associated with less optimism / more pessimism. In sum, VALUEEXP can be viewed as a measure of homeowner pessimism regarding property value changes in the neighborhood over a five-year horizon.

The survey data indicate that a vast majority of sampled homeowners (89 percent in Wooster, 81 percent in Minneapolis) expect no substantial deterioration or improvement in their neighborhood in the next one to two years.[2] In both samples slightly more homeowners are optimistic than are pessimistic in this regard. In contrast to a national 1978 survey of all households, which asked respondents to assess expected changes in neighborhood housing conditions, physical conditions, and social environment, the Wooster and Minneapolis homeowners expect much higher levels of stability, with fewer optimistic and pessimistic responses.[3] This raises the possibility that modeling expectations here may be unsuccessful due to relatively limited variation in the dependent variables.

There are theoretical and empirical reasons why two seemingly similar expectations are modeled separately. Theoretically, the broader indicator of future qualitative neighborhood changes (NEIGHEXP) should measure the homeowner's assessment of how she or he personally perceives the future neighborhood as a place to live. Thus, independently of investment motivations, the homeowner as an individual consumer of housing should be interested in the neighborhood's future because, as shown in chapter 3, the anticipated marginal utility from consuming extra units of housing capital may be altered. On the other hand, the specific measure of property value expectations (VALUEEXP) should capture the homeowner's assessment of how she or he perceives the market's evaluation of the area in the future, and hence changes in expected home equity at the time of sale. These perceived market evaluations may affect the homeowners' housing maintenance efforts through pure investment-strategy calculus, regardless of the homeowner's personal (consumer) evaluation of the desirability of the residential environment. Furthermore, in chapter 3 it is demonstrated how strategic gaming behavior between homeowners is likely to be related in distinctive ways to expectations about neighborhood quality and property value changes. Thus, both types of expectations theoretically should be related behaviorally to home-upkeep activity, but for different reasons and in different manners.

On empirical grounds as well there is ample reason for distinguishing between the two types of expectations. There is a low degree of correlation between NEIGHEXP and VALUEEXP: .073 and .144 in Wooster and Minneapolis, respectively.[4] If expectations about qualitative neighborhood changes and property value changes were essentially identical beliefs, one would predict that virtually all observations would fall on the principal diagonal in the cross-tabulations of these two variables. But in fact there are significant and interesting exceptions to this prediction. In both samples, substantial numbers of homeowners expect their neighborhood property values to rise even though they expect no changes in their neighborhood: 61 percent in Wooster and 51 percent in Minneapolis. These results are undoubtedly produced by general inflationary expectations about the housing market. More surprising is that some homeowners believe their neighborhood property values will rise though they expect generally negative qualitative neighborhood changes: 3 percent in Wooster and 4 percent in Minneapolis. Conversely, a handful of pessimists foresee that property values will fall even in the face of expected neighborhood improvements: 0.6 percent in Wooster and 0.7 percent in Minneapolis. It is thus clear that the particular neighborhood-related expectation one considers for analysis makes an important difference empirically.

Before leaving this discussion of neighborhood expectations, it is interesting to note the more detailed types of changes that homeowners in both samples expected. Of those homeowners in Wooster who expect the neighborhood to improve qualitatively in the next few years, a vast majority (75 percent) foresee improvements in the physical condition of the neighborhood and/or in public facilities, infrastructure, and service delivery. By contrast, only 31 percent of Minneapolis homeowners attribute improvement expectations to this cause. Large proportions in Minneapolis expect improvements in social elements (predominantly younger homeowner families moving in), housing rehabilitation or new construction, and public-sector activities.[5] On the opposite side of the coin, 29 percent and 50 percent of Wooster homeowners expecting neighborhood declines attribute such to social conditions and neighborhood physical and public-service aspects, respectively. These are also the two most prevalent causes of expected decline cited by Minneapolis homeowners, both with 31 percent frequencies.

The two most surprising findings are: (1) the apparent lack of concern about changing social class or race, and (2) the inconsistency of evaluation of a given perceived change. Regarding the former, only five homeowners (9 percent) in the total foreseeing decline in both samples denote changes in neighborhood social class or racial composition as the main reason for their pessimism; and only three (4 percent) of those foreseeing improvements cite such changes as the main reason. These are unexpectedly low proportions, given the importance accorded to these factors in the social-science literature (e.g., Downs 1981). This result is undoubtedly a peculiar product of the two cities sampled, neither of which have experienced the more extreme forms of ghettoization, racial tipping, or the strong influx of low-income and minority in-migrants evidenced in other metropolitan housing markets.

It is also surprising to note how frequently the same expectation is evaluated both positively and negatively. In the Minneapolis sample, fourteen see increasing turnover and younger in-movers as a good thing; five see it as a bad thing.[6] Seven homeowners assess new housing construction positively; seven assess it negatively. The increase in nonresidential land use is evaluated positively by three and negatively by three.[7] Gentrification received an opposite evaluation by two homeowners. What all this means empirically is that in a regression explaining expectations it may be difficult to obtain meaningful coefficients for variables describing various physical and demographic aspects of the neighborhood if the evaluation of such aspects varies among homeowners. But, of course, these findings are perfectly understandable considering the conceptual discussion above. And, as we shall see below, estimates over stratified subsamples support this concern.

Independent Variables for Neighborhood Characteristics

Variables proxying for the physical-demographic and social-interactive dimensions of the neighborhood are virtually identical to those employed in the neighborhood satisfaction model described in chapter 6. The only exception is that the squared values of each are not included in the model. Unlike in the case of residential satisfaction where diminishing marginal utility should be evidenced, in the case of expectations there is no clear *a priori* rationale for a nonlinear relationship.

The predicted relationships between both NEIGHEXP and VALUEEXP and the variables of: neighborhood quality (both physical and socioeconomic status) (AREAQUAL, BLOCKQUAL, TRACTQUAL); longevity and owner occupancy (TENURE); nonresidential land use (NONRESID); and proportion black as seen by white (RACECOMPW) and by black (RACECOMPB) homeowners, are straightforward. Homeowners should be less pessimistic in neighborhoods of higher quality and of greater stability, hence negative coefficients for -QUAL variables and for TENURE. Conversely, the presence of nonresidential land uses may signal the possibility of further such encroachments in the future, yielding a predicted positive coefficient for NONRESID. In a similar vein, higher proportions of black neighbors may indicate to whites that eventual tipping (or at least further integration) is in the offing, yielding a positive coefficient for RACECOMPW. The sign of this variable for blacks (RACECOMPW) is harder to predict. Blacks, like whites, may be concerned about racial transition and the concomitant instability of property values, but this may be offset by their clear preference for approximately equal racial proportions in neighborhoods.

The two variables measuring the aggregate social-interactive dimension of the neighborhood (NIDENTIFY, NINTEGRATE) proxy for a more complex set of factors than did the physical-demographic dimension variables. As explained above, a cohesive, socially integrated community with strong solidarity sentiments is more likely to: (1) provide a dominant means of transmitting information about the residential environment (i.e., interpersonal, second-hand); (2) selectively color and interpret this information; (3) encourage a common evaluation of the information; and (4) generate a coherent collective response. Variations in any or all of these four functions should be inversely related to pessimistic expectations. In areas with high aggregate social interaction homeowners should be more confident that the neighborhood will quickly become aware of impending worrisome situations and will formulate an efficacious response.

There is solid theoretical justification for including all the aforementioned variables proxying for neighborhood characteristics in the model, and there are probably others that should be included as well. It is reasonable to posit that not only the current level of neighborhood conditions but also recent changes in these conditions influence expectations. Unfortunately, such data on recent trends in neighborhoods were not available to the present analysis. The omission of such variables leads to low explanatory power from the expectation model, although the coefficients of the remaining variables should not be biased unless they are highly correlated with the excluded variables.

Independent Variables for Public Policies

Public policies aimed at improving neighborhood confidence may have impacts upon the homeowner directly (e.g., through assistance to the individual) and indirectly (e.g., through improvements in the overall neighborhood environment). In the Minneapolis sample two measures of both types of potential effects are employed. If the individual had received within the last five years either a low-interest loan or a grant for housing rehabilitation or improvements, the dummy variables LOAN? and GRANT? take the value one, respectively (zero otherwise). Of the homeowners sampled, 10.8 percent had received such loans, and 7.4 percent had received grants.

The indirect effect is measured by the demarcation of observations into three distinct areas of the city: those that had not been denoted as qualifying for public Urban Renewal or Community Development Block Grants in neighborhood improvements (NOTQUALIFY); those that qualified for assistance but as of the time of the survey had received none, (QUALIFY); and those that had received assistance prior to 1980. The dummy variables NOTQUALIFY and QUALIFY denote the first two types of areas, and thus provide implicit comparison to the reference areas receiving assistance. The proportions of sampled Minneapolis homeowners in these two areas are 17.7 percent and 34.1 percent, respectively.

Public programs to assist in housing rehabilitation and improvements potentially should signal the commitment of the public sector to maintain and in some cases improve the quality of the residential environment. If an individual benefits directly from such programs the recognition of this effort is undoubted. Thus, one would predict that both LOAN? and GRANT? should be associated with less pessimistic expectations (i.e., a negative coefficient). Compared to those living in areas already receiving aid, those in ineligible areas would be more pessimistic, yielding a predicted positive coefficient for NOTQUALIFY. If it is the actual delivery of assistance, as opposed to its mere promise, that boosts confidence, one would predict a positive coefficient for QUALIFY as well.

Independent Variables for Homeowner Characteristics

As explained earlier, there are many reasons why different types of home-owners may express different expectations in the same residential context: (1) importance placed on certain attributes, (2) types of information acquisition and evaluation, and (3) general predispositions toward pessimism. The first reason cannot be adequately addressed in a simple additive (linear) regression model, because distinct interactions between homeowner types with particular preferences and particular neighborhood characteristics cannot be specified. This point will be addressed below, but suffice it to note that the same general technique used in chapter 6 will be employed here. Preliminary stratified models will suggest particular interaction terms to use in a subsequent synthesized model for the entire sample.

The latter two reasons above can, however, be explored in the context of an additive model. Controlling for the objective characteristics of the residential context, variations in expectations associated solely with homeowner characteristics must be attributed either to differences in the type or amount of information about this context that they possess and/or to differences in their predisposition to interpret the same information more optimistically or pessimistically. As for the former, homeowners with less (reliable) information would tend to have less certainty about the future. And since it is conventionally believed that people do not like excessive uncertainty, it follows that people would evidence greater pessimism in such circumstances. As for the third reason, people who hold a more fatalistic outlook on life would in any context be less likely to exude optimism than those who have a strong sense of personal efficacy.

Before dealing with specific household traits, one other conceptual factor must be considered: the likelihood of previous adjustment to pessimistic expectations. Those who have higher residential mobility potential (i.e., lower moving costs, more information about superior residential options, etc.) would be less likely to tolerate prolonged periods during which they expect their neighborhood to decline. Thus, at the time of the survey, there will be a bias against observing highly mobile homeowners with pessimistic expectations, because they will have moved already to neighborhoods about which they are more optimistic.

Given these considerations, predictions can be made for relationships between expectations and particular homeowner characteristics. Those with anomie are likely to express more pessimism in any residential context, hence the predicted coefficient for ALIENATED is positive. Homeowners with higher education and income are likely to be more self-efficacious, to have more information about any situation, and to have already made prior adjustments to earlier instances that engendered pessimism. The predicted coefficients of EDUCATION and INCOME are thus both negative. Conversely, one would expect a positive coefficient for BLACK homeowners, for all the opposite reasons. Those who have stronger solidarity sentiments with neighbors (IDENTIFY) are likely to be less pessimistic, because personal efficacy is enhanced via abetted confidence in the collective ability of the neighborhood to respond to potential threats.

For other homeowner characteristics no unambiguous prediction of coefficient signs can be made. Although it is likely that elderly (STAGE5) homeowners are more fatalistic and less mobile than STAGE1 homeowners, the relative pessimism levels for the other life-cycle stages cannot be predicted. Similarly, there is no *a priori* basis to expect pessimism differentials between married, female-headed and single-male-headed or multiple-headed households. Finally, though one would predict that those who interact more with neighbors (INTEGRATE) would get more information of the personal, second-hand variety, one cannot predict whether this would reduce uncertainty or abet it because of appeals to fear or emotion.

Summary of Expectations Model Specification

Given the aforementioned theoretical foundation and discussion of variables, the neighborhood expectations model to be estimated can be summarized symbolically below. Signs indicate predicted relationships between independent and dependent variables (see text or glossary for detailed definition of symbols).

$$\left.\begin{aligned} \text{NEIGHEXP} = \\ \text{VALUEEXP} = \end{aligned}\right\} \quad \begin{aligned} & C - (\text{AREA- TRACT- BLOCK-})\text{QUAL} - \text{TENURE} \quad\quad (7.1)\\ & + \text{NONRESID} + \text{RACECOMPW} \pm ? \text{RACECOMPB} - \quad (7.2)\\ & \text{NIDENTIFY} - \text{NINTEGRATE} + \text{NOTQUALIFY} +\\ & \text{QUALIFY} - \text{GRANT?} - \text{LOAN?} + \text{ALIENATED} -\\ & \text{EDUCATION} - \text{INCOME} - \text{MARRIED} \pm ? \text{FEMALE}\\ & + \text{BLACK} \pm ? \text{STAGE2} \pm ? \text{STAGE3} \pm ? \text{STAGE4} \pm ?\\ & \text{STAGE5} - \text{IDENTIFY} \pm ? \text{INTEGRATE} \pm ? [Z] + e \end{aligned}$$

Where C is a constant, e is a random error term with the usual assumed properties, and $[Z]$ is an unspecified vector of the variables showing the interaction between homeowner characteristics and neighborhood characteristics, which will be determined in the section presenting empirical results below. The sign before each variable denotes the expected sign of the coefficient, if any.

The next section describes the procedures used to estimate the parameters of the above model. First, ordinary least squares (OLS) regressions are estimated for equations (7.1) and (7.2) separately for the same homeowner strata as defined in chapter 6. Any strata demonstrating different relationships between the neighborhood characteristic variables and the expectations variables will be noted. Such results will then form the basis for defining new, interactive variables to be added to the model, which allow the coefficient of the given neighborhood characteristic to vary across strata. These interactive variables are then added to the basic model ([Z] in (7.1) and (7.2)) and the models are reestimated using both OLS and PROBIT specifications in order to check for sensitivity of parameter estimates. The reader interested only in the final results emerging from the foregoing steps should turn directly to the chapter summary.

Empirical Results for Expectations Models

Tests for Aggregation and Specification Biases

To assess whether there were significant differences across homeowner types in the relationship between expectations and aspects of the neighborhood context, separate regressions corresponding to equations (7.1) and (7.2) were estimated for the same twelve strata as analyzed in chapter 6.[8] Suffice it to note here that these results show that relatively few neighborhood characteristics are related to expectations in similar ways (in terms of both direction and statistical significance) across homeowner types and across samples, and that distinct sets of neighborhood characteristics explain variations in NEIGHEXP and VALUEEXP. These results suggest that not only are expectations about neighborhood quality in general and property values in specific shaped by different aspects of the residential environment, but that the particular aspects that are deemed salient in forming expectations vary dramatically across household types and across samples. Of course, this places great demands on empirical research. Nevertheless, the synthesized model discussed in detail below attempts to capture the key elements of this complexity.

The stratified expectations models provide the basis for developing a "synthesized" expectations model that avoids aggregation bias. As before, the goal is to estimate a single, aggregate expectations model that can easily fit as a component within the larger context of homeowners' housing investment behavior. Yet the model must still be robust enough to allow for significant variations in relationships across various homeowner groups, as indicated by the disaggregated stratified estimates above.

The procedure for accomplishing such a synthesis is identical to that followed in chapter 6. Strata groupings are first designated on the basis of similar coefficient signs in the stratified estimates of the expectations models. Each such grouping is then defined as a dummy variable, multiplied by the given neighborhood variable, and entered as a separate interactive variable [Z] in the given expectations model. Next, preliminary OLS regressions are run to ascertain which of these new homeowner and neighborhood interaction variables are statistically significant. Finally, after insignificant interaction variables are dropped, the result is a new synthetic model. In these models the interactive terms indicate those homeowner strata for whom the relationship between a given neighborhood characteristic and a given expectation differs significantly from the general relationship as given by the coefficient of the noninteractive neighborhood characteristic variable.

As in the case of satisfaction indexes, the expectational ordinal scales employed here as dependent variables are in some respects not appropriately analyzed with OLS. (These arguments are discussed in chapter 6 and will not be repeated here.) In order to assess the sensitivity of parameters to functional form, the synthesized expectations model is also specified as a PROBIT model. That is, one can posit the existence of a normally distributed but unobserved index of expectations that is assumed to be a linear function of the independent variables listed above in (7.1) and (7.2). Overall, the PROBIT estimates strongly support the conclusions drawn from the linear model. Similar patterns of coefficient statistical significance emerge, and when the PROBIT results differ from the OLS results they tend to clarify and resolve the unpredicted findings of the latter.

In order to increase confidence about which characteristics of homeowners and neighborhoods are consistently correlated with expectations irrespective of functional specification, the same two criteria used in chapter 6 are also employed here: statistically significant coefficients in the linear model must be corroborated by such in PROBIT; and marginally significant coefficients in the linear model must be corroborated by highly significant ones in PROBIT. The application of these criteria leads to the final, corroborated expectations model, which is discussed in detail in the next section.[9]

Results for Corroborated Models

Neither model has a great deal of explanatory power. In both samples the R^2 for the NEIGHEXP regression (OLS) is less than 10 percent; for the VALUEEXP regression it is about 20 percent. This is due to several factors. First, as noted above, the stability of neighborhood expectations seem atypical in both samples. Second, the expectations measures are limited to ordinal measures on a narrow response scale, which further limits variation. Third, there are undoubtedly omitted independent variables (e.g., recent changes in the neighborhood), which *a priori* should be expected to affect expectations. Fourth, there is undoubtedly some aggregation bias remaining even in the synthetic model, given the large cross-strata coefficient variability. Nevertheless, the models represent a significant step forward in the complex task of unraveling expectation formation.

QUALITATIVE NEIGHBORHOOD EXPECTATIONS   The main results generated by the corroborated models of NEIGHEXP are presented in the middle columns of tables 7.1, 7.2, and 7.3. To facilitate cross-variable comparability of magnitude of relationships, the OLS regression coefficients (only if corroborated by PROBIT) are expressed as standardized beta coefficients.

First consider homeowner characteristics (table 7.1). Only a handful of homeowner characteristics prove to be statistically significant correlates of NEIGHEXP. In Minneapolis, stage 2, 3, and 4 homeowners tend to be 31 percent, 22 percent, and 8 percent less pessimistic than stage 1 homeowners, respectively, computed at the mean of NEIGHEXP. This could signify a stronger general sense of optimism associated with early child-rearing life-cycle stages, but this pattern was certainly not supported in the Wooster sample. In Wooster, married homeowners are 7 percent less pessimistic compared to single-male– or multiple-headed homeowners. Neither socioeconomic status, race, alienation, or individual social interaction or integration in the neighborhood prove to be predictors of qualitative neighborhood expectations, after controlling for current neighborhood and public policy characteristics.

In the final corroborated model several aspects of the neighborhood surprisingly prove not to be correlates of NEIGHEXP for the sample as a whole or for any strata grouping interactive variables (see table 7.2). The

Table 7.1   Beta Coefficients* of Homeowner Characteristics in Corroborated Expectations Models

	Dependent variable			
	NEIGHEXP		VALUEEXP	
Independent variables	Wooster	Minneapolis	Wooster	Minneapolis
ALIENATED	—	—	—	—
EDUCATION	—	—	—	−.18
INCOME	—	—	—	—
MARRIED	−.18	—	—	−.10
FEMALE	X	—	−.16	−.11
BLACK	—	—	.38	—
STAGE2	—	−.56	X	X
STAGE3	—	−.34	—	X
STAGE4	—	−.11	X	—
STAGE5	—	—	.24	.33
IDENTIFY	—	—	−.08	−.08
INTEGRATE	—	—	—	—

*using linear model's beta coefficients only when corroborated by PROBIT model
— = coefficient not statistically significant in linear model or PROBIT model
X = coefficient not corroborated by PROBIT model; significant in linear model

indexes of the physical and socioeconomic-status quality of the neighborhood are not strongly correlated with NEIGHEXP; if anything, their modest influence appears to abet more pessimistic general expectations. This finding probably is produced by the absence of variables measuring recent changes in such indexes. The neighborhood racial composition variables also have little explanatory power. In neither sample as a whole does RACECOMPW prove a significant correlate of NEIGHEXP (although for low-education Minneapolis homeowners they are modestly inversely correlated). RACECOMPB is insignificant in both samples in the final model. Undoubtedly, this finding cannot be generalized, given the atypical racial dimensions of both Wooster and Minneapolis markets.[10]

Other dimensions of the physical-demographic neighborhood prove more important, but sometimes in unexpected ways. The presence of nonresidential land uses on the block face, for example, is inversely related to NEIGHEXP in Minneapolis. The coefficient's magnitude is such that those having nonresidential uses nearby are 19 percent less pessimistic about future changes in the neighborhood, compared to those who do not,

Table 7.2   Beta Coefficients* of Neighborhood Characteristics in Corroborated Expectations Models

| | Dependent variable | | | |
| | NEIGHEXP | | VALUEEXP | |
Independent variable	Wooster	Minneapolis	Wooster	Minneapolis
AREAQUAL	—	NA	−.26	NA
BLOCKQUAL				
Total	NA	—	NA	—
Low income, low education	NA	NA	NA	−.21
TRACTQUAL	NA	—	NA	—
NONRESID	—	−.11	—	.11
TENURE	−.12	.10	—	—
RACECOMPW				
Total	—	—	—	—
FEMALE, STAGE4	NA	NA	.21	NA
EDUCATION (LOW), FEMALE	NA	NA	NA	.15
EDUCATION (LOW)	NA	−.05	NA	NA
RACECOMPB				
Total	—	—	X	—
STAGE1	NA	NA	NA	X
NIDENTIFY				
Total	—	—	−.12	−.12
STAGE2, 4	NA	NA	.61	NA
STAGE2, 3	−.75	NA	NA	NA
NINTEGRATE				
Total	—	—	−.10	−.06
STAGE2	−.36	NA	NA	NA
FEMALE	NA	.50	NA	NA

*using linear model's beta coefficients only when corroborated by PROBIT model
NA = not applicable; variable not used in given model
— = coefficient not statistically significant in linear model or PROBIT model
X = coefficient not corroborated by PROBIT model; significant in linear model

Table 7.3 Beta Coefficients* of Policy Characteristics in Corroborated
Expectations Models

Independent variables	Dependent variable (Minneapolis only)	
	NEIGHEXP	VALUEEXP
NOTQUALIFY	.15	.09
QUALIFY	—	—
LOAN?	—	—
GRANT?	—	—

*using linear model's beta coefficients only when corroborated by PROBIT model
— = coefficient not statistically significant in linear model or PROBIT model

measured at the mean NEIGHEXP. This is surprising since (as discussed in
chapter 6) only low-education and stage 1 homeowners see NONRESID as a
positive contributor to neighborhood satisfaction; other strata view it
negatively. Apparently those in areas with no current nonresidential uses
are more likely to fear the incipient entrance of such (and perhaps other
negative influences) than those who already live amid such land uses.

The TENURE variable proves to be a consistent correlate of NEIGHEXP
across strata, but with opposite coefficient signs in the two samples. In
Wooster the predicted negative coefficients are consistently observed, but
positive ones obtain in Minneapolis. This disparity is probably due to the
difference in the formulation of the TENURE index in each sample. In
Wooster the proportions of owner-occupants and of households living in
the current dwelling ten or more years are added; in Minneapolis only the
latter is counted in the index. Apparently, greater proportions of long-
term residents (mainly elderly) erode confidence, perhaps by generating
associated worries about what will happen to the neighborhood when
elderly homeowners move to different quarters or die? But the greater
stability implied by more owner-occupants (instead of absentee-owners)
offsets such worries and abets confidence, as suggested by the Wooster
results. The magnitude of the relationships is such that compared to
homeowners in areas having mean values of TENURE, those in areas with
the maximum values of TENURE are 6 percent less pessimistic in Wooster,
and 4 percent more pessimistic in Minneapolis.

Although not statistically significant for both samples as a whole, the
aggregate social-interaction variables are significant for particular strata
groupings. For Wooster stage 2 and stage 3 homeowners, those living in
areas with the maximum NIDENTIFY are 5 percent less pessimistic than
those living in areas with the mean value.[11] The consequences of greater
aggregate social integration appear to be different for different home-

owners. Wooster stage 2 homeowners in areas with maximum NINTEGRATE are 9 percent less pessimistic than their counterparts in areas with the mean value.[12] Conversely, Minneapolis female homeowners living in areas with maximum NINTEGRATE values are 8 percent more pessimistic than those in areas with the mean value.[13] Clearly, one needs to know much more about the exact nature of neighborhood information being conveyed between different types of residents before any explanatory hypothesis can be offered for these results.

Of most potential interest are the results regarding public policy variables (see table 7.3). Residence in a Minneapolis area that does not qualify for Urban Renewal or CDBG neighborhoodwide housing assistance proves to be associated with 9 percent higher pessimism for homeowners as a group, compared to residence in an area that has received such assistance.[14] There are no statistically significant differences in NEIGHEXP between areas that qualify but have not yet received CDBG aid and those that have. One possible interpretation of this finding is that the mere designation of an area as eligible for CDBG funds is as effective in creating optimism as the actual expenditure of such funds in the area. This may, indeed, be true over the short run, but a long-run stream of empty promises seems unlikely to maintain optimism. An alternative explanation is that the results are due to spurious correlation. In fact, NOTQUALIFY designates areas that not only did not receive Urban Renewal or CDBG neighborhoodwide funds, but were not likely to contain property owners who were eligible for any individual home rehabilitation programs. On the other hand, individual recipients of subsidized grants and loans for rehabilitation appeared about equally common in all areas qualifying for CDBG, whether they received such funds or not. The upshot: the visible housing improvements engendered by the aggregated actions of those rehabilitating with public encouragement may have produced more optimistic expectations by homeowners in the area, whether they personally were recipients or not. But ironically, neither the direct receipt of a subsidized housing improvement grant or a loan (GRANT?, LOAN?) appears to have any significant effect upon the qualitative neighborhood expectations of the individual recipient. Regardless of which interpretation is correct, it is clear that public-sponsored neighborhood reinvestment efforts can abet optimism about the qualitative future of the area, whether the mechanism of impact is symbolic or real.

PROPERTY-VALUE EXPECTATIONS   The results generated by corroborated models of VALUEEXP are presented in the right-hand columns of tables 7.1, 7.2, and 7.3. Again, beta coefficients are used as summary measures.

Several homeowner characteristics are related to property-value expectations in the manner predicted by theory. In both Wooster and Minneapolis samples those possessing the mean level of identification with neighbors (IDENTIFY) can be expected to be 9 percent less pessimistic compared to those possessing the minimum level. Thus, independent of neighborhood cohesion, the individual's solidarity sentiments prove somewhat important in building confidence about property value changes. In both samples, stage 5 homeowners are more pessimistic than their counterparts in stage 1, *ceteris paribus*; the respective differences are 20 percent and 22 percent in Wooster and Minneapolis, measured at the mean of VALUEEXP in both samples. Female heads of households are less pessimistic than single males or heads of multiple-headed households, by 14 percent in Wooster and 7 percent in Minneapolis, measured at the mean. Finally, as predicted, Wooster blacks are 122 percent more pessimistic than whites, Minneapolis homeowners with college degrees are 10 percent less pessimistic than those who dropped out of high school, and married Minneapolis homeowners are 6 percent less pessimistic than single-male or multiple heads.

Less clear results are forthcoming from the other life-cycle stage variables. Their signs follow no clear pattern either over the life cycle within a sample or between samples for the same stage. Also noteworthy is the lack of statistical significance for the alienation, income, and personal social-integration variables in explaining VALUEEXP. Nevertheless, the existence of several patterns of statistically significant coefficients having predicted signs suggests that there are variations in certain homeowner characteristics that do seem to produce differences in property-value expectations, independent of the residential context. It is beyond the scope of the present study to attempt to discern, however, whether such variations are indicative of systematic differences in the means and extent of information acquisition, tolerance for uncertainty, sense of personal efficacy, or general tendencies toward pessimism. Further research in this vein should provide fruitful results.

Although physical and demographic conditions at the census-tract level appear to be irrelevant in shaping Minneapolis homeowners' expectations about short-term changes in neighborhood property values, such conditions have strong effects in smaller-scale areas (see table 7.2). Minneapolis homeowners on block faces having the highest value of BLOCKQUAL are, however, 33 percent less pessimistic than those on average-quality blocks (again computed at mean VALUEEXP). Wooster homeowners living in planning areas with the maximum AREAQUAL are 22 percent less pessimistic than their counterparts in planning areas with mean values of quality. The presence of nonresidential land use on the block face is associated with 27 percent more pessimism in the Minneapolis sample. Higher proportions of black households are also associated with more pessimism about future property values on the part of selected white homeowners. Compared to whites having the mean values of RACECOMPW, Minneapolis female and low-education homeowners and Wooster female and stage 4 homeowners in areas having the maximum values of RACECOMPW are 41 percent and 32 percent more pessimistic, respectively.

Overall, the results for nonresidential land use and to a lesser degree the quality-index neighborhood variables are exactly opposite those obtained for NEIGHEXP. This indicates once again that not only are expectations concerning neighborhood quality and property-value changes distinct empirically, but that identical neighborhood conditions can foster contrary expectations on these measures. Though these results appear counterintuitive, deeper analysis suggests a rationale. Homeowners residing in neighborhoods that would be designated as "higher quality" by conventional standards (i.e., high socioeconomic status, no deterioration, no nonresidential land use) may believe that qualitatively their area is currently as good as is reasonable to expect. Although such homeowners may be confident that they will continue to accumulate capital gains on their property, they may nonetheless be pessimistic about particular future deleterious changes in the area.[15] At the other extreme, homeowners in conventionally designated "lower-quality, mixed-use" neighborhoods have less confidence that the local home market will inflate. Indeed, deterioration and even abandonment nearby might provide tangible support for such skepticism. On the other hand, they may perceive that in terms of neighborhood quality, there's no place to go but up, and thus manifest less pessimism on this score.

In both samples the aggregate degree of social identification proves inversely associated with VALUEEXP. Compared to homeowners from areas where in general residents have the mean NIDENTIFY, those in areas having the maximum value are 6 percent and 5 percent less pessimistic in Wooster and Minneapolis, respectively. For Wooster stage 2 and stage 4 homeowners, however, the net relationship is opposite, with the corresponding estimate to the above values being 4 percent more pessimistic for those strata. In both samples higher aggregate levels of social integration also are inversely associated with VALUEEXP. Wooster homeowners in planning areas with maximum NINTEGRATE values are 9 percent less pessimistic than counterparts in areas with the mean value; the corresponding figure for Minneapolis is 3 percent. These findings indicate that regardless of the individual's own degree of social integration and identification with neighbors, he or she will tend to be marginally less pessimistic about future property value changes when he or she perceives that the neighborhood as a whole possesses these attributes, i.e., is cohesive. That this relationship is stronger in Wooster may be because in Wooster NINTEGRATE measures interneighbor familiarity and interaction in a somewhat larger geographic area than in Minneapolis (i.e., planning area instead of block face), and the attributes of this broader area are important in belief formation. A more provocative explanation is that values of *gemeinschaft* are more pervasive in a small-town setting and thus the weight placed on interpersonal communication media and communal information assessment is greater. Such would support Goetze's (1979) claim that the media's role is more important than interpersonally mediated sources for shaping expectations in larger cities.

As in the case of qualitative neighborhood expectations, only the distinction between neighborhoods that do not qualify for Urban Renewal or CDBG assistance and those that do qualify appears to affect property value expectations (see table 7.3). Homeowners in the former type of Minneapolis areas are 8 percent more pessimistic compared to others. Personal receipt of either grants or loans for housing improvements are unrelated to VALUEEXP. It thus appears that explicit public efforts to abet reinvestment have some success in stimulating optimism both about future neighborhood quality and property values, although in both circumstances the impact is small.

Summary and Conclusions

This chapter establishes a conceptual framework for understanding homeowners' neighborhood expectations that draws upon social-psychological theories of belief formation and information acquisition. This framework suggests that there likely will be interhomeowner variations in the relationship between external, objective data indicating changes in the residential environment and their subsequent translation into expectations. Such can be due to differences in: (1) the amount and type of both active and passive modes of information acquisition that are employed, and (2) whether new information is assessed both as valid and as important enough to warrant alteration of prior beliefs. The framework also suggests analogous variations in the formulation of expectations based on the social-interactive neighborhood context in which homeowners find themselves. These types of variations provide the rationale for the stratified estimations conducted, and ultimately prove of empirical importance.

Two distinct types of expectations are modeled, due to strong *a priori* theoretical justification. This modeling is supported empirically, in that expectations about changes in neighborhood quality and in property values prove not to be highly correlated. The variations in both measures are probably atypically small compared to those held in other urban areas, however. Multivariate analyses designed to explain these expectations indicate the following:

– Only a few current neighborhood characteristics predict expectations in similar ways across homeowner types and across samples, and distinct sets of neighborhood characteristics explain variations in both expectational measures. The implication is that future empirical research on expectation formation must take an approach that disaggregates not only by household type but especially by expectation type. The potential benefit from including measures of recent changes in the neighborhood is also large.

– For the most part, indicators of the current physical-demographic character of a neighborhood are poor predictors of homeowners' expectations about qualitative neighborhood changes. When they do hold even modest explanatory power, they suggest that homeowners in higher-quality neighborhoods that have no nonresidential land use are slightly more likely to be pessimistic about future changes in neighborhood quality. These indicators provide consistently strong predictors of expectations concerning property value changes as well, but in precisely the opposite fashion. This potent result suggests that identical neighborhood conditions simultaneously can foster optimistic expectations on some bases, but pessimistic expectations on others.

– Only certain small subsets of white homeowners view a higher proportion of blacks in the neighborhood as a basis for a more pessimistic outlook on property-value appreciation. Racial composition does not, surprisingly, generally affect expectations regarding general neighborhood quality. Because both samples originated in cities containing atypically low black concentrations, however, these findings may not be generalizable.

– Both the individual and collective degree of neighborhood identification and, to a large extent, social integration are strong contributors to optimism about property-value changes. This perhaps indicates that homeowners identifying with a cohesive neighborhood believe that, collectively, the area will be successful in warding off elements that could erode values. The stronger relationships in the Wooster sample suggest that those in small-town housing markets may rely more heavily on interpersonal, communally mediated sources of information when forming beliefs.

– Married and female heads of households are less likely to evaluate a given neighborhood condition pessimistically than are male heads or heads of multiple-headed households. The same can be said for life-cycle stage 2 to 4 homeowners versus those in stage 1 (at least in Minneapolis). Elderly homeowners (stage 5) were much more pessimistic in their expectations about property-value appreciation than any other stage, *ceteris paribus*. This last result is consistent with the hypothesis that those least likely to obtain large amounts of reliable housing market information, who are hence less certain, evidence greater pessimism. Unfortunately, we know too little about how the other groups noted above gather and evaluate information and form beliefs to identify the precise origins of their different expectations.

– Residents of areas that had never qualified for public Urban Renewal and/or CDBG programs in Minneapolis are more inclined to be pessimistic about both future neighborhood quality and property-value changes, compared to homeowners in areas qualifying for or receiving such aid. But because there was no significant difference in expectations between areas receiving such aid and those qualifying for it (but receiving none), it is possible to conclude that Urban Renewal and CDBG programs affect expectations only symbolically. An alternative explanation is that areas with recipients of individual home rehabilitation grants and loans benefit from the visible, aggregate consequences of these renovations, and it is these that abet confidence. Although the magnitude of the above relationships is somewhat smaller than that evidenced by neighborhood variables, such considerations may be important for policymakers.

8 Homeowners' Mobility Plans

The previous two chapters theoretically specify and empirically estimate models of homeowners' residential satisfaction and their expectations about the future of their neighborhoods. This chapter proceeds in analogous fashion in developing a model of homeowners' plans for leaving or remaining in their current residential situations. Two important determinants of these mobility plans will be the same residential satisfactions and expectations investigated previously. These mobility plans will, in turn, be modeled as explanatory variables in the ultimate housing reinvestment model to be specified in chapter 9. Because current housing-upkeep behavior is affected by homeowners' mobility plans, rather than by their actual mobility, this chapter will focus on their plans.

This chapter first presents a conceptual framework for comprehending the formation of mobility plans. This conceptual framework synthesizes and extends received theory in such a manner that shortcomings of past approaches are avoided. The central feature of this framework is the notion of the "comparative net advantages" of alternative feasible residential options as perceived by the homeowner. It is shown how these perceptions likely are influenced by characteristics of the household as well as the residential environment. Next, previous empirical studies of mobility intentions and actual moving behavior are reviewed and critiqued. Based on these theoretical and empirical discussions, a model of homeowner mobility plans is specified and empirically estimated. Both linear probability and PROBIT specifications are tested in order to produce a final, corroborated set of parameter estimates. The key findings are summarized in the chapter summary.

Conceptual Framework

Chapter 7 analyzes how people acquire information and form beliefs about themselves and their current residential environment, and how they form expectations about the future of that environment. Here we push farther

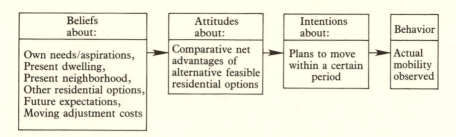

Figure 8.1 The Relationship between Mobility Beliefs, Attitudes, Intentions, and Behavior

along these cognitive pathways and connect these beliefs to ultimate behaviors. A simple schematic for comprehending this connection has been developed by Fishbein and Azjen (1975). The basic logic is this. Voluntary behavior presumes a prior intention to undertake such behavior. Intentions, in turn, are developed on the basis of attitudes—predispositions to respond favorably or unfavorably to certain hypothetical or real objects (events, persons, propositions, etc.). Finally, these attitudes are shaped by beliefs about the attributes that these objects possess. This schematic can be readily adapted for specific application to homeowner mobility. A visual summary of this adaptation is shown in figure 8.1.

At any given moment a homeowner will hold a multifaceted set of beliefs that help inform a potential option of moving from the current residence. For our purpose these beliefs may be categorized into six distinct subsets: (1) needs and aspirations, (2) characteristics of the present dwelling, (3) characteristics of the present neighborhood, (4) characteristics of alternative feasible residential options, (5) expectations of future aspects of items 1–4, and (6) adjustment costs associated with mobility.

The first three sets of beliefs have already been discussed extensively in the prior two chapters. But to these three sets is added here a fourth set of beliefs concerning other residential locations, about which the homeowner has varying degrees of information but nevertheless judges to be "feasible" in terms of affordability.[1] For present purposes it is not important whether these beliefs about other dwellings and neighborhoods are certain or correct in any objective sense; the "reality" is that as perceived by fallible people with imperfect information.[2] Another, fifth set of beliefs are expectational. These relate to future needs/aspirations and anticipated changes in present and alternative residential contexts. A sixth belief set concerns the costs that the homeowner's household could be expected to bear if an actual move were undertaken to one of the aforementioned feasible options. These costs come in many forms. Perhaps most obvious are the out-of-pocket expenses associated with home-selling (and often subsequent buying) transactions, the search for a different home, and physically moving people and belongings to the new location. There are also time expenditures associated with all the above activities. Finally, there may be substantial social and psychological costs of adjustment: valued proximate kin or friends may be left behind, new social networks must be established in unfamiliar surroundings, minorities may face harassment or ostracism in a different neighborhood, etc.

In conjunction, these six belief sets inform attitudes about the expected alterations in well-being that would be forthcoming from a move to a given residential location. The evaluative calculus can be thought of as proceeding in the following manner: Taking into account beliefs about the household's current and anticipated needs/aspirations, the homeowner comparatively evaluates the degree to which present and feasible alternative residential environments (both their current and future characteristics) may be expected to fulfill them over some extended time horizon.[3] If the perceived ability of a feasible alternative location to meet needs/aspirations exceeds that of the current location by more than the lost well-being associated with adjustment costs (all being appropriately time discounted), a favorable attitude toward mobility will be forthcoming.[4] The key element of this comparison can be summarized as "comparative net advantage," i.e., the relative well-being of alternative locations net of adjustment costs, as perceived by the given homeowner and as appropriately adjusted for the time horizons.

Now at any given moment some homeowners see the comparative net advantage as currently favoring a different residential location, and thereby develop the intention to move. This intention can be thought of as a desire and plan to move to the location with the highest comparative net advantage during a period in the near future. Others perceive that the comparative net advantage currently rests with their present home, but also foresee a period during which expected alterations in needs, aspirations, resources, or adjustment costs will likely upset this weighting. These homeowners will develop a longer-term mobility plan that is consonant with the time horizon at which they expect comparative net advantage to rest with another location. Finally, at the other extreme, some homeowners may perceive the comparative net advantage as overwhelmingly and permanently in favor of the current dwelling. Such people may be especially pleased with how the present residence fulfills their needs, or may face extremely burdensome adjustment costs that render moves to alternative residences, however attractive, inconceivable.

For the present study it is only these various mobility intentions or plans that are of interest, but for completeness the last element in the schematic should be mentioned. Intentions to undertake a certain behavior frequently, but not necessarily, lead to the actual behavior. Slippage can be caused by emerging constraints that render a prior intention infeasible (e.g., a homeowner is laid off, mortgage interest rates skyrocket) or by altered circumstances that swing the comparative net advantage in favor of the present site (e.g., a massive rehabilitation program in the current neighborhood). Studies have found high correlations between peoples' moving plans and their subsequent moving behavior, but these correlations are substantially less than absolute.[5]

The above conceptual framework may be compared with two theoretical perspectives that have dominated the scholarly literature on mobility for the last decade.[6] The first has arisen primarily from the disciplines of sociology and geography, and is represented in the works of Speare, Goldstein, and Frey (1974); Speare (1974); Duncan and Newman (1975); Morris, Crull, and Winter (1976); Newman and Duncan (1979); Seek (1983); and Varady (1975, 1982a, 1983, 1986, ch.6). It posits that mobility is a two-step process. In the initial stage, elements of the current residential environment interrelate with household characteristics to produce stress or dissatisfaction. If this dissatisfaction exceeds some (unspecified) threshold, then the household will develop a desire to move. In the second step, only those who have developed this desire will gather information so as to assess the relative benefits and costs of alternative residential locations, and they will make a subsequent decision to move or not, based on such information. In this view, then, background characteristics at both the individual and the residential context influence mobility desires and actions only through the intervening variable of current residential dissatisfaction.[7]

A contrasting view stems from the work of economists such as Goodman (1976); Quigley and Weinberg (1977); Cronin (1978); Hanushek and Quigley (1978); Mark, Boehm, and Leven (1979); and Weinberg, Friedman, and Mayo (1981). This perspective begins by positing that households attempt to maximize their well-being ("utility") by consuming an "equilibrium" level of housing, but because of varying degrees of market frictions (information and moving costs) households may be more or less in disequilibrium. Mobility[8] is seen as being directly related to the degree of such relative disequilibrium, and inversely related to search and moving costs. The decision to acquire more information about housing market alternatives is undertaken whenever the marginal expected benefits of such outweigh the marginal expected costs (see Cronin 1978; Weinberg and Atkinson 1979; Porell 1982a; and Weisbrod and Vidal 1981). And although the marginal expected benefits are seen as directly related to current degree of disequilibrium housing consumption, there is no implicit threshold of disequilibrium involved.

The theory employed here represents both a synthesis and extension of these two conventional views (cf. Brummel 1979). From the economics view, it adopts the contentions that: (1) the dominant force motivating mobility is not current stress in an absolute sense but a comparative assessment of current and feasible alternative residential sites, and (2) search may be forthcoming even before a threshold level of residential stress is exceeded. From the sociology-geography view, it adopts the contentions that: (3) mobility plans/intentions are usefully distinguished from actual mobility, and (4) expressed dissatisfaction with the current residential context is the appropriate concept for empirically proxying for mobility plans. (This is explained more fully below.) The theory here extends these views by explicitly modeling adjustment costs as a component of comparative net advantage and, hence, of the determination of a plan to move, and by positing that not only present conditions but also anticipated future conditions affect mobility plans. Keeping these theoretical contrasts in mind, we turn now to a critical review of past empirical research in the area.

Review of Previous Research

Most scholarly research has not focused on mobility plans as a topic in its own right, but rather as a predictor of actual mobility behavior.[9] Nevertheless, multivariate statistical studies provide a useful empirical background with which the current investigation may be contrasted.

First consider studies stemming from the sociology-geography approach noted earlier (see table 8.1 for a summary). Empirical research in this area can be categorized into three groups. The first attempts to explain variations in household mobility plans[10] solely in terms of household demographic and economic characteristics (see Roistacher 1975; Duncan and Newman 1975). These studies generally conclude that plans to move in the near future are more likely to be associated with younger, black, lower-income, lower-education, welfare-recipient, small-family households. The second group adds to these household characteristics objective features of the dwelling (and, less often, neighborhood) and the respondents' subjective evaluations of their residential environment (see Speare 1974; Speare, Goldstein, and Frey 1974; Varady 1975; Morris 1976; Morris, Crull, and Winter 1976; Ahlbrandt and Cunningham 1979; Boehm 1981; and Taub, Taylor, and Dunham 1984, ch.8). Although these studies usually confirm the inverse relationship between moving plans and age of and size of household, results for other household characteristics are decidedly mixed—variables proving statistically significant in one study prove not to be so in others. The objective measures of neigh-

Table 8.1 Summary of Research Findings on Predictors of Mobility Plans

Objective household characteristics	Objective contextual characteristics	Intervening subjective evaluations
−Age of oldest child: 6	+Slight (not great) excesses or surpluses of interior space: 6	−Yard satisfaction: 1
−Length of job tenure: 6,7		−# room satisfaction: 1
−Black head: 5,7*	+Dwelling needs repairs: 7	−House age satisfaction: 1
−Age of head: 3,5,7,8,9,10	−Neighborhood average home prices: 7	−Neighborhood satisfaction: 1*
+Small family: 5	−Interior space in house: 3*	−Community satisfaction: 1
+Very big family: 5*	+Abandoned bldgs on block: 9	−Residential satisfaction: 2
−Family size: 7,8	+Block deterioration: 9	−Dwelling satisfaction: 3,4,8
+Income: 5,8*	+Census-tract crime rate: 9	−Sense of community: 8
+Education: 5*	+Neighborhood 50%+ black (whites only): 10	+Perceived housing problems: 3
+Welfare: 5	Expected Contextual Characteristics	+Perceived neighborhood problems: 8
−Female Head: 4*	+Neighborhood 50%+ black in 5 years (whites only): 10	−Satisfaction with crime: 9
+Occupational status: 4		−Favor investment in neighborhood: 9
−Socializing in Neighborhood: 7,8*		
−Length of tenure in home: 3,7*		

1. Speare (1974); Speare, et al. (1974)
2. Butler, et al. (1969)
3. Varady (1975)
4. Morris, Crull, and Winter (1976); Morris (1976)
5. Roistacher (1975)
6. Duncan and Newman (1975)
7. Boehm (1981)
8. Ahlbrandt and Cunningham (1979)
9. Taub, Taylor, and Dunham (1984, ch. 8)
10. Wurdock (1981)
*contrary result (i.e., variable insignificant) found in another study cited.
Note: all results for combined owners and renters, except 8, 9 (owners only).

borhood quality and interior dwelling space are inversely related to short-term mobility plans,[11] but they lose independent explanatory power if subjective evaluations of these characteristics are also included in the regression. The most consistent finding is that respondents' expressed current satisfaction with their dwellings and/or neighborhoods is inversely related to their plans to move in the near future. The third category in the literature is uniquely represented by Wurdock (1981), the only researcher to investigate the role of expectations. He finds that whites are more likely to plan on moving if they expect their neighborhood to become 50 percent or more black within five years.

The two significant shortcomings of this empirical research are lack of solid theoretical foundation and failure to consider expectations. The lack of theoretical underpinning is most acute in the first strand of research above, for there is no reason to expect consistent interhousehold differences in mobility plans independent of the residential context in which households find themselves. The second strand avoids this pitfall with its inclusion of residential satisfaction measures, but errs in the specification of the model by including objective measures of the residential context and of the household. Yet the theory upon which these specifications are based explicitly posits that such objective contextual and household features affect mobility plans only via the intervening variable of residential satisfaction.[12] The fact that such objective household variables do, in fact, add explanatory power over and above residential satisfaction is inexplicable through their theory. This finding can be interpreted in the context of the theory presented here, however. The significance of household characteristics independent of satisfaction might well indicate that these serve as proxies for adjustment-cost differentials.

The second shortcoming is that neither theoretically nor empirically, with the exception of Wurdock (1981), has attention been paid to households' expectations. Mobility plans have been viewed only as responses to current situations, but there seems ample *a priori* justification for positing that households' expectations about the future of their neighborhoods should be influential factors as well.

The economics approach to mobility cited earlier has also produced several empirical works, although all have focused on explaining actual mobility instead of mobility plans (see Goodman 1976; Quigley and Weinberg 1977; Cronin 1978; Hanushek and Quigley 1978; Mark, Boehm, and Leven 1979; Weinberg, Friedman, and Mayo 1981). Nevertheless, they are relevant here because they explicitly attempt to construct a variable for measuring "household disequilibrium," or the degree to which the present residential environment diverges from the optimal one (see Golledge 1981; and Porell 1982b, ch.2). The common technique for constructing this measure is as follows. "Housing consumption" is treated as a flow of homogeneous, single-price units of "housing services," which emanate from the residential context in a perfectly competitive housing market. All individual attributes of the residential package are collapsed into this metric and, thus, housing consumption can be measured by expenditures on housing. "Equilibrium" housing consumption is operationally defined by regressing annual housing expenditures of recent-movers (who presumably have chosen an optimal amount of housing) on their background characteristics. These regression coefficients are, in turn, used to estimate equilibrium consumption expenditures for all households (based on their particular characteristics), which then can be compared to their current consumption expenditures to measure disequilibrium.[13] This variable is included in a multivariate probability model,[14] which explains mobility behavior along with household characteristics proxying for search and moving costs.

Although this economic approach to mobility behavior is theoretically superior to the sociology-geography approach insofar as it explicitly focuses on comparative well-being of alternative residential contexts, it still suffers empirical shortcomings. First, its assumption of homogeneous housing services renders the particular attribute mix of a dwelling package irrelevant to households. Yet, there is substantial evidence that preferences for particular residential attributes do vary across households (see Wheaton 1977; Galster 1979). And the evidence from chapter 6 clearly indicates that there are substantial differences between homeowners in how they translate various residential features into dwelling and neighborhood satisfaction. Second, it implicitly assumes that its objective measure of disequilibrium accurately proxies for this measure as subjectively perceived by the household. This assumption is unwarranted in light of the theory's own stress on imperfect information and evidence from the same studies on interhousehold variations on the likelihood of gathering housing market information (see, e.g., Cronin 1978; Hanushek and Quigley 1978). Third, their formulation allows no place for expectations about future degrees of disequilibrium to influence mobility.

The empirical specification employed here attempts to avoid the shortcomings of previous research in the following three ways. First, instead of the aforementioned technique for estimating disequilibrium, the residential satisfaction indexes analyzed in chapter 6 (NEIGHSAT, HOUSESAT) are employed as direct proxies for comparative net advantage. Recall from the theory of satisfaction in chapter 6 that a key determinant of one's need/aspiration level (against which the current residential context is evaluated) is the perceived available options in the local housing market. Thus, satisfaction-dissatisfaction should provide a superior measure of the gap between current and feasible alternative residential options as perceived by the individual homeowner than the conventional estimate of disequilibrium.[15]

Second, unlike the sociology-geography approach, only those household characteristics that serve as reasonable proxies for adjustment costs or anticipated future changes in needs/aspirations are included in the specification. Because objective characteristics of the residential context only theoretically influence mobility plans via their impact on satisfactions and expectations, including these latter subjective elements obviates the rationale for including the former. Third, the two measures of expectations about neighborhood qualitative and property-value changes analyzed in chapter 7 (NEIGHEXP and VALUEEXP) are included in the specification so as to overcome the omission of expectational controls in previous models. We now turn to a more detailed presentation of this specification.

Specification of an Empirical Model of Mobility Plans

Pursuant to making operational the theory above, this section explains the dependent and independent variables employed. The model consists of three equations, each of which explains the probability that a given homeowner will fall into a given category of mobility plans, ranging from short term to very long term. The independent variables fall into three categories: residential satisfaction measures, neighborhood expectation measures, and household characteristics proxying for adjustment costs.

Dependent Variables

The projected mobility of the sampled homeowners in Wooster and Minneapolis is assessed from responses to the question: "How long do you expect to live in this neighborhood?" Responses were coded in years, with the exception of some who could answer only in terms of categories: "No particular plans, I could move with opportunity," or "Never, I'll stay until I die." Approximately half the respondents in each sample responded in one of these two general categories (mainly the latter), which rendered problematic the construction of a single, ratio-level variable measuring years of expected tenure.

But besides this empirical problem, there is an even more powerful conceptual reason for not attempting to specify mobility plans in terms of a single, continuous variable. Recall from the theoretical discussion in chapter 3 that the likely relationship between expected length of tenure and intensity of upkeep activity is bell shaped. Because of this, and because mobility plans are being explored here only as a means to explain and predict upkeep behavior, this study specifies a series of dummy variables. The cost of such a specification is, of course, increased complexity and decreased ease of exposition of findings.

Having settled upon a specification involving categorical (dummy) variables, the next question involves how to collapse appropriately the responses to the above-expected mobility question. Several experiments with various formulations of the mobility-plan dummy variables were conducted to determine their role in predicting housing-investment behavior (see chapter 9). These experiments led to the collapsing of responses into four conceptually attractive categories.[16]

These categories denote respondent plans to remain: (a) two years or less; (b) three to ten years / has no particular plans to move; (c) eleven or more years (but a definite number); and (d) always or until death. Specified as dummy variables, these categories are defined as STAY0–2, STAY3–10, STAY10+, and STAYPERM. These categories can be interpreted as a progression from short term, medium term, long term, to permanent. Frequency distributions of these categories for both samples show them to be very similar, with large pluralities (in the fortieth percentile) in both the medium-term and permanent categories of expected tenure. As predicted based on other, national surveys of moving plans comparing large to small towns, somewhat more Minneapolis than Wooster homeowners plan to move within two years (7.9 percent and 6.6 percent, respectively). But in either case this incidence of short-term mobility plans is dramatically lower than the national average for homeowners, which is 21 percent.[17]

Independent Variables

Consider initially various measures of present and projected future proxies for comparative gross advantages. As argued above, homeowners' expressed satisfaction with both their dwelling and their neighborhood should embody implicitly a prior current comparison between the present and perceived feasible alternative residential environments. As such, the variables HOUSESAT and NEIGHSAT should provide a proxy for the present comparative gross advantage of the status quo. (Note that net advantage involves factoring in adjustment costs, which are discussed below.) It follows that homeowners with greater HOUSESAT or NEIGHSAT would be less likely to form short-term mobility plans versus all longer ones, *ceteris paribus*.

Distinctions between degrees of longer-term plans are more complicated to model, because they revolve around comparative advantages in the future. Those who do not plan to move in the near future have sizable variations in their estimates of when they will move, based on their differing estimations of when the comparative net advantage will likely tip in favor of an alternative location. Holding needs, aspirations, adjustment costs, and other homeowner characteristics constant over time, the balance could tip if the present residential environment were to deteriorate absolutely. Whether such an eventuality is perceived by the homeowner should be measured by the indexes of pessimistic expectations for neighborhood quality (NEIGHEXP) and property values (VALUEEXP). Based on this discussion, it could be predicted that NEIGHEXP and VALUEEXP should be inversely associated with the expected length of tenure, as they represent one proxy for future comparative gross advantage.

Of course, comparative advantage can switch even if residential environments remain constant, due to internal changes in occupying homeowners. If, e.g., one projects that in five years the household's needs or resources will dramatically alter in such a way as to render the current location suboptimal, a mobility plan of medium term will be formed. How to measure directly such anticipated personal changes is problematic, but some reasonable proxies may be suggested. Life-cycle stage is one. (see Clark and Onaka 1983). Those in pre– or early–child-rearing stages can likely project that their current dwelling or neighborhood, though now entirely satisfactory, will not continue to be so five to ten years hence. They are thus less likely to form long-term plans. Conversely, homeowners in the last life-cycle stage should not anticipate future changes in their family needs, and therefore form permanent plans. Married homeowners may predict that someday they will reside without their spouses (due to separation, death, etc.) and thus will have altered housing needs. Although the exact timing of this event is unknown, it is safe to predict that permanent mobility plans are less likely for MARRIED. A similar argument can be made for large households (OCCUPANTS).

Having considered measures of both current and future comparative gross advantage of the present residential context, the remaining conceptual element to be controlled for is adjustment costs. Unfortunately, accurate prospective adjustment costs are difficult to obtain in surveys, and no direct measures are utilized here. But a variety of household characteristics hopefully can provide reasonable indirect measures of such costs, at least costs of near-term adjustments.

Several homeowner classifications can be predicted to have higher adjustment costs, *a priori*. Because of the implicit larger quantity of household items involved, homeowners who are married (MARRIED), who have larger households (OCCUPANTS), and who are in child-rearing life-cycle stages (STAGE2 through 4) should have to bear higher near-term out-of-pocket moving expenses (see Weisbrod and Vidal 1981). STAGE2 through 4 households may also perceive an added psychologcial cost associated with the disruption of friendship ties and schools for their children. Homeowners who are FEMALE or BLACK may project comparatively higher costs of acquiring information and higher psychological adjustment costs for all future periods. Both groups may face discrimination in the housing market, which may hinder their ease of searching the housing market and their adaptation to new circumstances (see Courant 1978; Zonn 1979, 1980; Weisbrod and Vidal 1981; Porell 1982a; Newburger 1984). Homeowners who have stronger social ties with their neighbors (measured by IDENTIFY, INTEGRATE) should perceive greater psychological adjustment costs as well. Finally, the elderly (STAGE5) may perceive greater physical and psychological trauma associated with moving than those in STAGE1.

Note that MARRIED, OCCUPANTS, and STAGE2 through 4 serve two functions in the specification. As adjustment-cost proxies they should show a direct relationship to expected length of tenure. As future comparative gross advantage proxies, they should show an inverse relationship to extremely long-term plans. Their net impact on the probability of a homeowner manifesting one of the four mobility plan categories is likely curvilinear across the categories; i.e., an inverted U-shape pattern of the characteristic versus expected length of tenure.

Other types of households may perceive less onerous adjustment costs. Those with more education probably are more efficient searchers and thus have lower costs of acquiring market information, both now and in the future. Therefore, EDUCATION should be inversely related to expected length of tenure (see Weisbrod and Vidal 1981). Homeowners with higher effective income (INCOME) may be less deterred by out-of-pocket expenses for moving or data acquisition.[18]

Two other homeowner characteristics are included that might reasonably proxy for a wide range of unspecified adjustment costs. Those who have remained in their present dwellings for a long period (LONGEVITY) may have higher current and future adjustment costs. For one thing, they are likely to be less market oriented, and thus have a lower reservoir of current market information. For another, they may have developed strong psychological bonds to neighbors or to the neighborhood that would impose severe costs if ruptured. On the contrary, homeowners who have made a large number of moves in the last five years (NUMMOVES) should perceive lower adjustment costs for any potential subsequent move for all the opposite reasons.

Finally, public policies designed to encourage home improvements in Minneapolis may affect mobility plans, but possibly in two contrary ways. If the homeowner has received a loan (LOAN?) or grant (GRANT?) for such improvements recently, he or she may feel some increased desire to stay in the home for a longer period in order to personally recoup the consumption value of the investments, or perhaps out of a sense of commitment or gratitude to the public aid-granting authority. In addition, certain grant and loan programs included financial incentives to remain in the home.[19]

On the other hand, investment-oriented homeowners may have perceived such assistance as a means (perhaps as the only means, if bank financing was unavailable) for inexpensively engaging in an activity that could markedly increase home value. If short-run investment motives dominate, one would expect the receipt of assistance to be positively correlated with short-term mobility plans so that the capital gains can be quickly recouped. Even though the signs of LOAN? and GRANT? in the mobility plan models are ambiguous, therefore, they have enough intrinsic interest to be included.

Summary of Mobility-Plan Model Specification

As formulated in terms of a probability model where $P(\ )$ signifies the probability that a particular mobility plan will be held, the model to be estimated can be expressed symbolically as:

$$
\left. \begin{array}{l} P(\text{STAY0--2}) \\ P(\text{STAY3--10}) \end{array} \right\} = \begin{array}{l} C_j - \text{NEIGHSAT} - \text{HOUSESAT} + \text{NEIGHEXP} \\ + \text{VALUEEXP} - \text{MARRIED} - \text{FEMALE} - \text{BLACK} \\ - \text{OCCUPANTS} - \text{STAGE}(2,3,4,5) + \text{INCOME} \\ + \text{EDUCATION} + \text{NUMMOVES} - \text{LONGEVITY} \\ - \text{IDENTIFY} - \text{INTEGRATE} \pm ?\text{LOAN}? \pm ?\text{GRANT}? + e \end{array}
\qquad \begin{array}{l} (8.1) \\ (8.2) \end{array}
$$

$$
\left. \begin{array}{l} P(\text{STAY10+}) \\ P(\text{STAYPERM}) \end{array} \right\} = \begin{array}{l} C_j + \text{NEIGHSAT} + \text{HOUSESAT} - \text{NEIGHEXP} \\ - \text{VALUEEXP} \pm ? \text{MARRIED} + \text{FEMALE} + \text{BLACK} \\ + \text{OCCUPANTS} \pm ? \text{STAGE}(2,3,4) + \text{STAGE5} \\ - \text{INCOME} - \text{EDUCATION} - \text{NUMMOVES} \\ + \text{LONGEVITY} + \text{IDENTIFY} + \text{INTEGRATE} \pm ?\text{LOAN}? \\ \pm ?\text{GRANT}? + e \end{array}
\qquad \begin{array}{l} (8.3) \\ (8.4) \end{array}
$$

where C is a constant, e is the error term, and signs are those predicted for a given variable's coefficient based on the discussion above. The precise functional form of (8.1)–(8.4) will be discussed below. Note that unambiguous sign predictions can be made only in the two extreme longevity categories STAY0–2 and STAYPERM; the precise intermediate category in which the sign reversal occurs cannot be predicted. As a result, two-tailed tests of statistical significance will be employed for all coefficients in the STAY3–10, STAY10+ equations.

Empirical Results for the Mobility-Plan Model

The parameters of equations (8.1)–(8.4) as estimated by two alternative techniques are discussed in the following section. Initially, the equations are specified as linear probability models and the parameters are estimated via ordinary least square (OLS). (Note that unlike in the previous two chapters, the theory presented here does not suggest that various strata of homeowners should respond differently to the same residential contexts when formulating mobility plans. Thus there is no need for stratified regressions.) Next, the four equations are specified as a PROBIT model and the parameters estimated via nonlinear, maximum-likelihood techniques, so as to test the sensitivity of results to alternative specifications. Only those results that are corroborated by both techniques form the basis of the discussion of quantitative impacts that variables have upon mobility plans, both directly and indirectly by means of their effect on satisfactions and expectations. Readers less interested in the specification bias tests and detailed model results may turn directly to the chapter summary.

Tests for Specification Bias

The appropriate statistical technique for estimating the relationships between the independent and dependent variables in (8.1)–(8.4) depends on the assumptions one makes about the probability of a homeowner choosing one of the four mutually exclusive mobility plan categories discussed above (see Pindyck and Rubinfeld 1981, ch.10). One simple and conventional assumption is to assume that the probability of an individual holding a given plan is a linear function of the aforementioned independent variables. With this assumption the specification becomes one regressing a dummy variable denoting a particular plan category (STAY0–2, STAY3–10, STAY10+, or STAYPERM) on the set of independent variables and estimating parameters using OLS. In such a model the resulting coefficients may be easily interpreted as the change in the conditional probability of the homeowner holding the given mobility plan associated with a unit change in the given independent variable. Unfortunately, in such a specification the variance of the error term e is not constant for all observations, which violates the assumptions required to render OLS the best linear unbiased estimator. The resulting heteroscedasticity results in a loss of efficiency but does not result in biased or inconsistent parameter estimates. Although heteroscedasticity can be corrected for by using other statistical adjustments, these adjustments introduce their own difficulties. Thus it is now conventionally believed most appropriate to use OLS in estimating linear probability models, especially with large sample sizes.[20]

Unfortunately, the linear probability model has an added difficulty: it is possible that estimated parameters can lead one to make numerical predictions outside the 0–1 interval.[21] To avoid this conceptual difficulty one can transform the original model in such a way that predictions must fall in the 0–1 interval for all values of independent variables. As in previous chapters, a cumulative normal probability function is employed for such a transformation. More specifically, the assumption is made that there exists some unobserved, normally distributed index of homeowners' mobility plans M. Based on the implicit value of this index, a homeowner responds in one of the corresponding ordinal categories: 1 if STAYO–2; 2 if STAY3– 10, 3 if STAYIO+, 4 if STAYPERM. The probability that M falls into a particular category can be computed from the cumulative normal probability function evaluated at the appropriate integral limits. This probability is, in turn, assumed to be a linear function of the independent variables predicting mobility plans discussed in the previous section.

The disadvantage of the second, PROBIT, specification is that coefficients are not directly interpretable in an intuitively pleasing fashion and the calculation of indirect effects (i.e., combined-path coefficients) is difficult. Because the model is already complex, the strategy chosen is to focus attention on the linear probability model, and to use the cumulative normal probability model as a check on the sensitivity of results to statistical estimating technique.

Parameter estimates for both the linear probability model and the PROBIT model yield, with only a few exceptions, the same conclusions about those variables that are statistically significant predictors of mobility plans.[22] In addition, the relative magnitudes of coefficients for these variables were highly consistent between the two specifications. These results allow one to have more confidence about which variables have consistent relationships with mobility plans, regardless of functional specification. The same criteria used in the previous two chapters are employed here to identify these variables. In all cases, coefficients that did not prove statistically significant in PROBIT also were not significant at the 5 percent level or better in the linear probability model. These corroborated results are the basis of the remarks and analyses that follow.

Results for Corroborated Model

OLS estimates of the parameters of the linear probability model of mobility plans as specified in equations (8.1)–(8.4), and corroborated by PROBIT, are presented in table 8.2 in the form of beta coefficients.[23] Most statistically significant coefficients shown correspond to *a priori* expectations. Given this, the expositional strategy employed here will be to highlight the major findings.

First, consider homeowner demographic characteristics. Compared to households headed by single males or multiple heads, MARRIED homeowners are .08–.10 less likely to have short-term mobility plans, .11–.12 more likely to hold medium-term ones, and marginally less likely to hold any longer ones. This inverted U-shaped pattern is exactly what would be expected if MARRIED were proxying for both adjustment costs and the

Table 8.2 Beta Coefficients* of Homeowner Characteristics, Satisfaction, and Expectations in Corroborated Mobility-Plan Model

Homeowner characteristics	Dependent variable							
	STAY0–2 Wooster	Minn	STAY3–10 Wooster	Minn	STAY10+ Wooster	Minn	STAYPERM Wooster	Minn
EDUCATION	.09	—	—	.16	—	—	−.08	−.17
INCOME	—	—	—	—	—	—	—	—
MARRIED	—	−.14	.10	.11	—	—	−.14	—
FEMALE	—	−.13	.15	—	—	—	−.14	—
OCCUPANTS	—	—	—	—	—	—	−.13	—
BLACK	—	—	—	—	—	—	—	—
STAGE2	−.24	X	—	—	—	—	.13	—
STAGE3	−.21	—	−.18	—	—	—	.26	—
STAGE4	−.25	—	−.17	—	—	—	.25	—
STAGE5	−.28	—	−.30	—	—	—	.43	.14
NUMMOVES	.13	—	—	.11	—	—	—	−.08
LONGEVITY	−.06	—	−.13	—	—	—	.19	.12
IDENTIFY	—	—	—	—	X	—	—	—
INTEGRATE	—	—	−.13	—	.10	—	.08	—
Subjective Intervening Variables								
HOUSESAT	−.18	−.11	—	—	—	.13	—	.08
NEIGHSAT	−.11	—	−.08	−.13	—	—	.11	.19
NEIGHEXP	X	—	−.15	—	—	.16	.13	—
VALUEEXP	—	—	—	—	—	−.10	—	—

*using linear model's beta coefficients only when corroborated by PROBIT model
— = coefficient not statistically significant in linear model or PROBIT model
X = coefficient not corroborated by PROBIT model; significant in linear model

likelihood that housing needs/aspirations would change within a ten-year planning horizon. Surprisingly, the same curvilinear pattern is manifested by the FEMALE coefficients as those for MARRIED, suggesting that it also proxies for more than adjustment costs.

The results for the life-cycle–stage variables indicate strong monotonic direct relationships between stage and expected length of tenure, although almost exclusively in Wooster. As expected, compared to STAGE1 home-owners, STAGE5 homeowners demonstrate the strongest relationship: they are .14–.22 less likely to hold short- or medium-term plans (in Wooster), and they are .43 and .14 more likely to hold permanent mobility plans in Wooster and in Minneapolis, respectively. Compared to STAGE1, the child-rearing groups (STAGE2 through 4) in Wooster are .12–.18 less likely to have short-term plans, .09–.30 less likely to have medium-term plans, and .19–.32 less likely to have permanent plans. These life-cycle–stage findings are consistent with those of Clark and Onaka (1983), and are easily applicable in the context of the foregoing theory if they indeed are serving as proxies for projected changes in comparative net advantage. The fact that there are fewer statistically significant differences in mobility plans across life-cycle stages in Minneapolis indicates the presence of a substantially lower rate of shorter-term mobility plans for the reference (STAGE1) group—a difference not being adequately captured by other control variables in the model. One reason may be that this group in Minneapolis is dominated by young urban professionals who view their current residence not as a temporary stopping-off place but as a more per-manent residence.[24] Another is that younger homeowners may have felt more locked into their current dwelling in 1980 than in 1975 due to more stringent financial constraints, such as greater housing inflation, higher mortgage interest rates, etc. In such an environment they would be less able to consider moving on from their starter home.

As for the socioeconomic characteristics of homeowners, EDUCATION does demonstrate the predicted inverse relationship with time horizon of mobility plans in both samples, although the magnitude of the correlation is modest. For example, compared to a homeowner with a high school diploma only, one with a college degree is .05 and .11 less likely to hold permanent plans in Wooster and in Minneapolis, respectively. This result is consistent with Weisbrod's and Vidal's (1981) evidence, and supports the hypothesis that education is associated with lower information and adjustment costs. In no equation is INCOME a statistically significant pre-dictor, suggesting that the financial cost of moving does not generally inhibit the formulation of mobility plans. That BLACK proves not to be significant is likely attributable to the paucity of black homeowner obser-vations and the relative absence of ghettos in both samples.

Past housing-market experience variables frequently prove to have statistically significant coefficients of the signs to be expected if they were proxying for adjustment costs. Higher numbers of prior moves made during the last five years (NUMMOVES) are generally associated with greater probabilities of nearer-term plans. Conversely, increased LONGEVITY leads one to predict longer-term mobility plans.

Only one of the two personal social-interaction variables holds any consistent predictive power for mobility plans. The degree to which homeowners assess their familiarity and communication with their neighbors is directly related to more extended mobility plans, at least in Wooster. Compared to those with the mean value of INTEGRATE, those two standard deviations above the mean should be .12 less likely to have middle-term plans, .05 more likely to have long-term plans, and .08 more likely to have permanent plans. This finding is contrary to the claim of Haggerty (1982) that the social attachment between neighbors has little effect upon mobility plans.

The residential satisfaction variables consistently perform as predicted in both samples, being directly related to the planned duration of residency. Compared to a homeowner having the mean level of dwelling satisfaction, one with the maximum HOUSESAT should be: .02–.04 less likely to have short-term plans, and .01–.02 more likely to have long-term or permanent plans (using coefficient ranges in both samples). Similarly, compared to a homeowner having the mean level of neighborhood satisfaction, a homeowner with the maximum NEIGHSAT should be: .02 less likely to have short-term plans, .02–.05 less likely to have middle-term plans, and .03–.08 more likely to have permanent plans. Although comparatively modest in terms of magnitude, these findings are consistent with the conventional wisdom (see Speare 1974; Public Affairs Counseling 1975, 15; Ahlbrandt and Cunningham 1979, ch.7, and Taub, Taylor, and Dunham 1984, 176). And they are certainly consistent with the position argued earlier that satisfaction affects mobility plans through its proxying for gross comparative advantages of feasible residential alternatives, as perceived by homeowners. Finally, note that both neighborhood and dwelling satisfaction are correlated with plans in roughly the same magnitude. This provides further foundation for the model developed in chapter 3 and for a persistent theme echoing throughout this work: homeowners' behaviors cannot be comprehended within a four-walls framework—the neighborhood is of crucial import.

Interestingly, expectations about future property values (VALUEEXP) does not prove to be a statistically significant predictor of mobility expectations, with one exception. In Minneapolis those who are most pessimistic are .08 less likely to have long-term plans than those having the mean value of VALUEEXP. That expectations about neighborhood property values typically does not influence mobility plans lends credence to the assumption employed in the upkeep model of chapter 3: homeowners may adjust optimal home investments according to changes in VALUEEXP, but do not simultaneously adjust their planning horizon.

Neighborhood quality expectations (NEIGHEXP) demonstrate an unexpected relationship with mobility plans. Compared to homeowners with average pessimism, those with maximum pessimism in Wooster are .23 less likely to have middle-term plans and .19 more likely to have permanent plans. A similar comparison shows that Minneapolis homeowners with maximum pessimism are .08 more likely to have long-term plans. These results are difficult to interpret if the implicit direction of causality is retained; i.e., more pessimism about the future quality of their neighborhood causes some people to lengthen their plans to remain. One alternative possibility is that the above causation may be reversed for some homeowners; i.e., those who have decided on other grounds to remain in their neighborhoods for longer periods may for some reason tend to evaluate more harshly any expected changes therein.

Another possibility is that the quality-expectation variable is framed in too short a time horizon to be relevant to the formulation of mobility plans.[25] If attitudes about the comparative net advantage of the residential environment are formed gradually and are modified even more slowly, their relationship with current expectations about near-future events would be low. And this is precisely the case in both samples here, where the two attitudinal variables HOUSESAT and NEIGHSAT are virtually uncorrelated with NEIGHEXP.[26] If this hypothesis is correct, then the above relationship between the quality-expectation variable and mobility plans is spurious (although the source of this spurious relationship is unidentified in either sample). Whether the above hypotheses are correct or not, it is clear that this study represents the first attempt to investigate and quantify the relationship between neighborhood quality and property-value expectations and mobility plans. The results are curious enough to serve as a springboard to further, more refined tests.

Finally, the two public home-improvement–assistance variables prove statistically significant (two-tailed test) only once. The receipt of a loan for home rehabilitation (LOAN?) is directly related to short-term mobility plans, suggesting that short-term capital gain recouping is a (perhaps unintended) side effect of such a policy. Homeowners who have personally received subsidized home-improvement loans in the past five years are .08 more likely to hold short-term mobility plans than others, *ceteris paribus*.

Direct and Indirect Determinants of Mobility Plans

Table 8.2 presents those variables that might be labelled direct correlates (or, presuming causality, determinants) of homeowners' mobility plans.

But it should be recalled from chapters 2, 6, and 7 that four of those direct determinants—HOUSESAT, NEIGHSAT, NEIGHEXP, and VALUEEXP—are themselves functions of a variety of objective characteristics of the home-owners, their dwellings, and their neighborhoods. This means that, via their presumed influence on these intervening satisfaction and expectation variables, a large number of additional variables have indirect (presumed causal) relationships with mobility plans. In order to assess the full impact of one of these characteristics on mobility plans, one must consider both direct and indirect effects. These variables are categorized into the same four sets employed before for the purpose of exposition: homeowner characteristics, dwelling characteristics, neighborhood characteristics, and policy characteristics.

A summary of direct and indirect relationships for these variable sets is presented in tables 8.3, 8.4, and 8.5. In each table the direct relationship is measured by the beta coefficient of the given variable in the given linear mobility plan model. In each table the indirect relationship is measured by the product of the beta coefficient of the given variable explaining a given intervening satisfaction or expectation variable and the beta coefficient of that intervening variable in the given linear mobility-plan model. The total relationship between a given objective characteristic and a given mobility plan probability is the sum of the direct (if any) plus indirect (if any) beta coefficients.

Consider first the results of total relationships between mobility plans and homeowner characteristics, as shown in table 8.3. These show that, for the Wooster sample, the strongest predictors of mobility plans are life-cycle stages—even more than satisfaction or expectation measures. Compared to those in STAGE1, those in later stages have much longer-range mobility plans, and the magnitude of the difference grows as one considers successively older stages. For the longest-term–plans part of this life-cycle effect, all of the impact occurs directly; for the short-term component generally 15 to 20 percent of the total occurs via housing satisfaction. This same qualitative pattern is manifested in Minneapolis, but the magnitudes of the total relationships are much smaller.

Virtually all the household characteristics that were noted above as holding strong predictive power for mobility plans operate directly. The exceptions are MARRIED and FEMALE, which achieve some effect on plans indirectly via satisfaction. And IDENTIFY evidences a positive relationship with longer length of expected tenure solely through its indirect path via NEIGHSAT. That is, those who share common solidarity sentiments with neighbors are more likely to hold very long-term mobility plans because they are more satisfied with their neighborhood. Without exception, however, the magnitude of any indirect effects of household characteristics are far smaller than the magnitude of direct effects.

Table 8.3   Direct and Indirect Relationships* between Homeowner
Characteristics and Mobility Plans

				Dependent
	STAY0–2		STAY3–10	
Characteristics	Wooster	Minn	Wooster	Minn
EDUCATION	.09	—	—	.16
	(−.01)[1]	(—)	(—)	(—)
INCOME	—	—	—	—
	(—)	(—)	(—)	(—)
MARRIED	—	−.14	.10	.11
	(.02)[2]	(—)	(.04)[2,3]	(—)
FEMALE	—	−.13	.15	—
	(—)	(.01)[1]	(—)	(.01)[2]
OCCUPANTS	—	—	—	—
	(NA)	(NA)	(—)	(—)
BLACK	—	—	—	—
	(—)	(.02)[1]	(—)	(—)
STAGE2	−.24	—	—	—
	(−.03)[1]	(−.01)	(—)	(—)
STAGE3	−.21	—	−.18	—
	(−.05)[1]	(−.02)[1]	(—)	(−.02)[2]
STAGE4	−.25	—	−.17	—
	(−.05)[1]	(−.02)[1]	(—)	(−.01)[2]
STAGE5	−.28	—	−.30	—
	(−.08)[1]	(−.03)[1]	(—)	(−.03)[2]
NUMMOVES	.13	—	—	.11
	(NA)	(NA)	(NA)	(NA)
PRIORHOME	NA	NA	NA	NA
	(—)	(—)	(—)	(—)
EARLYHOME	NA	NA	NA	NA
	(—)	(.01)[1]	(—)	(—)
LONGEVITY**	−.06	—	−.13	—
	(—)	(−.02)[1]	(−.02)[2]	(−.04)[2]
IDENTIFY**	—	—	—	—
	(−.03)[2]	(—)	(—)	(—)
INTEGRATE**	—	—	−.13	—
	(—)	(—)	(—)	(—)
ALIENATED	NA	NA	NA	NA
	(.01)[2]	(—)	(.01)[2]	(—)
HOUSESAT	−.18	−.11	—	—

variables

	STAY10+		STAYPERM	
Wooster	Minn		Wooster	Minn
—	—		−.08	−.07
(—)	(.03)[4]		(—)	(.01)[1]
—	—		—	—
(—)	(—)		(—)	(—)
—	—		−.14	—
(—)	(.01)[4]		(−.04)[1,2]	(—)
—	—		−.14	—
(—)	(−.01)[1,4]		(—)	(−.04)[1,2]
.13	—		−.13	—
(—)	(—)		(—)	(—)
—	—		—	—
(—)	(−.02)[1]		(—)	(−.01)[1]
—	—		.13	—
(—)	(−.07)[1,3]		(—)	(.01)[1]
—	—		.26	—
(—)	(−.03)[1,3]		(—)	(.04)[1,2]
—	—		.25	—
(—)	(.01)[1,3]		(—)	(.03)[1,2]
—	—		.43	.14
(—)	(.01)[1,4]		(—)	(.07)[1,2]
—	—		—	−.08
(NA)	(NA)		(NA)	(NA)
NA	NA		NA	NA
(—)	(—)		(—)	(—)
NA	NA		NA	NA
(—)	(−.01)[1]		(—)	(−.01)[1]
—	—		.19	.12
(—)	(.03)[1]		(—)	(.02)[1]
—	—		—	—
(—)	(.01)[4]		(.03)[2]	(.06)[2]
.10	—		.08	—
(—)	(—)		(—)	(—)
NA	NA		NA	NA
(—)	(—)		(−.01)[2]	(—)
—	.13		—	.08

(*continued*)

Table 8.3   (*Continued*)

	Dependent			
	STAY0–2		STAY3–10	
Characteristics	Wooster	Minn	Wooster	Minn
	(NA)	(NA)	(NA)	(NA)
NEIGHSAT	−.11	—	−.08	−.13
	(NA)	(NA)	(NA)	(NA)
NEIGHEXP	—	—	−.15	—
	(NA)	(NA)	(NA)	(NA)
VALUEEXP	—	—	—	—
	(NA)	(NA)	(NA)	(NA)
LOAN?	NA	.08	NA	—
GRANT?	NA	—	NA	—

Note: Indirect relationship via: 1 = HOUSESAT; 2 = NEIGHSAT; 3 = NEIGHEXP; 4 = VALUEEXP. Indirect shown in parentheses.
*using linear model's beta coefficients only when corroborated by PROBIT model

Consider next the relationships between dwelling characteristics and mobility plans, which are, by their nature, indirect via dwelling satisfaction (see table 8.4). Because HOUSESAT is only a statistically significant predictor of STAY0–2 in the Wooster sample, all indirect impacts of dwelling characteristics are confined there. In Minneapolis these indirect relationships are more widespread, being absent only in the STAY3–10 equation. The most important indirect relationships are shown by the structure age variables. Homeowners in older homes are more likely to have shorter-term mobility plans, due to their lower satisfaction with their dwellings. These relationships between age of structure and mobility plans are orders of magnitude stronger than those for quantitative or other qualitative dwelling feature variables. But in all cases the magnitudes of the beta coefficients are small—.03 at the largest.

The neighborhood characteristic variables can have only indirect relationships with mobility plans, but can manifest such via their relationship with either NEIGHSAT, NEIGHEXP, and/or VALUEEXP. As shown in table 8.5, the connection with neighborhood satisfaction is more prevalent than with expectations. Once again, these indirect relationships are more frequent in the Minneapolis sample than in the Wooster sample, although in neither

variables

	STAY10+			STAYPERM	
Wooster	Minn		Wooster		Minn
(NA)	(NA)		(NA)		(NA)
—	—		.11		.19
(NA)	(NA)		(NA)		(NA)
—	.16		.13		—
(NA)	(NA)		(NA)		(NA)
—	−.10		—		—
(NA)	(NA)		(NA)		(NA)
NA	—		NA		—
NA	—		NA		—

**using both linear and squared terms where appropriate; evaluated at means
NA = not applicable; variable not used in given model
— = coefficient not statistically significant in linear model or PROBIT model

sample do they occur often in the STAY0–2 equation. Nevertheless, some generalizations can be made. The physical and socioeconomic quality indexes at the study area, block, and tract level all tend to be positively correlated with comparatively longer-term mobility plans, typically due to their positive correlation with neighborhood satisfaction. On the other hand, the presence of nonresidential land use, larger proportions of long-tenure neighbors, and larger proportions of black neighbors are all negatively correlated with longer-term mobility plans, primarily due to reduced satisfaction. In the Wooster sample, at least, the aggregate degree of communal identification in the neighborhood is positively associated with longer-run mobility plans via neighborhood satisfaction. Although in most cases the size of these indirect beta coefficients is in the minimal (.01 to .03) range, for certain homeowner strata they are larger. In addition, these magnitudes are generally larger than those for the dwelling characteristic variables (see table 8.4) and generally equal to those for the indirect relationships of homeowner characteristics (see table 8.3).

Finally, the indirect relationships for Minneapolis public policy variables are infrequent and small in size, as seen in the bottom panel of table 8.5. Homeowners in areas that do not qualify for home-improvement

Table 8.4   Indirect Relationships* between Dwelling Characteristics and Mobility Plans

Dwelling characteristics	Dependent variable							
	STAY0–2		STAY3–10		STAY10+		STAYPERM	
	Wooster	Minn	Wooster	Minn	Wooster	Minn	Wooster	Minn
YARD/OCC**	—	—	—	—	—	—	—	—
ROOM/OCC**	—	−.01	—	—	—	.01	—	.01
BATH/OCC**	—	−.02	—	—	—	.02	—	.01
BUILTPRE-20	—	.03	—	—	—	−.03	—	−.02
BUILT20-39	.03	.03	—	—	—	−.03	—	−.02
BUILT40-59								
Total	.03	.02	—	—	—	−.03	—	−.02
FEMALE, STAGE3,4	NA	−.01	NA	—	NA	.01	NA	.01
BUILT60-69								
Total	—	—	—	—	—	—	—	—
STAGE2	.01	NA	—	NA	—	NA	—	NA
NOHEAT	—	—	—	—	—	—	—	—
AIRCOND								
Total	—	—	—	—	—	—	—	—
FEMALE, STAGE4	NA	−.01	NA	—	NA	.02	NA	.01
GARAGE								
Total	−.02	—	—	—	—	—	—	—
STAGE2	.01	NA	—	NA	—	NA	—	NA
WOOD								
Total	—	—	—	—	—	—	—	—
STAGE3	.02	NA	—	NA	—	NA	—	NA

*using linear HOUSESAT model's beta coefficients only when corroborated by PROBIT model
**using both linear and squared terms where appropriate; evaluated at means
NA = not applicable; variable not used in given model
— = coefficient not statistically significant in linear model or PROBIT model

Table 8.5 Indirect Relationships* between Neighborhood and Policy
Characteristics and Mobility Plans

	Dependent variable							
Neighborhood characteristics	STAY0–2		STAY3–10		STAY10+		STAYPERM	
	Wooster	Minn	Wooster	Minn	Wooster	Minn	Wooster	Minn
AREAQUAL	$-.01^2$	NA	$-.01^2$	NA	—	NA	$.01^2$	NA
BLOCKQUAL								
Total	NA	—	NA	$-.02^2$	NA	—	NA	$.02^2$
Low inc, low ed.	NA	—	NA	—	NA	$.02^4$	NA	—
TRACTQUAL	NA	—	NA	$-.02^2$	NA	—	NA	$.03^2$
NONRESID								
Total	—	—	$.01^2$	$.03^2$	—	$-.03^{3,4}$	—	$-.04^2$
Low inc, STAGE 1	NA	—	NA	—	NA	—	NA	$—^2$
TENURE								
Total	—	—	—	—	—	$.02^3$	$-.02^3$	$.03^2$
MARRIED	NA	—	NA	$.05^2$	NA	—	NA	$-.04^2$
RACECOMPW								
Total	—	—	$.02^{2,3}$	$.01^2$	—	$.01^3$	—	$-.02^2$
FEMALE, STAGE4	—	NA	—	NA	—	NA	—	NA
FEMALE, EDUCATION (LOW)	NA	—	NA	—	NA	$-.02^4$	NA	—
EDUCATION (LOW)	NA	—	NA	—	NA	$-.01^3$	NA	—
RACECOMPB	—	—	—	—	—	—	—	—
NIDENTIFY**								
Total	$-.03^2$	—	$-.02^2$	—	—	$.01^4$	$.03^2$	—
STAGE2,4	—	NA	—	NA	—	NA	—	NA
STAGE2,3	—	NA	—	NA	—	NA	—	NA
NINTEGRATE								
Total	—	—	—	—	—	$.01^4$	—	—
STAGE2	—	NA	$.05^3$	NA	—	NA	$-.05^3$	NA
FEMALE	NA	—	NA	—	NA	$.08^3$	NA	—
Policy Characteristics								
NOTQUALIFY	NA	—	NA	—	NA	$.02^{3,4}$	NA	—
QUALIFY	NA	—	NA	—	NA	—	NA	—
LOAN?***	NA	—	NA	—	NA	—	NA	—
GRANT?***	NA	—	NA	—	NA	—	NA	—

Note: Indirect relationship via: 2 = NEIGHSAT; 3 = NEIGHEXP; 4 = VALUEEXP
*using linear model's beta coefficients only when corroborated by PROBIT model
**using both linear and squared terms where appropriate; evaluated at means
***direct relationships shown in table 8.3
NA = not applicable; variable not used in given model
— = coefficient not statistically significant in linear model or PROBIT model

assistance are slightly more likely to hold long-term mobility plans because they have more pessimistic neighborhood expectations. Thus, the only noteworthy impact of these particular types of public policy upon mobility plans appears to be directly, via the association between short-term plans and rehabilitation-loan recipients.

Summary and Conclusions

This chapter develops a model of homeowner mobility plans that centers on the concept of perceived "comparative net advantage." Homeowners evaluate their relative well-being at their current residence and at other feasible alternative residences, net of various adjustment costs such as out-of-pocket and time expenses and social-psychological burdens. Homeowners who, on the basis of their limited information, now perceive their comparative net advantage as resting with another dwelling will form short-term mobility intentions. Others may not currently perceive such an imbalance, but project a time in which altered needs, aspirations, resources, or adjustment costs will likely shift so as to tip the scale in favor of another dwelling. They will indicate longer-term mobility plans. Still others may perceive such extreme advantages from their present location or such burdensome adjustment costs that moving is ruled out, thereby producing permanent mobility plans.

The key empirical claim is that residential satisfaction represents a superior proxy for the homeowner's perceived current comparative gross advantages of alternative feasible residential environments. Characteristics of homeowners should predict mobility plans insofar as they proxy for adjustment costs (thereby producing comparative net advantage) or future anticipated changes in needs and aspirations that will tip the future comparative advantage in favor of an alternative dwelling. Expectations about neighborhood quality and value changes are modeled as proxies for future comparative gross advantage.

The empirical estimates generally provide strong support for the conceptual approach. Specifically:

– Marital status of homeowners is related to the probabilities of various mobility plans in a curvilinear fashion that is clearly explicable on the grounds that it serves as a dual proxy for both adjustment costs and anticipated changes in housing needs and aspirations. Married homeowners are most likely to anticipate that the comparative net advantage of their present dwelling will cease in three to ten years. Any life-cycle stage is more likely to hold permanent plans and less likely to hold shorter-term plans compared to young, childless households. And the magnitude of these differences tends to grow as progressively older stages are compared.

Homeowners with less education are more likely to hold permanent plans than short-term ones, compared to those with more education, as would be expected if education proxies for adjustment costs. All of these relationships are approximately equal in magnitude, and are as large as those manifested for the satisfaction variables. Between-sample variation in results suggests, however, that the apparent importance of life-cycle stage is minimized when childless homeowners under age forty-five are upper-status professionals, and when skyrocketing mortgage rates and home prices lock such homeowners into their starter homes.

Both neighborhood and housing satisfaction prove directly related to expected length of tenure in roughly the same magnitude as each other and as the aforementioned homeowner characteristics. The relationships were highly generalized between samples, as would be predicted if they were proxying for perceptions of gross comparative advantage.

– The objective characteristics of the dwelling (like structural age) and of the neighborhood (like quality indexes) provide only a minor degree of explanatory power for mobility plans, as their impacts are channeled through the intervening variables of dwelling satisfaction and neighborhood satisfaction, respectively.

– Property-value expectations show virtually no relationship with plans. Qualitative neighborhood expectations are related to mobility plans in a counterintuitive manner that defies easy explanation. The most plausible is that the results are spurious. If so, this means that homeowners' projections of future comparative net advantage are formulated almost entirely on the basis of expected changes in their household needs, and not on the relatively short-term expectations as modeled here. In any event, because the effort to model expectations empirically is in its infancy and these preliminary results are curious, extreme caution is warranted in drawing any conclusions on this matter.

9 Homeowners' Housing Upkeep Behavior

Now that all the component submodels of satisfaction, expectations, and mobility plans have been specified and estimated, we can consider empirically the ultimate concern of this research: the expenditures by homeowners on maintenance, repairs, and improvements of their dwellings. Extended theoretical discussions of the determinants of this housing upkeep behavior are provided in chapter 3 and are not repeated here. Rather, the chapter commences with a review and critique of relevant previous empirical studies. Then an empirical model of homeowners' housing upkeep behavior is specified that follows directly from the theory presented in chapter 3 and that incorporates the earlier behavioral submodels of expectations and mobility plans. Three different measures of upkeep efforts serve as dependent variables in this model: (1) the probability of adopting a positive upkeep strategy; (2) the amount of expenditure given such a strategy; (3) the probability of adopting an upkeep strategy producing visible exterior home defects. Finally, parameters of the probability models are estimated empirically using both LOGIT and ordinary least squares (OLS) techniques, so as to test for the robustness of parameter estimates. As in previous chapters, readers wishing to skip detailed discussions of empirical issues and model results should turn directly to the chapter summary.

Previous Research on Homeowners' Housing Upkeep Behavior

There have been a sizable number of empirical investigations of homeowners'[1] housing upkeep behavior that have employed sophisticated multivariate statistical analyses: Winger (1973), Mendelsohn (1977), Chinloy (1980), Struyk and Soldo (1980), Shear and Carpenter (1982), Shear (1983), Taub, Taylor, and Dunham (1984), Myers (1984), McConney (1985), Stewart and Hyclak (1986), Varady (1986), and Boehm and Ihlandfeldt (1986). Although the exact form of the dependent variable, the specific investment in question, and the type of sample have varied across these studies, reasonably consistent conclusions have been reached about the most important homeowner and dwelling characteristics. See table 9.1 for a summary of these alternative specifications and their findings. As for homeowner characteristics, the relationship between upkeep and age appears to be an inverted U-shape, although there is disagreement over exactly at which middle-aged category the maximum occurs.[2] Upkeep efforts appear positively correlated with household education, size, and especially income; inversely correlated with black or female homeowners and duration of occupancy. Independent of these homeowner characteristics, older dwellings are positively associated with repairs, but negatively associated with additions and alterations. Higher valued homes have higher amounts of various upkeep activities, although there is obvious simultaneity involved in such a relationship. Smaller dwellings evidence larger expenditures for additions and improvements, but smaller expenditures for repairs.

Regarding objective neighborhood characteristics and homeowners' subjective evaluations, there is far less consistency in results, though few models have incorporated such variables. Several studies discern no appreciable relationships between upkeep investments and qualitative aspects of the neighborhood environment. Others find diametrically opposed results concerning, e.g., the role of deterioration on the block face. There is also a potpourri of implications that can be drawn from variables measuring perceptions of various neighborhood attributes (see table 9.1).

The above inconsistencies are likely produced by the weakness shared by previous research in this area: specification bias. First, existing models typically omit variables controlling for social-interactive neighborhood characteristics, homeowners' expectations about both qualitative and property-value changes in their neighborhood, and homeowners' mobility plans, in spite of the strong theoretical justification for including them.[3] Second, no studies have specified a model that allows for expectations to have different impacts on home investment, depending on the character of the neighborhood. As explained in chapter 3, such variation in impact can be predicted theoretically and offers an intriguing vehicle for understanding variants of strategic interactions among homeowners.

Four of the aforementioned studies have, however, made significant advances in obviating some, but not all, of these criticisms. Shear and Carpenter (1982) and Shear (1983) implicitly control for short-term mobility plans by estimating the joint probabilities of various types of homeowners' housing investments between 1974 and 1976 and whether they actually moved between 1976 and 1979. The authors find that although the set of significant explanatory variables for housing upkeep investments vary across mobility categories, there is not a statistically significant dif-

Table 9.1   Summary of Results from Previous Housing Upkeep Investment
Studies

Homeowner Characteristics
Age: compared to those under age
   25:*
      −age 25–34: 1
      +age 45–54: 1
      −age 65+: 1, 10
Age: compared to those under age
   30:*
      −age 30–39: 7
      −age 40–49: 6, 12, 13, 14
      −age 50–59: 6, 12, 13, 14
      −age 60+: 6, 12, 13, 14
Age: compared to those under age
   35:*
      +age 35–44: 2
      −age 45–64: 2
      −age 65+: 2, 10
+Education: 1, 13, 14, 15
−Education: 12, 15
−Black:* 2, 7, 13, 14
+Income: 2, 4, 5, 6, 7, 8, 9, 11–15
−Duration of occupancy:* 2, 5, 6, 13,
   14, 16
+Growth in household size: 12
+Household size:* 4, 5, 6, 14, 16
−Female head: 12, 14
+Married with children (versus single
   or childless): 8, 10
−Married with children: 15
+Desire to move due to bad neigh-
   borhood: 14
0 Expected mobility: 4
+Unskilled worker: 16
−Housepayment burden: 16

Market Characteristics
−Construction cost index: 4

Dwelling Characteristics
+House value: 2, 5
+Age of house: 2, 3, 4, 7, 14, 16
−Age of house: 6, 12
−# bathrooms: 13
−# rooms: 5, 6
+# rooms: 4, 7
−Good condition: 4, 15
+Good condition: 15
−Interior problems: 14

Neighborhood Characteristics
+Commercial parcels on street: 15
0 Bad sidewalks, roads, litter: 4, 15
0 Abandoned buildings on block: 6,
   7, 12, 13, 14
−Property tax rate:* 6
+Property tax rate:* 16
−Central city residence: 6
+Block deterioration (whites only): 8
+Median income of tract: 9
−% black in tract:* 9
+% structures with no defects: 4
−Vacant parcels on street: 15
+Rehab. actions of neighbors: 15, 16

Subjective Assessments
−Satisfaction with dwelling: 16
−Race prejudice (whites only): 8, 16
+Satisfaction with property value
   trends: 8
0 Satisfaction with neighborhood:* 9,
   10
0 Respondent rating of neighborhood
   quality: 6, 9, 10, 16
−Perceived crime problem: 4
0 Adequacy of schools: 4
+Social problems in area: 15
−Physical problems in area: 15

Social Characteristics
+Membership in local organizations
   (whites only): 8
+# family members who visit
   monthly: 9
0 Social interaction, cohesiveness: 16

Table 9.1   (*Continued*)

*no significance for this variable found by at least one other study cited
+ = variable positively associated with housing upkeep
− = variable negatively associated with housing upkeep
0 = variable not associated with housing upkeep

Key: author; dependent variable(s); data base (all one-family houses, homeowners)

1. Winger (1973); $ maintenance, replacements, improvements; national survey of Consumer Finances, 1964–65
2. Mendelsohn (1977); prob(nonzero $) and $ repairs, alterations; national Census Bureau Special Survey, 1971–72
3. Chinloy (1980); ratio of maintenance $ to property value $; London and St. Catherines, Ontario, 1974
4. Boehm and Ihlanfeldt (1986); expenditure on maintenance and improvements; survey of 20 cities' National Housing Services (NHS) neighborhoods, 1978–79
5. Myers (1984); prob.(improvements 1974–79) and frequency of maintenance, 1974–79; National Annual Housing Survey, 1974–79
6. Shear (1983), and Shear and Carpenter (1982); prob.(alterations, additions, replacements, 1974–76; for those not moving 1976–79; National Annual Housing Survey, 1974–79
7. Shear and Carpenter (1982); as 6, but prob.(repairs)
8. Taub, Taylor, and Dunham (1984, ch.6); prob.(spending $1,000 on home); Chicago survey, 1978
9. Struyk and Soldo (1980, ch.4); prob.(repairs); 1975 Survey of Maintenance and Repair Activity by Elderly Homeowners (5 SMSA sample of elderly only)
10. Struyk and Soldo (1980, ch.4); as 9, but # repairs done by self
11. Struyk and Soldo (1980, ch.4); as 9, but # repairs done by hired labor
12. Stewart and Hyclak (1986); prob.(additions in prior year); National Annual Housing Survey, 1976–77
13. Stewart and Hyclak (1986); as 12, but prob.(alterations)
14. Stewart and Hyclak (1986); as 12, but prob.(repairs)
15. McConney (1985); $ rehabilitation expenditures; CDBG neighborhoods in Corpus Christi and Birmingham, 1979–80
16. Varady (1986); $ spent on home, Urban Homesteading Demonstration neighborhoods, 1977–79

ference in mean investment propensities among them (1982, 44). Shear (1983) also specifies dummy variables indicating whether the homeowner perceives the neighborhood to be getting better or worse. For movers the proxy for optimism is associated with more alterations but fewer replacements. For neither movers nor nonmovers do these variables strongly predict the probability of various investment behaviors, however. Unfortunately, no variables measuring social interaction or expectations about property-value changes are included in this model.

Using a similar specification and data base as Shear, Stewart and Hyclak (1986) employ two variables denoting if the homeowner desires to move due to inadequacies in either the home or the neighborhood. The former proves not to be statistically significantly related to the probability of engaging in any sort of upkeep activity. The latter is associated with a greater likelihood of replacements and repairs only. Once again, however, potentially important proxies for expectations and neighborhood social interaction are omitted.

Taub, Taylor, and Dunham (1984, ch.6) make a useful contribution by including in their model a crude measure of social interaction: home-owner's membership in local organizations. As predicted, this measure is associated with a greater probability of making major home investments. A possible proxy for owners' expectations (i.e., satisfaction with property-value trends) also evidences this association. It is ironic that a model unique in specifying certain variables is beset by a paucity of controls for homeowner characteristics. Even more serious, no attempt is made to control for mobility plans, characteristics of the sampled dwellings, or the demographic character of the neighborhood.

An important recent advance is made by Varady (1986). His housing repair model not only contains a wealth of neighborhood physical charac-teristics and features of the homeowner and the dwelling, but measures of neighborhood expectations, social interactions, and cohesiveness as well. None of these latter variables prove statistically significant, although all likely suffer from measurement shortcomings. Expectations are proxied for by a "neighborhood confidence" dummy variable that combines cur-rent and future assessments in defining the "optimistic" respondents. Social interaction and cohesiveness are both measured by three-item scales that limit variation and tap only two dimensions of the constructs (Varady 1986, appendix table 1). Mobility plans are not controlled for. Finally, it is difficult to generalize from Varady's results because the sample is drawn only from Urban Homesteading Demonstration neighborhoods.

In summary, previous work in the area of homeowners' housing upkeep activity has fallen short of empirical specifications that meet the minimal requirements of theory. As a result, we know little about the roles played by either the physical-demographic or social-interactive dimensions of neighborhood, by various sorts of expectations, or by homeowners' mobil-ity plans. The present study attempts to remedy this shortcoming.

Specification of an Empirical Model of Housing Upkeep Behavior

Dependent Variables

There are at least three distinct ways to measure the housing upkeep behavior of homeowners: the frequency of various types of investments; the dollar expenditure on such investments; and the result of such expenditure in terms of augmented quantities of housing capital and or qualitative condition of the dwelling.[4] The relationships among these three alternative measures can be better understood with reference to the theory in chapter 3, which deals with four alternative housing upkeep strategies: upgrading improvements, positive maintenance, zero maintenance or improvements, and downgrading (subdividing the dwelling). For each strategy there is a corresponding optimal level of expenditure (this will be zero and negative, respectively, in the case of the latter two strategies). This choice of optimal strategy per expenditure will, in turn, specify the alterations in units of housing capital that will occur during the period and, thus, the new level of housing services that will flow from the residential package over time. In the present research all three elements are considered: the choice of upkeep strategy, the expenditure associated with the chosen strategy, and the consequences for exterior dwelling quality resulting from the strategy and expenditures.

The following specific information is obtained from the Wooster and Minneapolis surveys about these three elements. First consider the choice of upkeep strategy and expenditure on it. Recall that the sample is limited to homeowners living in single-family dwellings, thus confining attention to those who in the recent past have not pursued a downgrading (dwelling subdivision) strategy. The homeowner respondents were asked to list their expenditures during the past year for each of the following maintenance categories: interior and exterior repairs, interior and exterior repainting, yard and driveway upkeep, and repairs (not replacement) of plumbing or heating equipment.[5] Respondents were also asked to list their expenditures during the last five years (or however long they've lived in current dwelling) on the following upgrading or improvement categories: interior remodeling, exterior improvements (e.g., aluminum siding, insulation, new roof), structural additions (e.g., extra bedroom, garage, swimming pool), and alterations or replacements of plumbing, heating, cooling, or electrical systems.

The obvious shortcoming of these maintenance and improvement data is that they are estimates of past housing upkeep activity, whereas all other variables in the model are estimates of present characteristics of households, dwellings, and neighborhoods. In the absence of follow-up surveys, which are not financially feasible, some assumptions must be made about how this information can proxy for current housing upkeep strategies and expenditures. It is assumed that those homeowners who have neither made expenditures on maintenance in the prior year or on improvements during the previous five years are continuing to pursue a zero-upkeep or passive-undermaintenance strategy. (In terms of figure 3.1, these individuals are assumed to be operating at point F.) But given the nature of the data, it cannot be known unambiguously whether those who are pursuing a different strategy are in fact pursuing a maintenance-only or a maintenance-and-improvements strategy. Thus, because no distinction can be made between these alternative strategies involving positive upkeep investments, a dummy variable UPKEEP? is specified taking the value one if either of these two strategies for positive upkeep expenditures are indicated, and zero otherwise. As a proxy for the expenditure involved in the assumed current positive housing-upkeep strategy, the dollars expended on the prior year's maintenance activities and one-fifth of the dollars expended on improvements during the previous five years are added to form UPKEEP$.[6] In sum, the current model considers the choice between a zero-upkeep strategy and a positive-upkeep strategy (the downgrading strategy being controlled for by sample selection), and considers for those choosing the latter the size of expenditure involved.

Frequency distributions and descriptive statistics for the housing upkeep strategy and expenditure variables reveal that a much higher percentage of homeowners were pursuing a zero-upkeep strategy at the time of the survey in Wooster than in Minneapolis: 9 percent versus 2 percent.[7] For those sampled who were pursuing a positive-upkeep strategy, the expenditures were much higher on average in Minneapolis than in Wooster: $1,805 versus $642 (in current dollars). This is also true relative to property value: the ratio of estimated annual upkeep expenditure to property value was 2 percent in Wooster but 3.3 percent in Minneapolis. Comparisons with national data for upkeep expenditures show that both samples are above the national average for the comparable year, however.[8]

The final measure of housing upkeep activity employed in this study focuses on the qualitative results of the above upkeep efforts in terms of the housing capital alterations in the dwelling. Specifically, the variable DEFECTS? is defined as a dummy variable taking the value one if the interviewer assesses the dwelling as having one or more of the following external residential defects: broken or boarded-up windows; trash or litter on premises; badly peeling exterior paint; broken steps, railings, or siding; missing shingles or sagging roof; cracked or sagging foundation. There were so few dwellings in the sample having multiple defects that the specification of DEFECTS? as a ratio-level variable proved impractical.[9]

The presence of such defects is a clear signal that the homeowner has not invested sufficiently in upkeep to offset the deterioration of the dwelling, at least in its external manifestations. In terms of chapter 3, the optimal level of upkeep being pursued in the face of depreciation produces amounts of structural capital increments ($\bar{A}_t$) that are significantly less than the amounts of structural capital decrements ($\bar{A}_{t-1}(1-d)$) that are lost to depreciation. The variable DEFECTS? also indicates something of the nature of whatever upkeep expenditures are invested: are they devoted primarily to exterior or interior sorts of structural capital? Thus, DEFECTS?

gives us a distinct measure of the adequacy and composition of housing upkeep behavior that is not necessarily reflected in either UPKEEP? or UPKEEP$. And it is, in some respects, the most crucial measure of upkeep, because it is the presence of exterior defects that potentially produces negative externalities and subsequently altered housing upkeep behaviors for neighbors.

The data show that 4.5 percent of the Wooster dwellings and 15.1 percent of the Minneapolis dwellings sampled have DEFECT? present.[10] This may appear to contradict the earlier statistics indicating that Minneapolis homeowners have higher propensities of positive upkeep strategies and spend more real dollars on such than Wooster homeowners. But this need not be contradictory if the exterior condition of the sampled Minneapolis housing stock several years prior to the survey was so inferior to that of the Wooster stock that even superior upkeep efforts were insufficient to erase the difference. This is consistent with earlier comparisons in chapter 5 that note the relative age differentials in the two stocks. It may also be the case that those pursuing zero-upkeep strategies in Wooster have been doing so for a relatively shorter period than those doing so in Minneapolis, so that the clear external indicators of such a strategy are not yet visible at the time of the survey in Wooster.

Independent Variables of Homeowner Characteristics

Households of higher socioeconomic status are expected to invest more often and more heavily in positive upkeep strategies (see chapter 3). Those with more education or income may perceive their dwellings as crucial symbols of their achieved status. These factors are reflected as more housing-intensive preferences, with a concomitant greater probability of home upkeep activity and greater expenditure. In addition, those with higher incomes have lower financial constraints on their upkeep expenditures and may perceive lower costs of major home improvements that entail borrowing because of greater tax savings from interest deductions. However, there is a countervailing effect to this. Higher-income homeowners may attach a higher implicit wage to the time they personally invest in housing upkeep, which tends to reduce the probability of positive upkeep and expenditure on it. Thus, one can predict that EDUCATION should be directly related to UPKEEP? and UPKEEP$, and normally one would expect that INCOME will be directly related to both these variables. Both measures of socioeconomic status should be inversely related to DEFECTS?

Life-cycle stage also creates a variety of impacts on the model. One expects that the extent of housing-intensive preferences will follow a bell-shaped path over the life cycle. This means that, compared to childless homeowners, those in child-rearing stages will be more likely to choose a positive-upkeep option and will spend more on such having chosen it. Just the reverse will be true for the elderly, both because they more likely have excess amounts of housing capital remaining as a vestige of earlier child-rearing periods and because of their lesser concern about long-term investment considerations. In addition, there are probably differences in the perceived costs of upkeep that vary systematically over the life cycle. Compared to the young, middle-aged homeowners may have more experience with home repairs and thus be more efficient with time and out-of-pocket expenses involved in upkeep. This effect renders those in middle stages more likely to do upkeep than the young, but to spend less in doing so. Those in the last life-cycle stage may perceive higher costs of upkeep due to their own physical impairments and the concomitant need to hire professional contractors. Healthy retirees, on the other hand, may place a low implicit wage on their own labor, so the net effect is ambiguous regarding the ability of the elderly to transform maintenance inputs into housing capital. One would thus expect the preference effect noted above to dominate for those in STAGE5.

The net result of the above factors is that those in middle life-cycle stages (STAGE2, 3, 4) are more likely to engage in positive upkeep strategies and to have fewer home defects, but will spend more or less doing so, compared to those in early stages. The elderly (STAGE5) are less likely to make upkeep investments, are more likely to have exterior defects, and unless they often resort to professional labor for upkeep, they will likely make fewer expenditures.

Married homeowners likely have more housing-intensive preferences than single-male or multiple-head homeowners, and they may place more weight on longer-term investment considerations. There is no reason to believe *a priori* that this is also true for female homeowners. Female homeowners may, however, have less experience or skill in undertaking many home repairs, and thus may perceive relatively higher costs of such. One would predict on the basis of these arguments that, compared to single male or multiple-head homeowners, married homeowners (MARRIED) are more likely to have a positive upkeep strategy, to spend more accomplishing such, and to have homes with fewer defects; female homeowners (FEMALE) are less likely to have positive upkeep, more likely to have defects, but comparative expenditures for those doing upkeep are ambiguous.

There are few *a priori* reasons for expecting the race of the homeowner to affect housing upkeep. One possibility is that blacks may face greater constraints when attempting to borrow to make home improvements, because of lending-institution discrimination (see Schafer and Ladd 1980; and Black and Schweitzer 1980). If such were the case, it would decrease blacks' probability of positive upkeep (especially improvement) strategies and the optimal amount of expenditures once having chosen such. This, in turn, may result in the observation of greater frequencies of exterior defects in black-occupied homes. Although there is some evidence of interracial differences in the preferences for particular attributes of the housing package (Galster 1979), there is none to suggest that there are such for housing versus nonhousing consumption.

The number of occupants in the household likely affects both housing preferences and upkeep transformation functions in three distinct ways. First, household size should be directly related to intensity of housing preferences, and hence directly related to positive upkeep strategies, expenditures, and absence of defects. Second, larger households may have more (inexpensive) labor to call upon to accomplish upkeep activities and thus enhanced abilities for efficient upkeep. This would encourage positive upkeep and fewer defects, but has ambiguous consequences for expenditures. Finally, household size is probably directly related to greater wear and tear and structural depreciation (McGuire 1974). As explained earlier, greater depreciation is often associated with greater numbers of defects, but has an ambiguous relationship with choice of and expenditures on upkeep. The net effect of these three elements is that the coefficient signs of OCCUPANTS in any of the three equations are all ambiguous.

The final homeowner characteristic to be controlled for is a variable that has not previously entered the discussion. CONTRACT is a dummy variable taking the value one if the homeowner hired a professional contractor to perform any maintenance or improvement activities during the previous five years; zero otherwise. It is assumed here that, given a positive upkeep strategy, the use of a contractor would lead to greater expenditures on upkeep, though it should not affect numbers of defects.[11]

Independent Variables of Dwelling Characteristics

In discussing independent variables for the upkeep models in this and subsequent sections the theoretical propositions derived in chapter 3 and summarized in table 3.2 will be used to predict coefficient signs. Only heuristic summaries of these propositions are presented here; for the more rigorous analysis the reader is referred to chapter 3.

Two sets of characteristics of the sampled homeowner's dwelling are included in the model. The first set controls for different rates of structural depreciation: the vintage dummy variables (BUILT—) and the dummy denoting wood clapboard exterior construction (WOOD). The second set controls for different absolute levels of depreciation: the number of rooms (ROOMS) and the front footage of the lot (YARD). It is assumed that older and wooden structures have faster rates of depreciation[12] and thus, controlling for the initial amount of structural capital embodied in the dwelling, these structure types should have larger absolute declines in units of housing capital during a given period. Similarly, for a given rate of depreciation, larger dwellings have a larger absolute drop in housing capital during a given time period. As was explained in more detail in chapter 3, greater depreciation creates three distinct and offsetting effects in the model. First, greater depreciation means bigger lump-sum loss of structural capital, i.e., more things need repairing in the structure, and thus the homeowner needs to spend more on upkeep to restore an optimal mix of housing and nonhousing consumption. Second, in accomplishing such repairs there are fewer diminishing technical returns (and perhaps in the case of older dwellings enhanced opportunities to save utility costs), so the ability to transform upkeep inputs into increments of housing capital is enhanced. Third, faster depreciation means that any increments in dwelling capital invested by maintenance or improvement will erode faster in the future and therefore have a shorter utility-providing lifespan. The first effect tends to increase expenditures, the second tends to increase the probability of a positive upkeep strategy and the third tends to increase the probability that a zero-upkeep strategy is chosen and to decrease expenditures on positive upkeep strategies. But regardless of which of these effects predominates, the model predicts that upkeep investments (if any) will become progressively less able to completely offset the results of faster depreciation. Thus, dwellings experiencing higher depreciation should be observed to have a greater number of exterior defects.

Therefore, for both UPKEEP? and UPKEEP$ no unambiguous prediction can be made for the coefficient signs of WOOD, ROOMS, YARD, and BUILT-variables. But in the DEFECTS? equation all these variables' coefficients should have a positive sign.

Independent Variables of Neighborhood Characteristics

The physical-demographic dimension of neighborhood potentially affects upkeep behavior in two ways. If, as explained in chapter 3, the neighborhood and housing services interact multiplicatively in producing utility, homeowners in better-quality neighborhoods (as they perceive it) will be encouraged to undertake positive upkeep strategies and to expend more having chosen such, because every increment of structural capital they provide will enhance their consumption payoffs. Second, the extra asset value gained from a marginal amount of housing alterations is greater the higher the market's ultimate valuation of the neighborhood when the dwelling is sold. Assuming a direct correlation between the present state of the neighborhood and the market's eventual valuation, and assuming that the home-equity component of homeowners' utility functions is nonzero, one would predict a direct relationship between current neighborhood quality and upkeep. To conclude, the expected coefficient signs of all the previously defined variables measuring presumably positive attributes of the physical-demographic neighborhood (AREAQUAL, BLOCKQUAL, TRACT-QUAL, TENURE), should be positive in equations predicting UPKEEP? and UPKEEP$, and negative in the equation predicting DEFECTS? Just the opposite would be predicted for RACECOMPW, RACECOMPB, and NONRESID.

The social-interactive dimension of the neighborhood should, however, ultimately encourage the adoption of nonzero upkeep strategies, enhanced expenditures on such strategies, and a lower incidence of observed exterior defects (see chapter 3). The social-interactive dimension has the potential to create more housing-intensive preferences by providing positive psychological feedback when upkeep strategies are pursued and negative reinforcement when undermaintenance occurs. These positive and negative consumption reinforcements may affect individuals in the short run, and may affect their perceptions about longer-run investment payoffs as well. If homeowners have confidence that the future aggregate social-interactive mechanisms of their neighborhood will continue to encourage not only their own upkeep but that of *others* in the neighborhood, they will more likely perceive enhanced capital gains from housing investments, again assuming a non-trivial contribution of housing equity to utility.

These two dimensions of neighborhood are likely to be related to upkeep in the same general way, but the precise mechanism by which these effects may be accomplished differs, which supports distinct variable specifications. The impact of the physical-demographic neighborhood transpires through the individual. That is, it is only how individual homeowners assess the residential environment (both from their own and the market's perspective) that matters. By contrast, the social-interactive dimension of neighborhood operates through individual-collective interactions. In chapter 6, measures of the individual's neighborhood social interaction (IDENTIFY, INTEGRATE) and the aggregate degree of such evidenced by the neighborhood as a whole (NIDENTIFY, NINTEGRATE) were employed as separate, additive variables explaining the individual's neighborhood satisfaction. But clearly such a specification would be inappropriate here, for it would imply that there are no synergistic interactions. Put differently, an additive specification would suggest that: (1) highly social-interactive individuals perceive the same encouragement for home upkeep in weakly and highly cohesive neighborhoods alike; and (2) highly cohesive neighborhoods elicit the same upkeep behavior from all sorts of homeowners within it.

A much more reasonable *a priori* position is that individual and aggregate degrees of social interaction interact, but in a highly nonlinear, even discontinuous fashion. Individuals with low levels of social interaction and identification are not likely to be affected by social sanctions and solidarity sentiments even in neighborhoods where, on the whole, cohesion is high. Similarly, even individuals who interact frequently and identify closely with neighbors are unlikely to get much encouragement or discouragement in areas where none of the other neighbors share these communications and sentiments. In the former case the messages conveyed by the neighborhood may be strong but will fall on deaf ears; in the latter case the receiver may be tuned in when no clear message is forthcoming from the neighborhood. This suggests that either individual or aggregate measures of the social-interactive neighborhood will have a discernible effect upon upkeep behavior only after a threshold degree has been exceeded on both individual and aggregate measures.

This leads to the specification of the following three social-interactive variables for the upkeep models.[13] COHESION1 is defined as the product of IDENTIFY and NIDENTIFY, but only for observations when both components are above their respective mean values; zero otherwise. COHESION2 is defined as the product of INTEGRATE and NINTEGRATE, but only for observations when both components are above their mean values; zero otherwise. In other words, COHESION1 tests for the interactive effects of the individual's sense and the neighborhood's sense of solidarity, presuming that the effect on upkeep is nil if either component is below the threshold point (assumed to be the mean). COHESION2 tests for the interactive effects of the individual's degree of contact and familiarity with neighbors and the neighborhood's aggregate degree of such, also presuming that the effect is nil if either component is below the mean. The prediction for both variables is that they will be positively correlated with UPKEEP? and UPKEEP$, and negatively correlated with DEFECTS?.

Independent Variables of Public Policies

The direct effect of the Minneapolis public policies investigated herein on housing upkeep occurs through their impact on upkeep costs. (Their indirect effect through altered expectations and mobility plans was discussed in chapters 7 and 8). The receipt of a low-interest loan or an outright grant for structural replacements or improvements has the consequence of reducing the per-unit costs of maintenance or improvement inputs, thereby increasing the ability of the homeowner to transform such inputs into units of housing capital. More precisely, low-interest loans increase the relative probability that upgrading will be selected as an optimal strategy instead of positive or zero maintenance, thereby increasing total upkeep expenditures. Grants, depending on their specific purpose, could increase the probability of either maintenance or upgrading as the optimal strategy, but in either case would lead to increased housing expenditures and subsequently lower rates of exterior defects. A fuller theoretical exposition of the impact of such subsidies on upkeep behavior is undertaken in chapter 12.[14]

To measure these hypothesized effects, the variables GRANT$ and LOAN$ are defined as the average annual dollar value of the home improvement grants and/or low-interest loans, respectively, that the homeowner has received (if any) over the past five years (or however long the tenure in the unit if less than five years). Descriptive statistics of these variables show that 7.4 percent of sampled Minneapolis homeowners had received such grants, averaging $3,959; 9 percent received low-interest loans, averaging $13,409. It is predicted that GRANT$ and LOAN$ should be positively correlated with UPKEEP$ and negatively correlated with DEFECTS? Of course, these policy variables cannot be used in the UPKEEP? equation because they are not independent of the decision.[15]

Independent Variables of Neighborhood Expectations

The neighborhood-expectations variables modeled in chapter 7 enter the housing upkeep model because they proxy for the homeowner's perceptions of: (1) future parameter values that may affect the future marginal utility from consumable housing services that are produced by present alterations in the dwelling/neighborhood package (NEIGHEXP), and (2) future market evaluations of the capital value of the housing stock (VALUEEXP). The ability of NEIGHEXP to affect current upkeep behavior will depend on the influence of neighborhood conditions on the marginal consumption value of alterations. The ability of VALUEEXP to affect current upkeep behavior will depend on influence of long-term expected home equity value on the marginal value of alterations. In the general case where homeowners have positive weights on both elements, one would predict a negative correlation between pessimism (i.e., higher NEIGHEXP, VALUEEXP values) and upkeep activity.

The first potential exception to this predicted general pattern stems from strategic interactions among homeowners, as analyzed in chapter 3. Homeowners in initially low-quality neighborhoods are more likely to adopt a free-rider stance, regardless of the relative weights they give to consumption and wealth components of upkeep, because they are more likely to have originally pursued a zero-maintenance corner-solution strategy. This free-rider stance means that they likely will continue to pursue a zero-maintenance strategy even with sizable variations in their expectations, thus voiding any relationship between NEIGHEXP or VALUEEXP and the dependent variables for upkeep behavior. To test for this, two new variables, NEIGHX(LOW) and VALUEX(LOW), are defined that take the values of NEIGHEXP and VALUEEXP, respectively, but only in neighborhoods of low quality; zero otherwise. Low-quality neighborhoods are operationally defined as those having mean neighborhood property values less than one standard deviation below the sample mean. This means that neighborhoods in Wooster were made up of planning areas with average values below $20,200; in Minneapolis of block faces with average values below $39,100. Given this specification, the signs of NEIGHX(LOW) and VALUEX(LOW) are predicted to be positive and approximately equal in magnitude to those of NEIGHEXP and VALUEEXP, respectively, if the effect of the corner solution and free rider were dominant. Because the net coefficient for homeowners in low-quality neighborhoods is the sum of the respective two coefficients, the ultimate result for them is the predicted zero relationship.

There is a second complicating factor that applies to the prediction concerning VALUEEXP, however. This arises from the varying marginal utility of increments to the home equity value as such equity's relationship to the threshold-equity changes (see chapter 3). So long as the current perception of achieved equity remains well below the threshold, marginal utility via equity enhancement is gained from upkeep, and the relationship between VALUEEXP and upkeep is inverse (i.e., crowd-follower behavior). But if the threshold is consistently exceeded, the equity component of marginal utility is voided, and any alterations in expectations about property values yield no relationship with upkeep behavior (i.e., symmetric free-rider behavior). Finally, if revisions in value expectations alter the perceived relationship of achieved equity and threshold equity, a direct relationship between VALUEEXP and upkeep is predicted. That is, if as values unexpectedly inflate one perceives that the threshold equity can now easily be surpassed without further investments, an erstwhile upkeep strategy may be abandoned (i.e., asymmetric free-rider). Conversely, previous complacency about achieving the threshold may be reversed with newly pessimistic expectations, subsequently yielding more vigorous upkeep efforts (i.e., trend-bucker).

In sum, the foregoing suggests that the relationship between upkeep and property-value expectations cannot be predicted without more information about homeowners' earlier expectations and their threshold equity levels. Although such information is not available from the data set, a crude proxy may be the aforementioned VALUEX(LOW) variable. It is reasonable to posit that those buying originally in lower-quality neighborhoods hold more modest aspirations and expectations about long-term property appreciation rates, and that their threshold-equity levels are only slightly higher than their initial home equity at time of purchase. Homeowners in low-quality areas may be happy to get their initial money out and avoid a capital loss. Thus the relationship between threshold equity and perceived achieved equity is extremely sensitive to changing expectations, and there is a direct relationship between VALUEX(LOW) and measures of upkeep. Unlike the analysis above of the corner-solution effect in low-quality areas, however, the foregoing suggests that the coefficient of VALUEX(LOW) will be much larger in magnitude (as well as opposite in sign) than that of VALUEEXP, thereby producing a net direct relationship.

Independent Variables of Mobility Plans

The homeowner's mobility plans that were the focus of chapter 8 are employed here as explanatory variables for upkeep behavior. As shown in chapter 3, one would predict that in preference functions in which consumption considerations dominate investment considerations, expected length of tenure is directly related to upkeep activity until all present investments were completely depreciated. The exception is the homeowner who plans to reside in a dwelling permanently. Regardless of the actual length of expenditure, those who do not expect to be alive at the time of home sale likely place little value on investment considerations, and therefore have less upkeep activity than those with the same expected tenure but expectations of subsequent years of life. The predicted result: the relationship between expected tenure and upkeep effort is bell-shaped. What all this means is that (compared to STAY10+, the excluded reference category), the signs of STAY0–2, STAY3–10, and STAYPERM are negative in the UPKEEP? and UPKEEP$ equations, and positive in the DEFECTS? equation.

Summary Specifications of Housing Upkeep Models

The preceding discussion of the three components of the empirical upkeep models to be estimated is summarized in symbolic terms below (see glossary or text for symbol definitions).

$$P(\text{UPKEEP?}) = C \pm? \text{ WOOD } \pm? \text{ BUILT(—) } \pm? \text{ ROOMS } \pm? \text{ YARD} \quad (9.1)$$
$$+ \text{ EDUCATION } \pm? \text{ INCOME } + \text{ STAGE(2, 3, 4) } -$$
$$\text{STAGE5 } + \text{ MARRIED } - \text{ FEMALE } - \text{ BLACK } \pm?$$
$$\text{OCCUPANTS } - \text{ STAY0–2 } - \text{ STAY3–10 } - \text{ STAYPERM}$$
$$+ \text{ (AREA- BLOCK- TRACT-)QUAL } + \text{ TENURE } -$$
$$\text{NONRESID } + \text{ RACECOMPW } + \text{ RACECOMPB } +$$
$$\text{COHESION(1, 2) } - \text{ VALUEEXP } - \text{ NEIGHEXP } +$$
$$\text{VALUEX(LOW) } + \text{ NEIGHX(LOW) } + e$$

UPKEEP$
(given
$P(\text{UPKEEP?})$
= 1)
$$= C \pm? \text{ WOOD } \pm? \text{ BUILT(—) } \pm? \text{ ROOMS } \pm? \quad (9.2)$$
$$\text{YARD } + \text{ EDUCATION } + \text{ INCOME } \pm? \text{ STAGE(2, 3,}$$
$$\text{4) } -\text{STAGE5 } + \text{ MARRIED } \pm? \text{ FEMALE } - \text{ BLACK}$$
$$\pm? \text{ OCCUPANTS } + \text{ CONTRACT } - \text{ STAY(0–2,}$$
$$\text{3–10, PERM) } + \text{ (AREA- BLOCK- TRACT-)QUAL}$$

$$+ \text{TENURE} - \text{NONRESID} + \text{RACECOMPW}$$
$$+ \text{RACECOMPB} + \text{COHESION}(1, 2) - \text{VALUEEXP}$$
$$- \text{NEIGHEXP} + \text{VALUEX(LOW)} + \text{NEIGHX(LOW)}$$
$$+ \text{GRANT\$} + \text{LOAN\$} + e$$

$$P(\text{DEFECTS?}) = C + \text{WOOD} + \text{BUILT}(\text{---}) + \text{ROOMS} + \text{YARD} - \quad (9.3)$$
$$\text{EDUCATION} - \text{INCOME} - \text{STAGE}(2, 3, 4) +$$
$$\text{STAGE5} - \text{MARRIED} + \text{FEMALE} + \text{BLACK} \pm ?$$
$$\text{OCCUPANTS} + \text{STAY}(0-2, 3-10, \text{PERM}) - (\text{AREA-}$$
$$\text{BLOCK- TRACT-})\text{QUAL} - \text{TENURE} + \text{NONRESID} -$$
$$\text{RACECOMPW} - \text{RACECOMPB} - \text{COHESION}(1, 2) +$$
$$\text{VALUEEXP} + \text{NEIGHEXP} - \text{VALUEX(LOW)} -$$
$$\text{NEIGHX(LOW)} - \text{GRANT\$} - \text{LOAN\$} + e$$

where signs indicate predicted signs of the (implicit) coefficients, C is a constant term to be estimated, and equations 9.1 and 9.3 are to be estimated using two alternative specifications of probability models, as explained below.

Empirical Results for the Housing Upkeep Models

In this section the various parameter estimates for the upkeep models specified in equations (9.1), (9.2), and (9.3) are discussed. These results are presented in tables 9.2 and 9.3. The model components dealing with choice of positive upkeep strategy or zero upkeep strategy (UPKEEP?), and with likelihood of evidencing exterior home deterioration (DEFECTS?) may be framed in two alternative probabilistic terms, as has been done in previous chapters.[16] Here, two dummy dependent variables are first modeled as a linear function of the variables, and parameters are estimated using OLS regression techniques. Second, they are specified in terms of the cumulative logistic probability function wherein the dependent variable is simply the natural logarithm of the odds that a particular choice has been made. The parameters of this LOGIT specification are estimated using maximum-likelihood nonlinear estimating techniques.[17] As in prior chapters the models are compared as a check on potential specification bias.

In the case of the probability models, only those parameter estimates that prove statistically significant in both linear and LOGIT estimations are stressed. This leads to more confidence that the main conclusions are not based on statistical artifact. This section discusses patterns of statistical significance and qualitative results. Discussion of specific quantitative implications of parameters is conducted in the following section, and both direct and indirect relationships are brought to bear.

Table 9.2   Coefficients of Home Upkeep Activity Models

	P(UPKEEP?)					
	Linear model		LOGIT model		UPKEEP$	
	Wooster	Minneapolis	Wooster	Minneapolis	Wooster	Minneapolis
Homeowner Characteristics						
STAGE2	−.048	.021	.025	.749	−22.1	652.8
	(.612)	(.678)	(.035)	(.661)	(.108)	(1.33)*
STAGE3	−.100	.034	−.777	11.0	−181.4	152.7
	(1.31)*	(1.05)	(1.20)	(.005)	(.902)	(.295)
STAGE4	−.083	.039	−.744	13.1	−490.9	−203.3
	(1.09)	(1.09)	(1.16)	(.006)	(2.45)[b]*	(.351)
STAGE5	−.117	.019	−.903	.967	−266.9	−712.1
	(1.71)[b]	(.717)	(1.53)[b]	(1.10)	(1.48)[c]	(1.65)[b]
EDUCATION	.001	.001	.065	.002	1.27	58.3
	(1.90)[b]	(.385)	(1.913)[b]	(.018)	(.095)	(1.30)[c]
INCOME	−9.4E−6	−3.7E−8	−.08E−4	−.79E−5	.012	.024
	(.668)	(.081)	(.896)	(.328)	(3.21)[a]	(3.23)[a]
MARRIED	.097	.001	.422	−.096	−19.0	674.9
	(1.56)[c]	(.358)	(1.28)[c]	(.144)	(.110)	(1.91)[b]
FEMALE	.077	−.010	.311	−.400)	165.5	301.0
	(1.21)	(.361)	(.936)	(.504)	(.943)	(.661)
BLACK	.002	.010	9.03	6.54	−38.2	452.6
	(.006)	(.147)	(.000)	(.001)	(.036)	(.411)
OCCUPANTS	.010	.001	.046	−.019	16.0	−283.0
	(.647)	(.152)	(.377)	(.084)	(.394)	(2.54)[b]*
Dwelling Characteristics						
WOOD	−.023	−.002	−.186	−.249	−98.4	305.0
	(.816)	(.117)	(.961)	(.466)	(1.30)*	(1.17)
BUILTPRE-20	.130	−.034	.800	−12.6	438.4	324.7
	(1.71)[c]*	(.877)	(1.83)[c]*	(.004)	(2.06)[b]*	(.521)
BUILT20–39	.159	−.006	1.01	−11.6	677.9	277.7
	(2.35)[b]*	(.161)	(2.47)[b]*	(.004)	(3.60)[a]*	(.441)
BUILT40–59	.150	−.025	.880	−12.3	298.7	75.3
	(2.37)[b]*	(.621)	(2.53)[b]*	(.005)	(1.67)[c]*	(.116)
BUILT60–69	.148	−.004	.813	−4.13	161.3	95.0
	(2.26)[b]*	(.063)	(2.15)[b]*	(.001)	(.881)	(.095)
ROOMS	.013	−.001	.116	.043	30.4	142.6
	(1.16)	(.242)	(1.37)*	(.256)	(1.02)	(1.77)[c]*
YARD	3.3E−4	−3.8E−4	.003	−.017	1.58	5.0
	(.887)	(.700)	(1.02)	(1.38)*	(1.65)[c]*	(.570)

(*continued*)

Table 9.2 (*Continued*)

| | P(UPKEEP?) | | | | | |
| | Linear model | | LOGIT model | | UPKEEP$ | |
	Wooster	Minneapolis	Wooster	Minneapolis	Wooster	Minneapolis
Mobility Plans						
STAY0–2	−.035	.020	−.778	1.67	−66.0	−328.5
	(.448)	(.503)	(.920)	(.000)	(.330)	(.506)
STAY3–10	−.072	−.004	−1.11	−7.66	−63.6	346.0
	(1.20)	(.114)	(1.65)[b]	(.000)	(.414)	(.625)
STAYPERM	−.045	.001	−.921	−7.56	−110.4	111.8
	(.725)	(.006)	(1.35)[c]	(.000)	(.684)	(.195)
Expectations						
VALUEEXP	.014	−.010	.058	−.415	61.9	−32.5
	(.458)	(1.01)	(.290)	(1.27)	(.752)	(.204)
VALUEX(LOW)	−.016	−.008	−.094	−1.89	−61.4	−500.0
	(.344)	(.229)	(.300)	(1.07)	(.471)	(.902)
NEIGHEXP	.033	.024	.266	.714	109.1	−553.6
	(.757)	(1.47)*	(.949)	(1.28)*	(.935)	(2.03)[b]
NEIGHX(LOW)	.004	−.018	−.030	1.52	−4.49	329.4
	(.093)	(.353)	(.108)	(.623)	(.040)	(.407)
Neighborhood Characteristics						
AREAQUAL	−.005	NA	−.038	NA	14.8	NA
	(.135)		(.170)		(.146)	
BLOCKQUAL	NA	.011	NA	1.27	NA	−123.0
		(.843)		(1.13)		(.597)
TRACTQUAL	NA	−.008	NA	−.687	NA	−232.0
		(1.02)		(1.20)		(1.71)[c]*
NONRESID	.100	.047	10.25	13.9	94.8	125.8
	(1.15)	(.916)	(.002)	(.002)	(.426)	(1.53)
TENURE	.025	.009	.147	.334	−12.6	−210.7
	(1.30)[c]	(.859)	(1.20)	(.950)	(.242)	(1.27)
RACECOMPW	.009	7.5E−5	.044	−.072	53.1	−27.6
	(.556)	(.037)	(.395)	(.981)	(1.21)	(.826)
RACECOMPB	.045	3.0E−4	.342	.074	−12.1	−81.2
	(.277)	(.078)	(.000)	(.001)	(.029)	(1.32)*
COHESION1	−1.7E−3	−7.0E−4	−.015	−.088	10.0	31.5
	(.948)	(.514)	(1.17)	(1.42)*	(2.05)[b]	(1.43)[c]
COHESION2	1.2E−3	1.9E−3	.006	.119	.90	−7.1
	(.403)	(1.05)	(.318)	(1.15)	(.109)	(.243)
Policy Characteristics						
GRANT$	NA	NA	NA	NA	NA	2.62
						(8.21)[a]

Table 9.2 (*Continued*)

	P(UPKEEP?)				UPKEEP$	
	Linear model		LOGIT model			
	Wooster	Minneapolis	Wooster	Minneapolis	Wooster	Minneapolis
LOAN$	NA	NA	NA	NA	NA	.345 (4.32)[a]
Other Adjustments						
CONTRACT	NA	NA	NA	NA	NA	687.7 (2.69)[a]
Constant	.423 (2.02)[b*]	.938 (10.9)[a*]	4.06 (2.73)[a*]	26.9 (.006)	−393.1 (.688)	1560. (1.11)
R^2	.080	.050	—	—	.158	.454
F	1.276	.654	—	—	2.48	9.6

Note: asymptotic t-statistics for LOGIT model are shown in parentheses; t-statistics for others
a, b, c = coefficient statistically significant at 1%, 5%, 10% levels, respectively (one-tailed test unless *)
* = two-tailed test if no predicted coefficient sign or opposite predicted sign
NA = not applicable; variable not used in given model

Overall the equations explaining the choice of positive versus zero upkeep strategies performed least satisfactorily. In particular, there were too few observations of the latter strategy in Minneapolis to yield any highly significant coefficient estimates. Thus, the discussion focuses on those components of the model emphasizing intensity of upkeep in terms of annual expenditures, and the ultimate effectiveness of that upkeep in terms of eliminating exterior dwelling defects. Results for these components strongly attest to the importance of the social-interactive (and to a lesser degree, the physical and demographic) dimensions of the neighborhood, expectations, mobility plans, and the conventional characteristics of the dwelling and homeowner as separable influences upon housing upkeep behavior.

Homeowner Characteristics

The estimated parameters of homeowner characteristics correspond closely to *a priori* predictions, although there are several inconsistencies between the two samples. The only life-cycle stage variable to show any consistent statistical significance is STAGE5.[18] Wooster's STAGE5 homeowners are less likely to engage in a positive upkeep strategy, compared to STAGE1 homeowners. In Wooster and Minneapolis STAGE5 homeowners spend less than their STAGE1 counterparts after they have chosen a positive

Table 9.3   Coefficients of Home Exterior Defects Models

P(DEFECTS?)

	Linear model		LOGIT model	
	Wooster	Minneapolis	Wooster	Minneapolis
Homeowner Characteristics				
STAGE2	.044	−.060	.121	−.267
	(.788)	(.814)	(.178)	(.794)
STAGE3	.001	−.095	−.166	−.318
	(.021)	(1.23)	(.237)	(.905)
STAGE4	−.010	−.056	−.386	−.249
	(.193)	(.652)	(.513)	(.607)
STAGE5	−.014	−.066	−.505	−.366
	(.292)	(1.04)	(.760)	(1.22)
EDUCATION	−.005	.001	−.060	.027
	(1.35)^c	(.154)	(1.09)	(.794)
INCOME	−6.7E−7	2.1E−6	−.04E−3	.01E−3
	(.671)	(1.92)^{c*}	(1.26)^c	(1.83)^{c*}
MARRIED	−.059	−.110	−.423	−.427
	(1.33)^c	(2.10)^b	(.933)	(1.89)^b
FEMALE	−.025	−.105	−.141	−.459
	(.561)	(1.56)*	(.302)	(1.40)*
BLACK	.001	.163	−7.59	.980
	(.033)	(.979)	(.000)	(1.42)^c
OCCUPANTS	−.001	.055	.026	.226
	(.013)	(3.27)^{a*}	(.197)	(2.91)^{a*}
Dwelling Characteristics				
WOOD	.039	.117	.518	.480
	(1.91)^b	(3.03)^a	(1.59)^c	(2.57)^a
BUILTPRE-20	.033	.225	9.49	1.18
	(.610)	(2.40)^a	(.002)	(2.47)^a
BUILT20–30	.029	.286	9.47	1.48
	(.609)	(3.00)^a	(.002)	(3.00)^a
BUILT40–59	−.020	.175	8.72	.863
	(.447)	(1.79)^b	(.002)	(1.65)^b
BUILT60–69	−.012	.140	−.301	−9.02
	(.257)	(.929)	(.000)	(.001)
ROOMS	.001	−.027	.036	−.176
	(.699)	(2.26)^{b*}	(.335)	(2.66)^{b*}
YARD	1.6E−3	1.2E−3	.004	.008
	(.611)	(.942)	(.919)	(1.27)

Table 9.3   (*Continued*)

	Linear model		LOGIT model	
	Wooster	Minneapolis	Wooster	Minneapolis
Mobility Plans				
STAY0–2	.026	.194	.061	.899
	(.476)	(1.98)[b]	(.079)	(1.83)[b]
STAY3–10	.001	.139	.106	.795
	(.136)	(1.66)[b]	(.170)	(1.79)[b]
STAYPERM	.001	.158	.069	.974
	(.131)	(1.83)[b]	(.105)	(2.10)[b]
Expectations				
VALUEEXP	.010	−.018	.189	−.062
	(.464)	(.750)	(.572)	(.514)
VALUEX(LOW)	−.109	−.162	−.831	−.134
	(3.21)[a]	(1.94)[b]	(1.82)[b]	(1.51)[c]
NEIGHEXP	.028	.055	.288	.329
	(.895)	(1.38)[c]	(.576)	(1.73)[b]
NEIGHX(LOW)	.113	.245	.645	1.65
	(3.90)[a]*	(2.01)[b]*	(1.80)[c]*	(1.54)*
Neighborhood Characteristics				
AREAQUAL	−.003	NA	−.040	NA
	(.136)		(.893)	
BLOCKQUAL	NA	−.071	NA	−.577
		(2.30)[b]		(2.33)[a]
TRACTQUAL	NA	−.031	NA	−.115
		(1.55)[c]		(1.21)
NONRESID	−.081	.053	−9.77	.501
	(1.31)*	(.425)	(.002)	(.954)
TENURE	.006	−.010	.145	−.009
	(.442)	(.423)	(.670)	(.079)
RACECOMPW	.001	−.002	.084	−.017
	(.514)	(.433)	(.574)	(.686)
RACECOMPB	−.026	−.008	−.859	−.041
	(.221)	(.824)	(.000)	(1.05)
COHESION1	−1.6E−3	−6.1E−3	−.018	−.037
	(.859)	(1.84)[b]	(.632)	(1.88)[b]
COHESION2	.001	−.001	.006	−.003
	(.282)	(.027)	(.195)	(.107)

P(DEFECTS?)

(*continued*)

Table 9.3   (*Continued*)

P(DEFECTS?)

	Linear model		LOGIT model	
	Wooster	Minneapolis	Wooster	Minneapolis
Policy				
Characteristics				
GRANT$	NA	2.2E−5	NA	1.3E−4
		(.427)		(.654)
LOAN$	NA	1.9E−5	NA	7.0E−5
		(1.40)*		(1.27)
Constant	−3.8E−4	.045	−6.21	3.08
	(.003)	(.208)	(.001)	(2.64)^{a*}
R^2	.134	.222	—	—
F	2.27	3.35	—	—

Note: asymptotic t-statistics for LOGIT model are shown in parentheses; t-statistics for others
a, b, c = coefficient statistically significant at 1%, 5%, 10% levels, respectively (one-tailed
test unless *)
* = two-tailed test if no predicted coefficient sign or opposite predicted sign
NA = not applicable; variable not used in given model

upkeep strategy. In spite of this, however, the dwellings of STAGE5 homeowners do not have greater numbers of exterior structural defects.
Wooster's STAGE4 homeowners also spend comparatively less on upkeep,
but this may be explained by the households' availability of inexpensive
teenage labor and the relatively greater home-upkeep experience of the
adults present.

Socioeconomic status variables also prove important, and generally support findings of earlier studies. In Wooster, education is associated with a
higher probability of positive upkeep, and a lower probability of home
defects. In Minneapolis, education is associated with more annual expenditure by those adopting a positive upkeep strategy. In both samples
income is strongly associated with upkeep expenditures, but in neither
case with incidence of exterior defects.[19]

Marital status also appears to be related strongly to upkeep behavior.
Compared to households headed by single males or multiple heads, those
headed by married Wooster homeowners are more likely to adopt a
positive upkeep strategy, and those married Minneapolis homeowners
who adopt a positive upkeep strategy spend more annually on such. In
both samples the dwellings of these married homeowners have comparatively fewer incidences of exterior defects. The above qualitative pat-

tern is also true for female-headed households, but both coefficient magnitudes and levels of statistical significance are lower.

Unlike some earlier studies' findings, the current data offer virtually no support for the hypothesis that black homeowners have different home upkeep behavior than whites, *ceteris paribus*. In all components of the upkeep model and in all estimating techniques the coefficient of BLACK has low statistical significance.

The size of the household has a strong relationship to both upkeep expenditure and defects incidence in Minneapolis. In this sample the number of occupants is associated with less annual upkeep expenditure and, as a result, with a greater probability of having exterior defects. Such suggests that, in the Minneapolis sample at least: (1) the presumed intensified housing preferences of larger households is offset by accelerated wear and tear, and (2) the abundance of cheap household labor reduces expenditures on upkeep but is insufficiently applied to counteract the greater deterioration completely.

Finally, if a positive upkeep strategy is pursued in Minneapolis with the aid of contract labor, there are significantly higher outlays: $776 on average annually. The unavailability of this datum in the Wooster sample is partly responsible for the substantially lower R^2 in its UPKEEP$ equation as compared to that in Minneapolis.

Dwelling Characteristics

The results provide strong support for the theoretical proposition developed in chapter 3 that structural features of the dwelling contribute independently to upkeep behavior by shaping technical possibilities for transforming upkeep inputs into units of housing capital. In the Wooster sample, the age of the dwelling is strongly positively correlated with both choice of upkeep strategy and amount expended. Compared to homeowners in post-1970 homes, those living in homes built earlier are significantly more likely to have adopted a positive upkeep strategy, and having chosen such to spend more per year. The cross-vintage magnitude of the results indicates a curvilinear pattern of upkeep activity: steadily greater intensity of upkeep expenditures through successively older vintages until 1920, and somewhat reduced intensity subsequently (see also Stewart and Hyclak 1986). In the context of the theory in chapter 3, this can be understood as variation in the relative dominance of the three countervailing factors associated with depreciation. In moderately aged homes, more units of capital are eroding and need compensatory investments, but there is little corresponding sense that depreciation is so advanced that long-term future flows of housing services or capital value are threatened. For pre-1920 vintages, homeowners apparently begin to worry about the structure exhausting its useful lifetime and/or predict accelerating rates of future depreciation, whereupon both frequency and degree of upkeep is discouraged. It is also interesting to note, however, that both the enhanced frequency of upkeep and the amount expended on it in Wooster are sufficient to offset the visible signs of structural deterioration, as evidenced by the insignificance of vintage variables in the DEFECTS? equations.[20]

For the Minneapolis sample a different pattern of relationships emerges for the structure-vintage variables that, though not conforming to results of previous studies, is easily understandable in light of the theory. The vintage variables are not statistically significant correlates of either upkeep propensities or expenditures, and as a result they are significantly positively correlated with the incidence of structural defects. There are at least three reasons for these distinct differences in the relationships between structure age and upkeep behavior in Wooster and Minneapolis. First, due to climatic differences and/or unmeasured differences in architecture and construction materials, Minneapolis dwellings may have less favorable maintenance transformation possibilities. The latter possibility is indicated because: (1) sampled Minneapolis dwellings were less than half as likely to be of wood clapboard construction than those in the Wooster sample, and (2) nonclapboard homes were typically of stucco in Minneapolis, but of brick in Wooster. Second, there may be systematic differences in how homeowners in the two samples relate vintage to future useful lifetime of the dwelling. The results in Minneapolis are consistent with the hypothesis that sampled homeowners there have lost confidence in the duration of useful flows of housing services and/or capital value from older homes. Such an implied reduction in future utility from current upkeep investments leads to a domination of the substitution effect of depreciation as described in chapter 3. Third, for many years the property tax laws in Minneapolis were written and administered so as to favor older structures. But in January 1979 a tax-court case ruled that all dwellings be assessed at full market value. In order to keep effective property taxes from escalating, the city reduced the millage rates, but not enough to keep homeowners of older dwellings from bearing dramatically increased property tax bills in the year prior to the present survey. It is thus conceivable that these homeowners were especially reluctant to make sizable upkeep investments, especially in exterior repairs, out of fear of still further increments in a suddenly more burdensome property tax levy. Such a temporary reaction to an atypical event would tend to offset the normal age–upkeep effort relationship (evidenced in Wooster).

The other three variables measuring dwelling characteristics have less frequent statistical significance. Wood clapboard houses are associated with a higher incidence of exterior defects, as would be expected because of their greater rate of deterioration. Such dwellings do not, however, elicit larger frequencies or amounts of upkeep activities. The measure of yard frontage in both samples is associated with slightly more upkeep expenditure but also with somewhat higher incidences of defects, although these results all have very modest degrees of statistical significance. Finally, the number of rooms is directly related to frequency and amount of upkeep expenditure in both samples but, again, with modest statistical significance. The only result contrary to expectation is the statistically significant inverse relationship between ROOMS and DEFECTS? in Minneapolis. There may be some idiosyncratic, unmeasured aspects of the larger dwellings in the Minneapolis stock that produce their superior observed condition; e.g., if such homes were relatively scarce and thus commanded exceptionally high resale potential. Unfortunately, none of these results for ROOMS go far to clarify the contradictory findings of previous studies in this regard (see table 9.1).

Neighborhood Characteristics

A primary thesis of this study is that multiple physical, demographic, and social dimensions of the neighborhood have important impacts upon homeowners' housing upkeep behavior, and that previous theoretical and empirical work that overlooks these dimensions is therefore seriously misspecified. The empirical results for neighborhood-quality variables and social-cohesion variables support this thesis. The measures of the socioeconomic status and physical quality of the neighborhood (AREAQUAL in Wooster and BLOCKQUAL and TRACTQUAL in Minneapolis) are all inversely related to the incidence of exterior defects, although the first is not significantly so. However, none of these variables are significant correlates of the incidence of upkeep. This suggests that in better-quality neighborhoods homeowners are more likely to choose upkeep strategies that concentrate on repairing exterior structural defects, though overall, they engage in upkeep activities no more frequently. This finding is consistent with two entirely plausible, non–mutually exclusive hypotheses about homeowners' preference functions: (1) neighborhood conditions affect the marginal utility of housing alterations involving only exterior aspects of the dwelling, (2) current neighborhood conditions shape homeowners' estimates of how the market will value their homes at time of sale (and this asset value is of importance to them). Given that upkeep expenditure is not significantly enhanced by neighborhood, however, the magnitude of these hypothesized interactions must be relatively modest.

Interestingly, in Minneapolis TRACTQUAL proves inversely related to both the incidence and magnitude of upkeep, albeit at modest levels of statistical significance. Because the quality of the block face is being controlled for, higher qualities of census tracts mean an increased likelihood that a given dwelling will be located in a block that is below the average tract quality. Apparently in such situations homeowners engage in upkeep less intensively, perhaps because the qualitative evaluation (from their personal and/or the market's perspective) of the immediate neighborhood (block face) is made not on an absolute scale but relative to the larger area (tract). The validity of this relativistic view of how homeowners evaluate neighborhood quality is reinforced by recalling that the BLOCKQUAL and TRACTQUAL variables load heavily on socioeconomic status attributes, which inherently involve relative, not absolute, comparisons. This result is consistent with the hypothesis that the relative quality or status of the block face influences: the marginal utility of housing services, and/or the homeowner's perception of how the market will value the home at time of sale (and such resale value influences utility). However, because coefficients for BLOCKQUAL and TRACTQUAL are not highly statistically significant in the UPKEEP? and UPKEEP$ equations, conclusions must be tentative.

Other measures of the physical-demographic dimension of neighborhood show only low levels of statistical significance, perhaps because most are not preponderantly measures of block-face conditions. The presence of nonresidential land use (NONRESID) is such a block-face measure, but it never proves statistically significant, which indicates that it may have less to do with neighborhood upkeep levels than is conventionally believed (see, e.g., Downs 1981, 19). As was the case with the black homeowner dummy variable, the overall racial composition of the neighborhood (RACECOMPB, W) provides no explanatory power for either black or white homeowners, which contradicts conventional wisdom (see, e.g., Peterson et al. 1973, 67). This finding supports the contention of Taub, Taylor, and Dunham (1984) that it is not race *per se* that affects housing investment, but rather factors that are associated with integration in the minds of some owners. But once again, given the special racial dimensions of both sampled housing markets, firm conclusions about such racial effects cannot be drawn.

Perhaps most dramatic are the results for the interactive effects of individual and aggregate levels of social identification, which attest to the importance of this heretofore unanalyzed dimension of the neighborhood. In both samples the interaction between individual and aggregate degrees of group identification (COHESION1) significantly augments the expenditures on upkeep for those choosing such a strategy. There is also a reduced incidence of exterior defects associated with COHESION1. Apparently it is the aspect of solidarity sentiments embodied in COHESION1 that carries the burden of the social-interaction theory propounded in chapters 2 and 3, because the degree of familiarity and contact with neighbors (COHESION2) never proves statistically significant in any models.

Public Policies

As predicted, there is a strong positive correlation between the amount of low-interest loans and/or grants received for home improvements and the expenditures on such in Minneapolis.[21] These are, obviously, important results, and will be analyzed much more extensively in chapter 12.

Neighborhood Expectations

The general pattern across all Minneapolis neighborhoods is that pessimistic expectations about qualitative changes in neighborhood conditions (NEIGHEXP) are associated with less expenditure and a greater incidence of exterior defects.[22] Even more dramatic is the powerful result for NEIGHX(LOW): in lower-valued neighborhoods in both samples, more pessimism is associated with a much larger incidence of exterior defects. This is opposite to the prediction forthcoming if one surmised that a threshold effect (i.e., behavior of a free-rider) ensuing from an initial corner solution would be more likely in such areas. Instead, the findings suggest that it is in such lower-valued neighborhoods where expectations about future neighborhood quality affect the marginal utility from housing investments most potently. And the behavior indicated is that of the crowd-follower: pessimism about the aggregate conditions leads to increased incidence of defects in the individual's dwelling, and vice versa for optimism.

The results for the property-value expectation variables are similarly revealing about the geography of homeowner strategic behavior. Outside of lower-valued areas the VALUEEXP variable provides no explanation of upkeep behavior. Apparently homeowners in higher-valued neighborhoods remain confident that their home equity threshold is or will be exceeded, in spite of alterations in their outlook about neighborhood property values over the next five years. Therefore, they perceive comparatively less extra utility from prospective capital gains produced by added home investments. Thus there is little sense in radically revising their optimal upkeep strategy in light of new expectations about how changing property values could render such capital gains slightly higher or lower. The observed insignificance of VALUEEXP follows. But once again in lower-valued neighborhoods, a consistent, statistically significant pattern emerges in both samples. Greater pessimism about future neighborhood property values (holding expectations about neighborhood quality constant) is associated with a reduced incidence of exterior home defects. Note that the net coefficient for such areas (i.e., that of VALUEEXP plus that of VALUEX(LOW)) is negative, again suggesting that corner-solution free-riders are not as prevalent. On the contrary, the relationship clearly supports the asymmetric free-rider and trend-bucker behaviors described in chapter 3. The optimists in lower-valued areas apparently feel that they can attain their home equity thresholds with reduced investments in exterior maintenance, because of general housing inflation. The pessimists apparently grow increasingly concerned about not meeting their thresholds, so they intensify their exterior upkeep efforts in an attempt to salvage some home equity.

Mobility Plans

The predicted signs of coefficients for homeowners' mobility plans are almost universally confirmed by the results, although the general levels of statistical significance are quite low. The only results in which any confidence may be placed occur in the DEFECTS? equation for the Minneapolis sample. Here those with short-term, middle-run, and permanent mobility plans are equally much more likely to evidence home defects than those planning to remain more than ten years (but a finite period). These results suggest that those with long-term plans are least likely to let their properties visibly run down and thereby plant the seeds for neighborhood decline. They also suggest that both consumption and asset dimensions of home upkeep are important to most homeowners, at least to some degree. If only consumption benefits contribute to utility, there is no reason for an upkeep differential between those with long-term and those with permanent mobility plans. But if the latter group places less weight on the ultimate asset value of the home, the observed differential will result.[23]

Direct and Indirect Determinants of Housing Upkeep

The previous section contained a qualitative discussion of statistically significant variables as they affect housing upkeep behavior directly. But many variables also have indirect effects on such behavior through their presumed influence on intervening variables in the complete model: dwelling and neighborhood satisfaction, expectations, and mobility plans. (See figure 2.1 for a review of the overall conceptual model.) The combination of these direct and indirect relationships allows the estimation of the full magnitude of the relationship between a given explanatory variable and upkeep behavior. It is this quantitative dimension that will be stressed here.

The indirect relationships with upkeep are ascertained by examining the relationship of a given variable with one (or more) intervening variable(s), and these variables' subsequent relationships with upkeep. Note that in order to have an indirect relationship with upkeep in the present specification a variable must somehow be related to either expectations, and/or mobility plans, because these are the only intervening variables that appear as explanatory variables in equations (9.1), (9.2), and (9.3). As in the previous chapters, standardized beta coefficients are employed to measure the strength of these relationships in order to facilitate direct comparisons of correlation magnitudes across variables. The beta coefficients of the linear (OLS) models are used here, but only if they are statistically significant in both the linear and LOGIT models. In addition to the separate beta coefficients denoting direct and indirect relationships, the following sections present the net relationships of a given variable with upkeep behavior through the more intuitively pleasing device of calculating predicted changes in a given upkeep variable associated with a unit change in the given explanatory variable.

Satisfaction, Expectations, and Mobility Plans

It was noted above how mobility plans are significantly correlated with upkeep behavior only in the Minneapolis sample, but here they are strongly so. As shown in tables 9.4 and 9.5, Minneapolis homeowners who hold mobility plans other than long term (i.e., to stay more than ten years but a finite span) are expected to evidence from 14 percent to 19 percent higher incidence of exterior home defects, *ceteris paribus*. Indeed, the betas are on the same order of magnitude as those for expectations, and are larger than those of other homeowner characteristics. It is thus clear that factors leading to changes in mobility plans likely have potent impacts on housing upkeep behavior, but only when such factors alter the likelihood of holding long-run plans. Alterations of plans between the other mobility categories apparently made little difference.

The impact of neighborhood expectations on upkeep appears to be entirely direct, and of large magnitude. In all Minneapolis neighborhoods, those who are one unit more pessimistic on the NEIGHEXP (three-unit) scale are expected to spend $542 less annually on upkeep than those who are one unit less pessimistic, and to have an incidence of exterior defects 7 percent higher. In lower-valued areas the comparison is even more dramatic: a 30 percent higher incidence of defects in Minneapolis, an 11 percent higher rate in Wooster.

Expectations about property values in the neighborhood also appear to affect upkeep directly, and not by influencing mobility plans. Compared to homeowners in lower-valued areas who are one unit more pessimistic in the VALUEX(LOW) scale, comparable homeowners are likely to evidence a 16 percent higher frequency of exterior defects in Minneapolis, and an 11 percent higher rate in Wooster.[24]

Finally, residential satisfaction proves to have a comparatively small,

Table 9.4 Direct and Indirect Relationships* between Intervening Variables and Upkeep Behavior

| | Dependent variables | | | | | |
| | UPKEEP? | | UPKEEP$ | | DEFECTS? | |
Characteristics	Wooster	Minn.	Wooster	Minn.	Wooster	Minn.
HOUSESAT	NA	NA	NA	NA	NA	NA
	(—)	(—)	(—)	(—)	(—)	(.03)[7]
NEIGHSAT	NA	NA	NA	NA	NA	NA
	(—)	(—)	(—)	(—)	(—)	(.02)[6,7]
NEIGHEXP	—	—	—	−.08	—	.07
	(—)	(—)	(—)	(—)	(—)	(—)
NEIGHX(LOW)	—	—	—	—	.48	.30
	(—)	(—)	(—)	(—)	(—)	(—)
VALUEEXP	—	—	—	—	—	—
	(—)	(—)	(—)	(—)	(—)	(—)
VALUEX(LOW)	—	—	—	—	−.39	−.23
	(—)	(—)	(—)	(—)	(—)	(—)
STAY0–2	—	—	—	—	—	.15
	(NA)	(NA)	(NA)	(NA)	(NA)	(NA)
STAY3–10	—	—	—	—	—	.19
	(NA)	(NA)	(NA)	(NA)	(NA)	(NA)
STAYPERM	—	—	—	—	—	.22
	(NA)	(NA)	(NA)	(NA)	(NA)	(NA)

Note: Indirect relationship via: 1 = HOUSESAT, 2 = NEIGHSAT, 3 = NEIGHEXP, 4 = VALUEEXP, 5 = STAY0–2, 6 = STAY3–10, 7 = STAYPERM. Indirect shown in parentheses.
*using linear model's beta coefficients only when corroborated by PROBIT or LOGIT model
NA = not applicable; variable not used in given model
— = coefficient not statistically significant in linear model or PROBIT (or LOGIT) models

indirect influence on upkeep behavior. In Minneapolis, a homeowner who is least satisfied with the dwelling is 8 percent less likely to have home defects than one who is most satisfied,[25] since the latter more likely holds permanent mobility plans. For the same reason, those in Minneapolis who are least satisfied with their neighborhood are 12 percentage points less likely to have defects than the most satisfied.[26]

The above results confound the conventional wisdom, but the current theoretical model handles them neatly. First, this model shows excessively long-term, permanent plans to reside in the dwelling are a bad thing for neighborhood reinvestment; it increases the likelihood of undermaintaining the dwelling's exterior. Though shorter-term mobility plans result in

Table 9.5   Predicted Changes in Upkeep Behavior Associated with Unit Changes in Satisfaction, Expectations, and Mobility-Plan Characteristics

	Expected Value of UPKEEP$		DEFECTS	
Characteristics	Wooster	Minneapolis	Wooster	Minneapolis
HOUSESAT*	$0	$ 0	0	.02
NEIGHSAT	0	0	0	.03
NEIGHEXP	0	−542	0	.07
NEIGHX(LOW)**	0	−542	.11	.30
VALUEEXP	0	0	0	0
VALUEX(LOW)**	0	0	−.11	−.16
STAY0–2	0	0	0	.19
STAY3–10	0	0	0	.14
STAYPERM	0	0	0	.16

*unit change = 5 point change in 1–20 scale of HOUSESAT
**using net coefficient; see table 9.4

the same sorts of neglect, stretching out the horizon of mobility indefinitely does not produce unmitigated improvements in upkeep efforts. Second, neighborhood optimism in general does not necessarily abet upkeep. Indeed, expectations about qualitative changes in the area may improve upkeep, but exactly the opposite effect ensues from optimism about property inflation, at least in lower-value neighborhoods. Third, higher levels of residential satisfaction may be desirable on numerous grounds, but they do not stimulate more upkeep activity. On the contrary, because such satisfaction increases the likelihood of homeowners adopting plans to reside permanently in that location it can lead to a higher incidence of exterior dwelling defects.

Homeowner Characteristics

Summary results of direct, indirect, and net relationships involving homeowner characteristics are found in tables 9.6 and 9.7. Marital status of the homeowner generally proves to have the largest quantitative impact on upkeep behavior, especially in Minneapolis. Compared to households headed by single-males or multiple-heads, households headed by married homeowners have a $662 higher expected value[27] of annual upkeep expenditures; the corresponding Wooster figure is $62. In lower-valued neighborhoods, married homeowners have a .10 and .04 lower incidence of

Table 9.6 Direct and Indirect Relationships* between Homeowner Characteristics and Upkeep Behavior

Dependent

Characteristics	UPKEEP?		UPKEEP$	
	Wooster	Minneapolis	Wooster	Minneapolis
EDUCATION	.11 (—)	— (—)	— (—)	.11 (—)
INCOME	— (—)	— (—)	.18 (—)	.14 (—)
MARRIED	.15 (—)	— (—)	— (—)	.10 (—)
FEMALE	— (—)	— (—)	— (—)	.14 (—)
BLACK	— (—)	— (—)	— (—)	— (—)
STAGE2	— (—)	— (—)	— (—)	— (−.04)[3]
STAGE3	— (—)	— (—)	— (—)	— (−.03)[3]
STAGE4	— (—)	— (—)	−.23 (—)	— (−.01)[3]
STAGE5	−.21 (—)	— (—)	−.15 (—)	−.13 (—)
OCCUPANTS	— (—·)	— (—)	— (·)	−.13 (—)
IDENTIFY	NA (—)	NA (—)	NA (—)	NA (—)
INTEGRATE	NA (—)	NA (—)	NA (—)	NA (—)
NUMMOVES	NA (—)	NA (—)	NA (—)	NA (—)
PRIORHOME	NA (—)	NA (—)	NA (—)	NA (—)
EARLYHOME	NA (—)	NA (—)	NA (—)	NA (—)
LONGEVITY**	NA (—)	NA (—)	NA (—)	NA (—)
ALIENATED	NA (—)	NA (—)	NA (—)	NA (—)
COHESION1***	— (NA)	— (NA)	.12 NA	.06 NA
COHESION2***	— (NA)	— (NA)	NA (—)	NA (—)

Note: Indirect relationship via: 1 = HOUSESAT, 2 = NEIGHSAT, 3 = NEIGHEXP, 4 = VALUEEXP, 5 = STAY0–2, 6 = STAY3–10, 7 = STAYPERM. Indirect shown in parentheses.
*using linear model's beta coefficients only when corroborated by PROBIT or LOGIT model
**using both linear and squared terms where appropriate; evaluated at means
***combination homeowner and neighborhood characteristic

variables

	DEFECTS?		
Wooster		Minneapolis	
$-.09$	$(—)$	$—$	$(.03)[1,4-7]++$
$—$	$(—)$	$.12$	$(—)$
$—$	$(-.09)[3]+$	$-.15$	$(.02)[4-6]++$
$—$	$(.06)[4]+$	$—$	$(-.01)[1,2,4-7]++$
$—$	$(-.15)[4]+$	$—$	$(0)[1,5]$
$—$	$(—)$	$—$	$(-.13)[1,3,5]$
$—$	$(—)$	$—$	$(-.07)[1-3,5-7]$
$—$	$(—)$	$—$	$(-.02)[1-3,5-7]$
$—$	$(-.09)[4]+$	$—$	$(-.05)[1,2,4-7]++$
$—$	$(—)$	$.22$	$(—)$
NA	$(.03)[4]+$	NA	$(.02)[4]+$
NA	$(—)$	NA	$(0)[2,6,7]$
NA	$(—)$	NA	$(0)[6,7]$
NA	$(—)$	NA	$(—)$
NA	$(—)$	NA	$(0)[1,5,7]$
NA	$(—)$	NA	$(.03)[1,5,7]$
NA	$(—)$	NA	$(—)$
$—$	(NA)	$-.10$	(NA)
$(—)$	NA	$(—)$	NA

$+$ = only in low-value neighborhoods
$++$ = includes low-value neighborhood effect
NA = not applicable; variable not used in given model
— = coefficient not statistically significant in linear model or PROBIT (or LOGIT) models
$(0)^n$ = beta coefficient less than .01 but greater than zero

Table 9.7   Predicted Changes in Upkeep Behavior Associated With Unit Changes* in Homeowner Characteristics

Characteristics	Expected value of UPKEEP$		DEFECTS?	
	Wooster	Minneapolis	Wooster	Minneapolis
EDUCATION	$ 6	$ 57	−.01	0**
INCOME	10	24	0	0**
MARRIED	62	662	(−.04)	(−.10)
FEMALE	0	0	(.03)	(−.01)
BLACK	0	0	(−.18)	0
STAGE2	0	−285	0	−.11
STAGE3	0	−242	0	−.07
STAGE4	−448	− 98	0	−.02
STAGE5	−243	−699	(−.04)	(−.05)
OCCUPANTS	0	−278	0	.06
NUMMOVES	0	0	0	0**
LONGEVITY	0	0	0	.02

Note: Parenthetical terms indicate changes in low-value neighborhoods only; zero otherwise
*unit change = $1,000 for INCOME; for all dummy variables it means having the given characteristic
**less than .01

home defects in Minneapolis and Wooster, respectively.[28] These latter impacts transpire through indirect relationships involving neighborhood expectations and mobility plans (see table 9.6).

Life-cycle stage apparently also produces some sizable differences in upkeep behavior. In both samples those in STAGE 4 and STAGE 5 spend from $100 to $700 less than those in STAGE 1. Ironically, through multiple indirect linkages (see table 9.6), those in STAGE 5 in lower-valued areas have a 2 to 5 percent lower incidence of exterior defects. In Minneapolis, homeowners in STAGE 2 and STAGE 3 spend less as well, due primarily to their greater pessimism about qualitative neighborhood changes, but their houses evidence fewer exterior defects. This pattern in Minneapolis is likely due to the predominance of young urban professionals in the STAGE 1 reference category, in conjunction with high interest rates and home inflation rates observed in 1980. Financial exigencies, commuting costs, and current fashions all conspired to make many STAGE 1 couples' first starter home one located in an inner-city neighborhood that needed a good deal of rehabilitation. Many of these homeowners were in the process of renovating older homes at the time of the survey, and thus had spent more than their counterparts in later stages. But their efforts had not yet succeeded in eliminating the comparatively higher incidence of exterior defects associated with their homes before renovations began. The upshot is that the conventional life-cycle pattern of home investments (evidenced in Wooster) may be modified in housing markets undergoing substantial inner-city rehabilitation generated by young, childless homeowners (as in Minneapolis).

The socioeconomic status variables virtually have their entire apparent impact upon upkeep expenditures directly. Comparing, e.g., college graduates to those with only an eighth grade education, the former would have $48 and $456 higher expected values of annual expenditures in Wooster and Minneapolis, respectively. For each $1,000 difference in adjusted income, one would predict an $11 and $24 higher expected annual value for the homeowner with the larger income in Wooster and Minneapolis, respectively. Interestingly, though, income has no relationship with exterior defects, suggesting that lower-income homeowners are no more likely to let their homes visibly decay, *ceteris paribus*. Black homeowners in Wooster's lower-valued neighborhoods have a .18 lower incidence of exterior defects because they are more likely to be pessimistic about future property-value appreciation. Although there are too few blacks in either sample to make compelling generalizations, the evidence fails to support the conventional notion of the relatively inferior upkeep efforts of black homeowners compared to white.

Of the remaining homeowner characteristics, only the number of occupants has any sizable impact upon upkeep. Compared to a one-person household, one having four persons has an $834 higher expected value of annual upkeep expenditure and a .18 higher incidence of exterior defects in Minneapolis. The direct impact of female-heads and the indirect impacts of number of previous household moves, alienation, previous residential experiences, and length of tenure in the home are negligible and inconsistent between samples.

Dwelling Characteristics

Certain dwelling characteristics indirectly affect upkeep behavior by influencing dwelling satisfaction and thus both short-run and permanent mobility plans. Other dwelling characteristics directly affect upkeep through their presumed proxying for technological transformation possibilities embodied in the structure. See tables 9.8 and 9.9.

Examples of the former include per capita numbers of rooms and bathrooms and the presence of air-conditioning. In Minneapolis all such aspects are directly related to dwelling satisfaction, which is in turn in-

Table 9.8   Direct and Indirect Relationships* between Dwelling Characteristics and Upkeep Behavior

Dependent

Characteristics	UPKEEP?				UPKEEP?			
	Wooster		Minneapolis		Wooster		Minneapolis	
YARD/OCC**	NA	(—)	NA	(—)	NA	(—)	NA	(—)
ROOM/OCC**	NA	(—)	NA	(—)	NA	(—)	NA	(—)
BATH/OCC**	NA	(—)	NA	(—)	NA	(—)	NA	(—)
BUILTPRE-20	.15	(—)	—	(—)	.18	(—)	—	(—)
BUILT20–29	.24	(—)	—	(—)	.39	(—)	—	(—)
BUILT40–59	.26	(—)	—	(—)	.19	(—)	—	(—)
Total STAGE3,4, FEMALE	.26	(NA)	NA	(—)	NA	(NA)	NA	(—)
BUILT60–69	.18	(—)	—	(—)	—	(—)	—	(—)
Total STAGE2	.18	(—)	NA	(NA)	NA	(—)	NA	(NA)
NOHEAT	NA	(—)	NA	(—)	NA	(—)	NA	(—)
AIRCOND	NA	(—)	NA	(—)	NA	(—)	NA	(—)
Total FEMALE, STAGE4	NA	(NA)	NA	(—)	NA	(NA)	NA	(—)
GARAGE	NA	(—)	NA	(—)	NA	(—)	NA	(—)
Total STAGE2	NA	(—)	NA	(NA)	NA	(—)	NA	(NA)
WOOD	—	(—)	—	(—)	—	(—)	—	(—)
Total STAGE3	NA	(—)	NA	(NA)	NA	(—)	NA	(NA)
ROOMS	—	(NA)	—	(NA)	—	(NA)	.08	(NA)
YARD	—	(NA)	—	(NA)	.09	(NA)	—	(NA)

Note: Indirect relationship via: 1 = HOUSESAT and mobility plans, 5 = STAY0–2, 6 = STAY3–10, 7 = STAYPERM. Indirect shown in parentheses.
*using linear model's beta coefficients only when corroborated by PROBIT or LOGIT models
**using both linear and squared terms where appropriate; evaluated at means

variables

	DEFECTS?		
Wooster		Minneapolis	
NA	(—)	NA	(—)
NA	(—)	NA	(0)[1,5,7]
NA	(—)	NA	(0)[1,5,7]
—	(—)	.33	(−.01)[1,5,7]
—	(—)	.46	(−.01)[1,5,7]
—	(—)	.26	(−.01)[1,5,7]
NA	(NA)	.26	(0)[1,5,7]
—	(—)	—	(—)
NA	(—)	NA	(NA)
NA	(—)	NA	(—)
NA	(—)	NA	(—)
NA	(NA)	NA	(0)[1,5,7]
NA	(—)	NA	(—)
NA	(—)	NA	(NA)
.08	(—)	.15	(—)
.08	(—)	.15	(NA)
—	(NA)	−.14	(NA)
—	(NA)	—	(NA)

NA = not applicable; variable not used in given model
— = coefficient not statistically significant in linear model or PROBIT (or LOGIT) models
$(0)^n$ = beta coefficient less than .01 but greater than zero

Table 9.9   Predicted Changes in Upkeep Behavior Associated With Unit Changes in Dwelling Characteristics

Characteristics	Expected value of UPKEEP$		DEFECTS?	
	Wooster	Minneapolis	Wooster	Minneapolis
YARD/OCC	$ 0	$ 0	0	0
ROOM/OCC***	0	0	0	0*
BATH/OCC***	0	0	0	.01
BUILTPRE-20	483	0	0	.21
BUILT20–39	720	0	0	.27
BUILT40–59				
Total	369	0	0	.18
STAGE3,4, FEMALE**	269	0	NA	.17
BUILT60–69	95	0	0	0
NOHEAT	0	0	0	0
AIRCOND				
Total	0	0	0	0
FEMALE, STAGE4**	NA	0	NA	.01
GARAGE	0	0	0	0
WOOD	0	0	.04	.12
ROOMS	0	0	0	−.03
YARD	0	0	0	0

*less than .01
**using net coefficient
***using linear and squared terms (latter evaluated at mean of variable)
NA = not applicable; variable not used in given model

versely related to short-term mobility plans and directly related to permanent mobility plans. Because such plans are themselves directly related to incidence of exterior defects, their net effect on upkeep is virtually nil.

Of all the other dwelling characteristics, the vintage of the structure is associated with the largest impacts, though not consistently so between samples. In Wooster older structures are associated with much larger expected values of upkeep expenditures: $369 for 1940–1969 vintages, $720 for 1920–1939 vintages and $483 for pre-1920 vintages. In Minneapolis there is no relationship between dwelling age and expected upkeep expenditures, either directly or indirectly. As explained above, this may be due to idiosyncratic property tax reassessment practices. The relative lack of upkeep in the face of faster depreciation results in substantially higher incidences of exterior defects for older Minneapolis dwellings: .18 to .27, depending on the exact vintage. Thus, although the Minneapolis results support a conventional wisdom about older houses being more prone to visible disrepair (see Muth 1969, 98; Public Affairs Counseling 1975, 12; Quigley 1979, 417), the Wooster results indicate that this relationship is not necessary.

The only remaining dwelling features having any sizable relationships with upkeep behavior are wood clapboard construction and number of rooms. In both samples WOOD is associated with greater incidences of exterior defects compared to other materials: .04 in Wooster and .12 in Minneapolis (both direct effects via the DEFECTS? equation). In Minneapolis each additional room is associated with a .03 decrease in the probability of defects, a result undoubtedly due to some idiosyncratic architectural features of stock not well proxied for by other variables, as explained earlier.

Physical-Demographic Characteristics of Neighborhoods

Direct, indirect, and net relationships between upkeep and various measures of the physical and demographic dimensions of neighborhood are presented in tables 9.10 and 9.11. The only measure of the physical and socioeconomic quality of the neighborhood to have the conventionally predicted relationship with upkeep activity is BLOCKQUAL. Compared to homeowners in lowest-quality block faces in Minneapolis, those in the highest quality ones are expected to have a .43 lower incidence of strategies that produce exterior defects. This effect is only half as large for low-income, low-education homeowners in low-value neighborhoods, however. Measures embodying larger geographic scales of neighborhood (the planning area in Wooster, tract in Minneapolis) do not evidence such direct effects and their indirect impacts are quite unconventional. In lower-value neighborhoods in Wooster, higher levels of AREAQUAL are associated with less pessimism about property-value appreciation and, hence, with a slightly higher level of exterior defects due to free-rider behavior. In all Minneapolis tracts (and especially lower-valued ones) higher values of TRACTQUAL are associated with higher neighborhood satisfaction, therefore with greater chances of being in the medium-run and permanent (STAY3–10, STAYPERM) mobility-plan categories and, ultimately, with greater incidence of defects. (To a smaller degree this same indirect effect tends to blunt the direct effect of BLOCKQUAL.) What the foregoing suggests is that conventionally predicted responses in homeowner upkeep are produced by socioeconomic and qualitative conditions only in the very localized neighborhood (i.e., block face). Conditions in larger spatial aggregations tend to produce contrary, negative effects on upkeep

Table 9.10   Direct and Indirect Relationships* between Neighborhood Characteristics and Upkeep Behavior

| | Dependent | | | |
| | UPKEEP? | | | |
Characteristic	Wooster		Minneapolis	
AREAQUAL	—	(—)	NA	(NA)
BLOCKQUAL				
Total	NA	(NA)	—	(—)
INCOME(LOW)	NA	(NA)	—	(—)
EDUCATION(LOW)				
TRACTQUAL	NA	(NA)	—	(—)
NONRESID				
Total	—	(—)	—	(—)
EDUCATION(LOW)	NA	(NA)	NA	(—)
STAGE1				
TENURE				
Total	—	(—)	—	(—)
MARRIED	NA	(NA)	NA	(—)
RACECOMPW				
Total	—	(—)	—	(—)
FEMALE, STAGE4	NA	(—)	NA	(NA)
FEMALE, EDUCATION (LOW)	NA	(NA)	NA	(—)
EDUCATION(LOW)	NA	(NA)	NA	(—)
RACECOMPB	—	(—)	—	(—)
NIDENTIFY**				
Total	NA	(—)	NA	(—)
STAGE2,4	NA	(—)	NA	(NA)
STAGE2,3	NA	(—)	NA	(NA)
NINTEGRATE				
Total	NA	(—)	NA	(—)
STAGE2	NA	(—)	NA	(NA)
FEMALE	NA	(NA)	NA	(—)
COHESION1***	—	(NA)	—	(NA)
COHESION2***	—	(NA)	—	(NA)

Note: Indirect relationship via: 1 = HOUSESAT, 2 = NEIGHSAT, 3 = NEIGHEXP, 4 = VALUEEXP, 5 = STAY0–2, 6 = STAY3–10, 7 = STAYPERM. Indirect shown in parentheses.
*using linear model's beta coefficients only when corroborated by PROBIT or LOGIT models
**using both linear and squared terms where appropriate; evaluated at means
***combination homeowner and neighborhood characteristic

variables

	UPKEEP$				DEFECTS?		
Wooster		Minneapolis		Wooster		Minneapolis	
—	(—)	NA	(NA)	—	(.10)[4]+	NA	(NA)
NA	(NA)	—	(—)	NA	(NA)	−.15	(.01)[2,6,7]
NA	(NA)	NA	(—)	NA	(NA)	−.15	(.05)[4]+
NA	(NA)	−.07	(—)	NA	(NA)	—	(.01)[2,6,7]
—	(—)	—	(−.01)[3]	—	(—)	—	(−.07)[2–4,6,7]
NA	(NA)	NA	(—)	NA	(NA)	NA	(0)[2,7]
—	(—)	—	(−.01)[3]	—	(−.06)[3]+	—	(.03)[3]
NA	(NA)	NA	(—)	NA	(NA)	NA	(0)[2,6,7]
—	(—)	—	(—)	—	(—)	—	(.02)[2,3,6,7]
NA	(—)	NA	(NA)	NA	(−.08)[4]+	NA	(NA)
NA	(NA)	NA	(—)	NA	(NA)	NA	(−.03)[4]+
NA	(NA)	NA	(.01)[3]	NA	(NA)	NA	(−.01)[3]
—	(—)	—	(—)	—	(—)	—	(—)
NA	(—)	NA	(—)	NA	(.05)[4]+	NA	(.03)[4]+
NA	(—)	NA	(NA)	NA	(−.18)[4]+	NA	(NA)
NA	(—)	NA	(NA)	NA	(−.36)[3]+	NA	(NA)
NA	(—)	NA	(—)	NA	(—)	NA	(—)
NA	(—)	NA	(NA)	NA	(−.13)[3,4]+	NA	(NA)
NA	(NA)	NA	(.04)[3]	NA	(NA)	NA	(.12)[3]
.12	(NA)	.06	(NA)	—	(NA)	−.10	(NA)
—	(NA)	—	(NA)	—	(NA)	—	(NA)

+ = only in low-value neighborhoods
++ = includes low-value neighborhood effect
NA = not applicable; variable not used in given model
— = coefficient not statistically significant in linear model or PROBIT (or LOGIT) models
(0)[n] = beta coefficient less than .01 but greater than zero

Table 9.11 Predicted Changes in Upkeep Behavior Associated with Unit Changes in Physical-Demographic Neighborhood Characteristics

Characteristics	Expected value of UPKEEP$		DEFECTS?	
	Wooster	Minneapolis	Wooster	Minneapolis
AREAQUAL	$0	NA	(.03)	NA
BLOCKQUAL	NA	$ 0	NA	−.07
INCOME(LOW), EDUCATION(LOW)	NA	NA	NA	(−.04)
TRACTQUAL	NA	229	NA	0
NONRESID Total	0	210	$0	−.18
STAGE1, EDUCATION(LOW)	NA	210	NA	0*
TENURE Total	0	−40	(−.01)	.01
MARRIED**	NA	0	NA	0*
RACECOMPW Total	0	0	0	0*
EDUCATION(LOW)	NA	6	NA	0*
FEMALE, STAGE4	0	NA	(−.02)	NA
FEMALE, EDUCATION(LOW)	NA	0	NA	(−.01)
RACECOMPB	0	0	0	0

Note: Parenthetical terms indicate changes in low-value neighborhoods only; zero otherwise
*less than .01
**using net coefficient
NA = not applicable; variable not used in given model

because of their complex impacts on satisfaction, expectations, and mobility plans.

The apparent effect of nonresidential land use upon upkeep behavior in Minneapolis is entirely indirect, mediated by neighborhood satisfaction, expectations, and the probability of holding medium-run and permanent mobility plans. In general, those having nonresidential land use on the block face have lower neighborhood satisfaction, and thus a reduced probability of planning to remain in the area permanently or from three to ten years. They are more pessimistic about the neighborhood's future property values, but less pessimistic about its quality. Together, this results in such Minneapolis homeowners having a .18 lower incidence of exterior housing defects,[29] and spending $210 more on upkeep annually. Thus, the results provide no support for the conventional hypothesis that the presence of nonresidential land use acts as a deterrent to housing upkeep activity; in fact, the opposite is strongly suggested.

The relationship between upkeep and the variable measuring the tenure characteristics of the neighborhood also is solely indirect through expectations about neighborhood quality. But because TENURE has an opposite relationship with expectations in the two samples, no consistent picture emerges.[30]

Although there are a few indirect influences of neighborhood racial composition upon upkeep, their magnitudes are negligible. Once again, one must conclude that neighborhood racial composition is not a noticeable determinant of housing upkeep behavior after other aspects of the neighborhood have been controlled for, at least for the two samples investigated. The reader is cautioned to recall, however, that both samples are drawn from cities with relatively small black populations, and little history of ghettos or racial tipping of neighborhoods.

Social-Interactive Characteristics

A major innovation of this research is the inclusion of the social-interactive dimension of the neighborhood in both theoretical and empirical models of housing upkeep behavior. The results for both individual and aggregate measures of this dimension reported in tables 9.6, 9.10, and 9.12 give strong affirmation to this inclusion. The largest effects of social-interactive characteristics come about through their contributions to the COHESION1 variable, which becomes operative in neighborhoods having above-average values of both individual and collective senses of group identification. Consider first the quantitative impact of COHESION1 on upkeep expenditures and rates of defects before analyzing the separate contributions of its two constituent parts: IDENTIFY and NIDENTIFY.

Compared to homeowners in noncohesive neighborhoods in Wooster, those living in minimally cohesive areas (i.e., mean values of both IDENTIFY and NIDENTIFY) should have a $146 higher expected value of annual upkeep expenditure; those in maximally cohesive areas (i.e., maximum value of COHESION1) should have a $241 higher expected value. The corresponding comparisons in Minneapolis produce higher expected values of $268 and $500, respectively. Note how large these dollar differences are in comparison to the impacts of other variables. In Wooster the differences between extrema are on the same order of magnitude as the most potent homeowner characteristic (STAGE5) and as an interhomeowner difference in income of $22,000! In Minneapolis the difference between extrema is somewhat smaller than the potent homeowner characteristics (MARRIED and STAGE5). But it is equivalent to an interhomeowner difference of five

Table 9.12   Predicted Changes in Upkeep Behavior Associated with Unit
Changes in Social-Interactive Characteristics

Characteristics	Expected Value of UPKEEP$		DEFECTS?	
	Wooster	Minneapolis	Wooster	Minneapolis
IDENTIFY				
Total*	$ 0	$ 0	.01	.01
via COHESION1[a]	34	74	0	−.01
INTEGRATE				
Total**	0	0	0	0
via COHESION2[b]	0	0	0	0
NIDENTIFY				
Total*	0	0	(.02)	(.04)
STAGE2	0	0	(−.03)	NA
STAGE3,4	0	NA	(−.01)	NA
via COHESION1[c]	41	116	0	−.02
NINTEGRATE				
Total	0	0	0	0
STAGE2*	0	NA	(−.01)	NA
FEMALE*	NA	−128	NA	.06
via COHESION2[d]	0	0	0	0
COHESION1	10	32	0	−.01
COHESION2	0	0	0	0

Note: Parenthetical terms indicate changes in low-value neighborhoods only; zero otherwise.
[a] = assuming IDENTIFY above mean, NIDENTIFY at mean value
[b] = assuming INTEGRATE above mean, NINTEGRATE at mean value
[c] = assuming NIDENTIFY above mean, IDENTIFY at mean value
[d] = assuming NINTEGRATE above mean, INTEGRATE at mean value
*only valid in lower-valued neighborhoods
**evaluated at mean INTEGRATE
NA = not applicable; variable not used in given model

years of education, two persons in the household, or $21,000 in income.
And it is larger than any of the differences between extrema associated
with the physical or demographic dimensions of neighborhood (except
TRACTQUAL), with satisfaction, or with expectations. Indeed, social cohesion must be considered when analyzing homeowners' upkeep expenditures.

These differences in cohesion in the group-identification aspect of social
interaction also affect observed rates of exterior defects in Minneapolis.
Compared to those living in noncohesive neighborhoods, those in minimally cohesive ones should have a .05 lower incidence of defects; those in

maximally cohesive ones should have .10 lower incidence. Although not nearly as large as the defect variations associated with extrema of MARRIED, OCCUPANTS, STAGE2, STAGE3, mobility plans, or BLOCKQUAL, the above values are on the same order of magnitude as those associated with extrema of NEIGHEXP, NEIGHSAT, NONRESID and ten years' difference in EDUCATION.

The relationships between the individual's sense of group identification (IDENTIFY) and the aggregate neighborhood's sense of such (NIDENTIFY) and upkeep behavior operate both separately through indirect influences and interactively through the direct impact of COHESIONI when the preconditions for the latter are fulfilled.[31] Perhaps the most effective way to portray these relationships is with the aid of graphs. Consider the implied impact upon expected values of upkeep expenditures as shown in figures 9.1 and 9.2.

These figures plot the variation in expected values of annual upkeep expenditures associated with variations in a given social-interaction variable. They show that there is a zero effect of increasing the given social-interactive characteristic until both it and the other characteristic reach their means. These threshold points specify when COHESIONI begins, and are indicated by M^* and W^* for Minneapolis and Wooster, respectively. Past these thresholds, the relationship between upkeep expenditure and the given social-interactive variable is direct, with the other social-interactive variable marking the parameters of both level and slope of the relationship. For simplicity the only relationships shown are those where the parameter takes the mean and the maximum value. The Minneapolis relationships are shown by dotted lines; the Wooster ones by dashed lines. The direct linear relationships continue until they reach the maximum sample value of the given social-interactive variable, M^{**} and W^{**} in Minneapolis and Wooster, respectively.

As can be seen from figure 9.1, in cohesive residential contexts in Wooster those having the mean individual sense of group identification (IDENTIFY) can be expected to have a $142 to $164 higher annual upkeep expenditure than those who are not in cohesive neighborhoods (regardless of the latters' level of IDENTIFY), depending on the corresponding level of NIDENTIFY in the cohesive area. The corresponding figures for Minneapolis homeowners are $266 to $329. Past these threshold points, further increases in IDENTIFY yield progressively higher levels of expenditures, the rate depending again on the associated aggregate level of NIDENTIFY for the cohesive neighborhood in which the homeowner lives. Those having the maximum individual level of IDENTIFY can be expected to have $67 to $77 higher annual upkeep expenditure (depending on NIDENTIFY) than those with the mean value of IDENTIFY in the same neighborhood. The corresponding range in Minneapolis is $110 to $136.

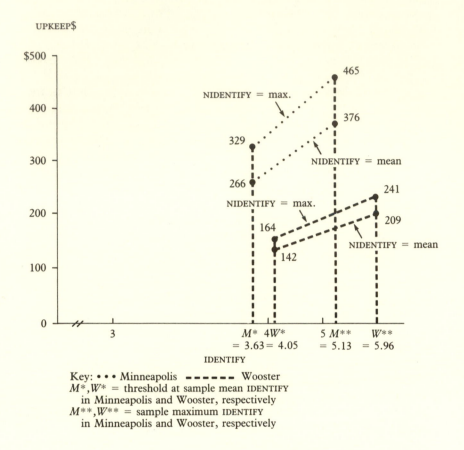

UPKEEP$

Figure 9.1 Relationship between IDENTIFY and Expected Value of UPKEEP$ (both samples)

Figure 9.2 shows a qualitatively similar pattern of variation in expenditure associated with changes in the neighborhood's aggregate sense of group identification (NIDENTIFY). Those at the threshold levels of minimally cohesive neighborhoods are likely to spend $142 to $209 more in Wooster and $266 to $376 more in Minneapolis than those in noncohesive neighborhoods. The exact magnitude of these differences depends again on the reinforcing effect derived from the associated level of group identification held by the individual homeowner. Past this threshold, stronger NIDENTIFY leads to a greater expected value of upkeep expenditure. Compared to those at the threshold cohesion levels, those living in areas with maximum NIDENTIFY are likely to spend $38 to $39 more in Wooster and $63 to $89 more in Minneapolis per year on upkeep, depending on the associated level of IDENTIFY.

To sum up, there is clear, consistent, and convincing evidence that in cohesive neighborhoods both the homeowner's and the aggregate level of communal norms and solidarity sentiments interact synergistically to encourage the investment of significant sums in home upkeep.[32] The homeowner with the strongest sense of social identification who also lives in an area with the strongest aggregate sense of such can be predicted to annually invest 28 percent more in Minneapolis and 45 percent more in

Figure 9.2 Relationship between NIDENTIFY and Expected Value of UPKEEP$ (both samples)

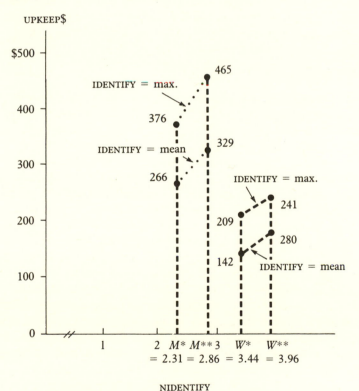

Key: • • • Minneapolis ▬ ▬ ▬ ▬ Wooster
$M*$, $W*$ = threshold at sample mean NIDENTIFY
    in Minneapolis and Wooster, respectively
$M**$, $W**$ = sample maximum NIDENTIFY
    in Minneapolis and Wooster, respectively

Wooster,[33] compared to an otherwise-identical homeowner living in a noncohesive area. The widespread view that housing upkeep behavior can be understood solely as a response to financial considerations is simply untrue.

Note finally that measures of the degree of social integration (either at the individual (INTEGRATE) or the neighborhood (NINTEGRATE) level) are not statistically significant.[34] Apparently, intense local interpersonal familiarity and interaction are not necessarily the means through which neighborhood standards and positive and negative reinforcements concerning upkeep are conveyed to individual homeowners. As Vaskowics and Franz (1984, 159) note, "integration . . . into a residential area cannot imply the adoption of a predominant value and norm pattern that is obligatory for all residents." The internalization of such local norms and values (in the aforementioned group-identification variables) seems to be the key. This corresponds closely to what has been called "community" in the sociological literature (Warren 1978, 9; Hallman 1984, 34).

Public Policies

Finally, consider the indirect and direct influences upon upkeep behavior generated by public policies in Minneapolis (see tables 9.13 and 9.14). Compared to areas designated as qualifying for some form of home improvement assistance (whether aid has actually been received or not), those areas not designated as such have a $65 lower expected annual value of upkeep expenditures and a .02 higher probability of exterior defects. These relationships are both generated indirectly, because homeowners in such nonassistance areas are associated with more pessimistic neighborhood quality expectations and shorter-run mobility plans. As noted earlier, the receipt of low-interest loans or outright grants for home improvements is associated with higher expected values of upkeep expenditures: $35 per $100 LOAN$ and $262 per $100 GRANT$. But as will be discussed in chapter 12, further analysis is needed to ascertain to what degree such figures provide guidelines for selecting appropriate rehabilitation subsidy policies. Nevertheless, the evidence even at this superficial level suggests that public policy can wield some nontrivial levers in encouraging neighborhood reinvestment, both directly and indirectly.

Summary

Previous empirical research has focused on uncovering the relationship between housing upkeep behavior and characteristics of homeowners and of dwellings, while generally overlooking social-interactive dimensions of

Table 9.13   Direct and Indirect Relationships* between Minneapolis Public Policy Characteristics and Upkeep Behavior

Characteristics	UPKEEP? Minneapolis	UPKEEP$ Minneapolis	DEFECTS? Minneapolis
NOTQUALIFY	NA (—)	NA $(-.01)^3$	NA $(.02)^{3,4}$
QUALIFY	NA (—)	NA (—)	NA (—)
LOAN?	NA (—)	NA (—)	NA (—)
GRANT?	NA (—)	NA (—)	NA (—)
LOAN$	NA (NA)	.24 (NA)	— (NA)
GRANT$	NA (NA)	.43 (NA)	— (NA)

Note: Indirect relationship via: 1 = HOUSESAT, 2 = NEIGHSAT, 3 = NEIGHEXP, 4 = VALUEEXP, 5 = STAY0–2, 6 = STAY3–10, 7 = STAYPERM. Indirect shown in parentheses.
*using linear model's beta coefficients only when corroborated by PROBIT or LOGIT model
NA = not applicable; variable not used in given model
— = coefficient not statistically significant in linear model or PROBIT (or LOGIT) models

Table 9.14   Predicted Changes in Upkeep Behavior Associated with Unit Changes* in Minneapolis Public Policy Characteristics

Characteristics	Expected value of UPKEEP$	DEFECTS?
NOTQUALIFY	$-65	.02
QUALIFY	0	0
LOAN?	0	0
GRANT?	0	0
LOAN$	35	0
GRANT$	262	0

*Unit change for LOAN$ and GRANT$ defined as $100

the surrounding neighborhood, homeowner's expectations about future changes in neighborhood quality and in property values, and homeowners' mobility plans. The statistical results reported in this chapter forcefully testify to the significance of these heretofore overlooked elements in explaining upkeep activity, and provide strong support for the theoretical model developed in chapters 2 and 3. The primary findings are as follows:

– Results suggest that particular assumptions about the structure of homeowners' preferences are appropriate. Both physical-demographic and social-interactive dimensions of the (present and expected future) neighborhood interact multiplicatively with housing capital so as to affect the marginal consumption utility derived from home alterations. The wealth aspect of home investment can also abet the marginal gain from home alterations, but apparently primarily in situations where the perceived achieved level of home equity falls below some threshold level of equity.

– Characteristics of a given homeowner are crucial in understanding upkeep behavior, because they proxy for preferences, financial resources, and relative prices faced in transforming expenditures into housing capital. These characteristics influence upkeep indirectly as well, in shaping satisfactions, expectations, and mobility plans. Specifically, households with higher income and educational attainment show much higher levels of upkeep expenditures. But lower-income owners are no more likely to allow their homes to visibly decay, all else equal. Married homeowners and those with smaller families spend more on upkeep and their homes have fewer exterior defects. Expenditures on home upkeep generally tend to decline with life-style stage, unless there is an unusual degree of revitalization activity undertaken by young, childless homeowners—as in Minneapolis. And, due to a host of complicated interactions with satisfactions, expectations, and mobility plans, the dwellings of homeowners in later stages tend to have fewer exterior defects, especially if the neighborhood is lower valued. There is no evidence that race *per se* is related to upkeep behavior.

– Dwelling age and construction type are the prime structural determinants of upkeep behavior. Older homes generally command increased frequency and expenditures of upkeep resources, although there is circumstantial evidence that such a relationship can be affected by concerns over how upkeep will affect property-tax bills. Homes of wood clapboard construction are more vulnerable to exterior defects during any given period. These results are consistent with the theoretical arguments that these variables proxy for the rate of depreciation and technological possibilities for transforming expenditures into housing capital. Yet it is clear that older structures do not inevitably decay, and that many homeowners invest enough in them to deter visible defects.

– The physical-demographic dimension of the neighborhood has a detectable direct impact upon upkeep behavior only when the neighborhood is defined at a very localized (i.e., block-face) geographic scale. Although the socioeconomic status and physical quality index of the local area is directly related to upkeep activity, as expected, less conventional results also appear. The presence of nonresidential land use on the block is associated with stronger upkeep efforts, indirectly due to its relationship with expectations and mobility plans. Virtually no impact of neighborhood racial composition on upkeep behavior by homeowners of either race is observed. There is also some evidence that the block-face conditions are assessed relative to those in larger scales of neighborhood; i.e., upkeep efforts are slackened the lower the block-face quality relative to the tract quality, while holding the former constant absolutely. That the assessment of the local neighborhood's quality (whether it be absolute or relative) has a positive correlation with upkeep supports the theory that the marginal utility of housing alterations is a function of neighborhood conditions.

– The degree to which the social-interactive dimension of the neighborhood produces both an individual and aggregate sense of neighborhood identification proves to be a consistent and crucial determinant of homeowners' upkeep efforts. Indeed, homeowners in highly cohesive neighborhoods in both samples annually spend hundreds of dollars more on home upkeep than otherwise-comparable homeowners in noncohesive contexts.

– Satisfaction with both the home and with the neighborhood have modest impacts upon upkeep behavior, but not in the conventionally predicted manner. Because those who are satisfied are more likely to hold permanent mobility plans, they more often tend to neglect the exterior condition of their dwellings.

– Variations in homeowners' planned length of tenure in the neighborhood do not appear to affect total upkeep expenditures, but rather the composition of those expenditures. Compared to those with long-term (i.e., a finite period but more than ten years) mobility plans, those with shorter-term plans are less likely to worry about repairing external home defects. As would be predicted by a model in which the weight placed on ultimate home equity varies with mobility plans, those with permanent plans are likely to manifest a similarly higher incidence of home defects.

– Expectations about changes in the quality of the neighborhood (independent of expectations about property values) relate to upkeep behavior in a way that, again, supports the notion that the neighborhood strongly affects the marginal utility of home investments as perceived by homeowners. Indeed, compared to Minneapolis homeowners who expect the neighborhood to stay the same, those who expect it to get worse are likely to spend over $500 less, on average, for annual upkeep, which results in more exterior defects. This sensitivity to expectations appears to be heightened in lower-valued neighborhoods in both samples. Thus, expectations about qualitative changes in the neighborhood engender crowd-following behavior on the part of individual homeowners, which tends to create self-fulfilling prophecies about neighborhood dynamics.

– Expectations about future neighborhood property-value changes have very different impacts than those about qualitative neighborhood changes. In lower-valued neighborhoods, higher levels of pessimism concerning property values are associated with greater efforts to repair and maintain the exterior quality of the dwelling, apparently so as to salvage home equity. Conversely, optimism is associated with more exterior defects, as homeowners anticipate reaping capital gains and cut back on upkeep efforts. As the theoretical model explains, the value placed on home upkeep investments varies according to the relationship of achieved home equity and minimal threshold equity. This suggests that in lower-valued areas at least, optimistic property-value expectations engender trend-bucking behavior, and pessimistic expectations engender free-rider behavior. In either case, the perceived momentum of neighborhood change is counteracted by the response of the individual homeowner.

– In Minneapolis, public policies do appear to affect upkeep behavior, both directly and indirectly. Directly, grants and loans to individual homeowners abet upkeep expenditures, though at varying degrees depending on the particular subsidy. Indirectly, housing investments through these subsidy programs have some modest positive effect on optimism about neighborhood conditions and, hence, on upkeep. A fuller exploration of these findings is undertaken in chapter 12.

and Housing Upkeep: A Summary of
Empirical Findings

The previous four chapters specify a complex empirical model of homeowners' housing upkeep behavior based on the theory presented in chapters 2 and 3. This model begins by positing that five distinct sets of
exogenous variables influence this behavior: homeowner characteristics,
dwelling characteristics, physical-demographic neighborhood characteristics, social-interactive neighborhood characteristics, and public policy
characteristics. In addition, three sets of intervening variables are seen as
important vehicles through which the influences of the above variables are
mediated: dwelling and neighborhood satisfaction, expectations about
qualitative and property-value changes in the neighborhood, and mobility
plans.

This chapter reviews the key findings that emerged from the estimation
of the parameters of the above model for data gathered in Wooster, Ohio,
and Minneapolis, Minnesota. It then applies these parameters to estimate
how the overall level of reinvestment of homeowners in a typical neighborhood is likely to change as the result of changes in neighborhood
demographic composition, social identification, expectations, or mobility
plans. Thus, the analysis applies what has been learned about individual
behavior to understand how behaviors in concert produce aggregate outcomes for a neighborhood. Particular attention is paid to three of the most
well-known phenomena in urban neighborhoods: succession, racial transition, and gentrification.

Key Parameters of Housing Upkeep Behavior

Homeowner Characteristics

The single most influential characteristic of the homeowner is marital
status. Compared to other household types with average characteristics,
married couples annually spend from 12 percent to 37 percent more on
home upkeep, regardless of age, children, dwelling, or neighborhood.

Socioeconomic status is also crucial. College graduates invest 9 percent to 26 percent more, on average, than do those with only an eighth-grade education. A difference in $10,000 income between otherwise-identical homeowners explains a 14 percent to 21 percent difference in their annual upkeep expenditures.

Variations in life-cycle stage have noticeable effects as well. Compared to younger homeowners who have no children, those with older teenage children invest less. And those over age forty-five with no children remaining in the home spend still less, by 39 percent–43 percent. Larger families invest more on upkeep, but this does not prevent them from evidencing higher rates of exterior home defects. These effects are modified somewhat in the Minneapolis sample, where young, childless homeowners spend 14 percent to 16 percent more than comparable homeowners in early and mid–child-rearing stages. This is undoubtedly due to demographic, financial, and employment conditions in Minneapolis, which have encouraged many young, childless people to buy and renovate homes in the inner city.

Dwelling Characteristics

Structural age is associated with progressively higher upkeep expenditures up to a point where expenditures slacken. Compared to a home built since 1969, annual average expenditure on a 1940–1969 vintage home is 70 percent more; on a 1920–1939 vintage is 136 percent more; on a pre-1920 vintage is 91 percent more. Such expenditures appear adequate to negate the higher rate of depreciation associated with age completely: older homes are no more likely to evidence exterior defects than others, all else equal. Homes sided with wood clapboards deteriorate fast enough that observed maintenance responses are too infrequent or insubstantial to prevent visible decay.

Physical-Demographic Neighborhood Characteristics

Quality characteristics produce conventionally predicted responses in home upkeep only on the geographic scale of the block face. Compared to similar homeowners living on lowest-quality blocks, those in highest-quality ones have a .43 lower likelihood of pursuing strategies that result in exterior home defects. The effect is only about half as large for homeowners in lower-value neighborhoods, however.

These same neighborhood features, when measured on larger geographic scales, produce the opposite effects, especially on lower-value blocks. Holding the quality of blocks constant, a one-standard-deviation quality improvement in the larger surrounding area is associated with 12 percent lower upkeep expenditures and .03 greater incidence of exterior home defects. These effects are generated by an amalgam of relativistic quality comparisons between block and larger areas and alterations in satisfaction, expectations, and mobility plans.

The impact of nonresidential land use on the block does not discourage housing reinvestment, as typically believed. As expected, homeowners having proximate nonresidential land use are less satisfied with their neighborhood. But because of this they are less likely to plan on remaining in their homes permanently, and this encourages upkeep. Such home-owners seem to be more pessimistic about future property values, but this encourages trend-bucking reinvestment behavior in lower-valued neigh-borhoods. In addition, they are less pessimistic about future neighborhood quality changes. The net effect: homeowners on blocks with nonresiden-tial use spend 12 percent more annually on upkeep and evidence a .18 lower incidence of exterior home defects, all else equal.

Social-Interactive Neighborhood Characteristics

The homeowner's degree of identification with neighbors holds immense explanatory power for home upkeep behavior, but only when that home-owner is situated in a cohesive neighborhood where most neighbors share the same solidarity sentiments. Compared to average homeowners in non-cohesive neighborhoods, owners in the most cohesive neighborhoods who identify most closely with their neighbors annually spend 28 percent to 45 percent more on upkeep, and evidence a .10 lower likelihood of exterior home defects. This impact is larger in magnitude than that associated with a $20,000 difference in homeowners' incomes.

Other subtleties are also of interest. The above consequences of neigh-borhood social identification are stronger in the Wooster sample, but are potent even in large, cosmopolitan Minneapolis. In neither context, however, does either the homeowner's own sense of identification with neighbors, nor the collective degree of such tend to influence behavior independently. Rather, both individual and collective identification must simultaneously be present to some threshold extent before home upkeep efforts increase. Finally, the level of social interaction in the neighborhood appears to have no impact on upkeep. Apparently interneighbor famil-iarity and contact are important only if collective solidarity sentiments result.

Public Policy Characteristics

All else equal, the homeowner's receipt of a low-interest loan or grant for home rehabilitation is associated with higher upkeep expenditures: $35 per $100 in loans and $262 per $100 in grants. There also seem to be modest indirect effects of such loan-grant policies on the neighbors of recipients. Homeowners who have not personally received a subsidy, but live in areas where such are allocated, have more optimism about the future quality of their neighborhoods. This, in turn, translates into a 4 percent larger upkeep expenditure stream and a .02 lower incidence of exterior home defects.

Residential Satisfaction

Homeowners are more satisfied with dwellings that have more rooms and bathrooms per occupant, although to a progressively smaller degree as the number of rooms and bathrooms rises. Occupants are generally less satisfied with older homes. The physical quality and socioeconomic status of the neighborhood are strong predictors of neighborhood satisfaction, regardless of whether the geographic scale of neighborhood is defined as small as a block face or as large as a census tract. Nonresidential land use on the block is evaluated differently by different homeowner groups. Both the individual's and the aggregate degree of neighborhood social identification strongly encourage neighborhood satisfaction. And regardless of residential context, those in later life-cycle stages are more satisfied.

Residential satisfaction, however, does not prove to be a prerequisite for home reinvestment. Quite the opposite, if anything. Satisfied homeowners are more likely to plan on residing in their location permanently, and this translates into a .08–.12 higher incidence of home defects.

Neighborhood Expectations

Neighborhood expectations are very difficult to predict. Theory suggests that two different sorts of experiences—those involving qualitative changes and those involving property-value changes—should be modeled, and indeed they turn out to be empirically distinct. Indicators of the current physical-demographic character of the neighborhood generally are poor predictors of qualitative changes, probably because no variables measuring recent trends were available. When they hold some explanatory power, they suggest that homeowners in higher-quality neighborhoods and those having nonresidential land use on the block are slightly more pessimistic. These same characteristics are related more strongly to property-value expectations, but in precisely the *opposite* fashion.

Both the individual and the aggregate degree of neighborhood identification are strong contributors to optimism about property-value changes. This probably indicates that homeowners identifying with a cohesive neighborhood believe that the area can collectively ward off those elements that could erode values.

Married and female homeowners are more optimistic about neighborhood conditions than multiple-headed or single-male–headed households. Those in child-rearing life-cycle stages are also more optimistic than others. Those in the post–child-rearing stage are more pessimistic about property-value appreciation.

Finally, homeowners in areas that received the bulk of subsidized loans and grants for home rehabilitation in Minneapolis are noticeably more optimistic about qualitative neighborhood changes than are those in other areas that have not been so affected. However, the personal receipt of such a subsidy has no additional effect on confidence. There were no higher levels of optimism in areas that received either large-scale Urban Renewal programs and/or CDBG infrastructure investments and those that did not. This suggests that place-oriented programs are less successful in promoting homeowner optimism than programs that directly subsidize investors.

The two sorts of expectations about the neighborhood's future produce different consequences in different types of neighborhoods. Across all sorts of neighborhoods, pessimistic expectations about qualitative neighborhood changes are associated with less home reinvestment. Compared to the most optimistic homeowners, the most pessimistic ones are likely to spend 61 percent less annually on their homes, and evidence a .14 higher incidence of exterior defects. In lower-valued neighborhoods the above comparison of defects incidences are greater: between .22 and .60 difference. These results suggest a crowd-following variety of interhomeowner strategic interaction. If homeowners perceive the quality of their area as improving, they will flow with the trend and intensify their own reinvestment behaviors. Just the opposite ensues with more pessimism. The upshot is that homeowner responses reinforce the qualitative changes the homeowners originally foresaw: the self-fulfilling prophecy.

Not so with expectations about property-value changes. For homeowners in moderate- and high-quality neighborhoods, variations in these expectations have no relationship to upkeep behavior, probably because these homeowners are confident that they will reap some minimally acceptable capital gain from their property. In lower-value neighborhoods such confidence is apparently less, because property inflation pessimism is directly related to the intensity of repair activity. Homeowners in a low-value neighborhood who are most pessimistic about capital gains will intensify exterior upkeep efforts and reduce external defects by .22 to .64, compared to homeowners who are otherwise identical but most optimistic. This seemingly irrational trend-bucking behavior can be comprehended by positing that the utility gained from home-asset value increments rises rapidly when capital value is expected to fall below a minimally accepted threshold upon which homeowner wealth accumulation plans were made. Conversely, homeowners in low-value neighborhoods respond to more optimism about capital gains by deferring external repairs, apparently believing that they can exceed their expected wealth target even while maintaining their home less. A free-rider strategy thus is adopted.

Mobility Plans

Homeowners' expected length of residence in their homes is strongly correlated with their marital and life-cycle characteristics. Married home-owners are most likely to anticipate that the comparative net advantage of their current residence will cease three to ten years hence, and to adopt a corresponding mobility timetable. Compared to young, childless home-owners, those in older life-cycle stages are less likely to hold short-run (one- to two-year) plans and more likely to hold plans of remaining perma-nently. And the magnitude of these differences grows as progressively older stages are contrasted. The importance of life-cycle stage is reduced, however, in a macroeconomic context of rapidly inflating home prices and high interest rates, which tend to freeze younger homeowners into erst-while starter homes.

Neighborhood satisfaction and dwelling satisfaction hold as much ex-planatory power as life-cycle stage. The consistent pattern of more satis-faction being associated with longer-run tenure plans suggests that it serves as a good proxy for homeowner perceptions of the gross com-parative advantages of their present residential context.

Neither sort of neighborhood expectations serves as a strong, consistent predictor of mobility plans. This suggests that homeowners' projections of future comparative net advantages between their current and alternative residences are formulated primarily on expected changes in their house-hold needs, not on relatively short-term expectations about the neighbor-hood.

Expected length of tenure is related to homeowners' upkeep behavior in a nonlinear fashion, with those planning on remaining a finite period but at least ten years evidencing the most intensive activity. By comparison, those planning to move in less than ten years and those planning to stay permanently are .14-.19 more likely to adopt strategies that result in exte-rior home defects.

Neighborhood Changes and Housing Reinvestment

Although the parameters estimated in the housing upkeep models dis-cussed above are based on individual homeowner observations, with some additional reasonable assumptions they can be employed to analyze changes that would predictably occur at the neighborhood level. Analysis of prospective alterations in upkeep activity at the aggregate neighborhood level provide an interesting alternative perspective on the relative impacts of various parameter changes, and also a basis for assessing policy alternatives in subsequent chapters.

In the following exposition a stylized, hypothetical neighborhood will be considered. It consists of a block face made up solely of single-family homes, each possessing the mean physical characteristics of the sample. All are owner occupied and are initially kept up at the mean investment levels of the sample.[1] Each of the following illustrative scenarios assumes that the characteristics of one-third of the homeowners are altered by a given amount (either by turnover or by some internal change); all else is held equal. Given this change, the parameters of the upkeep model in chapter 9 can be used to predict how the directly affected homeowners' upkeep expenditure behavior should be modified.[2] But any resulting changes in the visible exterior defects of their dwellings also change the average characteristics of the dwellings in the neighborhood; i.e., it creates negative externalities for others on the block. Specifically, here it will be assumed that each .01 increase in the average incidence of exterior home defects (DEFECTS?) in the neighborhood will increase the actual observed proportion of substandard dwellings on the block (DILAP) by one percentage point, and will lower the average property value on the block (AVEVALUE) by $1,000.[3] These DILAP and AVEVALUE variables are, of course, components of the physical quality index of the block (BLOCK-QUAL), and as such are directly related to the intensity of external maintenance undertaken by all homeowners on the block face, as described above in the upkeep model.[4] Thus, through their presumed impacts on aggregate neighborhood quality, any exterior-upkeep activities of the initially affected homeowners lead endogenously to altered exterior upkeep behavior by the other homeowners. Both direct and indirect (externality) effects of various hypothesized changes in homeowner characteristics are ascertained. In all cases the direct effects predominate, but in many cases the indirect, externality effects are also important.

Demographic Changes

First consider the predictable consequences of an alteration in the socioeconomic status of homeowners in our stylized neighborhood. Suppose that one-third of the homeowners move out and are replaced by ones having two years' less education. This is expected to lower the observed average annual upkeep expenditure in the neighborhood by only 2 percent, and there should be no visible difference in the incidence of home defects.

More potent results derive from a change in income. If one-third of the homeowners are replaced by those earning $10,000 less, the direct predicted impact is a reduction in average upkeep spending by 4.5 percent. Externalities are also generated to a small degree. Because the average income of the block has dropped, its indicated socioeconomic status has dropped as well.[5] The overall response is to reduce slightly the intensity of exterior upkeep. But a concomitant increase in exterior defects triggers still more externalities, which are reflected in lower average property values.[6] The ultimate impact would be an expected .008 (5 percent) rise in the incidence of homes needing exterior repairs in the neighborhood.

Consider next several hypothetical changes in household marital status and life-cycle stage, all of which produce qualitatively similar consequences to those described above. Should one-third of married homeowners be replaced by unmarried ones (female, single-male, or multiple heads), the predicted decrease in average neighborhood upkeep expenditure would be 11 percent. Furthermore, because nonmarried homeowners are more prone to having exterior home defects (by .10 per household), negative externalities are generated. These, in turn, spawn a further increase in average defects incidence of .01 across all in the area. The net result: a .04 (25 percent) higher average incidence of exterior problems in the neighborhood.[7]

On the other hand, if one-third of elderly, childless homeowners in the area are replaced by those in child-rearing life stages, average expenditures rise by 8 percent to 11 percent across the neighborhood. If the in-movers have young children, a .02 (13 percent) decrease in the overall incidence of exterior defects also transpires. And if young, childless homeowners replace the elderly, there is a sizable 13 percent increase in average expenditures. Finally, if one-third of the married homeowners with one child each are replaced by homeowners of the same age having three children each, the prediction for reduced average upkeep expenditure is 10 percent and the concomitant increase in incidence of defects is .046 (31 percent).

Thus it is clear that changes in the demographic composition of homeowners in a neighborhood can lead to substantial changes in the average upkeep behaviors. Of course, the foregoing is based on a moderate, *ceteris paribus* change in one particular characteristic of one-third of the homeowners. Actual situations could involve even more dramatic results if a larger proportion of an area's homeowners change several characteristics, all of which have mutually reinforcing consequences on upkeep behavior. This is considered in sections below. Nevertheless, it's clear in general that plausible changes in the family-status characteristics of a neighborhood's homeowners (e.g., marital status, life-cycle stage, family size) have just as sizable an impact on neighborhood investment levels as substantial changes in socioeconomic status characteristics, and a much larger impact on the exterior condition of the neighborhood's stock. Thus, for neighborhood reinvestment it matters not only how well-off homeowners are, but also what other characteristics they have.

Social-Interactive Changes

The empirical results show that the degree to which individual home-owners identify with their neighbors and the aggregate degree of such identification interact so as to specify a vital determinant (COHESION) of home upkeep behavior. However, this effect requires both individual and aggregate components (IDENTIFY and NIDENTIFY) to be above average levels. In our stylized neighborhood, consider what transpires if, for one-third of the homeowners, each of the five component items of their IDENTIFY indexes declines by one point on its respective five-point scale.[8] If initially all of the block's homeowners are at the highest value of IDENTIFY (and hence NIDENTIFY and COHESION are also at maximum), the individuals with reduced IDENTIFY spend $206 less (in Minneapolis). But because the aggregate NIDENTIFY also is now lower, the other homeowners are affected as well because COHESION for them has been reduced (COHESION = IDENTIFY × NIDENTIFY). These others similarly adjust downward their upkeep expenditures by $50 each. The combined result is that average annual expenditure in the neighborhood falls by 5 percent.[9]

The effect is intensified, however, if reductions in IDENTIFY result in either the individuals and/or the entire neighborhood dropping below the mean values of IDENTIFY and NIDENTIFY, respectively. In the former case, assume that a decline in IDENTIFY for the one-third occurs, and they indeed fall below the threshold needed for COHESION to operate. The effect is as if IDENTIFY has dropped to zero for them. Of course, as these home-owners' IDENTIFY drops, it lowers the aggregate NIDENTIFY, so the others reduce upkeep as well. The total effect here is a predicted drop of 9 percent in the neighborhood's average annual upkeep expenditures.[10] In the latter case, take a neighborhood in which initially all the homeowners have the mean level of IDENTIFY, and hence the neighborhood is minimally cohesive. In this case if any of the area's homeowners have a reduction in IDENTIFY, it reduces to zero the impact of COHESION on the whole neighborhood. This yields a drop in annual upkeep rates of 15 percent, on average.[11]

In sum, modest changes in homeowners' sense of identification with their neighbors have the potential for significantly altering the upkeep expenditure levels of an entire neighborhood. Especially if a neighborhood is barely beyond the threshold needed for the effect of cohesiveness to be operative, changes in only a few homeowners' social sentiments and collective norms prove sufficient to unravel the social-interactive fabric of the area. This reduces annual average upkeep expenditures by much greater amounts than the illustrative demographic changes described in the prior section.

Expectational Changes

Next suppose that some of the homeowners' expectations about the future quality of the stylized neighborhood become more pessimistic. For instance, let one-third of the homeowners who previously thought the neighborhood would get better now expect it to stay the same (i.e., a one-point increase in NEIGHEXP). This produces a 9 percent reduction in average annual upkeep expenditures, and a .02 (13 percent) increase in the average incidence of exterior defects. If the hypothetical neighborhood in question is one of lower value (i.e., falling one standard deviation or more below mean property values), the predicted impact on average incidence of DEFECTS? is more sizable: .10 (66 percent).

In such lower-valued areas the effect of expectations about property-value changes are quite the opposite. Let one-third of the homeowners who originally thought that neighborhood values would stay the same now believe that they will rise (i.e., a one-point decline in VALUEEXP). In such a situation free-rider behavior produces a .05 (33 percent) higher average incidence of exterior defects in the neighborhood.

Thus, even moderate changes in expectations have quantitative impacts upon neighborhoodwide upkeep expenditure levels and incidences of exterior defects that are as potent as those generated by the demographic and social-interactive changes considered earlier. And in lower-valued neighborhoods expectations about both neighborhood qualitative and property-value changes are the single most powerful determinants of exterior upkeep behavior, although their impacts are diametrically opposed.

Mobility Plan Changes

Finally, consider what occurs in our stylized neighborhood if one-third of the homeowners who originally planned to remain fifteen years now alter their plans so that they plan either to move out within ten years or to remain forever. The model's parameters suggest that such an alteration leads to a .05 to .06 (33 percent to 40 percent) increase in the average incidence of exterior home defects in the area. These magnitudes are sizable, being greater than any except those described for changes in expectations. This implies that alterations in mobility plans and, presumably, actual turnover rates can have considerable impacts on neighborhood exterior upkeep levels even if in-movers have identical demographic characteristics as out-movers. But this effect is apparent only when the net result is an alteration in the proportion of homeowners planning to reside a finite length of time but ten years or more; changes in the distribution of those across other categories have relatively little impact.

Succession and Filtering

"Succession" is a term conventionally employed in the human ecology literature to describe a process whereby the residents of a given neighborhood are replaced over time by those of lower socioeconomic status (see Grigsby et al. 1987). An oft-used synonym is "filtering" (see Grigsby et al. 1987; Weicher and Thibodeau forthcoming). Homes (and presumably neighborhoods) filter down to progressively lower income groups. The fundamental force triggering filtering is a reduction in the real value of property in the given neighborhood (for detailed discussion, see Grigsby et al. 1987). Typically such a decline can be traced to metropolitanwide or even national factors that ultimately produce either a lower demand for the types of dwelling present in a given neighborhood or to a greater supply. One factor could be a loss of employment and subsequent out-migration of residents from the metropolitan area. Another might be a deterioration of public schools and other city services provided by the jurisdiction containing the neighborhood. Metropolitan employment locations and transportation systems can change, thereby altering the accessibility features of the given neighborhood. New subdivisions may offer close substitutes for the dwellings in the given neighborhood. Whatever its cause, succession has clearly been a common feature of American urban neighborhoods for generations.

What happens to the physical quality of the housing stock when residents of lower income move in is less well understood, either theoretically or empirically (Grigsby et al. 1987, ch.6). The conventional view is that successive waves of progressively lower income residents will produce a deterioration of the housing stock eventually (see, e.g., Ahlbrandt and Brophy 1975, 5; Public Affairs Counseling 1975, 11–12; Leven et al. 1976, 38–39). If so, then the long-standing belief about filtering's improving the housing standards of poorer groups is called into question. For if neighborhoods always deteriorate to match the initial drop in real price that triggered the succession, lower-income households end up getting no more quality for their money than they ever did.

The parameters of the model estimated in this book can provide insights into the filtering phenomenon. Of course, the analysis does not examine neighborhoods over time as succession progresses, and confines itself to cross-sectional comparisons of areas occupied by different socioeconomic classes. In addition, it considers only homeowners.[12] Yet, under some reasonable assumptions, provocative implications can be drawn nonetheless.

The first is that there is no evidence that changes in the incomes of homeowners in a neighborhood produce any observable difference in the incidence of home defects. Controlling for other factors, in neither sample is income related to the incidence of litter, peeling paint, or external structural damages on property. Indeed, lower-income homeowners spend less on overall upkeep (as described above), but it apparently occurs in the additions, alterations, and improvements components of upkeep, not on the exterior maintenance. If lower-income areas appear more run-down, this appearance must be due to some factors that are spuriously correlated with income—perhaps larger families, more pessimism about neighborhood changes, shorter-term mobility plans, more clapboard houses, etc.

What the foregoing suggests is that the steady-state condition of lower-income neighborhoods is not necessarily visible decay. But the dynamic process by which a given neighborhood filters from one socioeconomic group to another may well promote such decay. That is, the initial lower-income in-movers into the neighborhood undergoing succession likely have no more propensity to let their homes decay than those they replace. But the relatively higher-income homeowners still residing there probably change *their* upkeep behavior, for several reasons suggested by the model.

First, more of them likely become more pessimistic about the future of the neighborhood. Most believe that the quality of residential life is directly related to the socioeconomic status of neighbors (see, e.g., HUD 1978). Many undoubtedly believe that the newcomers will not maintain their property as well as their predecessors. As we have seen above, such pessimism can prove devastating to upkeep expenditures and the incidence of exterior defects of homes (see Varady 1986). And of course, such reactions tend to encourage the very decay that was feared.

Second, homeowners may believe that a cohesive social fabric is unraveling if newcomers are perceived to have different traits, behaviors, and values. Indeed, it is this insecurity fostered by socioeconomic class diversity that frequently propels homeowners to choose homogeneous neighborhoods in the first place (Birch et al. 1979). And as shown above, if either the individual or the aggregate sense of identification with neighbors erodes, upkeep expenditures suffer. Reduced identification and cohesion also reduce the satisfaction of homeowners, and thereby encourage them to leave the area sooner than they had originally planned. This, of course, creates still more opportunities for succession.

Third, but of least quantitative importance, is the negative externality effect. Entering homeowners of lower socioeconomic status reduce the quality of the neighborhood by lowering its average income. As shown above, this quality decline induces homeowners previously in the area to defer exterior maintenance.

A reduction in home reinvestment by owners previously in the area creates corresponding reactions from the in-movers. They, too, now may perceive less cohesion and less upkeep in the neighborhood. And they, too, might temper their optimism about their new residential environment. Ironically, they may be induced to undertake certain upkeep strategies that they had not originally contemplated when moving in, but that subsequently were made rational by the responses of previous homeowners.

The upshot is that succession may indeed be causally associated with physical neighborhood decay, though the source of such decay must be traced to the behaviors of the prior residents as well as to those of the in-migrating owners of lower socioeconomic status. The discouraging implication of this analysis is that these deleterious consequences for the residential quality of life in urban neighborhoods undergoing succession are, to a large extent, the result of self-fulfilling prophecies.

Racial Transition

Few phenomena conjure up as strong an image of neighborhood decline as when formerly all-white areas become significantly racially integrated. And there are solid empirical studies that indicate that racial integration is indeed a powerful predictor of decline in the physical conditions of a neighborhood (see Little 1977; Vandell 1981). But this conventional wisdom must be treated very carefully in light of the findings presented here.

In brief, in neither sample was there any indication that black and white homeowners engaged in different home upkeep behavior when all else was held equal. Similarly, neither black nor white homeowners in areas of higher black proportions demonstrated weaker reinvestment efforts than their counterparts in all-white neighborhoods. If anything, white, lower-education, and female homeowners invested slightly more and evidenced fewer home defects in integrated neighborhoods than in all-white neighborhoods (see table 9.11). Of course, the present analysis was conducted for samples where more virulent forms of segregation, rapid transition and tipping of neighborhoods, and ultimate ghettoization has not been observed historically. But this is precisely what provides a clue as to why integration in other contexts has produced different results: particular expectations formed by white homeowners whose neighborhoods have been penetrated by minorities.

If whites associate lower socioeconomic status with blacks, then for them integration is tantamount to the onset of succession. And we have seen above how such perceptions can undercut home reinvestment. Similarly, many white homeowners believe that the desirability of the neighborhood is eroded by the presence of minorities, given stereotypical prejudices about the behaviors and mores of minorities. They thus view integration as a harbinger of neighborhood quality decline, with the resulting destructive behaviors outlined above.[13] This expectation possibly also reduces their expected length of tenure, further eroding reinvestments.[14] In the extreme case of "block busting" or panic selling, so many homes in the area are put on the market in such a short span that prices fall. This, in turn, encourages more succession and concomitant decay.

In other words, this study suggests that an integrated neighborhood has no less home upkeep than a comparable all-white one. But the transition of a neighborhood from all-white to integrated can lead to reduced upkeep and physical decay if the white homeowners in the area develop certain expectations. With pessimistic expectations, founded on prejudices and stereotypes about what happens in integrated neighborhoods, the neighborhood will probably decay physically and become predominantly black as well. But the reactions of the original white owners, not the behaviors of the initial minority in-movers, plant the seeds of deterioration.

Gentrification

Much public attention has been devoted to what has variously been called "central city revitalization," "urban renaissance," "the back-to-the-city movement," or what shall be used here, "gentrification" (Laska and Spain 1980; Palen and London 1984). As conventionally defined, gentrification is a process by which low- to moderate-income households are replaced in a neighborhood by higher economic status, typically younger, childless, multi-earner homeowners. In this sense gentrification could be called "reverse succession." A correlate of reverse succession has been large-scale rehabilitation of the housing stock of some neighborhoods.

Of interest here is not why gentrification occurs or what neighborhoods it focuses on, but rather on how the housing reinvestment upsurge occurs. This model suggests that there are both direct and indirect effects to be considered.

The direct effects are straightforward. The gentrifying homeowner typically replaces one of older age and lower socioeconomic status. If, for example, an elderly, high school–educated homeowner earning $15,000 were replaced by a gentrifier who was young, childless, college educated, and earned $35,000, the annual dwelling investment would be predicted to rise by 79 percent (see table 9.7).

The indirect effects, which transpire through alterations in the upkeep behavior of homeowners who remain in the area, are more complex. On the one hand, the socioeconomic status and physical quality of the neighborhood has risen, and these positive externalities may encourage homeowners to repair exterior defects. If they also become more optimistic about future neighborhood quality, even greater reinvestments are predicted.

On the other hand, if homeowners who remain in the area become more optimistic about capital gains, they may free ride and defer exterior repairs. In addition, the preexisting social cohesion of the neighborhood may be destroyed by the turnover. Valued social attachments of the remaining homeowners may be severed by the displacement of their compatriots. Finally, fears about forthcoming property-tax reassessments may be forthcoming. All of these plausible effects work to erode upkeep activity.

The net result of gentrification on the home upkeep behavior of the homeowners who remain is thus ambiguous.[15] There is little doubt, however, that an individual dwelling that transfers hands from one sort of household to a radically different sort is endowed with significantly more reinvestment.[16]

Summary and Conclusions

No single factor explains the degree to which homeowners invest in their homes and, thus, how the quality of their neighborhoods will change. Homeowners' demographic and socioeconomic characteristics, expectations, mobility plans, and solidarity sentiments shared in a cohesive neighborhood context all are crucial determinants of upkeep. Approximately the same increase in upkeep investments occurs whenever: (a) an unmarried homeowner is replaced by a married one, (b) an elderly one is replaced by one with a young child, (c) one with three children is replaced by one with only one child, and (d) one is replaced by another with both two years' more education and $20,000 more income. If any such changes occur in one-third of the owner-occupant households in an average neighborhood, aggregate levels of home investments will rise 10 to 11 percent, and the incidence of home exterior defects will fall 10 to 31 percent. If one-third of the homeowners in a neighborhood become more pessimistic about trends in the neighborhood's physical-demographic character, aggregate upkeep expenditures falls 9 to 18 percent, and the incidence of exterior defects rises 13 to 26 percent (even more in lower-quality neighborhoods). If one-third of the homeowners in lower-quality neighborhoods become more optimistic about property value trends, the incidence of exterior defects rises 33 to 66 percent. If one-third of those who hold either short-term or permanent mobility plans are replaced by homeowners planning to reside in the neighborhood 10 or more years, the incidence of exterior defects falls 33 to 40 percent. Finally, if one-third of the homeowners in a highly cohesive neighborhood lose some of their solidarity sentiments for their neighbors, aggregate upkeep expenditures fall 5 to 9 percent; if such occurs in a neighborhood barely above the cohesion threshold, the fall is three times as large.

Of course, the above refers to predicted changes that occur if only one feature of homeowners changes. In actual neighborhoods several homeowner characteristics simultaneously change in the aggregate. Yet, the above disaggregated estimates allow analysts and policymakers for the first time to decipher the welter of data flowing from neighborhoods and make quantitative predictions of the overall trends in housing conditions that will ensue.

For example, the results make it clear that any deterioration of housing that transpires as a result of neighborhood income succession or racial transition is primarily the result of self-fulfilling prophecies made by the original homeowners. There is no evidence that lower-income or black homeowners are less likely to undermaintain their homes' exteriors than are higher-income or white homeowners. Racial integration per se does not affect the home upkeep behavior of either race. Yet, the dynamics of succession and transition can generate expectations (often based on unfounded prejudices) that the physical and/or socioeconomic quality of the neighborhood will fall. Neighborhood cohesion may also suffer. As a result, the homeowners originally in the neighborhood reduce their upkeep investments and postpone exterior repairs. Ironically, it is the behavior of the in-migrating households that is conventionally (if erroneously) cited as the key cause of neighborhood deterioration.

III Policy Analyses

In past decades, various levels of government have employed a clear-cut interventionist approach to the issues of neighborhood reinvestment. At the federal level this is most visibly evidenced by the common thread running through such initiatives as the Model Cities program, the Community Development Act, the Community Reinvestment Act, and the Urban Homesteading program. Activism at the local level has taken an even wider variety of forms, as will be discussed below. In recent years, however, an unambiguous trend toward public disengagement has developed, especially at the federal level. The doctrine of *laissez faire* is now frequently used to justify a minimalist government response.

This trend toward noninterventionism raises important issues that policy analysts ignore at their peril. Exactly what sorts of outcomes does the unfettered urban residential marketplace produce? Are these outcomes efficient? Equitable? Does public intervention hold any promise for improving the efficiency or equity of the outcome? If so, which policy will likely produce the greatest positive response for a given investment of public resources?

As basic as these questions are, there have been few answers in the field of homeowners and neighborhood reinvestment. This chapter employs the results gleaned from the current model to evaluate the outcome produced by the private market for home upkeep, and to assess whether the necessary conditions for public intervention—inefficient and/or inequitable market outcomes—are met. It then analyzes which sorts of interventions have the greatest potential for improving efficiency or equity, and thus should be enacted. The possibilities are: (1) public investments in the physical conditions of neighborhoods; (2) land-use zoning regulations; (3) fostering neighborhood social cohesion; (4) building neighborhood confidence about the future; (5) ensuring adequate loan flows into the area; and (6) stabilizing neighborhood populations. Two other policy alternatives, rehabilitation grants and loans and encouraging homeownership, are sufficiently complex to warrant separate treatment in chapters 12 and 13, respectively.

The upshot of this chapter is that much of the conventional wisdom concerning policies for neighborhood reinvestment is rife with myths, half-truths and overblown generalizations. Throughout, the presentation is nontechnical so as to be accessible to a wide range of analysts and policymakers concerned with this vital issue.

A Rationale for Neighborhood Reinvestment Policy

Earlier chapters have explored theoretically and empirically how urban homeowners reach decisions about how to invest in their homes. But if these individual decisions produce outcomes that are not in the best interests of the city as a whole, at least a necessary condition for the intervention of the local public sector is established.

The two traditional criteria employed for assessing the outcomes of market behaviors are efficiency and equity. Social efficiency is achieved when a particular activity is undertaken at a level such that net social benefits (i.e., total benefits minus total costs to all parties who directly engage in this activity or indirectly are affected by it) are maximized within the constraints of resources available. Social equity is achieved when the various benefits and costs of an action are distributed across members of some society in a "fair" manner, as determined by the collective's norms and as expressed through the political (policy-making) process.

Both criteria are not likely to be fulfilled in the case of homeowners' housing upkeep behaviors. The analysis has revealed two distinct sources of inefficiencies: externalities, and strategic interactions among homeowners. Neighborhood externalities occur because homeowners decide how much upkeep investment to undertake so as to maximize their own well-being, but do not consider that their potential investments provide well-being to other proximate residents (see chapter 3). As a result, they invest too little from a broader social perspective. Results in chapter 6 provide some confirmation for this externality effect by showing that conditions of properties on the block-face, planning-area, and census-tract levels of neighborhood are all directly related to neighborhood satisfaction.

A commonly used statistical procedure allows one to place a dollar valuation on this externality effect. By regressing home market value on a variety of structural, lot, public service, and neighborhood characteristics, one can discern how each of these characteristics separately is valued by the market. Because market values reflect differences in the capitalized stream of net benefits presumably flowing to the occupants, they are conventionally employed as proxies for social benefits (see Rothenberg

1967, Pines and Weiss 1976, Chung 1973, Diamond and Tolley 1982, and Brueckner 1983). This procedure is followed for the Minneapolis sample, with home value being regressed on all the dwelling and neighborhood variables employed earlier in the upkeep analysis. Of most interest is the coefficient of the variable denoting the proportion of other houses on the block face having exterior defects (DILAP). A 10 percentage point higher value of DILAP is associated with an an average 2.7 percent reduction in property value per dwelling, or $1,215 for dwellings valued at the median of the lowest third of the property-value range, $45,000.[1] The implication is that if a homeowner decides to renovate a dilapidated property it likely induces an aggregate increase in neighboring property values of $10,000 to $15,000, given typically sized block faces. As found in other studies (Varady 1982b), the magnitude of this externality generated by a single property may not seem staggering, but aggregated over thousands of deteriorated dwellings on hundreds of different blocks in an average city, the implied inefficiency is not trivial.

An even more important source of inefficiency is the strategic interaction among homeowners. Even if there were no externalities from upkeep, because each individual's investments are decided based on expectations of proximate others' investments, the sum of these individual investments (and resulting group well-being) may be much less than would be possible if decisions were collectivized. In other words, if each homeowner could be assured that all other homeowners will reinvest, the individual's neighborhood optimism and subsequent upkeep expenditures would be encouraged. Unfortunately, because of uncertainty and decentralized decision making, each individual tends to hold back, waiting for the behaviors of others to signal intentions. This conservative, crowd-following behavior retards neighborhood revitalization and hastens decay. As shown in chapter 10, if homeowners expect neighborhood quality to decline, they cut back upkeep, thereby hastening the deterioration of their dwellings. If such decay becomes visible, pessimism and concomitant cutbacks follow from neighboring owners. This ultimately leads to a self-fulfilling prophecy of neighborhood decay: a result no individual homeowner desires but cannot rationally avoid in a fragmented decision-making context. Similar inefficiencies occur in lower-valued neighborhoods when optimism about future property values increases. On such occasions, free-rider behavior retards the upgrading of properties and improvements in the quality of the residential environment.

The foregoing chapters provide little direct evidence relevant to the equity criterion, but justification for intervention can be made on other grounds. Fundamental to such an argument must be a normative judgment that every household is entitled to a minimal quality of residential environment, which includes the dwelling and the neighborhood context.

Such a norm is explicit in the national goal expressed in the 1949 Housing Act to provide a suitable home and a decent living environment for all Americans. At the local level, this norm can be applied to justify public actions aimed at raising the dwelling quality or neighborhood quality of residents who have been adjudged to fall below minimal environmental standards, or to prevent such a decline in the first place.

In sum, both efficiency and equity standpoints provide necessary conditions for public-sector interventions in the arena of neighborhood housing reinvestment levels.[2] Necessary conditions need not be sufficient for adoption, of course. Whether a particular policy can be justified depends crucially on whether it promotes the desired level of housing upkeep. It is precisely this question that is investigated for a variety of policies below and in chapters 12 and 13.

Alternative Neighborhood Reinvestment Policy Responses

There is a long-standing history of public-sector attempts to affect housing reinvestment and thereby stabilize or revitalize neighborhoods. Most seem superficially sensible, but few have been rigorously scrutinized. In light of the empirical research reported in previous chapters, this section evaluates six such conventional areas of policy responses: neighborhood physical investments, land-use zoning, fostering social cohesion and neighborhood confidence, ensuring adequate loan flows, and stabilizing neighborhood populations. Two other policy responses are treated in the next two chapters: rehabilitation grants and loans, and inducements for homeownership.

Improving Neighborhood Physical Conditions

An oft-cited public-policy strategy for encouraging housing investment is to improve the physical conditions in neighborhoods through, e.g., housing code enforcement, demolition of abandoned structures, and investments in local public infrastructure. Proponents of such a strategy implicitly accept the conventional view that the presence of deteriorated surroundings discourages the individual from undertaking housing upkeep strategies (see Stegman 1972; Public Affairs Counseling 1975, Ahlbrandt and Brophy 1975, Hollister et al. 1978, Clay 1979, Downs 1981). But several recent empirical studies have questioned this implicit assumption. Ahlbrandt and Cunningham (1979, 159) and Birch et al. (1979, 119) have presented cross-tabular evidence suggesting that the physical condition of the neighborhood is of little import to upkeep behavior. Struyk and Soldo (1980, ch.4) find no relationship between elderly homeowners' assessments of neighborhood quality and their repair activities. Shear and Carpenter (1982), Shear (1983), and Stewart and Hyclak (1986) find that, *ceteris paribus*, the presence of abandoned buildings on the block is not a significant correlate of upkeep expenditures. Taub, Taylor, and Dunham (1984, ch.6) show in a multivariate analysis that the state of neighborhood (i.e., multitract community area in Chicago) deterioration is positively correlated with the probability that a homeowner has spent over $1,000 on upkeep during the previous two years. This relationship is shown to vary, however, depending on the degree of optimism about trends in neighborhood property values: for optimists, upkeep is lower in deteriorated areas (see table 9.1).

The results of this study provide a means of reconciling this debate. The results reported in chapters 9 and 10 suggest that physical conditions on the surrounding block face have very small impacts on homeowners' upkeep behavior, as measured through incidence of exterior defects (and even less if measured as expected value of expenditure).[3] Suppose, for example, that a host of neighborhood infrastructure investments were undertaken such that it boosts the average property values on some representative block face by $10,000. Compared to an otherwise-identical block (but with $10,000 lower values) homeowners in the improved area are expected to manifest only a .012 reduction in exterior defects due to intensified upkeep behavior. For an average block face, this represents just an 8 percent reduction in such incidence.

Of course, the above estimate is based on a cross-sectional analysis, and it is not necessarily the case that the result of dynamic changes from one state of quality to another will produce identical behaviors to those exhibited in one static state versus another. Yet this study finds that there are no differences in the expectations held by homeowners in areas that have received large amounts of community development infrastructure funds and by those in similar, but unfunded, areas (see chapter 7), suggesting that such investments are not terribly effective generators of optimism.[4] Nevertheless, even if such temporary expectational dynamics are highly efficacious for upkeep, the parameters indicate that the longer-run differences in steady-state upkeep levels between improved and unimproved blocks will likely be modest.[5]

Even more cause for skepticism concerning the efficacy of infrastructure improvements arises when one considers impacts generated in areas surrounding improved blocks. Recall that all the spatial levels of neighborhood tested—block face, multiblock planning area, and census tract—contribute equally to homeowners' evaluations of the quality of residential environment (see table 6.6). Also, the current conditions on both the block-face and planning-area scale appear to affect homeowners' expectations about future property-value trends (see table 7.2).

Consider what the foregoing means for any of a variety of possible public programs that succeed in improving the physical quality on the one block in a lower-value area upon which the funds are expended, but not other blocks nearby. The neighborhood satisfaction of homeowners on and well beyond the immediate targeted block are enhanced. Confidence about property-value appreciation is increased within a several square-block area around the targeted block, though not so widely as the satisfaction effect. But, as indicated by tables 9.4 and 9.5, both enhanced optimism about capital gains and satisfaction is predicted to increase the likelihood of undermaintaining dwelling exteriors. Thus, if the goal is to abet neighborhood satisfaction or optimism about property values, policies that improve the condition of one block have considerable positive geographic spillovers. On the other hand, the geographic spillovers appear as negative consequences if the program goal is enhanced housing upkeep. Indeed, the net effect of infrastructure investments on housing conditions may prove deleterious when viewed over a broader area.

In conclusion, public investments in neighborhood infrastructure are unlikely to induce homeowners on the impacted block faces to undertake significant amounts of exterior home repairs. Although those on adjacent blocks may be more satisfied with and optimistic about their neighborhood's property values, this proves indirectly to be harmful to their levels of upkeep. The result: such public investments are not recommended as a device for encouraging private housing reinvestment.

Land-Use Zoning Regulations

The conventional wisdom suggests that encroaching nonresidential land use typically produces deleterious effects on housing upkeep investment in the affected neighborhoods (see Muth 1969, 118–19; Clay 1979, 82; and Downs 1981, 19, 67–68). As a result, there have been strong pleas for intensified application of land-use zoning as a tool for stimulating upkeep (see Clay 1979, ch.7; Hallman 1984, 215). Yet there has not been any convincing empirical evidence to back up this policy.

The empirical results of this study provide strong refutation for the conventional position (see tables 9.10 and 9.11). Controlling for other features of the residential environment and characteristics of the homeowner, the presence of nonresidential land use on the block face is not significantly correlated with the choice of upkeep strategy, upkeep expenditures, or the probability of home defects, in either the Wooster or the Minneapolis sample. In the Minneapolis sample there is, however, an indirect, negative correlation between nonresidential land use and housing defects mediated by neighborhood satisfaction, expectations, and mobility plans. First, although nonresidential land use generally produces lower neighborhood satisfaction for most household groups (as conventionally predicted), this does not discourage upkeep. Rather, it reduces the likelihood that the homeowner will hold permanent mobility plans, and thereby enhances the chances of exterior upkeep. Second, this relationship is strengthened by another indirect relationship: those with nonresidential land use on their block faces are less pessimistic about their neighborhood's future, contrary to conventional wisdom. This increased optimism both decreases the likelihood of observing exterior home defects and increases upkeep expenditures. Finally, those with nonresidential land use in lower-valued areas are more pessimistic about property-value appreciation, but respond with trend-bucking behavior, which lowers the incidence of exterior defects (see table 7.2). The net result is that homeowners on blocks with nonresidential land use on average spend 12 percent more on upkeep and evidence a .18 lower incidence of disrepair—a figure larger than the sample mean!

In conclusion, the evidence indicates nothing that would commend land-use zoning as a potent reinvestment-stimulating policy in most neighborhoods. This conclusion should not be construed as an assertion that no actual or anticipated change in land use affects housing upkeep investment. Undoubtedly there are instances when the introduction of severe nuisance-creating uses (polluting factories, transport modes, etc.) into a residential neighborhood or the widespread anticipation of a major development converting large tracts from residential to nonresidential use has had such an effect. But the results indicate that residential areas do not need to be protected from the retail, commercial, and even light industrial land uses that are often present in neighborhoods similar to those surveyed in Minneapolis. Unfortunately, one cannot tell from these data precisely what these nonresidential uses are, so conclusions about specific zoning regulations cannot be drawn.

Fostering Social Cohesion

In recent years a rising chorus has been heard arguing that public policies must not look solely at economic and physical aspects of home upkeep, but must also consider the social-interactive dimension of the neighborhood. That local social pressures to conform and the commitment wrought from participation in local social organizations can encourage upkeep has been claimed by Clay (1979, ch.3), Goetze (1979, ch.6), Ahlbrandt and Cunningham (1979, chs. 1, 3, 12), Downs (1981, 11), Hallman (1984, 41), and Taub, Taylor, and Dunham (1984, ch.6). Particular programmatic means for building this social cohesion have been described by Ahlbrandt and Cunningham (1979, ch.12), and Hallman (1984, part 4).

Although the present research provides little guidance as to how the weaving of local social fabric should be accomplished, it strongly supports such action, at least as far as home upkeep goes. And the results suggest which social dimensions of the neighborhood should and should not be striven for. First, interneighbor social interaction should not be seen as a desirable goal in itself. Neither the individual's nor the neighborhood's average level of interpersonal name familiarity or frequency of contact has any salutary effect on promoting upkeep. (For female homeowners it even appears to discourage it by fanning pessimistic expectations.) It is only when local social interaction serves as a means for promoting a sense of neighborhood identification that it becomes a reasonable goal of public reinvestment policy. Second, both the individual's and his/her neighbor's sense of group solidarity are important independent contributors to housing investment in neighborhoods. Any community organizing or informational efforts that serve to enhance owners' beliefs that their neighbors have fundamentally common interests to their own are thus to be commended. But those pursuing such efforts must be aware that the positive individual-group synergism that leads to improved upkeep will be forthcoming only after a certain threshold of group identification has been attained. Put differently, reinvestment payoffs of policies to build neighborhood cohesion may reap rapid returns in marginally cohesive areas, may require sizable efforts in areas with less collective identification, and may be virtually impossible to attain in highly fragmented contexts. Clearer evidence on the efficacy of creating neighborhood cohesion through exogenous intervention is certainly needed before one can estimate precisely how scarce resources should be used in such an effort.

The data do suggest, however, something of the character of sampled areas that prove to be cohesive in the sense of strong collective identification. Cohesive and noncohesive neighborhoods differ dramatically on numerous dimensions.[6] Cohesive areas in both samples have higher physical quality, higher socioeconomic status, higher property values, larger proportions of white and of long-time residents, lower incidence of nonresidential land use, and fewer deteriorated structures. The comparative characteristics of homeowners in the two types of areas indicate that in both samples the cohesive areas have larger proportions of married homeowners and significantly greater mean levels of residential satisfaction.[7] Interestingly, there are not statistically significant differences between cohesive and noncohesive areas in terms of proportions with short-term, medium-term, or long-term mobility plans, or in terms of general neighborhood expectations.

As a final caveat, the evidence supporting augmented neighborhood cohesion is limited to its impact on housing upkeep behavior only. There may be other undesirable side effects from increasing cohesion: intensified parochialism, racial and socioeconomic segregation, and political "balkanization" (see Clay 1979, 69–71). Obviously, we need to learn more about how these potentially undesirable features may be minimized before we make significant public attempts to increase neighborhood social cohesion. Nevertheless, the salutary effects of cohesion on neighborhood reinvestment undoubtedly commend it as an objective of public policy.

Building Neighborhood Confidence

There has been little quarrel among members of the academic and planning communities about the investment-shaping potential of owners' optimistic expectations or confidence in the future of the neighborhood (see Stegman 1972, 98; Ahlbrandt and Brophy 1975, 10–14; Kain and Quigley 1975, 35; Ahlbrandt and Cunningham 1979, 155; Clay 1979, 79–80; Downs 1981, 16–19; and Grigsby and Corl 1983). Until recently, however, there has been only impressionistic evidence to support the conventional wisdom that confidence and upkeep go hand in hand. Taub, Taylor, and Dunham (1984, ch.6) are the first to suggest that not only the type of expectation matters, but also the neighborhood in which it occurs.

The present study not only supports these last provocative findings, but also sheds light on hitherto uninvestigated dimensions of expectations and housing upkeep that contradict the conventional wisdom. The most important result is that there are at least two quite independent types of expectations held by homeowners, and that they have dramatically opposite consequences for upkeep behavior, depending on the neighborhood. The results for neighborhood quality expectations support the conventional predictions cited above in all sorts of neighborhoods.[8] For policymakers this means that any sorts of actions that promote optimism about neighborhood quality can be commended for any sort of neighborhood as a potentially potent generator of home reinvestment. Unfortunately, neither previous work nor the analysis in chapter 7 provides any guidelines about what specific programs might be most successful in this effort.

The task confronting policymakers in neighborhoods of lower property value (presumably where most efforts would be concentrated) is considerably more complex. In such areas optimism about future property capital gains results in a weakening of upkeep efforts. The elusive goal is to abet optimism about neighborhood quality without simultaneously abetting optimism about property values. Whether this is possible is problematic. Suppose that a city embarks on a concerted campaign of both symbolic (e.g., public relations gimmicks) and real (e.g., infrastructure invest-ments) gestures that succeed in making homeowners in certain lower-value target neighborhoods more optimistic about their neighborhoods as places to live. Even if this campaign somehow avoids simultaneously in-flaming their expectations about property inflation (a large assumption indeed), consider the likely consequences. The now-more-optimistic homeowners are expected to invest considerably more sums in their homes and to maintain their exteriors more intensively. But the model's results indicate that such physical home improvements will generate optimism about capital gains, even if the initial public efforts did not. This optimism encourages free-rider behaviors that counter the exterior renovation ef-fects. The net result is that there likely will be a period of comparatively static exterior quality of the neighborhood's homes until the consequences of neighborhood quality expectations begin to dominate. Of course, there is no guarantee that they always will.

The programmatic implications are that, at best, policymakers can ex-pect only rather halting, fitful overall improvements in the visual ap-pearance of neighborhoods targeted for confidence building.[9] And it is easily conceivable that well-intentioned policies can produce unintended consequences in this regard (see Goetze and Colton 1980). Given the lack of understanding about how expectations are altered and the evidence of their volatile, unpredictable consequences for home upkeep, intentionally attempting to build neighborhood confidence cannot be recommended as a key element of neighborhood investment policy (cf. Goetze 1976).

Ensuring Adequate Loan Flows

Most of the previous analysis has focused on understanding the circum-stances when a homeowner would or would not like to make home invest-ments. Here attention is turned to the circumstance when a homeowner wishes to make a sizable home improvement, but is unable to obtain the requisite financing. Some analysts and many community groups have al-leged that applications for home improvement loans often have been de-nied on the basis of discriminating criteria (e.g., the sex or race of the applicant, the racial composition or age of housing stock in the neigh-borhood). Since the passage of the Community Reinvestment Act and the Home Mortgage Disclosure Act in the late 1970s there has been only limited empirical evidence that such illegal lending policies are continuing (see Schafer and Ladd 1980, Listokin and Casey 1980, King 1980, Black and Schweitzer 1980, and Ryker et al. 1984). If such illegal practices were to prove to be curtailing the flow of reinvestment funds into a particular neighborhood, local authorities in conjunction with the appropriate federal regulatory agencies should seek legal redress as a matter of course.

The more important financing issues revolve around whether legal, responsible lending practices are foreclosing socially desirable home reinvestments by willing homeowners. It is not illegal to deny loans on properties that are fairly adjudged to be weak collateral, based on their prospective resale potential. But what such rational decisions on the part of a single lending institution overlook is that individual institutional portfolio risks can be minimized if all lenders act in concert. The interinstitution strategic behaviors and resulting social inefficiencies are analogous to those among homeowners described earlier. In neighborhoods with uncertain futures, individual lenders are loath to take the risk of approving a sizable home improvement loan, fearing that other institutions will be more conservative and, as a result, the neighborhood will decay and the value of the collateral will be eroded. Of course, if all institutions do this, the self-fulfilling prophecy occurs. The task of the public sector is, then, to devise ways of coordinating lender decisions and boosting institutional confidence in a neighborhood so as to render the issuance of loans there a sound business practice.

One of the most widely adopted and acclaimed schemes for accomplishing this is the Neighborhood Housing Services (NHS) model (see Ahlbrandt and Brophy 1975, and Ahlbrandt and Cunningham 1979 for a complete description and evaluation of NHS). In brief, NHS organizers in conjunction with local government officials select as target neighborhoods those areas that have predominantly owner-occupied, structurally sound dwellings, but that are beginning to show signs of decay or to need significant investments to meet housing codes. A consortium of lending institutions is assembled and a common pool of revolving loan funds is earmarked for the target area. The local public sector typically commits itself to infrastructure improvements, selective code enforcement, and program outreach in the target areas. The overall goal is to coordinate decisions about reinvestments and reassure all parties, so as to avoid the inefficiencies associated with the prisoner's dilemma scenario noted above.[10]

Virtually all evaluations of NHS have indicated that it does, indeed, promote home rehabilitation. It is less clear, however, whether this transpires through increasing: (1) voluntary homeowner demand for loans, (2) involuntary homeowner demand for loans (through code enforcement), or (3) financial institutions' willingness to supply loans. Such clarification is crucial for proper policy formulation. If, e.g., many homeowners want to borrow but cannot obtain financing, either a collective private loan pool or loans directly from the public sector (as described in chapter 11) might be sufficient. If, however, the underlying demand is not there, no abetted availability of private or public loans will induce reinvestment. This may be especially true in neighborhoods that already have deteriorated. Other sorts of "carrots and sticks" are then needed to induce homeowners to take advantage of the available financing.

In sum, public efforts to avert inefficient strategic behaviors by lending institutions are to be commended in circumstances where the unavailability of loans is the binding constraint on home reinvestment. Such efforts alone are unlikely to be sufficient in many neighborhoods, however.

Stabilizing Neighborhood Populations

There have been several claims (Goetze 1976, Public Affairs Counseling, 1975) that one key to maintaining adequate reinvestment levels in decent neighborhoods is to stabilize their populations. Unfortunately, what "stabilizing their populations" means precisely is seldom spelled out. Yet one must be precise in this regard, because different interpretations yield wildly different conclusions.

Even if stabilization is viewed in nonracial terms, numerous alternatives remain. If one views stabilization as a process ensuring that in-movers have the same overall profiles as out-movers from a neighborhood, then indeed it follows logically that consistent upkeep efforts should persist indefinitely in that area. But such a situation is virtually impossible to achieve. We know too little about how mobility patterns are affected by public interventions to contemplate seriously the formulation of discretionary mobility policies that would regulate flows of households between neighborhoods. Even if such tools were developed, achieving such stability across all neighborhoods is impossible in principle if the aggregate socioeconomic or demographic profile of the metropolitan population is changing. For example, one cannot keep the same number of middle-income households moving into all erstwhile middle-income neighborhoods simultaneously if half the city's middle-income households have moved to another region of the country.

Stabilization could mean reducing excessive turnover of homeowners by somehow encouraging all to remain longer in their current residences than they might otherwise. In principle this is plausible, at least from a metropolitanwide perspective. But again, such a suggestion is not pragmatic. As we have seen, inexorable change in family life-cycle stage is the prime motivator of mobility, and it is hard to imagine how such motivation could be altered without fundamental changes in cultural norms. Furthermore, the analysis suggests that such stability would not necessarily be an unmitigated good, even if somehow it was achieved. Certainly if we could induce those who plan to reside in their homes for short periods to remain for more than a decade, we would expect intensified home upkeep efforts on their part. But the most stable homeowners—those who plan to remain permanently—also tend to undermaintain their homes. This suggests that one would need to stabilize some homeowners and destabilize others in the same neighborhood if reinvestment efforts are to be maximized.

Finally, nonracial stabilization can be interpreted as dispersing the lowest-income population (Downs 1973). Implicit here is the assumption that the filtering down of a neighborhood to this group will lead to its inevitable decay, as the multiple, complex pathologies of a concentrated poverty population come to bear. Also assumed is that these low-income households will not set off deleterious reinvestment reactions by owners in the neighborhood into which they are placed if they are somehow dispersed widely enough. Neither assumption commands unambiguous empirical support (see Grigsby et al. 1987, chs.6, 8). But even if they did, the programmatic implications of such a stabilization through dispersal would necessarily be massive housing subsidy programs such as rent vouchers or scattered-site subsidized dwellings. Although it is conceivable that the metropolitanwide levels of neighborhood reinvestment in such a hypothetical regime are superior to the status quo, it seems inadvisable to recommend such a dispersal effort on these grounds. It is also a highly impolitic means for encouraging reinvestment, given the current reluctance to continue, let alone expand, public transfer programs.

Neighborhood stabilization can also, however, have racial overtones. To the segregationist it means that blacks and other minorities are kept out of all-white neighborhoods so as to avoid the disruptive effects of threatened tipping on home upkeep levels, as described in chapter 10. But there is clear evidence that most minorities prefer to live in substantially integrated areas, and that large numbers have the economic wherewithal to occupy homes in most white neighborhoods.[11] The implication: if white neighborhoods are to be racially stabilized, discriminatory barriers must prevent minorities from making housing market choices that they are willing and able to make.[12] Of course, such barriers are illegal, so consideration of this form of stabilization is dismissed out of hand.

Another racially conscious notion of stabilization involves already-integrated neighborhoods. If these can be prevented from rapidly tipping and resegregating, then the associated spasmodic declines in reinvestment might be avoided.

The ultimate means for achieving the stabilization of integration can be found only in a metropolitanwide context. The goal must be that all neighborhoods in all political jurisdictions in a metropolitan area are truly open to any household that can afford to live there. Without this systematic elimination of discrimination, minority housing demands will be focused on those few communities that are perceived to be open. The result is that in these communities the demand for vacancies is disproportionately made up of minorities, and the tendency to tip persists.

The policy implication is clearly that there must be sustained efforts to achieve residential freedom of choice through the rigorous enforcement of fair housing laws (see Yinger et al. 1979). Shorter-run policies can be aimed at balancing racial housing demands in integrated areas through such devices as affirmative marketing aimed at white homeseekers or special public infrastructure investments designed to thwart conventional expectations about what happens to the physical condition of such neighborhoods. If these efforts produce visible, stable, integrated neighborhoods of high quality, they will serve to erode white stereotypes about such areas, rendering racial transition less likely elsewhere. Thus the two-pronged strategy of promoting metropolitanwide fair housing and shoring up integrated neighborhoods proves mutually reinforcing, and ultimately reduces the likelihood of underinvestment associated with racial transition.

Of course, neither prong of the above strategy is easy to implement. The former is especially difficult in fragmented political jurisdictions within a metropolitan area. A jurisdiction that wishes to stabilize its integrated neighborhoods has little leverage for encouraging others to adopt an open-housing posture. And metropolitanwide private fair-housing groups, even when present, are underfunded for the task of ensuring freedom of choice throughout the region. States and the federal government clearly have more potential policy tools to bring to bear in this regard (see Downs 1973), although at present the political will to exercise this potential is sadly missing. Whether localities can exercise the second prong, when the first is absent, to achieve any significant stabilization of integrated areas is problematic, although a limited number of successful cases can be cited.[13]

Summary and Conclusions

This chapter argues that unfettered individual behaviors in the market for home upkeep often produce outcomes that are not socially optimal. Individual behaviors are likely to produce an inefficiently low level of housing reinvestment as a result of strategic interactions and, to a lesser extent, as a result of the externalities produced by upkeep. These outcomes are also typically inequitable, because the burdens of neighborhood deterioration fall most heavily on those in lower socioeconomic groups. Thus, the necessary conditions for public sector intervention in the realm of home upkeep are established.

Unfortunately, many of the conventional means of public intervention are neither effective nor practical. Analysis of policies based on the theory and evidence presented earlier suggests that:

– Public investments to improve the neighborhood infrastructure or physical conditions will have only minimal positive impacts on the upkeep behavior of homeowners on the targeted block face. Upkeep expenditures are unlikely to be affected, and exterior defects will be reduced only by a small amount; overall optimism will not be improved. Consequences in areas surrounding the targeted area are likely to prove detrimental to upkeep activities there. The aggregate net result of reinvestment may not, therefore, be positive.

– Zoning restrictions designed to create and maintain areas of homogeneous residential land uses will have no salutary impact on upkeep in areas so affected. In Minneapolis, intensifying land-use segregation will reduce housing upkeep efforts by certain homeowner types.

– Promoting social cohesion of a neighborhood will likely produce sizable gains in upkeep expenditures and in exterior dwelling conditions, but only if: (1) identification (rather than interaction) with neighbors is abetted, and (2) the neighborhoodwide level of identification rises sufficiently to reach the threshold of cohesion. Unfortunately, we know little about how to promote social cohesion, and negative, unintended consequences may follow from such promotion.

– Building neighborhood confidence in lower-valued neighborhoods will have both negative and positive effects, because manipulations of expectations must simultaneously abet optimism about qualitative neighborhood changes and discourage it in connection with neighborhood property-value changes. It is doubtful that this can be accomplished, especially given the low level of understanding about how expectations may be manipulated through policy efforts.

– Public efforts to coordinate actions of individual lending institutions can, in principle, increase the availability of home improvement funds by eliminating gaming dimensions that produce the prisoner's dilemma. Increasing loan availability will be insufficient to generate much reinvestment, however, if there is no underlying demand for such loans.

– Efforts to stabilize neighborhood populations using nonracial criteria appear to be fruitless. It is impossible from a metropolitanwide perspective to ensure that in-movers have the same profiles as out-movers in all neighborhoods. Reducing turnover rates can increase upkeep, but there are no policy tools to stabilize such homeowners without simultaneously encouraging offsetting permanent mobility plans. Dispersing low-income populations might increase metropolitanwide upkeep levels, but even rough empirical estimates cannot be made on this. Such an effort would require massive housing subsidies supplied by some level(s) of government above the local public sector—subsidies that cannot reasonably be predicted.

– Efforts to stabilize the racial composition of a neighborhood will promote upkeep by avoiding the negative reactions to tipping. But racial stabilization by excluding minorities from white areas is illegal. Stabilization of already-integrated areas requires both metropolitanwide open-housing efforts and direct efforts to stimulate white housing demand in integrated neighborhoods. It is doubtful whether the latter effort can be successful alone if the former has not been achieved. In any case, these efforts are often beyond the influence of a single municipality.

12 Directly Encouraging Neighborhood Reinvestment through Public Subsidies

Attempting to encourage property maintenance by providing earmarked grants or low-interest loans is a policy option that has been employed frequently in various forms under both federal and local auspices.[1] The main empirical question is whether this option is effective in generating additional private investments in the existing housing stock. Put differently, do public subsidies merely substitute for private dollars that would have been spent in the absence of subsidies? Both the theoretical framework and the empirical results of previous chapters provide the means for addressing this question in a far more rigorous way than has yet been attempted.

First, the model of homeowner housing upkeep behavior developed in chapter 3 is employed below to show how grants and loans affect upkeep decisions. Whether public grants replace private housing investment is shown to depend on homeowners' preferences and on the relative marginal rates of transformation of upward conversion versus positive maintenance. Whether low-interest loans encourage more rapid rehabilitation efforts depends on the degree to which homeowners' marginal rates of substitution for upward conversion alterations and nonhousing consumption are altered. This treatment is technical and should be omitted by readers not thoroughly familiar with chapter 3.

Next, particular Minneapolis subsidy policies are outlined and empirical results from the Minneapolis sample are used to quantify their impacts. First, parameters of the home upkeep functions of homeowners directly receiving subsidies (as reported in chapter 9) are used to estimate the direct leveraging generated by the subsidies. Second, there is an empirical estimation of the indirect leveraging effect that occurs when subsidies to some homeowners in an area encourage other nearby homeowners to increase their investments, due to abetted confidence about the neighborhood (see chapter 7). Third, positive externalities accruing to nearby households as a result of the above reinvestments are quantified.

All these program benefits are compared with program costs both to society and to the local public sector, and a formal benefit-cost analysis is conducted to ascertain which subsidy policies provide the highest net benefits.[2] Three Minneapolis policies—grants, low-interest loans, and no-interest, deferred loans—are considered. The results are used to make detailed program recommendations about how subsidies might be packaged so as to obtain the maximum payoff from a given amount of public resources.

Theoretical Analysis of Rehabilitation Grants and Loans

Consider a theoretical analysis of the expected impact of subsidies on homeowners' upkeep behavior that employs a graphical analysis similar to that employed in chapter 3. Figures 12.1 and 12.2 are analogous to the situation portrayed in figure 3.1, with a set of representative homeowner indifference curves (U_i) showing marginal rates of substitution between alterations in housing structural capital ($\bar{A}_t$) and nonhousing consumption (Z_t). The presubsidy transformation function for maintenance is DF; for upward conversion it is GJ.

Matching Rehabilitation Grants

Consider a matching grant that is designed to help defray a portion of the homeowner costs of performing various maintenance activities. Minneapolis's "fix and paint" 50 percent matching grant program is representative. Graphically in figure 12.1, such a policy causes the pivoting of the positive-maintenance transformation function clockwise around point F, say to the extent shown by $D'F$.[3] Assuming that the original upkeep strategy being pursued was positive maintenance at point E, the new optimum at E' unambiguously is associated with greater housing capital alterations $\bar{A}_t$. Given the presumed normality of both goods in question, it is also likely that the income effect of a reduced price of $\bar{A}_t$ will dominate the substitution effect. This means that the postsubsidy expenditure of the homeowner's own funds will be less than the presubsidy expenditure, by the amount $\$P_Z(Z_1 - Z_4)$ in figure 12.1. This replacement of public for private funds is greater the lower the price elasticity of $\bar{A}_t$ versus Z.

Note, however, that if the presubsidy global-optimum strategy was zero maintenance, the consequence of the matching grant is potentially much more efficacious. If in terms of figure 12.1 the presubsidy optimum was F and the postsubsidy optimum is E', there is no replacement of private funds with public ones. Indeed, there is $\$P_Z(Z_0 - Z_1)$ extra private expenditure on maintenance that has been directly stimulated by the policy. Of course, it is possible that the matching grant does not reduce the

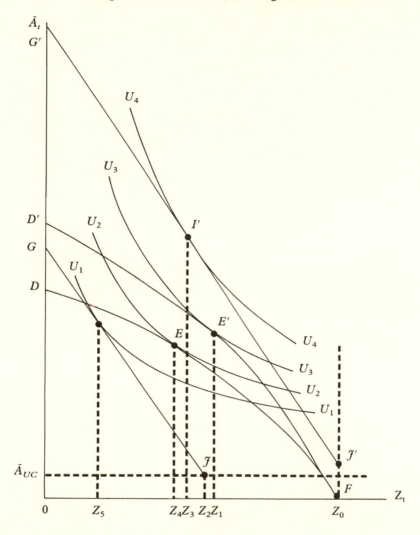

Key: U_n = homeowner indifference curves
DF = pregrant transformation function for maintenance
$D'F$ = postgrant transformation function for maintenance
$G\mathcal{J}$ = pregrant transformation function for upward conversion
$G'\mathcal{J}'$ = postgrant transformation function for upward conversion

Figure 12.1 The Effects of Grants on Home Upkeep

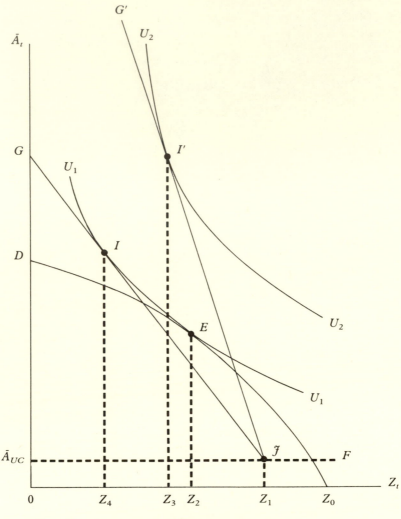

Key: U_n = homeowner indifference curves
DF = preloan transformation function for maintenance
$G\mathcal{J}$ = preloan transformation function for upward conversion
$G'\mathcal{J}$ = postloan transformation function for upward conversion

Figure 12.2   The Effects of Subsidized Loans on Home Upkeep

price of upkeep sufficiently to move homeowners from their prior zero-upkeep strategy. In this event, we observe qualifying homeowners choosing not to participate in the program.

Full Rehabilitation Grants

A policy that provides earmarked 100 percent grants for particular kinds of upward conversions, such as Minneapolis's grants for correcting code violations, has a different effect in the model. Recall that the model posits some minimal amount of alteration (and corresponding Z expenditure sacrifice) to qualify as upward conversion, $\bar{A}_{UC}$. Now suppose this $\bar{A}_{UC}$ initially requires a minimum investment of $\$P_Z(Z_0 - Z_2)$, as shown by point J on the upward-conversion transformation function GJ. If the grant program provides sufficient funds to cover such minimum expenditures only partially (e.g., \$500 for a heating-system replacement costing \$700), the new transformation function shifts (parallel to GJ) to the right, but attaining the requisite $\bar{A}_{UC}$ still requires some expenditure of private funds. Unless such a shift in GJ is sufficient to allow the homeowner to attain indifference curve U_2, accepting the grant is inferior to the utility gained from the original positive maintenance strategy at E. In this case we predict nonparticipation of eligible homeowners.

But consider a larger grant that provides more than the minimum-needed upward-conversion expenditure. Such is shown by upward-conversion transformation function $G'J'$ in figure 12.1, with a total grant amount of $\$P_{\bar{A}_t} (J' - F)$.[4] In this case the homeowner gets some free $\bar{A}_t$ without any sacrifice of Z_t, so of course the strategy is desirable for all homeowners who are able to participate in the program. If, as shown in figure 12.1, the new $G'J'$ dominates the positive-maintenance transformation function, the global optimum switches from positive maintenance to upgrading at I', with an associated expenditure of private funds $\$P_Z(Z_0 - Z_3)$.[5] Of course, some private funds would have been spent on maintenance in the absence of the grant, so the question is which expenditure is larger? No general answer can be given. If the initial optimum was at E', the initial expenditure of $\$P_Z(Z_0 - Z_1)$ is less than the postgrant expenditure. Just the opposite is true if the initial optimum was at E. Ultimately the answer depends on both homeowner preferences and shapes of the two transformation functions. The greater the income elasticity of $\bar{A}_t$ (i.e., the slope of locus II') relative to the price elasticity of $\bar{A}_t$ (i.e., the slope of locus EE'), the greater the likelihood that the grant will lead to an increase in private expenditures, as shown in figure 12.1. The smaller the marginal rate of transformation (i.e., the greater the diminishing returns) of the maintenance function compared to that of the upward-conversion function, the greater the likelihood of the grant stimulating more private expenditures.

In sum, the precise consequences of a rehabilitation grants program vary depending on characteristics of the program, the participating homeowners, and their dwellings. The likelihood of participation is enhanced the larger the outright grant or the matching fraction employed, and the stronger the homeowner's preferences for housing. Matching grants always tend to replace at least partially some private funds that would have been spent on housing otherwise, unless the grant induces homeowners to abandon zero-maintenance strategy. Thus the consequences of outright grants vary depending on participants' preferences, their pregrant strategies, and the dwelling characteristics that define structural transformation functions.

Low-Interest and Deferred-Repayment Rehabilitation Loans

Low-interest (or deferred-repayment) loans for home rehabilitation have distinct theoretical impacts compared to grants. Unlike grants, loans must be repaid eventually. Hence they ultimately represent private expenditures on housing. What low-interest or deferred-repayment loans provide is a chance to restructure the intertemporal sequence of housing expenditures. As explained in chapter 3, lower interest rates in general shift the optimal timing of expenditures toward nearer-term periods. Here, however, this effect is limited to the intertemporal pattern of housing expenditures only, because the lowered effective rate is confined to such. Another complication is that the programs typically constrain the loans to particular types of expenditures on upward-conversion activities.

The consequence is portrayed diagrammatically in figure 12.2. Suppose that the initial indifference curve mapping is represented by curves U_1 and U_2, and the maintenance and the upward-conversion transformation functions by DF and GJ, respectively. With the institution of a low-interest loan program, the homeowner perceives that the cost of upward conversion has fallen, thereby pivoting GJ clockwise around J to $G'J$ in figure 12.2. Now the decisionmaker must reassess the optimum intertemporal pattern of housing upkeep strategies over the planning horizon in order to ascertain whether undertaking upward conversion (financed by inexpensive loans) during one or more periods will improve well-being during the overall time span. In fact, the homeowner will choose not to participate in the program.

If so, the situation is shown in figure 12.2, where optimum at I' is superior to any of the pre-program options: zero maintenance at F, positive maintenance at E or (unsubsidized) upward conversion at I.[6] The effect on the intertemporal pattern of expenditures is as follows. If the homeowner originally would have chosen E but now chooses I' after the loan becomes available, (private) expenditure on housing during the period t shown in figure 12.2 rises by $\$P_Z(Z_2 - Z_3)$. If the homeowner originally would have upgraded the dwelling anyway, the consequences are a fall in expenditure on housing during t of $\$P_Z(Z_3 - Z_4)$. Finally, in periods during the planning horizon subsequent to the subsidized upward conversion, there is a modified budget constraint that reflects the new intertemporal pattern of rehabilitation loan repayments. (If the public loan defers all payments until the time of dwelling sale there are, of course, no new payments, but other repayment schedules are influenced by the interest rate charged on the subsidized loans.) If this results in a more binding constraint (as is likely for those who are induced to undertake upward conversion by the program), future expenditures on $\bar{A}_t$ (and Z) are lower than originally, thus offsetting somewhat the effect during t. Just the opposite is likely for those originally planning a privately financed upward conversion who gain through the program a less-binding budget constraint in periods after t.

In sum, as measured over some period t to t^*, the success of a subsidized loan program in stimulating more private housing expenditures by recipients depends on a variety of programmatic and personal characteristics. Success will be enhanced: (1) the smaller the per-period loan repayments, and (2) the greater the price elasticity of demand for $\bar{A}$ relative to Z.

Housing Rehabilitation Subsidy Programs in Minneapolis

There are two different grant programs and four different low-interest or deferred-repayment loan programs that were administered by Minneapolis before and during the period of study in an attempt to stimulate owner-occupied–dwelling rehabilitation. An overview of these programs is given here.[7]

In general all programs are limited to correcting code violations, although a few in targeted areas include energy conservation, exterior painting, and other limited categories of improvements. Although an explicit delineation of the goals established specifically by the city of Minneapolis for the programs cannot be found in written form, documents clearly suggest that the preeminent goal is a reduction in the number of substandard dwellings. Representative is the following statement by the Planning

Department (Minneapolis 1980, 26): "Neighborhood appearance is important to Minneapolis residents. City policies should be directed toward remedying the problems identified in the city-sponsored 1979 homeowner survey within each neighborhood. . . . Concentrated programs targeted to these neighborhoods where the assessment of the neighborhood as 'poor' was common are needed to combat relatively isolated conditions of blight."

The grant programs are funded by both the city of Minneapolis (through CDBG) and the Minnesota Housing Finance Agency (MHFA), with the former being responsible for about two-thirds of total disbursements through 1980. The loan programs are funded by the above two sources and the federal HUD Section 312 program, with disbursement ratios of 2:1:1, respectively, through 1980.

Minneapolis city resources for its loan programs come from the selling of general obligation bonds. The bond program started in 1974, and by the end of 1977, the city had reached its $10 million ceiling on such issuances. Added funds of $8.5 million were secured through credit agreements with local private lending institutions (MHRA 1980). The Minneapolis grant program received its funding from the Community Development Block Grant (CDBG). Beginning in 1979, CDBG also funded a special, interest-free loan program for qualified residents of the Neighborhood Strategy Areas (NSAS) only. The Minnesota Housing Finance Agency, created by the state legislature in 1970, began working with Minneapolis in 1975 to help provide support for both the grant and loan programs (MHRA 1980).

Eligibility for most programs is citywide, except for one administered under the aegis of CDBG that is focused only on NSAS. All programs have owner-income eligibility guidelines, typically with a $18,000 to $19,250 ceiling (approximately 80 to 85 percent of the city's mean income).

The grants are for a maximum of $6,000. The exception is the NSA fix-and-paint program, which specifies a $100 to $2,000 matching grant on exterior repair projects costing from $200 to $4,000. Loan maxima vary considerably across programs—$15,000 is the highest, with no loans made in excess of home market value less mortgage outstanding. Repayment schedules also vary by program—typical interest rates are 8 percent maximimums but are income graduated. About half of all MHFA loans were in the 6 percent to 7 percent range through 1980 (MHRA 1980, figure IV). Some programs defer all repayments of principal and interest to the time of home sale.

In total, these grant and loan programs injected substantial funds into the Minneapolis housing market prior to the time of the survey. By the end of 1980, 8,306 loans had been approved, totalling $59.5 million or $7,158 per loan, on average. A total of 3,836 grants were made of $18 million cumulative value, or $4,685 per grant, on average.

Estimating the Impact of Minneapolis Rehabilitation Programs

Program Benefits to Recipients and Nonrecipients

Ideally, one would wish to analyze each of the six Minneapolis rehabilitation programs separately, and for each to ascertain the degree to which it stimulated changes from a zero-maintenance strategy and changes in private housing expenditures. Unfortunately, limitations in the data force a less ambitious analysis. First, relatively few sampled Minneapolis homeowners had participated in any of the rehabilitation programs during the past five years: thirty-two received grants and thirty-nine received loans.[8] As a result, these two sets of homeowners are analyzed collectively, instead of subdividing them into unreliably small subsamples of participants in particular programs. Second, 98.2 percent of the sampled homeowners were engaged in a nonzero-upkeep strategy, resulting in a weak predictive equation for UPKEEP? in Minneapolis (see chapter 9). This means that only the direct-expenditure effects of subsidies occurring when homeowners are already investing some private funds in their dwellings can be estimated reliably.

DIRECT LEVERAGING EFFECTS   Given these limitations, the direct leveraging effects of rehabilitation policies upon actual recipients are estimated in a straightforward manner by examining the coefficients of GRANT$ and LOAN$ in the UPKEEP$ equation reported in table 9.2. These coefficients, 2.62 and .345, respectively, indicate that homeowners engaged in upkeep investment strategies spent $2.62 more for each $1 in grants they received and $.345 for each $1 in subsidized loans they received, *ceteris paribus*.[9] Recall that all these figures are calculated as annual averages over the prior five-year period (or for however long the owner had resided there, if less).

The stimulation effect implicit in these coefficients must be interpreted differently depending on whether a grant or a loan is being considered. In the case of grants, the test is whether the coefficient is (significantly) greater than one. If the coefficient is less than one, it means that the grant (partially) substituted for private investments that would have been forthcoming had the grant not replaced them. If the coefficient equals one, it means that the homeowners spent the grant plus what they had planned on spending originally, with no stimulation of additional private investment. But here the 2.62 coefficient means that the homeowners spent $1.62 more of personal funds (plus $1 of public funds) for each dollar of grant received. The average grant had an annual value of $1,260, thus the average stimulus in private upkeep spending was $2041 annually.[10] This is, indeed, a sizable direct "leveraging" effect from grants. In terms of the theoretical discussion above, the grants policy can be portrayed in figure 12.1 as generating a switch from a modest-expenditure maintenance strategy such as E' to a large-expenditure upward-conversion strategy such as I'. This is entirely plausible, given that most grants were directed toward correcting code violations.

In the case of loan recipients, the stimulation effect is revealed by a coefficient that is greater than zero. Because the loans (presumably) are repaid they ultimately represent private expenditures. As shown above, subsidized loans encourage recipients to shift their intertemporal pattern of expenditures toward nearer-term periods, but do not increase the total amount of financial resources available over their entire planning horizon, as does a grant. Thus, if this intertemporal switching effect is minimal, each dollar borrowed from the city will simply substitute on a one-for-one basis for homeowners' savings or loans from other sources, and the coefficient will be zero. But here the .345 coefficient indicates that for each dollar homeowners were able to borrow from the city they spent $.345 more on upkeep than if this option was unavailable to them. Since the average annual value of a subsidized loan was $3,611, each loan produced an average annual private expenditure of $4,857.[11]

That the coefficient for the LOAN$ variable proves statistically significant means that there are three (non–mutually exclusive) possibilities for recipients: (1) some who otherwise would have undertaken only modest maintenance activities during the period were convinced to undertake major upgrading activities; i.e., to move from E to I' in figure 12.2; (2) some who otherwise would have undertaken upward conversion only during some future, unobserved period were convinced to advance spending toward the near-term and undertake it during the period under observation; (3) some who otherwise would have undertaken upward conversion during the period anyway reinvested some of the money they saved from the low-interest loan in other upkeep activities during the period.

These conclusions correspond with the implications drawn from Rafter's 1985 opinion survey of recipients of low-interest home improvement loans in Wisconsin. He found that 50 percent of the recipients would have "delayed work" and 18 percent "never would have done the work" in the absence of the subsidized loans. By contrast, only 13 to 14 percent would have used a private bank loan and 7 percent would have used their own savings otherwise. In sum, there indeed appears to be a substantial direct private upkeep stimulus generated by the loans strategy.

INDIRECT LEVERAGING EFFECTS   The previous section indicates that both grants and loans succeed in encouraging recipient homeowners to invest more of their own funds in their homes than they would have otherwise.

But the empirical results of chapters 7 and 9 indicate that there is an additional payoff from these policies: homeowners who do not directly receive subsidies but live near those who do also alter their behavior. Homeowners in areas that have more rehabilitation grant or loan recipients tend to be less pessimistic about the future quality of life in their neighborhoods. This, in turn, results in these areas having an annual average of $65 more upkeep expenditure per homeowner. Unfortunately, the results do not allow one to quantify precisely how the neighborhood expectations of one homeowner is related to the number and location of rehabilitation grant or loan recipients in the surrounding area. But they do suggest that nontrivial sums of private expenditures may be leveraged indirectly from those living near homeowners who participate in a moderately scaled public program, through their enhanced confidence in the future quality of the neighborhood.

Suppose that only one homeowner receiving a grant or a loan is sufficient to generate and maintain boosted optimism for other homeowners on the block, by the above amount witnessed across all aided areas. Given a block face consisting of fifteen homes, the above figures suggest an aggregate indirect leveraging of $910 annually per block, or $.38 per $1 grant or loan on that block.[12] If one is more conservative and assumes that targeting three aided homeowners is required before blockwide confidence is boosted, then one obtains an indirect leveraging effect of $.10 per $1 subsidy, a figure comparable to that estimated by Ginsberg (1983) and McConney (1985).

PROPERTY-VALUE EFFECTS FROM LEVERAGING   The prior two sections indicate how sizable amounts of private dollars are leveraged both directly and indirectly through housing rehabilitation subsidies. But in order to quantify their ultimate benefit, their impact on enhancing property values must be considered. The means for doing so involves first assessing how property values are affected by the presence of certain home defects, then estimating how much expenditure is required for the repair of such defects.

The former assessment is accomplished by regressing Minneapolis single-family–home property values on the corresponding dwelling and neighborhood characteristics. Examination of coefficients of various dummy variables indicating the presence of particular structural shortcomings reveals that a given property's value is reduced: (1) 21 percent by severe interior cracks or holes, (2) 5% by peeling paint or exterior structure damages, (3) 19 percent by the absence of central heat.[13] Using a representative $45,000 dwelling as benchmark, the above translate into a range of $2,000 to $9,000.

Precise information is not available to assess precisely the costs of re-

Table 12.1   Comparative Leveraging Benefit Assumptions: Grants and Loans
(Leveraging Benefit = $M \times D$ per $ Subsidy)

Increment in value per $ expenditure (M)	Increment in home upkeep $ per $ subsidy (D)			
	Grants		Loans	
	$2.62*	$3.00**	$.345*	$.725**
$1	$2.62	$3.00	$.345	$.725
$3	$7.86	$9.00	$1.035	$2.175

*estimated direct leveraging effect only
**estimated direct plus indirect leveraging effects = $.38

pairing the above shortcomings. But general cost estimates suggest that the most conservative reasonable assumption would be that $1 worth of repairs of the above items improves the property's value by $1. The most liberal assumption would be that this ratio of repair to value in dollars is 1:3.[14]

The alternative estimation of how repair expenditure is translated into increments in property value (call it M) may be combined with the alternative estimates of leveraging effects (call it D) to give a plausible range of values for the leveraging benefits derived from the subsidies. This matrix of alternative parameter values is presented in table 12.1. Using the most conservative assumptions (i.e., M = 1:1, and D = direct leveraging effect only) each dollar of grants produces $2.62 in property-value gains, and each dollar of loans produces $.345 in property-value gains. The corresponding figures using the most liberal parameters (i.e., M = 1:3 and D = direct plus indirect leveraging effects) are $9.0 and $2.175, respectively.

PROPERTY-VALUE EFFECTS FROM EXTERNALITIES   The previous three sections have discussed programmatic benefits in terms of enhanced property values stemming from induced rehabilitation expenditures. There may be additional property-value benefits as well that flow from the fact that such expenditures of both private and public funds improve the physical quality of the residential environment. These positive externalities are discussed and quantified in chapter 11. Suffice it to recapitulate here that the total of such benefits that might be expected to accrue from a grant or loan program that rehabilitates one visibly deteriorated dwelling are on the order of a $10,000 aggregate increase in property values on the block face. Of course, virtually all grants received by sampled homeowners are earmarked for correcting code violations, which typically do little for enhancing exterior condition. Though subsidized loans are more flexible in their allocation, it is unclear precisely how often they are used to rehabilitate home exteriors, thereby generating the maximum positive externalities. Given this and the average size of subsidy received, it is reasonable to posit that externality benefits are, at most, $.50 in aggregate property-value enhancement per $1 subsidy, and probably are considerably less (Varady 1982b, 1986).

PROPERTY VALUES AND SOCIAL BENEFITS   Most benefit-cost analyses evaluating public capital projects estimate the annual flow of benefits over the project's useful lifetime, then capitalize the stream so as to obtain a discounted present value of benefits. In the case of home rehabilitation subsidies the task is simpler because the increments to property values are precisely the desired proxy for present values of social benefits.

The ultimate social benefit here is the improved quality of life for the present and future occupants of the rehabilitated dwellings and their neighbors. Such improvements generate a fillip in housing demand for properties in the rehabilitated area, which, in turn, is reflected in higher real property values. It is precisely the market's evaluation of the present discounted value of the enhanced stream of residential benefits flowing from the rehabilitated areas that is represented in the observed increment in real property values.[15] This use of property-value gains as a proxy for social benefits is well established in the field (see Rothenberg 1967, Chung 1973, Pines and Weiss 1976, Segal 1979, Diamond and Tolley 1982, and Brueckner 1983).[16]

In sum, the per-subsidy-dollar benefits (B) from either a grant or a loan may be expressed:

$$B = (V + W) + E = (M \times D) + E \qquad (12.1)$$

where V is the increment in value of the rehabilitated home per $ subsidy received, W is the increment per $ subsidy in aggregate values of neighboring homes whose owners invest more due to abetted optimism stemming from the subsidy program, D is the increment in aggregate home upkeep expenditure per $ subsidy (i.e., the sum of direct and indirect leveraging effects), M is the increment in home value per $ upkeep expenditure, and E is the increment in aggregate neighboring property values generated via rehabilitation externalities per $ subsidy.

Program Costs to Society and the Local Public Sector

How one computes the costs of a public policy depends on one's frame of reference. On a broad, societal perspective, a policy's costs are the opportunity costs of the real human and nonhuman resources that are consumed by the policy. In the context of home rehabilitation subsidies, social costs involve primarily the labor and raw materials that were devoted to the actual rehabilitation actions, all valued at their full social (i.e., market) value.[17] The distinction between private and public financing of such resources is irrelevant.

On the other hand, from the perspective of a budget-conscious local public official, financing is of central importance. From such a local public-sector budgetary view, the cost is the ultimate budgetary allocation to the program.[18] Any additional private funds that can be leveraged are counted as benefits. What is more, loans do not cost as much as grants, because they are repaid and thus ultimately represent a smaller budgetary impact.

More specifically, the budgetary cost (C) to the local public sector of each \$1 rehabilitation loan with a simple interest rate of I as applied to N equal principal repayment installments over T periods (when first repayment occurs in period $T - N + 1$) is:

$$C = 1 - \sum_{t=T-N+1}^{T} [(1 + I)^t / N] / (1 + R)^t \qquad (12.2)$$

where R is the discount rate (the opportunity cost of funds loaned out). Ideally, R represents the maximum social return available from all alternative uses of the public funds. Practically, this figure might be set at the interest rate that could be earned by the local public sector should it invest in safe financial instruments.

Although the budgetary cost of a loan is less than that of a grant because the former funds can be reinvested after repayment, the present value of the repaid funds is reduced by the difference in discount rate and loan interest rate. Thus, the most expensive loan from the local public sector's perspective is the deferred loan (when the repayment is at the time of home sale at T) at zero interest. In such a case (12.2) simplifies to: $1 - 1 / (1 + R)^T$. Perhaps the least expensive policy that might still be considered a subsidized loan is a loan at 8 percent repayable in T annual installments. These two extrema are employed to bound the estimates in the following benefit-cost analyses. They are also representative of the range of programs operating in Minneapolis in 1980. A more typical, moderately expensive loan policy is also analyzed below: T annual principal installments at 5 percent simple interest.

Both social and public-sector views of costs have validity, depending on the frame of reference chosen. Both will be considered below in the benefit-cost analyses.

**Benefit-Cost Analyses of Minneapolis
Rehabilitation Programs**

The Social Perspective

From the perspective of the entire society, the benefit-cost analysis is simple. Any program that encourages resource investments in home rehabilitation is net beneficial if the aggregate gain in property values due to rehabilitation outweighs the rehabilitation expenditures, i.e., if social benefits exceed the value of the resources devoted. Symbolically, net benefits will be positive if $(M + E)$ is greater than one, i.e., if per dollar of upkeep investment the aggregate value of the rehabilitated and adjacent properties increases by more than one dollar.

Given that the aforementioned range of estimates for M is one or more, and for E is positive, the conditions for adjudging both Minneapolis grants and loans programs as socially net beneficial are fulfilled. Of course, one cannot infer that such programs represent the best use of resources, because other housing programs (e.g., new-construction subsidies) may have proven even more net beneficial.[19]

The Local Budgetary Perspective

Of course, from the perspective of the local public official, the above social benefit-cost analysis overlooks the central relevant question: which policy yields the biggest programmatic "bang" per budgetary "buck." To answer this question we must consider the differential leveraging benefits and the differential costs of both grants and loans, as described above.

GRANTS   Because the budgetary cost of each dollar of rehabilitation grant awarded during the current period is simply $1, the net-benefit estimation is an assessment of whether B in (12.1) is greater than one. Even if one is extremely conservative and assumes: (1) rehabilitation expenditure translates into property value at a one-for-one ratio (i.e., $M = 1$), (2) there are no indirect leveraging effects (i.e., $D = 2.62 =$ direct effect only), and (3) there are no externality effects (i.e., $E = 0$), one obtains benefit-cost ratios of over 2:1. The precise net benefits from any particular grant vary according to how the money is spent: exterior improvements abet E, but some interior improvements better enhance the dwelling's own value per dollar expended. In any case it seems safe to conclude that grants were extremely net beneficial from the perspective of the city of Minneapolis.

LOANS   A somewhat more complicated benefit-cost analysis must be conducted for alternative types of loans, based on the benefits shown in table

12.1 and the costs as given by equation (12.2). For each type, three alternative payback periods ($T = 5$, 10, 20 years), four alternative discount rates ($R = .06, .09, .12, .15$), and three alternative benefit estimates ($B = .345, 1.50, 2.675$) are considered. The benefit estimates range from those produced by the most conservative assumptions (one-for-one expenditure-to-value ratios, no indirect leveraging, no externalities) to the most liberal assumptions ($M = 3$, $D = .725$, $E = .5$, respectively), with a moderate estimate included for comparison as well.

First consider the benefit-cost ratios for the expensive (no-interest, deferred) loan policy, as shown in panel A of table 12.2. Estimates suggest that with a moderate benefit estimate ($B = 1.5$) such loans do not prove net beneficial if the loan is repaid over ten years or more, unless discount rates are near 6 percent. Even with the most liberal assumptions about benefits, no-interest deferred loans repayed in twenty years are unlikely to be net beneficial unless discount rates are extremely low.

By contrast, the loans involving T repayments at either 5 percent or 8 percent simple interest have a much wider parameter range of net benefits.[20] Moderate benefit assumptions produce net benefits even with twenty-year repayment schedules, given single-digit discount rates (see panels B, C in table 12.2).

The foregoing indicates that no definitive claims about the net benefits of any type of loan can be made without a clear estimate of an appropriate discount rate. In terms of the situation facing the city of Minneapolis during the 1976 to 1980 study period, the opportunity cost of funds as represented by U.S. Treasury Department three to five year bond returns[21] ranged from 6.7 percent to 11.6 percent, with an average of 8.6 percent.

So assuming a 9 percent discount rate, it is clear from table 12.2A that unless extremely liberal benefit assumptions are applied, no-interest deferred loans that were repaid after five years are probably not net beneficial.[22] On the other hand, the moderately expensive loans (table 12.2B) appear to be net beneficial even when repaid over twenty years, unless extremely conservative benefits are assumed. And of course the inexpensive loans (table 12.2C) appear to produce large net benefits, regardless of benefit assumptions and repayment schedules.

COMPARING THE RELATIVE EFFICIENCY OF GRANTS AND LOANS   The final benefit-cost analysis does not consider the absolute benefit-cost ratios of an individual policy, but rather contrasts the ratios for grants to those for loans. Such an analysis is useful when, e.g., it has been determined that both programs are net beneficial, and the policymaker is interested in packaging the mix so as to obtain the greatest payoff.[23] The approach here

Table 12.2   Budgetary Benefit-Cost Ratios for Alternative Loan Policies (Under Various Benefit Assumptions)*

A. Expensive Loans (assuming one loan repayment, at interest rate = 0%)

Repayment period (T)		Public discount rate (R)			
		.06	.09	.12	.15
5 Years					
Benefit:	.345	0.55	0.32	0.21	0.15
	1.50	2.3	1.37	0.92	0.67
	2.675	4.23	2.45	1.63	1.19
10 Years					
Benefit:	.345	0.31	0.19	0.13	0.10
	1.50	1.36	0.83	0.58	0.44
	2.675	2.42	1.49	1.04	0.79
20 Years					
Benefit:	.345	0.20	0.13	0.10	0.08
	1.50	0.87	0.59	0.44	0.36
	2.675	1.55	1.04	0.79	0.64

B. Moderately Expensive Loans (assuming T loan repayments, at interest rate = 5%)

Repayment period (T)		Public discount rate (R)			
		.06	.09	.12	.15
5 Years					
Benefit:	.345	4.22	0.92	0.46	0.29
	1.50	18.33	3.98	2.02	1.28
	2.675	32.69	7.10	3.60	2.28
10 Years					
Benefit:	.345	2.34	0.53	0.28	0.18
	1.50	10.16	2.30	1.22	0.80
	2.675	18.11	4.11	2.17	1.42
20 Years					
Benefit:	.345	1.26	0.31	0.18	0.12
	1.50	5.49	1.35	0.76	0.53
	2.675	9.78	2.41	1.36	0.95

(continued)

Table 12.2 (*)Continued*)

C. Inexpensive Loans (assuming T loan repayments, at interest rate = 8%)

Repayment period (T)		Public discount rate (R)			
		.06	.09	.12	.15
5 Years					
Benefit:	.345	**	3.53	0.79	0.41
	1.50	**	15.36	3.41	1.77
	2.675	**	27.39	6.09	3.15
10 Years					
Benefit:	.345	**	1.96	0.45	0.24
	1.50	**	8.50	1.97	0.91
	2.675	**	15.17	3.52	1.89
20 Years					
Benefit:	.345	**	1.06	0.27	0.15
	1.50	**	4.59	1.15	0.66
	2.675	**	8.19	2.06	1.18

*social planning horizon assumed = 20 years
**negative-cost policy since $R < I$

is to take the ratio of the benefit-cost ratio (BC) for the grants policy (G) to the comparable ratio for a particular loan policy (L). Symbolically:

$$BC(G \ / \ L) = [(MD_G + E) \ / \ (MD_L + E)] \ [1 - \ (\sum_{t=T-N+1}^{T} (1 + I)^t \ / \ N) \ / \ (1 + R)^t]$$

(12.3)

The expression (12.3) has strong intuitive appeal. It indicates that grants will be superior to loans only if the higher direct leveraged expenditures of the former are not outweighed by its higher budgetary costs. Values of BC greater than one indicate the relative superiority of grants.

The results of the comparative benefit-cost ratios given by (12.3) when grants are contrasted with the expensive loan program are presented in table 12.3, panel A. Two sets of estimates are shown. One assumes minimal upkeep expenditures to value increment ratios and no indirect leveraging or externalities;[24] the other, parenthetical one assumes most liberal

Table 12.3   Relative Budgetary Benefit-Cost Ratios: Grants versus Loans*

A. Expensive Loans (assuming one loan repayment, at interest rate = 0%)

	Public discount rate (R)			
	.06	.09	.12	.15
5 Years	1.92	2.66	3.21	3.65
	(.90)	(1.24)	(1.54)	(1.79)
10 Years	3.35	4.39	5.15	5.72
	(1.57)	(2.05)	(2.41)	(2.67)
20 Years	5.23	6.24	6.81	7.13
	(2.44)	(2.92)	(3.18)	(3.33)

B. Moderately Expensive Loans (assuming T loan repayments, at interest rate = 5%)

	Public discount rate (R)			
	.06	.09	.12	.15
5 Years	0.21	0.80	1.31	1.77
	(.10)	(.37)	(.61)	(.83)
10 Years	0.38	1.38	2.18	2.83
	(.18)	(.64)	(1.02)	(1.32)
20 Years	0.71	2.35	3.47	4.25
	(.33)	(1.10)	(1.62)	(1.99)

C. Inexpensive Loans (assuming T loan repayments, at interest rate = 8%)

	Public discount rate (R)			
	.06	.09	.12	.15
5 Years	**	0.21	0.78	1.28
	(**)	(.10)	(.36)	(.60)
10 Years	**	0.37	1.34	2.13
	(**)	(.17)	(.63)	(1.00)
20 Years	**	0.69	2.30	3.40
	(**)	(.32)	(1.07)	(1.59)

Note: calculations assume twenty year public sector time horizon and $E_L = E_G$
*assuming: $M = 1$, $E = 0$ and indirect leveraging effects = 0; parenthetical terms assume: $M = 3$, $E = .5$, indirect leveraging = .38
**loan superior to grant since loan has negative cost ($R < I$)

values for all parameters. Assuming a discount rate of 9 percent and conservative benefit assumptions, the analysis shows that during the 1976 to 1980 period, grants had a 2.66 to 6.24 times higher benefit-cost ratio depending on repayment period than an interest-free deferred loan. Even with liberal benefit assumptions (which most favor expensive loans[25]), they appear more efficient than grants only when they are repaid in one to three years.

The results of the comparative analysis when grants are contrasted with a moderately expensive loan program are presented in panel B of table 12.3. This shows a considerably larger region of superiority for loans, although it is highly sensitive to benefit assumptions. Assuming a 9 percent discount rate and the liberal benefits most favorable to loans, grants are inferior unless the loans are not repaid within eighteen years. The comparable repayment period is only seven years if indirect leveraging and externality effects are assumed to be nil, however. The inexpensive loan policy shown in table 12.3C appears relatively superior to grants, regardless of benefit assumptions and repayment schedules (assuming a 9 percent discount rate).

The conclusion is clear. Interest-bearing, periodic-repayment loans can be significantly superior to grants in producing net benefits to the local public sector, but such superiority is sensitive to the terms of the loan and to the assumptions made about leveraging and externality benefits. The more conservative one is about estimating program benefits to those other than direct recipients, the higher the interest rate the loan must carry (or, to a lesser extent, the faster it must be repaid) in order to remain superior to grants. Because most Minneapolis rehabilitation loans carried terms of 5 to 8 percent interest and fifteen- to twenty-year repayment periods, it is likely that those involving the most generous repayment terms were a slightly inferior use of public funds than similarly sized grants (assuming moderate benefits and a 9 percent discount rate).

This important conclusion provides a cautionary note to conventional wisdom: loans are cheaper for the local public sector because the money is repaid and available for subsequent lending. Indeed, loans are cheaper in this sense, but they are also much less beneficial in terms of the extra private rehabilitation investment that they directly induce. The superior cost characteristics of loans outweigh their inferior benefit characteristics only when the loans are repaid over a short period or when they carry an interest rate near the discount rate. Otherwise, the future repayment streams are discounted too heavily to affect sufficiently the present values of the funds. In the case of Minneapolis in the late 1970s it appears that loans of at least 6 percent interest and maximum fifteen-year repayment schedules were superior to grants, unless extremely small indirect benefits are assumed.

Implications for Designing Home Rehabilitation Subsidy Policy

The program implications echo from the analysis above. From a social perspective, grants or loans likely produce comparable net benefits. From a local public sector budgetary perspective, however, the two do not produce equivalent results for the same expenditure. Neighborhood policymakers should thus consider developing an integrated rehabilitation grant and loan program wherein the mix of grants and loans for individual applicants is varied so as to enhance public-sector efficiency. The central principle of the scheme suggested here is to require that subsidy recipients who can afford to do so take out loans on terms that are more net beneficial than grants, before any grants are given to the recipient.

Such a program might be administered as follows. First, as is typically done now, income eligibility guidelines and types of eligible property improvements would be established and a maximum interest rate and repayment period for rehabilitation loans set. Then, for each rehabilitation-subsidy applicant one would need to ascertain not only eligibility but also (presumably via the same documentation): (1) total value of eligible home repairs, or maximum subsidy (S), and (2) the maximum extra periodic payment she or he could afford (P). One reasonable guideline would be to set P so that total housing expenses (utilities, mortgage payments, taxes, etc., plus P) equalled 30 percent of periodic income.

If P is not positive,[26] the entire expense (S) of requested (eligible) property improvements should be met by grants. That is, only a deferred loan would not exceed the affordability constraint. Yet table 12.3A shows that such a loan package will more than likely offer inferior net benefits compared to a comparable grant. If P is larger, one needs to investigate whether a loan package involving interest rate (I) and repayment period (T) can be designed that simultaneously: (1) does not exceed programmatic maxima for I and T, (2) produces periodic repayments of principal and interest less than P, and (3) involves (I, T) terms such that the relative benefit-cost ratio of the loan package exceeds that of a grant for the same principal (see table 12.3). Obviously, if S is relatively small and P relatively large, it should be possible for the entire amount of the subsidy S to become the principal in a loan package that neither exceeds the affordability constraint of the recipient nor is so generous in terms that it renders the loan inferior to a grant. For intermediate cases, assessing the options is somewhat more complicated, because the loan's principal, interest rate, and repayment periods all can be varied so as to render a periodic repayment less than P and still satisfy the other two constraints. If the resulting principal is less than the eligible subsidy S, the remainder is tendered in the form of a grant.

The above administrative principles can be illustrated by a simplified hypothetical scenario. Suppose that a loan repayment period T has been fixed, with each of T periodic repayments consisting of that fraction of the subsidy loan principle (S_L / T) plus accrued simple interest $(1 + I)^t$. Now the net benefit to the local public sector of this loan of amount S_L is simply the difference between per dollar B_L and C, as given in equations (12.1) and (12.2), multiplied by total S_L dollars (where $B_L = MD_L + E$):

$$\text{Net loan benefit} = [B_L - 1 + \sum_{t=1}^{T} ((1 + I)^t / T) / (1 + R)^t] S_L \quad (12.4)$$

Assume that the affordability constraint here is that the loan recipient can repay no more than $P(t)$ dollars in principal and accrued interest on that principal per period t (i.e., a graduated repayment scheme):

$$\text{Affordability constraint} = S_L (1 + I)^t/T \le P(t) \quad (12.5)$$

If the policymaker wishes to extract the maximum net benefits from the subsidy package, the optimal S package mix (S_L, S_G) must be determined. At first blush it might seem obvious to set I equal to program maximum and let $S = S_L$. But such might well produce such a high periodic repayment that (12.5) was violated. Given (12.5), the policymaker must realize that the greater the share of the eligible subsidy devoted to S_L, the lower must be the I charged and, hence, the lower the net benefit gained from S_L. Furthermore, the extra or marginal net loan benefit gained by reducing I enough so that $1 more S_L can be afforded declines as S_L rises. This can be seen as follows. The marginal net benefit is simply the partial derivative of (12.4) with respect to S_L, i.e., the bracketed term. But substituting from (12.5) we can rewrite this constrained marginal net benefit as:

$$\text{Marginal net loan benefit} = B_L - 1 + \sum_{t=1}^{T} (P(t) / S_L) / (1 + R)^t$$

$$(12.6)$$

To optimize the (S_L, S_G) package the policymaker should keep allocating dollars to loans until the marginal net benefit from doing so (as given by (12.6)) no longer exceeds the marginal net benefit gained by allocating a dollar to a grant $(B_G - 1)$.[27]

This algorithm can be usefully explicated with the aid of figure 12.3. It shows various possible relationships between dollars of marginal net benefits accrued by the local public sector and various sizes of rehabilitation subsidies, depending on whether the subsidy takes the form of a grant or a

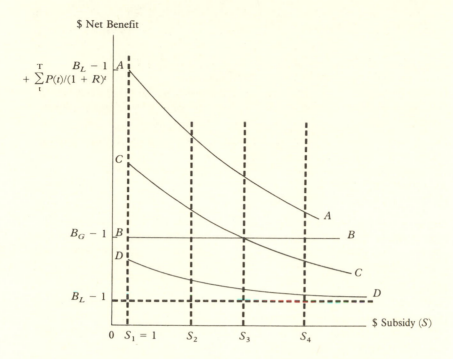

Figure 12.3   Illustrative Marginal Net Benefit Functions for Grants and Loans for Determining Optimal Grant/Loan Package

loan. The marginal net benefits obtained from giving a dollar of grant is shown by line BB; corresponding relationships for loan dollars are shown by the other lines. Line AA represents a situation where P is relatively large and thus each subsidy dollar lent can command a high I; line DD portrays an opposite situation.[28] Now if the the relevant loan function was AA and S_4 was the total eligible subsidy, maximization of net benefits would suggest that all subsidy dollars be given as a loan. Since all parameter values except I are predetermined and S_L is now established, the interest rate on this loan could be computed via solving for I in (12.5). On the other hand, given S_4 but CC, optimization suggests that only S_3 of the total should be allocated to loans, and $S_4 - S_3$ be allocated to grants. Of course, if the eligible subsidy were lower, say S_2, then even with moderate marginal loan net benefits like CC it would be preferable to loan out the entire amount. Finally consider if affordability constraints were excessive, as in DD. In such a circumstance P would be too small to render a loan of any amount superior to a grant.

In this fashion the integrated strategy of grant and loan administration described above attempts to exhaust all possibilities of packaging some or all of the eligible subsidy in the form of a loan that is more net beneficial than a grant, before any grant component is given. Note the key difference here from the way grant and loan programs have been administered traditionally. Instead of dealing with recipient-affordability constraints by making loan terms more generous, the above does so by tendering appropriate amounts of the subsidy as a grant. The clear advantage of doing so is that it avoids issuing loans that are inferior to grants in terms of net benefits to the local public sector.

Of course, other issues besides the maximization of net benefits for the local public sector are relevant in the development of an optimal grant and loan policy. One is the degree of homeowner participation. Obviously, the success of any program depends on widespread participation by eligible homeowners. The above suggests that the neediest applicants likely would receive a rehabilitation-subsidy package made up primarily of grants, and thus would likely participate. Survey evidence suggests that such grant programs are, in fact, widely praised by lower-income homeowners (Ahlbrandt and Cunningham 1979, ch.8). For subsidy packages involving larger loan components participation may be more sporadic, and policymakers should realize the inherent tradeoff here indicated by benefit-cost analysis. Enhancing the attractiveness of the package and thus likelihood of participation by extending repayment terms and reducing interest charges conflicts with the net social benefit gained from such a loan. Experimentation is suggested in order to ascertain the appropriate tradeoff in each locale. There may be, in particular, a problem of nonparticipation among elderly homeowners, especially if they qualify only for predominantly loan packages. As shown in chapter 8, their asset-enhancing motive for home investments is often eroded by their more frequent plans to reside in the dwelling until death and by their unwillingness to accrue more debt. One programmatic option may be to extend eligibility for grants by redefining "affordability" if the applicant is elderly.[29]

A second and closely related programmatic concern is political feasibility. Local fiscal austerity measures are so predominant that policymakers may be reluctant to consider initiating or expanding the scope of housing-rehabilitation grant and loan programs. But the foregoing benefit-cost analysis suggests strongly that a well-designed program can be touted as a fiscally prudent strategy. If the increases in program-generated property values are reflected in higher property tax assessments and, ultimately, revenues, it is not inconceivable that a rehabilitation program can be self-financing. Taking the most conservative assumption about grants benefits ($B = \$2.62$), a reasonable assumption about property depreciation rates (3 percent) (see Chinloy 1980), the current Minneapolis effective property-tax rate (3.8 percent), and a 9 percent discount rate, the present discounted value of the incremented stream of property-tax revenues derived from each dollar of rehabilitation grant equals unity in forty years. That is, on a forty-year time horizon, each dollar of grant repays itself. If one boosts the benefit assumption above to a modest $B = \$5$, the payback period drops to less than ten years. And grants still can be self-financing, though over a longer period, even if properties are not reassessed upward equal to B. Of course, capturing all program benefits through higher taxes may be fiscally enticing, but may once again dampen program participation if pursued too vigorously (see Peterson et al. 1973). Ideally, grant and loan strategies could be pursued wherein benefit-cost ratios are so high that self-financing could occur while capturing only a fraction of the gain to homeowners.

A final concern is the appropriate scale of the rehabilitation policy. On the one hand, it is obvious that there is some logical point where programmatic diminishing returns set in and both the direct and indirect leveraging impacts and the neighborhood externalities wane because the most egregious home defects have been rehabilitated. On the other hand, it is clear that in Minneapolis there remain substantial numbers of eligible homeowners with major rehabilitation needs that are not served by the program at its current scale. And the estimates provided by this research suggest that there are opportunities for expanding grant and loan programs well beyond conventional scales that would nevertheless be significantly net beneficial and potentially self-financing.

These results contribute heavily to resolving the long-standing debate over the merits of housing improvement subsidies. Ahlbrandt and Brophy (1975)[30] and Clay (1979, 79 and ch.7) have argued for the efficacy of this strategy. But others have suggested that this approach, by concentrating on a "four-walls" view of the residential environment, overlooks other key components of residential satisfaction and, hence, overall upkeep levels (see Ahlbrandt and Cunningham (1979, ch.12); and Leven et al. 1976, ch.10).

The findings of this study reject the latter criticisms. Certainly other contextual factors affect the individual homeowner's residential satisfaction (see chapter 6), but grants and loans nevertheless stimulate significant amounts of new upkeep activity independently of these contextual factors. Even more important, in a dynamic context the intensification of upkeep efforts physically enhances and abets optimism about the overall neighborhood environment, thereby providing positive externalities beyond the four walls of the individual aid recipient. In summary, subsidized grants and low-interest loans for home improvements are in a large number of contexts an effective strategy for stimulating homeowner upkeep efforts, if one may generalize from the results in Minneapolis.

Summary and Conclusions

This chapter first analyzes theoretically how the impacts of various re-habilitation grant and loan programs vary, depending on the particular characteristics of the policy, the participants, and their dwellings. Em-pirical estimates indicate that in the case of the policies pursued by Min-neapolis between 1976 and 1980, these impacts stimulated additional pri-vate upkeep expenditure over and above what would have been forth-coming in the absence of the subsidies. For each dollar of grant received, participating homeowners spent $1.62 more of their own funds, both expressed as annual averages. The comparable figure for loans was $.345. Besides this direct leveraging effect, the awarding of grants and loans to some homeowners in a neighborhood stimulates other nearby homeowners to augment their upkeep investments by an annual average of $65, because their confidence in the future quality of the neighborhood is abetted. In addition, positive externalities are created for nearby households. Thus, it is apparent that both directly and indirectly, grant and loan policies for subsidizing home rehabilitation can have significant effects on neigh-borhood quality.

Whether such policies represent a wise use of public funds is investigat-ed through several cost-benefit analyses. From a broad societal perspec-tive, both grants and loans seem to generate equal net benefits, with benefits outweighing costs by a probable maximum ratio of 3:1. From the perspective of the local public sector trying to maximize property values with the least public expenditure, important differences emerge between grants and loans, however. From the analysis of the single-family housing rehabilitation grants and loans programs sponsored by Minneapolis be-tween 1976 and 1980 one may conclude that:

– The grants program generally was net beneficial, with a plausible range of benefit-cost ratios of 2:1 to 10:1.

– The no-interest, deferred repayment loan program generally was not net beneficial, unless loans were repaid within a few years. Only if one makes extremely liberal benefit assumptions can one conclude that such loans were net beneficial if repaid much beyond ten years.

– The low-interest, periodic repayment loan program generally was net beneficial, even when loans were repaid over a twenty-year period, unless one makes extremely conservative assumptions about benefits.

– The grants program was significantly superior in budgetary efficiency to any sort of deferred-loan program in which loans were repaid over four years or more. Low-interest loans with periodic repayments up to ten years were superior in budgetary efficiency to grants, if very conservative assumptions are not made about leveraging and externality effects on property values. If interest rates on such loans were 8 percent and discount rates were in single-digit ranges, loans repaid in up to twenty years were superior to grants, regardless of benefit assumptions.

If one can generalize from these results, the common view that loans are a more fiscally responsible means of stimulating neighborhood reinvestment is true only for a subset of loans possessing a particular range of repayment terms. What policymakers should consider is developing an integrated rehabilitation grant and loan program wherein the mix of grants and loans for individual applicants is varied so as to enhance budgetary allocative efficiency. The central principle of the scheme should be to require that subsidy recipients who can afford to do so take out loans on terms that are more net beneficial than grants, before any grants are awarded. In such a fashion the subsidy can be packaged so as to enhance net benefits per budgetary dollar, while simultaneously considering aspects of recipient affordability and program participation.

13 Indirectly Encouraging Neighborhood Reinvestment through Expanding Homeownership

In the previous chapters of this book the focus is on understanding the determinants of homeowner-occupants' housing upkeep behavior. Here the focus shifts a bit to encompass absentee-owners as well. The question asked is whether the overall home upkeep performance of owner-occupants is superior to that of absentee-owners and whether such superiority can be traced to differences in tenure *per se*. If so, a clear policy implication is that an indirect means of encouraging higher levels of investment in the existing housing stock entails expanding opportunities for homeownership by renters.

This chapter begins by briefly reviewing the few rigorous studies that have investigated the aforementioned question. Next, it presents a conceptual model to help elucidate the potential sources of cross-tenure differences in home upkeep behavior. Third, empirical analyses employing the Wooster data base are used to assess whether tenure independently influences the likelihood and magnitude of upkeep expenditures and the incidence of exterior defects. Parameter estimates are then used to estimate the consequences for neighborhood housing upkeep of changing the tenure status of occupants. Readers wishing to omit discussion of conceptual and empirical issues can proceed directly to the sections discussing empirical results and their implications.

Previous Research on Tenure and Home Upkeep

For decades it has been widely believed that owners occupy higher-quality dwellings than renters, and that a major reason for this difference is the superior investment in home maintenance undertaken by owner-occupants.[1] Grigsby (1963, 235–36), Sternlieb (1966; 176, 227), Taggart (1970, 123), Sternlieb and Burchell (1973, 306–8), Peterson et al. (1973, 46–47, 63), Schafer (1977), and Mayer (1981) find that owner-occupants generally spend more on maintenance and engage in maintenance activities more frequently than absentee-owners. The implications of these studies are ambiguous, however, because a variety of other factors besides tenure, which could have explained the observed differences, are not controlled for.

The conventional wisdom is challenged in a rigorous empirical study by Ozanne and Struyk (1976, 54–77) that examines dwelling conditions in a multivariate analysis. They claim that:

> If one controls . . . for differences in the characteristics of occupants and neighborhood condition, the advantages of owner-occupancy (in dwelling condition) largely vanish. This suggests only small differences in the "efficiency" of owner-occupants as producers. . . . The superior level of housing services associated with owner-occupancy results to an important degree from the larger units and better neighborhoods which they inhabit. . . . Owner-occupants are demanding more housing and related services than comparable renters, and they maintain this housing at rates at least equivalent to landlords in similar circumstances (55).

In the Ozanne-Struyk view, owners do not occupy qualitatively superior dwellings compared to comparable renters and thus, by implication, do not engage in superior maintenance activities. Though the Ozanne-Struyk analysis represents an important methodological advance, the veracity of their conclusions may be questioned because the effects of important structural features (type of construction, age, floor and lot size) and occupying household (age, sex, education of head) are not controlled for, and no direct tests of maintenance effort are performed.

The purpose of this chapter is to report on empirical analyses that avoid these shortcomings. The specific two hypotheses tested are that at any given moment, when comparing single-family dwellings of similar construction, age, and size, located in similar neighborhoods, occupied by households of similar socioeconomic and demographic characteristics: (1) the physical condition of the owner-occupied dwelling will be superior to the renter-occupied one; (2) there is a greater probability that the owner-occupied dwelling will have had maintenance performed on it during the previous year and that such will have cost more than $100.

Specification of an Empirical Model of Cross-Tenure Differences in Home Upkeep Behavior

Conceptual Framework

A simple model of dwelling unit condition, maintenance effort, and depreciation will help clarify the role played by owner-occupancy, as well as other influences that may confound the observation of this role. At the end of a given time period (say, a year) t, the condition of any given dwelling, C_t may be expressed in terms of the following relationships:

$$C_t = i(K_t) \tag{13.1}$$

$$K_t = (1-d)K_{t-1} + K_M \tag{13.2}$$

$$d = f([A], [OC], [N]) \tag{13.3}$$

$$K_M = g(M) \tag{13.4}$$

$$M = h(K_{t-1}, [A], [OW], [N], P_M) \tag{13.5}$$

where:

K_t = measure of capital stock embodied in dwelling

d = annual rate of gross depreciation

K_M = measure of dwelling capital stock gained during year via maintenance efforts

$[A]$ = vector of architectural and structural features of building

$[OC]$ = vector of characteristics of occupying household related to intensity of use, such as family size, age, marital status, etc.

$[N]$ = vector of characteristics of neighborhood in which dwelling is located

M = interval measure of maintenance effort expended by owner during year, in terms of time and out-of-pocket expenses

$[OW]$ = vector of characteristics of the homeowner related to investment behavior such as preferences, income, expectations, etc.

P_M = price per unit of materials and/or labor utilized in maintenance efforts

i, f, g, h = functions of unspecified form

This set of equations specifies that the qualitative condition of a dwelling at a given time is a function of the depreciated stock of housing capital at that time and the flow of maintenance efforts invested during some previous time.[2]

In the context of this model, several mechanisms have been alleged whereby owner-occupancy results in greater maintenance effort (M) and thus, in greater dwelling quality (C_t), *ceteris paribus*. First, because owner-occupants rent to themselves, they can predict the demand for their dwelling with more certainty than can an absentee-owner, who is supplying for an anonymous mass market. Such certainty may increase the chances of the owner-occupant's perceiving a sufficient payback period for any contemplated housing investments, thereby altering a component of $[OW]$ above. This argument has been made in rigorous theoretical terms by Sweeney (1974). Second, if owner-occupants are both more likely to use their own time in maintenance activities and to value it at lower implicit cost than the time of professional contract labor (i.e., reducing the P_M term above), they will engage in more of the activity than absentee-owners (see Ozanne and Struyk 1976, 54; and Sweeney 1974, 136). Third, occupancy in the owned unit may increase pride in the dwelling, and these more housing-intensive preferences may lead to greater maintenance efforts (see Peterson et al. 1973, 64). Finally, owner-occupants are more likely to have stronger social identification with their neighbors, and hence, to be more likely to conform to neighborhood norms for acceptable maintenance levels (see chapters 2, 3, and 9). Both these last possibilities are modeled as an alteration in the [OW] vector and/or the h function above.

The unambiguous empirical identification of these potential mechanisms, which are inherent in owner-occupancy itself, is potentially confounded by cross-tenure differences in occupancy, structural, and neighborhood characteristics. As a result, there may exist systematic, cross-tenure differences in both the gross depreciation rates (d) and the transformation function of maintenance effort into structural quality (g), which are not, however, intrinsically caused by the mode of tenure. Observations of cross-tenure differences in dwelling conditions (C_t) are likely to be unreliable indicators of M differences unless [OC], [A], and [N] are controlled for. For example, if renter-occupiers tend to be younger, have larger households, and live at higher densities than owner-occupiers, the dwellings of renters will likely depreciate more rapidly due to greater wear and tear. They will thus evidence poorer conditions, even if the absentee-owner provides maintenance quality (K_M) comparable to the owner-occupant's.[3] A similar result follows if a larger proportion of renter-occupiers live in older structures and those made of less durable construction materials, or in neighborhoods where the chances of structural damage are greater due to vandalism or air pollution. Analogously, even if depreciation is the same, the types (multi- or single-family) of structures systematically differ between tenures. If multifamily structures yield less gain in quality (K_M) from a given maintenance effort (M), one might observe that renter-occupied dwellings are generally in poorer condition than owner-occupied ones, even if both sets of owners exerted identical maintenance efforts.[4] Of course, even if one tries to examine maintenance effort directly, multivariate controls are needed. If, for instance, owners occupy dwellings in neighborhoods having greater expected future increases in residential quality or dwellings that can be quickly and easily repaired, they will engage in larger M, although this is not the result of their tenure status. These considerations shape the specification of the empirical tests discussed below.

Variable Specification

Two types of empirical tests of the hypotheses are conducted. Both involve the estimation of variants of a reduced-form equation (13.1) and equation (13.5) through OLS multiple regression analysis. The first type pools tenures and uses a dummy variable to designate owner- and renter-occupancy. The second estimates separate regressions for each tenure, then uses the coefficients to predict housing upkeep in a scenario where tenure is altered.

The dependent variables to be employed are similar to those used to measure upkeep behavior in chapter 9, with slight modifications necessitated by the inclusion of renter-occupants in the sample. Because it is faulty to assume that the current renters occupying a sampled dwelling can give an accurate estimation of either the absentee-owner's precise upkeep activities or the funds expended on such during the past, UPKEEP? and UPKEEP$ variables are modified to alternative dependent variables in (13.5). Specifically, the likelihood of the owner engaging in nonzero upkeep activities is defined as a dummy variable denoting only whether maintenance and repairs were made during the prior twelve months; major renovations and improvements are not considered.[5] As for intensity of such maintenance and repair activities, the expenditure variable is also defined as a dummy denoting whether the estimated expense of such investments exceeded $100. It is assumed that renters are able to provide adequately accurate assessments of both whether the absentee-owner undertook home maintenance or repair activities during the previous year and whether such were likely to cost more than $100. The final dependent variable to be used as a proxy for dwelling conditions, C_t in (13.1), is the DEFECTS? variable employed in chapter 9; i.e., interviewer-assessed presence of exterior home defects such as peeling paint, trash on premises, or broken structural elements.

The independent variables are (with two exceptions) identical to those employed in the Wooster upkeep model described in chapter 9. In terms of equations (13.1) and (13.5), the independent variables to proxy for the structural attributes ([A]) vector include: number of rooms, front footage of lot, age of structure, and whether it was of wooden clapboard construction. The occupant characteristic ([OC]) vector includes: the age, marital status, sex, and education of household head; family income; number in household; and expected future length of residency. The neighborhood characteristic ([N]) vector is measured by the same indexes of neighborhood (planning area) quality used before.

Unfortunately, no means are available in the study for identifying absentee-owner characteristics ([OW]).[6] The only ownership distinction that can be made is through the use of a dummy variable identifying whether the dwelling is owner-occupied or not. And here is where the upkeep model specified here necessarily differs from that employed earlier. Because only the occupants were interviewed, their expectations or perceived social cohesion in the neighborhood are appropriate measures of the owner's characteristics only in the case of owner-occupants. As a result, the NEIGHEXP, VALUEEXP, and COHESION 1 and 2 variables are excluded from the present model. On the one hand, such exclusion may create some omitted-variable bias. On the other hand, the owner-occupancy dummy variable may capture a good deal of the impact of these excluded variables if there are sizable cross-tenure differences in their values. Indeed, in the case of COHESION there is no reason to suspect that this variable has any impact on absentee-owners, but chapter 9 demonstrates that it has a major impact on owner-occupants. Thus, although the coefficient of the tenure dummy captures an amalgam of factors, it should not be severely biased.

Data for all variables are obtained from the Wooster sample described in chapters 4 and 5. (No renter-occupied dwellings were sampled in Minneapolis.) Only those occupants who had lived in their dwellings for one year or more are selected here. In addition, so as to avoid making comparisons between structure types where the maintenance transformation function (g) is likely different, only single-family detached structures are employed in the analysis. The net result is that 487 owner-occupied dwellings and 85 absentee-owned dwellings are considered.

Empirical Results

Descriptive statistics for the two tenure subsamples indicate that 81 percent of Wooster owner-occupied dwellings had maintenance performed on them in the previous year; only 53 percent of absentee-owned dwellings did. Half of the owner-occupied homes had maintenance efforts of $100 or more; only 22 percent of absentee-owned dwellings had such investments. Finally, exterior defects were evident in 19 percent of the absentee-owned structures, but in only 4 percent of the owner-occupied ones. These results are consistent with all existing empirical work, including that of Ozanne and Struyk (1976). The key question is whether there is something about owner-occupancy in and of itself to which these results can be causally attributed.

Dummy Variable Specification

The initial regression estimates of the relationship between tenure and upkeep, which control for the effects of structural, household, and neighborhood characteristics, suggest an affirmative answer. Table 13.1 pres-

Table 13.1   Coefficients of Owner-Tenure Dummy Variable for Maintenance Effort and Housing Conditions by Income Strata (t-Statistics in parentheses)

Dependent variables	Full sample	Under $11,000 income	Over $11,000 income
Maintenance in prior year	.276	.297	.251
	(5.21)	(3.34)	(3.39)
Maintenance expenses $100+	.274	.362	.222
	(4.21)	(3.85)	(2.41)
Exterior problems	−.146	−.207	−.088
	(5.03)	(3.51)	(3.26)
Number of Owners	487	175	212
Number of Renters	85	42	43

Note: all coefficients are significantly different from zero at 1% level (one-tailed test)

ents the coefficients of the dummy variable that denoted if an observation was owner-occupied (estimated for the pooled sample of owner- and renter-occupants). All these coefficients prove highly statistically signifi-cant.[7] They indicate that, *ceteris paribus,* sampled owner-occupants have a .28 higher incidence of repairs during the previous year and a .27 higher incidence of spending over $100 doing so. Owner-occupied single-family dwellings were 15 percentage points less likely to have exterior problems at the time of the interview.[8] In all three cases of comparative upkeep measures, the coefficient of the owner-occupancy variables is almost as large as the respective cross-tenure difference in the means reported above. This means that virtually all the differences in upkeep between owner-occupied and absentee-owned single-family dwellings in the sample can be attributed to the character of ownership *per se,* not to cross-tenure differences in occupant characteristics, structural characteristics, or neigh-borhood characteristics.

The source of these dramatic cross-tenure differentials in upkeep behav-ior cannot be pinpointed precisely in this study, but the analysis of chapter 9 provides some useful hints. Recall that chapter 9 shows that Wooster homeowners can be expected to spend $142 more if they live in areas having the mean level of COHESIONI (i.e., if they have mean IDENTIFY and the area has mean NIDENTIFY), compared to if they do not. Of course, this figure applies to maintenance, repair, and upgrading expenditures. Given that 54 percent of annual upkeep expenditures in Wooster were for main-tenance and repairs only, however, it is reasonable to similarly adjust the above figure to $78 (= .54 × $142). In order to contrast this $78 figure to cross-tenure differences, some further assumptions must be made about the exact distribution of absentee-owners' maintenance expenditures. Assume that this distribution is identical to that evidenced by owner-occupants within the under-$100 and the over-$100 categories, respectively (allowing the distribution between the categories to match that described above).[9] In this case the average expected value of annual maintenance and repairs for sampled owner-occupants is $295, and that for absentee-owners is $158, a difference of $137. If these assumptions are tolerably correct, the implication is that 57 percent ($78) of the $137 cross-tenure difference in upkeep expenditures can be attributed to the absence of the neighborhood identification effect operating on absentee-owners. The remaining portion of the differential must be attributable to the combined effects of the other factors mentioned above. This finding provides quantitative support for the long-standing (if weakly substantiated) sociological tenet that homeownership is a key element in building neighborhood cohesion (see Gans 1967, Clark and Rivin 1977).

When regressions are estimated using observations stratified by income (bifurcated at the median household income of combined tenures: $11,000), the superiority of owner-occupant maintenance effort and housing condition persists, but more strongly so at lower-income levels (see table 13.1).[10] Several explanations are possible. First, lower-income owner-occupants may perceive a smaller opportunity cost for their time spent on maintenance. Second, for lower-income owner-occupants the home is likely the dominant means of indicating their status achievement, and therefore upkeep may assume greater relative importance (i.e., higher weighting in their utility functions compared to nonhousing expenditure; see chapter 3). Finally, lower-income owner-occupants demonstrate greater identification with their neighborhoods and familiarity with neighbors, and thus may be more subject to neighborhood pressures for maintenance through the COHESION effect noted above.

Stratified Specification

The above procedures assume that the behavioral relationships between the independent variables and the dependent variables are homogeneous with respect to tenure. To test this, separate regressions of the form described above (but omitting the tenure dummy variable) are estimated for each tenure, and a "Chow test" is performed (Chow 1960). The tests show that for all equations, one can reject the hypothesis of equality in the two sets of coefficients for owner-occupied and absentee-owned subsamples. This supports the position that the relationship between tenure and housing upkeep is more than simply additive, and is likely produced by the way in which the structural, neighborhood, and occupancy characteristics are evaluated and responded to by the owner.[11]

Table 13.2   Comparison of Actual versus Predicted Maintenance Efforts and
Housing Conditions by Tenure

	Maintenance in prior year	Maintenance expenses $100+	Exterior problems
A. Renter-occupied			
Actual proportion	.53	.22	.19
Predicted by owner function	.84	.51	.03
Difference	58%	132%	−84%
B. Owner-occupied			
Actual proportion	.81	.50	.03
Predicted by renter function	.63	.20	.15
Difference	−22%	−60%	400%

Given this result, the intuitive appeal of the second methodological
approach is clear. By substituting the mean values of all independent
variables for the absentee-owned subsample into the equation estimated
for owner-occupants and generating a predicted value for the dependent
variable, one can implicitly estimate what upkeep the average tenant
would undertake if he or she were an owner-occupant.[12] An analogous
procedure can be employed for owner-occupants. This produces an estimate of how the typical homeowner would behave if suddenly he or she
sold the home, but stayed on as a tenant.

Results of this second type of empirical test are presented in table 13.2.
Assuming that the relationships estimated are causal, if renters were to
relate structural, neighborhood, and occupant characteristics to upkeep in
the same manner that owner-occupants do, the maintenance efforts on
their dwellings will likely increase from 58 to 132 percent, and their
likelihood of having exterior housing problems will be 84 percent lower
(see panel A in table 13.2). Conversely, if current owner-occupants become tenants in their absentee-owned, single-family dwellings, the maintenance effort on their structures significantly drops and the likelihood of
dwelling problems increases by several orders of magnitude.

Discussion

The empirical tests reported here provide strong support for the two
hypotheses presented above. Owner-occupants do generally occupy dwellings of superior condition, *ceteris paribus*. This does not, of course, provide
prima facie evidence that owner-occupants maintain more. It could be that

those who choose to become owner-occupants have more housing-intensive preferences (not proxied for by the control variables employed) and thus consume a higher initial level of housing stock (K_{t-1}) than their renters. Though possibly valid, this objection is blunted by the finding that owner-occupants do exert stronger maintenance efforts. Owner-occupants, then, may start out with better dwelling conditions due to their stronger demand, but they continue to keep them superior through more intensive maintenance efforts. The superiority of owner-occupants' efforts prove nontrivial, and are especially strong when comparing lower-income households.

There is one major caveat concerning the results. Because absentee-owners are not interviewed in this study, the apparent maintenance superiority of owner-occupants may in part be due to the systematic under-reporting of the owner's maintenance efforts by renting respondents. Though there is no way to assess the severity of this potential bias, my belief is that it alone is not responsible for the significant cross-tenure differences observed. The fact that the sample is confined to households who have lived in a single-family structure, and for over a year, gives one increased confidence that the tenants would be aware if some maintenance had been undertaken, even if their estimate of the owner's expenses involved may be unreliable.

A final caution concerns interpretation of the results as proof that owner-occupancy *per se* causes higher maintenance effort. It may be that sampled owner-occupants possess systematic differences from absentee-owners that are responsible for their superior efforts yet are not the result of their tenure status. Some possible differences that are not controlled for in the present study include expectations, risk aversion, market information costs, use of contract labor, and personal efficiency in carrying out maintenance.

Policy Implications

If the foregoing results are indeed indicators of a general causal relationship between owner-occupancy and maintenance efforts, important policy implications follow. Panel B of table 13.2 indicates that if many homeowners move out of a neighborhood and are replaced by renters, the affected dwellings have dramatically less maintenance expenditures invested in them and more visible signs of external disrepair, even if the new tenants are otherwise identical to the former homeowners. This suggests that attracting and keeping a sizable number of homeowners is a crucial determinant of maintaining aggregate home upkeep levels in a neighborhood. Of course, if the total of homeowners stays constant over a given metropolitan housing market, this strategy produces a zero-sum game from the perspective of all neighborhoods.

A broader strategy that attempts to increase the total number of home-owners participating in a given metropolitan housing market is thus to be commended. A variety of programs at both local and federal levels have been instituted at varying degrees of intensity to accomplish this end, Urban Homesteading being the most visible.[13] Nontraditional forms of partial-ownership arrangements have also been experimented with, such as limited-equity cooperatives. Although it is beyond the scope of this work to evaluate the success of these programs, the results reported here strongly attest to likely substantial payoffs from programs that successful-ly expand homeownership.[14] As shown in panel A of table 13.2, for each renter who can successfully be induced into homeownership one reaps huge relative gains in the maintenance invested in the formerly rented dwelling. The incidence of exterior defects of such dwellings is also dra-matically reduced, which provides an added fillip to the upkeep efforts of neighboring homeowners. If nontrivial numbers of previously rented dwellings now converted to owner-occupancy are located in a given neigh-borhood, one can predict that the overall levels of upkeep in that area will be enhanced greatly.[15] The expected impact likely is of a much larger degree than would ensue even from dramatic increases in resident so-cioeconomic status, optimistic neighborhood expectations, or neigh-borhood cohesiveness (see chapter 10). Indeed, expanding the number of homeowners appears to be the single most potent means for encouraging the upkeep of dwellings in a neighborhood. And the differences are even more dramatic when considering lower-income occupants.

Summary and Conclusions

This chapter presents strong evidence that owner-occupants are better maintainers of single-family homes than are absentee-owners, even when controlling for differences in occupants, structure type and age, and sur-rounding neighborhood. If one can generalize from the Wooster results, compared to owner-occupants, absentee-owners are: (1) more than twice as likely to forgo maintenance and repairs during a year; (2) less than half as likely to spend $100 annually on maintenance or repairs; and (3) almost five times more likely to own dwellings having exterior defects.

It is estimated that about half of these cross-tenure differences in up-keep can be attributed to the effect of neighborhood social cohesion. If absentee landlords live outside the neighborhood in which their rental property is located, they likely will not be subject to the same sorts of social pressures and collective solidarity sentiments that have been shown to be such vital determinants of home upkeep efforts by homeowners.

The implication is that programs that encourage the net formation of owner-occupant households are to be recommended as instruments of neighborhood reinvestment policy. Indeed, expanding the number of homeowners appears to be by far the single most potent means of encouraging the upkeep of dwellings in a neighborhood. Unfortunately, recent national trends indicate that just the opposite is occurring for younger households. Homeownership rates for household heads under age twenty-five dropped from 23.4 percent in 1973 to 19.4 percent in 1983. For household heads age twenty-five to twenty-nine, homeownership during that period declined from 43.6 percent to 40.7 percent. Such trends do not bode well for neighborhood reinvestment, and they indicate the urgency of developing means for encouraging homeownership.

14 Conclusion: Toward a Holistic View of Homeowners and Neighborhood Reinvestment Policy

The quality of the residential milieu in which most Americans live is influenced by one group of decisionmakers more than any other: the owner-occupants of single-family dwellings. If we are to gain any measure of predictability about and, ultimately, a modicum of control over changes in urban neighborhoods, the housing upkeep behavior of such homeowners must be understood. The goal of this book is to expand this understanding through rigorous theoretical and empirical investigations. These investigations produce a variety of new insights into homeowners' housing upkeep behaviors and the means by which public policy efforts may influence these behaviors most effectively. In numerous cases, conventional wisdoms are shown to be fallacies. The main conclusions follow.

The Modeling of Homeowners' Housing Upkeep Behavior: What Has Been Learned and What Has Not

The task of developing a theory of homeowners' decisions about investing in the upkeep of their dwellings is a complex one indeed, given the multi-faceted nature of housing itself. Housing is durable, thus it provides not only current consumption benefits but also future asset value. It is fixed in location, thereby rendering its value vulnerable to the behaviors of other nearby propertyowners and to the public sector. The homeowner also therefore may be subjected to the social-interactive aspects of the neighborhood. Finally, housing is not perfectly malleable; upkeep decisions made now will limit what options are feasible in the future. Together, durability, locational fixity, and imperfect malleability imply that expectations about the future of the neighborhood are an important determinant of current upkeep behavior.

The theoretical model presented in this book captures the aforementioned complexity within the context of an intertemporal utility-maximizing framework. Homeowners act as if they are choosing a particular sequence of alternative upkeep activities over the period in which they plan to reside in their homes, so as to maximize the well-being flowing jointly from both consumption and asset dimensions of housing. The constraints faced are shaped by the homeowners' own financial resources, the technological possibilities for transforming the dwelling into various configurations, and the prices of various inputs used in these structural transformations.

The empirical evidence clearly suggests that the marginal consumption utility gained from additional upkeep investments is influenced by the expected future quality of the neighborhood and, to a lesser degree, by its current quality. Optimism about future neighborhood quality is thus directly related to intensity of home upkeep because the well-being homeowners derive from such expenditure is magnified in a superior residential environment. The evidence also implies that the marginal utility gained from enhanced asset value of the dwelling is not described by a continuous function. Rather, homeowners behave as if they have a threshold of target home equity, which, once exceeded, reduces their concern about further capital gains. In higher-quality neighborhoods homeowners seem confident about reaching this target, so only the consumption value of home upkeep matters much to them. But in lower-valued neighborhoods there appears to be a more tenuous balance between homeowners' target home equity and their perceptions of how well they're progressing toward it. This renders their upkeep behavior highly sensitive to alterations in their expectations about future neighborhood property values. In such lower-valued neighborhoods, homeowners who become more pessimistic about future property-value appreciation in the area apparently fear they will no longer reach their targets. This provides an extra fillip to the perceived value of housing investments and stimulates an increased effort to improve the exterior quality of their homes. The opposite response is forthcoming when such owners expect rapid property-value inflation. In such cases optimism about capital gains does not, as conventionally believed, intensify home investments; it reduces them.

These findings have strong relevance to the long-standing debate about what sorts of strategic interactions homeowners engage in. It is clear that such interactions can be predicted only after a particular sort of homeowner expectations and a particular residential context are defined. It appears that in all neighborhoods, homeowners' upkeep behavior responds to their expectations about future neighborhood quality changes (i.e., the upkeep behaviors of their neighbors) in such a way that expectation becomes a self-fulfilling prophecy. For example, if homeowners expect surroundings to decay they defer maintenance and, hence, stimulate decay. In this case the interactive behavior can be described as crowd following. In higher-valued neighborhoods homeowners show little concern that their own current actions plus those of others will threaten the attainment of their home equity target. As a result, variations in their expectations about neighborhood property values show no relationship with their upkeep behavior—a noninteractive result. On the other hand, in low-valued areas more pessimistic expectations about property values lead to intensified trend-bucking upkeep efforts, and more optimistic ones lead to a neglect of home exteriors (i.e., free-rider behavior). The relationships among particular sorts of expectations, neighborhood contexts, and strategic interactions are, therefore, considerably more complex than has heretofore been believed.

Attempting to model the formation of these expectations is difficult, especially given that the theory of belief formation suggests that there will be interhomeowner variations in the relationship between external, objective data indicating changes in the residential environment and their subsequent translation into expectations. The task is further hindered here by the unavailability of data on recent trends in the neighborhoods, necessitating reliance on current conditions. There is ample room for future research to probe more deeply into the realm of neighborhood expectation formation. Nevertheless, several conditions appear to be important as predictors. Current neighborhood quality is positively related to optimism about future property changes. Both the individual homeowner's and the neighborhood's aggregate degree of collective identification and social integration are strong contributors to optimism about neighborhood quality and (especially) property-value changes. Independent of context, however, certain homeowner types tend to evaluate the residential context in more optimistic ways than others: married and female-head homeowners and those in child-rearing life-cycle stages.

The planning horizon over which homeowners must assess the future of their residential milieus and develop appropriate upkeep strategies is defined as the length of time they plan to remain in their current dwelling. Interhomeowner variations in such mobility plans have an impact on observed upkeep behavior, quite independently of expectations and other characteristics of homeowners or residential contexts. Specifically, those who plan on residing in an area for a finite period but more than ten years undertake more intensive upkeep efforts than those with either shorter or longer (i.e., permanent) mobility plans. Ironically, a stable population is not, contrary to conventional wisdom, an unmitigated good for neighborhood reinvestment. Those most committed to the area are equally as likely to undermaintain as those who plan on remaining only a few years.

The origin of these mobility plans can be comprehended within the theoretical framework premised on the notion of comparative net advantage. The evidence is consistent with the view that homeowners evaluate their relative well-being at their current residence and at other feasible alternative residences, net of various adjustment costs. Homeowners ascertain an expected time of moving (if any) based on their estimate of when this comparative net advantage will tip in favor of an alternative residence. The main proxies for current gross comparative advantage (homeowner satisfaction with the dwelling and with the neighborhood) prove strong direct correlates of length of expected tenure. Characteristics of homeowners that proxy for both adjustment costs and future anticipated gross comparative advantage also help in predicting plans. Married homeowners are most likely to hold a three- to ten-year planning horizon. Life-cycle stage is directly related to length of expected tenure. Less-educated homeowners tend to evidence very long-term (even permanent) mobility plans. Short-term expectations about the neighborhood do not, however, appear to have strong and consistent impacts on the formulation of homeowner mobility plans, suggesting that future projections of comparative net advantage are developed almost entirely on the basis of anticipated changes in household needs, not in the residential context. Whether longer-run expectations about the residential environment affect mobility plans can be fruitfully investigated in the future.

Although residential satisfaction plays some part in the broader determination of upkeep behavior, its role proves to be circumscribed and of small magnitude. Both dwelling and neighborhood satisfaction positively affect length of mobility plans, but mobility plans are related to upkeep in a curvilinear fashion. The net relationship between satisfaction and upkeep thus is such that higher satisfaction will modestly stimulate home upkeep if it induces homeowners to defer erstwhile short-term moving plans, but will reduce it if it makes homeowners want to stay forever, thereby rendering moot concerns about ultimate home equity values. Contrary to widespread opinion, then, residential satisfaction is hardly the key to adequate home upkeep activity.

So, as predicted by the model, homeowners' housing upkeep behavior is influenced by two distinct types of expectations, by their expected length of tenure in the dwelling, and to a lesser degree by their current residential satisfaction. And all these intervening variables are, themselves, determined by characteristics of the homeowners, their dwellings, and their neighborhoods. But do these three sets of exogenous characteristics play a role in upkeep beyond their mediated influence through the above intervening variables? The answer is clearly yes. Homeowner characteristics like income, education, marital status, household size, and life-cycle stage all have direct impacts on upkeep behavior, even when controlling for expectations and mobility plans, as would be predicted if they proxied for housing preferences and financial constraints. Neither race of the homeowner nor racial composition of the area has any significant impact on home upkeep, however, contrary to popular impressions. Similarly, dwelling age and construction type apparently capture aspects of structural depreciation rates and transformation possibilities that directly affect upkeep, independent of homeowner characteristics. There is no evidence, however, that older homes inexorably decay, or inevitably plant the seeds for neighborhood deterioration.

Equally important are variables related to the neighborhood encompassing the given dwelling. Factor analyses of numerous variables characterizing this neighborhood aspect indicate that they can be unambiguously grouped into distinct physical-demographic and social-interactive dimensions. In addition, three distinct geographic scales of empirical variation of areal features can be distinguished.

Overall the results for the physical-demographic neighborhood variables indicate that different geographic scales of neighborhood are employed by homeowners in formulating different evaluations, expectations, and behavioral plans. Conditions on the immediate block face, on the several-square-block surrounding area, and on the census tract as a whole affect perceived satisfaction with neighborhood. On the other hand only the first two, smaller scales of neighborhood apparently are important in formulating expectations about neighborhood property-value changes. And only block-face conditions influence exterior maintenance behavior. Finally, relative conditions on the block face compared to those in a wider area may affect upkeep expenditure decisions. Most surprisingly, the presence of nonresidential land use on the block does not deter home upkeep; if anything, it tends to encourage it in certain homeowner groups.

The social-interactive dimension of the neighborhood, a hitherto uninvestigated aspect of housing upkeep behavior, proves to have major influences, both indirectly through expectations and directly. Specifically, both the individual homeowner's and the aggregate neighborhood's degree of identification with the group interact synergistically to produce a cohesive context. There is an apparent threshold level of such cohesion; if either an individual or the group falls below it, there will be no net effect of social identification on the upkeep behavior of the individual. But past the threshold, successively greater amounts of either individual or collective solidarity sentiments produce ever-higher upkeep expenditures. It thus is apparent that such social cohesion provides a means by which homeowners can exercise some collective control over the behavior of other homeowners in the neighborhood. In this manner social cohesion tends to minimize damaging strategic interactions among homeowners and to internalize the externalities associated with home upkeep activities. Thus, a widely held position that home upkeep is purely a matter of economics is definitely rejected. Future research can profitably be aimed at better understanding how such cohesive neighborhoods can be formed and maintained.

All of the foregoing conclusions prove to be quite general between both the Wooster, Ohio, and Minneapolis, Minnesota, samples of homeowners. Where the results differ noticeably provides some provocative hints about how upkeep behavior may differ across metropolitan housing-market contexts. First, the way in which dwelling age translates into upkeep effort is very different in the two samples, suggesting that the particular architectural features or construction materials associated with a city's housing vintages may be more important than age *per se*. Unfortunately, data were not available in this study to explore these potential structural idiosyncrasies more fully. Second, whether homeowners in child-rearing stages manifest distinct upkeep behaviors from those in the younger, childless stage depends on to what extent the latter comprises upwardly mobile, dual-income urban homeowners. This group apparently can make such exceptional home rehabilitation investments (at least in a regime of high interest rates and property-value inflation) that the conventional life-cycle pattern is invalidated. Additional research into the effect of macroeconomic conditions on home upkeep is clearly warranted. Third, informal social interaction with neighbors is a stronger determinant of more optimistic property-value expectations in Wooster than in Minneapolis, suggesting that reliance on interpersonal, communally mediated sources of market information are more important in smaller housing markets. Similarly, the effect of social identification on upkeep expenditures is larger in proportional terms in Wooster. It is nevertheless highly significant in Minneapolis, suggesting that even in a major urban area vestiges of *gemeinshaft* and its concomitant consequences may not be totally eroded. The relationship between city size and sociological attributes has been frequently investigated, but not as yet with an eye toward home upkeep levels.

Some final caveats about the generality of these findings are in order. Both samples are drawn from comparatively stable, homogeneous housing markets. Neither city has extreme slums or ghettos, and rapid socioeconomic succession or racial tipping of neighborhoods is absent. As a result, the importance of neighborhood racial and class composition and of expectations about changes in such compositions may well be more important determinants of housing upkeep elsewhere than they prove to be here. Further research is obviously needed in this vein.

Homeowners' Upkeep Behavior and Neighborhood Reinvestment

Moving from the individual to the aggregate perspective of an urban neighborhood, the foregoing empirical findings provide the means for quantitatively predicting how overall home investment levels in an area will change if attributes and beliefs of its occupying homeowners change. For instance, in some archetypical neighborhood if one-third of the homeowners were replaced by ones earning $20,000 less, this alone would be expected to produce an average 9 percent drop in upkeep expenditures and a 10 percent increase in the number of dwellings with exterior defects across the neighborhood. Comparable orders of magnitude of impacts would be predicted if one-third of the married homeowners were replaced by female heads or single-male ones, or if one-third of those in child-rearing stages were replaced by elderly homeowners. Thus it is clear that for neighborhood reinvestment it matters not only how wealthy homeowners are, but also what other characteristics they have, including life-cycle stage and marital status.

Equally important are changes in the social-interactive dimension of neighborhood. In a neighborhood that initially had the maximum observed value for cohesion in the present sample, if one-third of the homeowners were replaced by those having only the average level of local group identification, the mean annual upkeep expenditures would drop at least 5 percent. If enough turnover occurred so that the neighborhood as a whole fell below the minimal threshold for cohesion, a drop in expenditure of at least 15 percent would be predicted.

Finally, changes in expectations also induce potent consequences. For instance, if one-third of the homeowners in a typical neighborhood who previously thought that neighborhood quality would improve now expect it to stay the same, a 9 percent reduction in average upkeep expenditures and a 13 percent increase in exterior defects will transpire. The impact will be even greater in lower-valued areas. Though opposite in direction, changes in expectations about capital gains are equally powerful in lower-valued areas. Should one-third of the homeowners who originally thought that property values would stay the same now believe that they will rise, a 33 percent higher incidence of exterior defects will result due to free-rider behavior.

By synthesizing the results from these hypothetical scenarios, new insights can be gained into the three most prevalent neighborhood dynamic phenomena: succession, racial transition, and gentrification. As for succession, the evidence indicates that new, lower-income in-movers to a neighborhood will not evidence any higher incidence of home defects, although they will tend to spend less on alterations and additions. The visible deterioration that typically ensues is due instead to the home upkeep activity reductions of the homeowners who have remained in the neighborhood, generated either by their increasing pessimism about neighborhood quality of life or by an unraveling of the previously cohesive social fabric. The discouraging implication is that deleterious consequences for the residential quality of life in urban areas undergoing succession are to a large extent the result of self-fulfilling prophecies.

Racial transition may erode neighborhood reinvestment, but the evidence clearly suggests that stable, racially integrated neighborhoods have no different upkeep levels than comparable all-white ones. Again, the differential is due to perverse expectational dynamics initiated by the residents who have remained in the neighborhood. If whites are prejudiced, they will regard integration as tantamount to socioeconomic class succession and will expect an inevitable decline in the quality of the neighborhood. Such pessimistic expectations, in conjunction with reductions in their expected length of tenure and in social cohesion, can produce sizable reductions in their upkeep activity. If the dynamics of disinvestment and turnover are especially rapid, property values in an area of racial transition can plummet, thereby abetting socioeconomc succession and, ultimately, additional physical decay.

The improvement in housing quality in neighborhoods undergoing gentrification transpires both directly and indirectly. The direct effects occur as the gentrifying homeowner typically replaces one who is older and of lower socioeconomic status. The indirect effects, if any, occur through alterations in the reinvestments of homeowners who remain in the area, but such are impossible to predict *a priori*. On the one hand, upkeep may be abetted through positive externalities and increased optimism about neighborhood quality. On the other hand, more optimism about capital gains may produce free-rider behavior. A disintegration of the pregentrification social fabric may also deter investment. Thus the aggregate increase in neighborhood reinvestment is dominated by the direct effects of the gentrifiers themselves, the indirect effects on remaining owners being variable across contexts.

Evaluating Policies for Promoting
Neighborhood Reinvestment

The findings provide a wealth of input for those concerned with developing policies to maintain and rehabilitate neighborhood quality. They point to a series of indicators that can predict changes in neighborhood housing upkeep levels and, hence, target intervention efforts. Of course, it is one thing to predict neighborhood changes, and another to modify them in socially beneficial ways. Three general programmatic strategies for accomplishing this can be evaluated in the context of this research. The first tries to improve in a variety of ways the residential context surrounding homeowner-investors, and thereby to stimulate their home upkeep efforts. The second tries to subsidize upkeep activities directly through grants or low-interest loans intended to defray costs of home improvements. The third tries to augment neighborhoodwide upkeep levels indirectly by increasing the number of dwellings that are owner-occupied. Only the latter two hold much potential as potent tools of neighborhood reinvestment policy.

Policies for improving the residential environment may be viewed in the context of the conceptual model as an attempt to alter the values of certain neighborhood-related variables believed to influence homeowners' decision calculus. Improvements in public neighborhood infrastructure like those accomplished under the auspices of the Community Development Block Grant program do not appear to have major effects in this regard. The physical quality and property values of the targeted block face may be improved, but such variables affect the upkeep behavior of homeowners on that block face only minimally. Furthermore, their optimism about the future of the neighborhood is not abetted significantly. Beyond the block face the consequences likely prove deleterious, because homeowners on nontargeted blocks may perceive that the relative quality of their own areas has now fallen, and they are more likely to engage in free-rider behaviors. The aggregate net result on reinvestment may not even be positive, therefore.

Land-use zoning regulations are another potential policy option for influencing the physical environment. But the results give no indication that areas currently with mixed land use have lower home upkeep levels than areas with homogeneous residential uses. Indeed, for certain homeowners the effect is just the opposite.

As for altering the social-psychological milieu of the homeowner, the evidence is more mixed. Indeed, manipulating public opinion in a way that encourages optimism about the neighborhood as a place to live significantly enhances upkeep. But, unfortunately, in lower-valued neighborhoods, if such optimism also carries over into property-value expectations, the results are virtually negated. Thus the prickly policy problem here is how to engender crowd-following behavior through optimistic qualitative neighborhood expectations without simultaneously engendering free-rider behavior due to optimistic property-value expectations. Building neighborhood confidence thus is a policy prescription rife with half-truth, and a prescription we have no proven policy instruments to fill successfully.

Assisting in the maintenance and creation of neighborhood cohesion also appears to be a double-edged policy sword. On the one hand, neighborhoods with strong solidarity sentiments and collective identification clearly produce far superior levels of homeowner upkeep activity. They improve efficiency by providing a means for internalizing upkeep externalities and simultaneously coordinating otherwise-destructive strategic gaming behaviors by homeowners in the area. On the other hand, the

dangers of intensified neighborhood parochialism that may attend enhanced cohesion may be nontrivial. Again, it is doubtful whether we have
mastered the manipulation of neighborhood social dynamics sufficiently
so as to attain only benefits from a potential program. Nevertheless, the
potential payoffs for stabilizing neighborhood investment levels appear so
great as to warrant significant amounts of further study.

Other context-alteration strategies, such as ensuring adequate home
improvement loan flows and stabilizing integrated neighborhoods, have
no apparent negative side effects. But in themselves they cannot constitute
cornerstones of neighborhood reinvestment policy. Coordinating lenders'
behaviors can profitably reduce their prisoner's-dilemma situation and
spur financial resource availability, but the ultimate impact on rehabilitation depends on the desire by owners to take advantage of these resources.
Even if efforts to stabilize integrated areas are successful, other all-white
or all-minority areas may have insufficient reinvestment levels, which
must be dealt with through other means.

Thus it is apparent that the first overall neighborhood reinvestment
strategy of altering the context surrounding individuals' upkeep decisions
has little to recommend it. There is no evidence that changes in the
physical surroundings of homeowners will induce them to undertake significantly more home investments. Changes in the socio-psychological
context have more potential for shaping upkeep behavior. Unfortunately,
the programmatic means for influencing expectations and social cohesion
in controlled, beneficial ways have yet to be developed. And the possibilities of major unintended consequences spawned by public policy
blunders in this area are rife. Policies to augment home improvement loan
flows and to stabilize integrated neighborhoods may have positive effects,
but have limited applicability for dealing with reinvestment issues in all
sorts of neighborhoods.

The second general policy approach of directly subsidizing homeowners' upkeep efforts appears, by comparison, far more effective and less
fraught with unintended outcomes. It is clear that both rehabilitation-
grant and low-interest or deferred-loan programs in Minneapolis generated major increases in upkeep expenditures that would not have been
forthcoming otherwise. Directly, recipient homeowners' efforts were
stimulated. And indirectly, unlike public infrastructure investments,
those residing around the subsidy recipients also were encouraged to invest more, following from the optimism that was stimulated by the direct
allocation of subsidies to neighbors. Whether such increments to property
upkeep prove to be worth the allocation of public monies depends on the
assumptions one makes about: (1) how such upkeep increments and
positive externalities ultimately become capitalized into property values,
(2) the public sector's discount rate, and (3) the terms and conditions of

the grants and loans. Under wide ranges of plausible parameter assumptions it appears that both rehabilitation loans and especially grants have benefit-cost ratios in excess of one, regardless of whether one takes a broad social perspective or the viewpoint of a local public official. However, most loans that are repaid over terms exceeding about five years are unlikely to be net beneficial from a local public-sector budgetary standpoint. The relative superiority of grants to loans in terms of comparative budgetary benefit-cost ratios depends on the public discount rate (opportunity cost of funds), and the terms of the loan. Grants will generally be the recommended option the: (1) longer the deferment of loan repayment, (2) higher the discount rate, (3) lower the loan's interest rate, and (4) lower the indirect leveraging and externality effects of the subsidies. Even with a loan interest rate of 8 percent, a discount rate of 9 percent and liberal indirect leveraging and externality effects, loans are superior to grants only if they can be repaid within ten years. This, of course, may be financially impossible for many homeowners whom policymakers would wish to participate in such a program. Thus, future rehabilitation subsidies should seek to package subsidies in such a way that, whenever possible, recipients who can afford to do so receive loans that have superior benefit-cost ratios to grants. Grants would then be used in ranges where affordability concerns suggest that only inefficient loans could be offered otherwise.

In sum, directly influencing homeowners' reinvestment calculus through public subsidies commends itself as an important tool of neighborhood reinvestment strategy. If packaged correctly, a grant and loan program can generate far-larger increments of residential benefits than budgetary costs. And because such benefits are reflected in enhanced property values in the jurisdiction, it is conceivable that such a rehabilitation program could be self-financing in the long run. That is, even if only part of the property-value gains are reassessed for tax purposes, property-tax revenues will likely increase enough to offset the original subsidy provided.

The third broad category of neighborhood reinvestment policy options does not take as given the number of homeowners, as do the previous two categories. This third approach tries to produce a net increase in the number of homeowners (with a concomitant reduction in absentee-owners) throughout the metropolitan housing market—especially among lower-income households. This strategy is recommended because owner-occupants maintain their single-family dwellings at levels far superior to those evidenced by absentee-owners of such dwellings, controlling for cross-tenure variations in occupant, dwelling, and neighborhood characteristics. No specific programmatic means for enhancing rates of home-ownership are evaluated here. But it is clear that if these can be developed at moderate cost the payoff in the form of enhanced property upkeep will be dramatic.

The Broad View: Systems within and among Neighborhoods

Thus far, the policy analysis in this book has focused on programs' impacts on the housing upkeep behavior of individual homeowners currently residing in a particular target neighborhood. But before leaving the subject of neighborhood reinvestment policy, it is crucial to recognize that the housing upkeep behavior of homeowners in a given neighborhood is framed in the broader context of a metropolitanwide system of competing neighborhoods. Thus, the formulation of public policies to abet the upkeep efforts of individual homeowners in an individual neighborhood must not be myopic or static. It must explicitly recognize and account for the systemic, dynamic interactions among different neighborhoods (see Grigsby et al. 1987). Some of these interactions have been alluded to above. Here the purpose is to view them holistically within a single, overall framework.

These interindividual and interneighborhood connections are portrayed schematically in figure 14.1. The elements of the system are analogous to those delineated in figure 2.1, except that their interrelationships are portrayed in a dynamic context. In addition, the impact of characteristics of households and neighborhoods outside the neighborhood of concern are included explicitly. Figure 14.1 can be understood in the context of the empirical modeling effort represented here. When observing a given neighborhood at a given moment, its social-interactive, demographic, and physical characteristics may be taken as predetermined variables (see the left-hand rectangles in figure 14.1).[1] These characteristics (arrows 1, 2, and 3) influence the overall degree of residential satisfaction (arrow 4, as analyzed in chapter 6), the expectations of all households currently living in the neighborhood (arrow 5), and the expectations of homeowners in particular (arrow 14, as analyzed in chapter 7). Plans currently held by households to leave or stay in the neighborhood are influenced by these evaluations and expectations (arrows 6 and 7, as analyzed in chapter 8). In conjunction, all these current dimensions of the neighborhood (arrow 11), expectations (arrow 15), and mobility plans (arrow 10), affect the housing upkeep behavior of constituent homeowners (as analyzed in chapter 9).

This one-dimensional view of causality is satisfactory when considering only a given neighborhood at a given point in time. There are, however, patterns of circular causation that emanate over time within a given neigh-

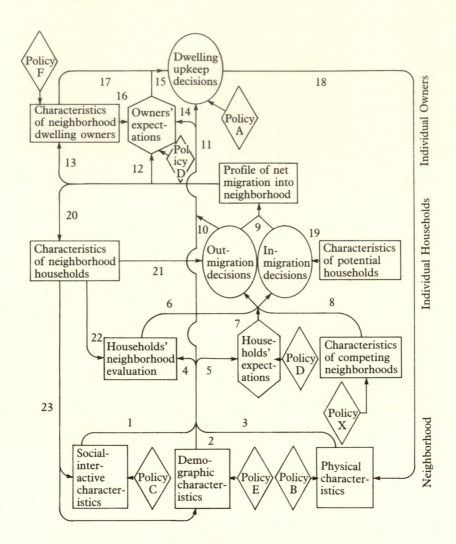

Figure 14.1 Systems within and among neighborhoods

borhood and that connect the given neighborhood to others in the metropolitan area through household mobility (shown as double-outlined rectangles in figure 14.1). For example, as discussed in chapter 10, in
aggregate the dwelling upkeep decisions of owners will determine over
time the physical character of the neighborhood, as suggested by the
feedback arrow 18 along the right side of figure 14.1. The out-migration
decisions of current residents in the neighborhood (arrow 21) are not only
a function of the current and expected absolute quality of the residential
environment (arrows 6 and 7) but also of its quality relative to known
comparisons, through the principle of comparative net advantage (arrow
8). Put differently, households need not be pushed out of their neighborhoods, they may be pulled elsewhere as well. Conversely, households that
are potential in-movers to a given neighborhood are also assessing it relative to other, substitute neighborhoods (arrow 19). Together, those who
choose to leave and those who choose to move into a given neighborhood
will determine a demographic and socioeconomic profile of net migration
(arrow 9). If the aggregate characteristics of in-movers differ in some way
from those of out-movers, the overall demographic and socioeconomic
character (renters and owners together) of the area will be altered (arrows
20 and 23), as will the likely characteristics of homeowners in particular
(arrow 13). How the in-movers evaluate the neighborhood may differ from
out-movers' evaluations (arrow 22).

This alteration in the profile of a neighborhood's residents has, of
course, further repercussions. Original owners who remain in the neighborhood may adjust their own expectations (arrow 12) and upkeep efforts
(arrow 15) accordingly. The new owners who have recently moved into the
neighborhood may adopt significantly different upkeep strategies than the
previous owners because their personal characteristics (e.g., housing preferences, incomes, and especially tenure) are different (arrow 17), and
because they form different expectations (arrow 16). Aggregate changes in
the neighborhood's housing upkeep investments ultimately will alter the
physical characteristics of the area (arrow 18), thereby spawning further
adjustments in owners' satisfaction, expectations, mobility plans and upkeep behavior, and in the subsequent type of migrating households that
will view the area as their best feasible alternative.

The public sector potentially can impinge directly on this nexus of
interrelationships at a variety of points. Again assuming that the object is
to improve the upkeep levels in the neighborhood pictured in figure 14.1,
the public sector could attempt to alter housing upkeep decisions through
home-improvement loans or grants (see policy A in figure 14.1). Alternatively, it could try to affect upkeep by altering the neighborhood's
physical environment (see policy B). Or, it could attempt to stimulate local
social organizations and neighborhood cohesion (policy C) or heighten

confidence (policy D). Stabilizing racially integrated areas would be tanta-mount to altering demographic characteristics (policy E). Finally, a policy encouraging more homeownership would impinge on the area's aggregate homeowner characteristics (policy F). The potential efficacy of all these strategies for directly abetting reinvestment in a given neighborhood has already been considered above. But the upshot of the previous systemic considerations is that public policy can have great indirect impact on a particular neighborhood through its efforts to alter characteristics of other, competing neighborhoods (which is shown as Policy X in figure 14.1).[2]

Imagine a hypothetical municipal policy that seeks to physically re-vitalize a particular graying inner-city neighborhood. In order to accom-plish this, suppose the city plants new trees, repaves the streets and side-walks, installs new lighting, builds a new elementary school, strengthens police foot patrols, and organizes local social and political organizations. Suppose these efforts are such that they significantly improve the per-ceived quality of the neighborhood in the eyes of its current residents. Though these residents are now less likely to voluntarily move elsewhere, there normally will be significant numbers of involuntary dwelling turn-overs spawned by deaths, changes of employment, or landlords increasing rents in response to the enhanced environmental quality.

These vacancies are filled by households not originally living in our hypothetical revitalized neighborhood. Now that the area has improved, not only current residents' perceptions but those of potential residents are altered. This means that the profile of net migration into our target neigh-borhood is different because of the effects of the revitalization policy. Earlier it was noted how such altered profiles change subsequent behavior in our target neighborhood. But the point here is that now the profiles of in-movers to other neighborhoods are affected. For instance, in the ab-sence of efforts to improve our target neighborhood, middle-class house-holds who have recently formed or who have just moved into the metro-politan area would not locate here; now they do. Or, our target area may become so attractive that residents in neighborhoods elsewhere in the city are pulled to it, and their intensive bidding eventually pushes original residents out. In either case, the net-migration profiles of other neigh-borhoods that compete with our target neighborhood are modified. And, as we have seen above, such modifications have the potential of drastically altering upkeep behavior in those areas.[3]

The central point is that policies to encourage neighborhood housing upkeep must not be geographically myopic. They must recognize that alterations in the absolute quality of a given neighborhood that is the target of upkeep incentives will affect the perceived relative quality of other neighborhoods (Grigsby et al. 1987). Thus, systemic neighborhood policy making is akin to walking a tightrope. A policy so modest that an inferior neighborhood remains so in everyone's perception will not leverage significant private investments. But a policy that is overly successful in revitalizing one neighborhood may so severely erode the relative attractiveness of other neighborhoods that, on balance, citywide housing upkeep levels are unaffected: the zero-sum game. In either case, the policy is inefficient.

Toward a People-Oriented Neighborhood Reinvestment Strategy

What does the systematic view of urban neighborhoods say about neighborhood reinvestment strategy? Simply put: Policies that focus on improving the neighborhood environment as a place will not be as successful as those that focus on altering the financial and tenure characteristics of people.

Consider what we have found earlier about place-oriented strategies of improving the residential context. They have little prospect of substantially improving the upkeep behavior of existing homeowners in target areas. From the perspective of the last section, however, it could be the case that such public efforts might improve the absolute attractiveness of a target area enough to alter migration flows.[4] This, in turn, could change the homeowner characteristics of the target area and thus aggregate reinvestment behavior there. But is this ultimately sensible?

Certainly not if the net result is a mere reshuffling of residents across different neighborhoods within the same jurisdiction. In such a case there is a zero-sum outcome: improvements in upkeep in targeted areas are exactly offset by declines in upkeep in nontargeted areas.[5] Only if the aggregate proportion of high-upkeep homeowners (i.e., higher income and education, married, child-rearing) can be increased does the overall upkeep level increase.

A single local jurisdiction can attempt to do this by public investments designed to market its neighborhoods to such desired residents. But if it is successful in doing this from its own perspective, from the broader social perspective the zero-sum result persists—the desired homeowners were pirated from other jurisdictions whose neighborhoods, by implication, now receive less reinvestment. Of course, if all jurisdictions follow suit and make investments so as to compete for desired households, the overall result is a waste of public resources, with little gain to any jurisdiction.

Thus, in principle, focusing attention on a set of target neighborhoods and attempting to improve them is a strategy fraught with peril. It has the potential of significantly affecting upkeep in the target area by altering who lives there. But the tools have not yet been developed to allow planners to guide mobility so precisely as to avoid a zero-sum outcome within their own jurisdictions. Even if a zero-sum outcome were somehow avoided in the targeted area, it still would hold over a larger, cross-jurisdictional set of neighborhoods. Competing jurisdictions would likely respond with their own version of neighborhood-marketing strategies, and the efficacy of the given program would dwindle.

All of these systemic difficulties are sidestepped by neighborhood reinvestment strategies that subsidize rehabilitation efforts by those who otherwise would be unable to maintain their dwelling in decent repair, and that promote homeownership.[6] This book shows that such people-oriented strategies produce sizable improvements in the condition of neighborhoods. And these are net-gain improvements, ones that are not counterbalanced by losses in upkeep elsewhere. Of course, the relative rankings of neighborhood quality may be altered, as might be future mobility. But such zero-sum–game producing dynamics become less relevant at this point, because the main fillip to neighborhood reinvestment has already occurred.

A strategy that provides subsidies attacks a major source of inefficiently low reinvestment levels: strategic gaming among owners. A strategy that expands homeownership establishes at least the prerequisite for abetted social identification and cohesion at the neighborhood level, which intensifies reinvestment. Thus, the analysis of homeowners and of the systems within and among neighborhoods points to people-oriented strategies as the cornerstone of successful public policy making.

Notes

2 Neighborhoods, Homeowners, and Housing Upkeep

1 Mobile homes as yet represent a small fraction of America's housing stock.
2 This framework is sometimes called a "path model" by sociologists, and a "recursive system" by economists. A complementary and similar conceptual model has been presented by Ahlbrandt and Cunningham (1979, figure 5.1).
3 For a historical review, see Urban-Suburban Investment Group (1977).
4 Indeed, the functions of the urban neighborhood are numerous; see Keller (1968), Suttles (1972), Hunter (1974, 1979), Appleyard (1979), Hallman (1984).
5 This is a common, though typically unsubstantiated, claim in the literature. See Ahlbrandt and Cunningham (1979, ch.1), Downs (1981, 11), Hallman (1984, 41, 151), Taub, Taylor, and Dunham (1984, 140).
6 See, e.g., Davis and Whinston (1967), and Rothenberg (1967). The former discuss "free-riders" (owners who refrain from improving even when others nearby are doing so and nevertheless reap capital gains); the latter discusses why there is a bias against spontaneous upgrading and toward undermaintenance in the housing market.
7 The presentation of such a general model was initiated by Granovetter (1978) and applied to housing upkeep by Taub, Taylor, and Dunham (1984, ch.6).
8 The ability of a neighborhood to deter counterproductive individual behaviors has been discussed in terms of "homeostasis" by Goetze (1979, ch.6) and in terms of a "civil class" by Clay (1979, ch.3).
9 For more detailed accounts of this process, as well as other neighborhood dynamic scenarios, see Public Affairs Counseling (1975), Downs (1981, 61), and Grigsby et al. (1987).
10 This is a conventional position; see Public Affairs Counseling (1975).

3 A Model of Housing Upkeep Behavior by Homeowners

1 Sweeney (1974) relates the length-of-tenure consumption desires of owner-occupants to their dynamic housing-investment decisions. Mendelsohn's (1977) and Galster's (1981) static formulations specify the asset value of the dwelling as an argument in the household utility function. Kau and Keenan's (1981) model involves intertemporal utility maximization based on an optimal stock of housing. Shear and Carpenter (1982) specify a three-period model and derive an optimal rehabilitation-investment rule for non-

movers in the first period. Chinloy's model (1980) also represents a hybrid of consumption-investment behavior, but does not derive optimal-maintenance rules. For a contrasting specification that separates these two behaviors, see Struyk (1976).

2   This specification is similar to that employed by Kau and Keenan (1981).

3   Equation 1 could equally well be written as a Stone-Geary utility function where each of the H, Z terms would be: $(H_t - \hat{H}_t)$, $(Z_t - \hat{Z}_t)$. For notational simplicity this is omitted.

4   Dildine and Massey (1974) and MacRae (1982) similarly view housing services as being solely a function of the quantitative and qualitative aspects of the structure and parcel. Locational and amenity characteristics of the neighborhood are seen as influencing the price of housing services. By contrast, Shear and Carpenter (1982, 11–12) and Ingram and Oron (1977, 275) do consider physical attributes of structure and neighborhood as jointly producing housing services. Note that for simplicity no explicit attention is given here to operating inputs in the production function for housing services in the present formulation.

5   There is ample evidence to suggest the relationship between neighborhood conditions and property values. For a selection, see Kain and Quigley (1970), Ingram and Oron (1977), Chinloy (1980), MacRae (1982). At this point the distinction between owner and market perceptions of N is unimportant; its potential significance is discussed later.

6   It may be that there is some average social-interactive dimension of neighborhood that the market presumes to exist for all dwellings when market price is computed, but even so this is probably not equal to that perceived by the current owner. Only after a particular buyer occupies the dwelling for some time does that homeowner's perception have the potential for diverging from this average.

7   This model assumes that upkeep decisions are made based on a prior decision about expected duration of residence in the unit. For a different treatment of these two decisions, see Shear and Carpenter (1982).

8   For simplicity it is assumed that r is constant over the planning horizon and equal to the real rate of interest; all results can be easily modified to encompass a varying rate of time preference which is not equal to the interest rate.

9   It is obviously a simplication to assume that the utility function is separable both across time and between the consumption and wealth arguments. In other words, it seems unlikely that a consumption pattern of, say, $50,000 in the first period and $0 in the next yields comparable utility to one of $25,000 in both periods. The qualitative conclusions of the model do not, however, depend on this assumption of separability. The simplification is adopted primarily so the reader can more easily recognize that the utility gained from a marginal unit of $\bar{H}$ increases both consumption and wealth opportunities in the future, as well as current consumption.

10 Again, r is assumed constant for the planning horizon in question for simplicity of notation.

11 The terms W_0 and W_T are negative if a net debtor position is extant. The limit to such debt is undoubtedly constrained by the homeowner's expected income, in combination with institutional borrowing restrictions, although these constraints are not modeled explicitly. It is assumed throughout that debt constraints are not violated by optimal consumption patterns implied by the first-order conditions.

12 Note that even if some maintenance expenditure is undertaken, it need not necessarily succeed in keeping the original housing stock constant if the added structural capital provided by maintenance does not offset that lost via depreciation.

13 A "unit of maintenance" can be thought of as consisting of a predefined combination of certain amounts of labor time and materials (wood, cement, paint, etc.).

14 The decision whether to contract out maintenance work has been modeled by Ozanne

and Struyk (1976) and Mendelsohn (1977). It is beyond the scope of the present work to do so. It is assumed the prices of contract labor and materials do not vary significantly in a local housing market. Evidence by Mayer (1981) supports this assumption.

15 Varying productivity of workers not only refers to differences between owner-occupants who perform M themselves, but also between professionals who may be hired by occupants. Of course, such differences may also be associated with differences in labor costs making up P_M. Birch (1979) has found that skilled craftsmen homeowners undertake more maintenance activities, as would be expected with their higher productivity, *ceteris paribus*.

16 This assumption is also conventional in the literature; see Moorhouse (1972), Dildine and Massey (1974), Sweeney (1974), Ozanne and Struyk (1976), Ingram and Oron (1977), McDonald (1979, ch.4), Shear and Carpenter (1982, 9).

17 As a final word on upward conversion, there is an idiosyncratic financial aspect to be mentioned. It is likely that a sizable upward conversion necessitates borrowing by the typical homeowner. Particular homeowners may be unable to obtain the requisite loan for an envisioned upward conversion, either due to their own credit-unworthiness or due to personally discriminatory or spatial red-lining actions by lenders. In such cases a quantity constraint would need to be added to the homeowner's choice calculus that would effectively rule out some foreseeable upward conversions. For simplicity this is omitted here.

18 It must be assumed here that whatever upkeep strategy is chosen it will not affect whether the homeowner is a net borrower or lender.

19 Put differently, one must account for the fact that expenditures for additions to the stock, $P_{\bar{A}t}\bar{A}_t$ for maintenance or upward conversions, also improve ultimate home equity E_T by the depreciated amount of the discounted present value of the added stock. Thus, the true financial constraint represented by such expenditure must have this equity-enhancement term (represented by the fourth term on the left-hand side of (3.13)) subtracted. Conversely, downward conversion of stock $\bar{H}_{t*} = k^{-1}(\bar{A}_{t*})$ creates "negative expenditures" (added rental revenues as shown in (3.11)) but simultaneously decreases the asset value of the entire dwelling by the difference in per unit capital stock values, $(P_{\bar{H}T} - \bar{P}_{\bar{H}T})\bar{H}_{t*}$. Thus, the true financial constraint represented by downgrading rental revenues must be adjusted by the fifth term on the left-hand side of (3.13).

20 Note that the partial derivative of E_T with respect to $\bar{A}_t$ is precisely the same value (but opposite in sign) as the similar partial derivative of either of the last two terms in (3.13), whichever is relevant. Thus, the derivatives of the wealth-constraint components do not appear in (3.15).

21 It is mathematically possible, of course, to get multiple global optima, but it is assumed this has little practical application.

22 The $\bar{H}_{t-1}$ parameter is implicit in the f_{Ht} and j_{At} partial derivatives in (3.17). Homeowner characteristics would determine the f and w functions. The role of the other parameters is obvious from (3.17).

23 The role of the parameters is clear from equations (3.8), (3.9), (3.11) specifying price of housing alterations. Attributes of the homeowner can determine both his/her productivity as a potential laborer for $\bar{A}_t$ and the probability of contracting the work out; both influence $P_{\bar{A}t}$. They may also affect the $dY / d\bar{A}$ term in (3.15). Characteristics of the dwelling shape the maintenance g function and the downward conversion k function, as well as the $dC / d\bar{A}$ term in (3.15).

24 Any intermediate microeconomics text will contain a full description of these effects.

25 If Y^* extra disposable income is available during the period, points J, K, F will shift horizontally to the right by an amount Y^* / P_Z.

26 For example, the homeowner may perceive a constant neighborhood quality, but because of growing attractiveness of the larger metropolitan area, real property values in the neighborhood may be rising nevertheless.

27 For a fuller description of these dynamics, see Public Affairs Counseling (1975), and Grigsby et al. (1987). Downs (1981, 61) has discussed these phenomena in terms of neighborhood linkages that establish spillover or external effects linking the quality of life for one household to behavior of others living nearby.

4 Data Base and Sampling Methodology

1 Detailed data on Wooster were obtained in a housing study conducted by Garry W. Hesser and George C. Galster in 1975. Hereinafter cited as "Wooster Housing Study."

2 Recall that these 1975 median values represent those extant just as property values began to inflate dramatically nationwide.

3 Data on Minneapolis were obtained in a housing study conducted by Garry W. Hesser in 1980. Hereinafter cited as "Minneapolis Housing Study."

4 In 1980 only seven census tracts (of 127) in the city had a majority of black households, and these were scattered around the northwest, west, and southwest sectors of the city. Indeed, it is probably inappropriate to generalize from either sample about the racial aspects of housing markets in more typical cities.

5 Major sections of two books on interviewing were incorporated into this manual: Raymond L. Gordon (1975), and Survey Research Center (1969).

6 "Wooster Housing Study" and "Minneapolis Housing Study" questionnaires are available from the author.

7 The Census Bureau's standard definition of "housing unit" is used for this study: "a house, an apartment, a group of rooms, or a single room occupied or intended for occupancy as separate living quarters," i.e., those in which the occupants do not live and eat with any other persons in the structure and which quarters have either: (1) a direct outside entrance(s); or (2) private and complete kitchen facilities. See U.S. Bureau of Census (1972).

8 Systematic selection is characterized as "a method of selecting units from a list through the application of a selection interval, I, so that every Ith unit on the list, following a random start, is included in the sample. The interval, I, is readily determined by dividing the population size (N) by the desired sample size (n). The result is the inverse of the sampling fraction, f. $I = N / n = 1 / f$ (Warwick and Lininger 1975, 101; cf. Babbie 1973, 92 ff.).

9 Unequal probabilities of selection (UPS) is commonly used in area sampling. For example, the "first stage of primary sampling units (PSUs) are often defined by natural or administrative units such as blocks, political subdivisions, or segments marked out on maps and sketches. Such units will usually show marked differences in the number of elements within their boundaries. Rather than forcing the formation of sampling units with approximately equal numbers of elements, the researcher can control for size differences by adjusting the selection probabilities to each unit's size" (Warwick and Lininger 1975, 104).

10 In Minneapolis, cluster sampling facilitated a more efficient and feasible research strategy.

11 A map delineating the twenty-six Wooster study areas is available from the author.

12 The process involves the selection of a sample "in two or more successive, contingent stages. The first stage consists of two fundamental operations: dividing the target popu-

lation into many large groups or clusters of elements (primary sampling units—PSUs), and then using chance procedures to select a large number of these to represent the entire set. The first stage is intentionally designed so that the selected PSUs, such as city blocks or counties, will contain more elements than are needed for the final sample. The second (or final) stage involves subsampling within the selected PSUs to draw the sample of elements, such as individuals or dwelling units" (Warwick and Lininger 1975, 108; cf. Babbie, 1973, 96–102).

13 The use of blocks further satisfies the critical need for clear and unambiguous definition of the PSUs, i.e., clear boundaries and delineated PSUs.

14 The list of all such blocks was compiled. The initial starting point was selected using a table of random numbers, with every sixty-fifth block chosen starting with the thirty-third on the list. A map showing this and other neighborhood groupings is available from the author.

15 Starting with the randomly selected eleventh block, every twenty-fifth block was selected.

16 Starting with the randomly selected thirty-ninth block, every seventy-ninth block was selected.

17 In general, sampling statisticians recommend the selection of a relatively large number of PSUs in the initial stage. Warwick and Lininger (1975, 108) suggest that this liability can be minimized. "In cases where the possible number of PSUs ranges from several hundred to a thousand or more, it is often advisable to select from 50 to 100 PSUs to keep sampling error within reasonable bounds." Also see Babbie (1973, 98), who stresses the number of clusters and the homogeneity represented by the residents of a single block, thus decreasing sampling error.

18 "The success of a probability sample depends on the observance of predetermined rules for the last stage of sampling, the selection of respondents. Only rarely will sampling requirements be met by interviewing whomever happens to appear at the door. Usually the target population is defined as a specific set of individuals living within the dwelling units, such as heads of household, all women fifteen to forty-nine years of age, employed males, or female registered voters. The instructions to the interviewers should specify exactly who is to be interviewed and how they are to be chosen. A brief filter interview is often used to identify the habitual residents in the selected dwellings. It is worth emphasizing that all of the elaborate work of preparing a multistage sample can come to naught if proper procedures are not followed in selecting respondents. Interviewers should have extensive training and practice before being assigned to this task" (Warwick and Lininger 1975, 109; Babbie 1973, 98–99).

5 Characteristics of Sampled Owners, Dwellings, Neighborhoods, and Policies

1 Many researchers have employed a third aspect of status: occupational rank. In trial estimations here its use did not contribute significantly to the model, so for simplicity it is not considered.

2 It also would have been desirable to subtract other financial commitments such as insurance, property taxes, and other debt service, but these data were unavailable from the surveys.

3 Frequency distributions and other descriptive statistics for these and all other variables in both samples are available from the author.

4 There were insufficient subsample sizes to permit further separation between not married male homeowners and multiple, unrelated adult homeowners.

5 Enclosed garage could be for one or more cars, but the variable excludes covered carports.

6 Any system that effectively air-conditioned the majority of rooms in the dwelling is included.

7 Alternative exterior construction to WOOD includes: brick, asbestos shingle, masonry block, stone or stone veneer, aluminum or vinyl siding. All the latter are considered the reference category.

8 Basement and attic rooms are counted only if they are finished.

9 A full bathroom is defined as having a flush toilet, and bathtub or shower, and a washbasin with piped water. A half-bathroom has at least a flush toilet, and either a bathtub or shower, or washbasin.

10 Yard frontage was paced off and estimated by interviewer. Admittedly a superior measure of yard area would have been street frontage multiplied by yard depth. But gathering the latter data might have implied an invasion of homeowner privacy.

11 Assessed by interviewer. So few dwellings in the samples had multiple exterior defects that an index specifying number of defects was not employed. The most common defect observed was peeling paint.

12 Assessed by respondent owner-occupants. To obtain the DILAP and AVEVALUE variables for Wooster planning areas the individual interview responses in each area were simply averaged. Because a 15 percent random sample was taken in each planning area, both conditions of renter- and owner-occupied dwellings are measured by DILAP. Similarly, households of both tenures are considered in the DENSITY variable.

13 As in the Wooster case, the sample itself provided data for measuring DILAP, except that here only owner-occupied dwellings' conditions are assessed.

14 From U.S. Bureau of Census (1983); and estimated from unpublished Minneapolis City Planning Department data, respectively.

15 As in the case of aforementioned physical-neighborhood variables, the demographic variables for planning areas in Wooster and block faces in Minneapolis were aggregations based on the surveys described in chapter 4. In Wooster these demographic variables refer to the population as a whole; in Minneapolis only to owner-occupants.

16 From U.S. Bureau of Census (1983).

17 The 1978 national HUD survey asked a question (HUD 1978, item 8) similar to ACTIVITY:

People in this neighborhood	Total	Large cities	Small city (not suburb)	Owners
Keep to themselves	57.0%	69.1%	45.3%	53.5%
Get together quite a bit	27.5	17.9	34.8	29.9
Both	11.6	9.8	14.5	13.0

The proportions of neighbors who "keep to themselves" or "stress private activities (somewhat)" are comparable in Wooster and Minneapolis to the national sample.

18 The summary statistics and factor loadings produced after varimax rotation are available from the author. The technique of varimax rotation produces factors that try to maximize the loading of a given variable on one factor. This aids the heuristic interpretability of the resulting factor.

19 Recall that the original Wooster sample consisted of both renters and owners, and this full sample was used as the basis for estimating the aggregate physical and demographic aspects of Wooster neighborhoods. But because the subsequent regression analyses in

both Wooster and Minneapolis are concerned with homeowners only, all factor analyses of Wooster neighborhood variables are concerned only with homeowners.

20 As with other block-level variables in Minneapolis, TENURE measures characteristics of homeowners only.

21 The loadings on the varimax rotated factors are available from the author.

22 The procedure follows the suggestion of Smith (1975), who argues that cohesion should involve conceptually aspects of both interaction and identification. He also provides a full discussion of existing work on the topic of neighborhood cohesion.

23 The only relevant activity occurring in Wooster prior to this period was undertaken by the nonprofit Wooster Interfaith Housing Corporation (WIHC). Through the auspices of federal programs such as Sections 235, 236, and 8, WIHC did purchase and rehabilitate dwellings in several neighborhoods in the early 1970s, but less than a dozen dwellings were directly involved. After 1975 the City of Wooster did allocate several hundred thousand dollars of Community Development Block Grant funds to a program of loans and grants for property improvements and one of infrastructure modernization in selected neighborhoods.

24 A map delineating NSAs in Minneapolis is available from the author.

25 A complete list of all active housing programs in 1980 is available from the author.

6 Homeowners' Residential Satisfaction

1 Residential satisfaction has been used in the research and policy literature in at least four ways: (1) as a key predictor of individuals' perceptions of general quality of life, (2) as an evaluative measure for judging *ex post facto* success of housing developments, (3) as a guide for public housing policies, and (4) as an indicator of incipient residential mobility. It is especially the last aspect that will be important in this study; see chapter 8.

2 As yet there has been no empirical support for this, however. See Galster and Hesser (1981).

3 Galster and Hesser (1981) employ a similar aggregation procedure, but distinguish between qualitative and quantitative items. Speare (1974) employs a similar technique to derive an aggregate satisfaction index out of individual satisfaction items, except that individual components are not weighted equally. By comparison, Varady (1982a) employs as a measure of dwelling satisfaction the responses to a question about the home as a place to live: excellent, good, fair, poor.

4 Varady (1982a), and Ahlbrandt and Cunningham (1979) use an analogous question to measure neighborhood satisfaction: "How is your neighborhood as a place to live?" Excellent, good, fair or poor?

5 In the Minneapolis survey two questions were asked that provide a more explicit measure of overall satisfaction than those devised here. These questions asked the respondent, "How satisfied would you say you were overall with your (dwelling/neighborhood)?" Responses were coded 1 if very dissatisfied to 4 if very satisfied. Unfortunately, similar questions were not asked in the Wooster survey, so for the sake of comparability the specifications for HOUSESAT and NEIGHSAT explained in the text are used. It is interesting to note, however, that in the Minneapolis sample the two alternative measures of dwelling satisfaction are correlated at .41, and the two alternative measures of neighborhood satisfaction are correlated at .61. This gives confidence that the dependent variables employed here actually are good proxies for residential satisfaction.

6 Frequency distributions and descriptive statistics are available from the author. The poll results are shown below (HUD 1978):

Overall feelings	Total	Large city	Small city (not suburb)	Owners
About neighborhood?				
Delighted	14.4%	13.7%	14.9%	17.6%
Pleased	35.4	33.5	41.0	39.1
Mostly Satisfied	27.5	28.3	18.8	26.4
Mixed	12.8	13.9	16.2	10.9
Mostly Dissatisfied	5.2	5.7	1.2	3.4
Unhappy/Terrible	4.6	4.8	7.9	2.6
About house?				
Delighted	26.1%	18.9%	28.0%	31.5%
Pleased	38.3	36.8	37.8	40.8
Mostly Satisfied	20.7	24.6	19.2	18.7
Mixed	7.4	10.3	7.4	5.1
Mostly Dissatisfied	3.5	5.1	2.8	2.1
Unhappy/Terrible	3.8	4.2	4.8	1.8

7 If the Clark and Huff hypothesis is correct, a positive sign for the coefficient of LONGEVITY and a negative sign for that of LONGEVITY^2 would be predicted.

8 Such would imply that successively greater amounts of social interaction produce smaller (perhaps eventually negative) increments in satisfaction, as would follow from the Law of Diminishing Marginal Utility.

9 Descriptive statistics of all dwelling characteristic variables are available from the author.

10 In Wooster the highest proportion black in any given area is 16 percent; thus higher values of RACECOMPB should be associated with closer approximations to blacks' preferred racial mix. In Minneapolis, there are a handful of black observations in areas that are either two-thirds or three-quarters black. Although such observations perhaps exceed the optimal black percentage as perceived by these blacks, it is assumed that they do not confound the expected positive coefficient of RACECOMPB.

11 Descriptive statistics for all variables are available from the author.

12 HOUSESAT regressions for all strata in both samples are available from the author.

13 Algebraically this is obtained by taking the partial derivative of HOUSESAT with respect to ROOM/OCC, setting the result to the chosen value, and solving for the desired ROOM/OCC value.

14 It is also higher for the Minneapolis full sample, but this estimate is based on a (BATH/OCC)^2 coefficient that is of low statistical significance.

15 Detailed results are available from the author.

16 In spite of the cross-strata differences in the relationships between HOUSESAT and ROOMS/OCC and BATH/OCC noted above, none of the strata groupings for these characteristics prove statistically significantly different from the pattern evidenced by the entire sample.

17 Note this is true even though squared values of certain terms are included as independent variables.

18 For a more detailed discussion of the shortcomings of the linear model when using an ordinal dependent variable, see McKelvey and Zavoina (1975).

19 A more restrictive assumption is that S is a linear function of these variables over its

entire range. If this is assumed, a somewhat different PROBIT technique may be employed; see McKelvey and Zavoina (1975) and Amemiya (1981, 1513–16).

20 For an introductory discussion of PROBIT, see Pindyck and Rubinfeld (1981, ch.10).

21 For a discussion of these maximum-likelihood techniques, see Pindyck and Rubinfeld (1981, appendix 10.1). The algorithm provided by $SPSS - X$ is employed in the present analysis. Specification details are available from the author.

22 PROBIT model parameters are available from the author.

23 The application of these criteria has only one effect on the dwelling variables selected for the corroborated dwelling satisfaction model: the two strata groupings for NOHEAT are omitted due to their insignificance in PROBIT. Conversely, in the Minneapolis HOUSESAT model three variables are included due to strong results in PROBIT: EDUCATION, EARLYHOME, and LONGEVITY. In the neighborhood satisfaction model, four homeowner characteristic variables are excluded because of insufficient support from PROBIT: EDUCATION, BLACK, and INTEGRATE in Minneapolis; FEMALE in Wooster. None that were not originally significant in the linear model are included.

24 Measured at the mean HOUSESAT for each sample. The cross-sample difference in results here is probably because there are comparatively few blacks in the Wooster sample, and 81 percent of FEMALE in Wooster consist of stage 5 elderly women, who because of their life-cycle stage are prone to be more satisfied.

25 Both (ROOM/OCC)^2 and (BATH/OCC)^2 are statistically significant in the corroborated model for Minneapolis.

7 Homeowners' Expectations of Neighborhood Changes

1 Note that this variable is similar to that employed by Varady and Rose (1983) and Varady (1984a, 1984b, 1986), except that only future expectations are measured here.

2 Frequency distributions for both expectational variables for both samples are available from the author.

3 In the national *HUD Survey on the Quality of Community Life* (1978) the following responses were rated (both owners and renters): Question: In next two years will your community be:

	Response category		
	Better	Same	Worse
1. Housing Conditions Change?			
Total	29.9%	47.8%	15.3%
Large Cities	20.0%	38.7%	32.5%
Small Cities (not suburb)	39.5%	46.0%	8.8%
2. Physical Conditions Change?			
Total	23.8%	50.3%	19.4%
Large Cities	16.8%	41.9%	32.8%
Small Cities	31.4%	49.2%	12.3%
3. Social Environment Change?			
Total	14.7%	14.4%	13.9%
Large Cities	70.7%	62.5%	74.0%
Small Cities	7.6%	14.2%	5.1%

NOTE: Totals do not sum to 100% due to "unsure" responses. By contrast, the proportion of respondents foreseeing no neighborhood changes in Varady's (1984b) study is 56%.

4   Zero-order (Pearsonian) correlation coefficients; details and cross-tabulations available from author.
5   Distributions of foreseen changes were: 22 percent younger homeowners; 37 percent housing rehabilitation and new construction; 26 percent public-sector activities.
6   In this survey a more detailed annotation of expectations was recorded than in Wooster.
7   This is, of course, consistent with the findings for NONRESID in chapter 6.
8   The detailed results from those estimations (and others not shown in this chapter) are available from the author.
9   The application of the dual-significance criterion resulted in the omission of five home-owner characteristic variables in total in both expectations models, two of which were significant at the 5 percent level in the linear model. It also led to the omission of two neighborhood characteristic variables related to RACECOMP that were significant at the 5 percent level in the linear model. The four variables included by the second criterion of modest significance in the linear model abetted by strong significance in the PROBIT were: NONRESID (NEIGHEXP, Minneapolis); MARRIED (VALUEEXP, Minneapolis); FEMALE (VALUEEXP, Wooster); and IDENTIFY (VALUEEXP, Minneapolis).
10 By contrast, Varady (1984a, 1984b, 1986) finds expected racial changes to be key correlates of pessimism.
11 Because the coefficient of the noninteractive variable is not significant, the net coefficient for this interactive variable is taken to be its own coefficient solely.
12 Same as note 11.
13 Same as note 11.
14 The means for NOTQUALIFY and QUALIFY are .177 and .341, respectively. The means for GRANT? and LOAN? are .074 and .09, respectively.
15 Whether such VALUEEXP optimism remains today in a less inflationary real-estate market is questionable.

8   Homeowners' Mobility Plans

1   Affordability here takes account not only of housing prices, taxes, insurance, and household income, but also of the cost of refinancing mortgage money and closing costs.
2   This is consistent with the view of the symbolic interactionist school of sociology.
3   The earliest theoretical work on mobility (e.g., Brown and Moore 1971) assumes that an evaluation of alternative locations is not undertaken unless a household is already dissatisfied with its present context. But this is a limiting assumption. Clearly, people become aware of other residential options through myriad means of passive data acquisition, and are frequently making more or less rigorous comparisons.
4   Differences in well-being and adjustment costs must, of course, be appropriately time-discounted because they occur and recur over various periods. It is precisely this intertemporal treatment of estimated advantages that makes the inclusion of expectational beliefs necessary. Clark and Onaka (1983) supply supportive evidence in this regard.
5   Speare (1974) finds that only 37 percent of those expressing a desire to move actually did so during the following year. Duncan and Newman (1975) find that less than half of those respondents saying they "expected to move because of neighborhood or house-related reasons" moved within the next three-year period.

6   For a more detailed review of this literature, see Porell (1982b, ch.2), and Golledge (1981).

7   In some specific empirical applications of this model there are added intervening variables that measure subjective evaluations of particular features of the residential environment. These, in turn, are modeled as affecting overall measures of residential satisfaction. See, e.g., Newman and Duncan (1979), and Varady (1982a, 1983).

8   In this view there is no distinction between moving plans/desires and actual mobility.

9   Exceptions are Varady (1975), Morris (1976), Ahlbrandt and Cunningham (1979, ch.7), and Wurdock (1981). Other studies employing mobility expectations and behaviors in the same model have posited an analogous set of determinants for both, but have typically found differing sets of empirical correlates for each (see, e.g., Speare 1974; Morris, Crull, and Winter 1976). For a thorough review of both theories and empirical evidence related to actual household mobility, see Porell (1982b, ch.2).

10   Plans are typically assessed through a question like, "Do you plan to move in the next one to two years?" This is then coded as a dummy dependent variable.

11   The relationship between interior space and mobility plans appears not to be a linear one, however. See Duncan and Newman (1975).

12   See, e.g., Speare (1974, fig.1); Morris, Crull, and Winter (1976, fig.1); and Varady (1983, fig.1) for clear portrayals of their theoretical frameworks. The one exception is Newman and Duncan (1979, fig.1), but they give no theoretical justification for how/why objective features of households and context should affect mobility plans directly.

13   There are some technical differences in the way this disequilibrium is measured. Compare Hanushek and Quigley (1978) to Cronin (1978) and Weinberg, Friedman, and Mayo (1981).

14   Depending upon assumptions, either OLS, LOGIT, or PROBIT techniques are used to estimate parameters of these models.

15   Note that in this specification no implicit claim is made regarding the household's perceived need/aspiration level and equilibrium level.

16   More specifically, estimates of housing-investment activity are made that employ separate dummy variables for the mobility plan categories: (a) no plans but could move with opportunity; (b) will move in two to five years, (c) will move in six to ten years. All these variables prove to have virtually identical magnitudes and levels of statistical significance, hence their subsequent treatment as a single category.

17   The comparison is based on HUD's *Survey on the Quality of Community Life* (1978). In this national sample the percentages of respondents who "definitely or probably would move" in the next two years are: 30 percent (total), 35 percent (large cities), 28 percent (small cities, not suburbs), 21 percent (owners). See HUD (1978, 738ff.). Frequency distributions of mobility plans for both samples are available from the author.

18   Higher income homeowners may, on the other hand, place a higher implicit value on their time, hence this component of adjustment costs may be higher for them.

19   For example, the Stabilization Rehabilitation Program has a 100 percent payback if property is sold within seven years; only 50 percent if it is held seven years or more. City grants to correct code violations have no repayment if the property is held at least seven years.

20   See Pindyck and Rubinfeld (1981, 275–78). Johnston (1972: 182–86) notes that the loss of efficiency stemming from OLS is small in large samples.

21   Put differently, a linear regression line can be mathematically extrapolated beyond the 0–1 range of values for the dependent variable, even though such values have no meaning.

22 Parameter estimates of both models are available from the author.
23 Although the R^2 of this model appears at first glance to be relatively low (minimum .064 to maximum .282), one must remember that the maximum possible R^2 is considerably less than one when using dichotomous dependent variables. If one assumes, e.g., that the true possibilities of a choice being made are distributed uniformly across a given interval, then the maximum possible value for R^2 is .333. See Pindyck and Rubinfeld (1981, 301).
24 This suspicion is supported by comparative descriptive statistics of the STAGE1 groups in both samples:

Variable (means)	Wooster	Minneapolis
FEMALE	.083	.118
MARRIED	.667	.510
SINGLE/MULTI	.250	.372
EDUCATION	14.4	16.7
INCOME	$13,300	$22,100

25 NEIGHEXP considers changes in the next 1–2 years.
26 HOUSESAT is correlated with NEIGHEXP at .06 to .07 in the samples; the corresponding range for NEIGHSAT is −.01 to .07.

9 Homeowners' Housing Upkeep Behavior

1 Several other studies have investigated the correlates of landlords' housing investment behavior: Sternlieb (1966), Sternlieb and Burchell (1973), Stegman (1972), Moorhouse (1972), Peterson et al. (1973), Schafer (1977), Quinn et al. (1980) and Mayer (1981). Peterson et al. (1973, ch.4), Birch et al. (1979, ch.4), and Ahlbrandt and Cunningham (1979, ch.8) all investigate homeowners' reinvestment activities, but all use bivariate statistical methods that fail to provide simultaneous controls. For this reason they are not discussed here.
2 Cf., e.g., Winger (1973) and Mendelsohn (1977).
3 The statistical consequences are that coefficients of included variables are biased (but in an indeterminate direction) in direct relation to their correlation with excluded (omitted) variables. That these variables are important predictors of reinvestment and must be included is suggested by the findings of Ahlbrandt and Cunningham (1979, ch.8), who find that homeowners' "plans for major repairs in the next year or so" have positive bivariate correlations with their satisfaction with home and neighborhood, with the neighborhood's social fabric (perceived friendliness, frequency of interaction), perceptions of rising neighborhood property values, and expectations that government policies will improve the neighborhood.
4 For examples of the first, see Mendelsohn (1977), Struyk and Soldo (1980), Shear and Carpenter (1982), Myers (1984); of the second, see Winger (1973), Mendelsohn (1977), Chinloy (1980), Myers (1984); of the third, see Galster (1983).
5 Unfortunately, the labor time devoted by the household to such activities was not measured.
6 With an appropriate adjustment if the homeowner has resided in the current dwelling less than five years. Undoubtedly there are errors in homeowners' records and recollections concerning these expenditures, but such measurement errors are assumed to be

random. In such a case coefficients are not biased, although their standard errors and R^2 tend to be inflated.

7   Figures are available from the author. Slightly over 80 percent of homeowners in both samples reported positive maintenance expenses in the prior year; thus virtually the entire between-sample difference in frequency of positive upkeep strategies is due to higher rates of improvement activity in Minneapolis. This is not surprising, given that part of the Minneapolis sample is drawn intentionally from areas suspected to have high rehabilitation incidence.

8   The comparisons are: $530 for all owners on average in Wooster versus $382 nationwide in 1975; comparable for 1980 are Minneapolis $1,772 and nationwide $698. National data are found in U.S. Bureau of Census, *Construction Reports*, series C50 (various years).

9   Because many interviewers did not enter the dwellings, and those who did did not see similar numbers of rooms, their assessments of interior defects are judged unreliable.

10 In both samples by far the most frequent exterior problem was peeling paint.

11 Mendelsohn (1977) models the choice of own labor versus contract labor in his model of home maintenance. Unfortunately, data on CONTRACT were collected only in Minneapolis.

12 A positive correlation between age and depreciation rate has been found by Chinloy (1980).

13 Obviously, there are a wide variety of possible interactive variables that reasonably could be specified. Many others were tried, but the ones reported provided the greatest explanatory power.

14 More precisely in terms of chapter 3 and figure 3.1, a low-interest improvement loan would tend to pivot the upgrading transformation function up and to the right around point J, because it reduces the effective interest rate r as shown in equation (3.9). This, in turn, increases the probability of an upgrading strategy. Grants shift up the appropriate transformation function (not changing its slope) in figure 3.1 by increasing the financial ability to purchase upkeep inputs without any corresponding sacrifice of Z.

15 These variables obviously are highly correlated with UPKEEP?, but they are not so much a predictor of such as they are a result: everyone with positive GRANT$ or LOAN$ by definition must have UPKEEP? equal to one.

16 It is also possible to employ a TOBIT specification to a set of observations containing many points clustering at the zero value, as is the case here. Mendelsohn (1977) tests the efficacy of this TOBIT specification and concludes that the procedure employed here is more appropriate in the case of home upkeep expenditures.

17 Either the LOGIT or PROBIT transformations will produce virtually indistinguishable results in binary-choice models (Amemiya 1981, 1487). The former is chosen here because it is easier to convert parameters into more heuristically attractive magnitudes, and it renders results more easily comparable to similar studies in the literature. For an introductory discussion of the LOGIT model see Pindyck and Rubinfeld (1981, 287–300).

18 Although the results for STAGE5 are comparable to those of earlier studies, the insignificance of other life-cycle stages is distinct. Other studies indicate that these life-cycle effects may predominate only for certain types of upkeep activities. Thus the aggregate measure UPKEEP$ used here may not be appropriately sensitive in this regard. See table 9.1.

19 There is also an inexplicable positive association between INCOME and DEFECTS? in Minneapolis. It may be that the extra expenditures on upkeep are focused on internal rather than external upkeep, although why this may be the case is unclear.

20 In terms of figure 3.2, these findings suggest that in Wooster point R has only a slightly lower A value than X, but is associated with a significantly lower Z.

21 A more surprising result is that GRANT\$ and LOAN\$ are positively correlated with exterior defects, albeit at low statistical significance. Implicit causation is blurry here, and one should not interpret the results as if subsidies were causing more DEFECTS? One might normally expect those receiving public aid to be more likely to repair home defects than those not receiving aid. Unfortunately, the reference category for the above two variables can only be those not receiving aid. The result: those most likely to obtain aid are those who originally needed most desperately to repair a myriad of defects, but the subsidized investments may be insufficient to completely eliminate defects. In addition, many subsidies are earmarked for correcting code violations only, not external defects. A high correlation of these two sorts of inadequacies would explain the above results.

22 This is probably because there is much less variation in NEIGHEXP in Wooster; its standard deviation is 25 percent lower than in Minneapolis.

23 This implication does not contradict that drawn earlier for VALUEEXP. To say that those with STAYPERM place much less utility on asset dimension than those with STAY10+ is not to suggest that those in higher-value areas place so much value on this dimension that differences in VALUEEXP result in radically different upkeep strategies.

24 Recall that VALUEEXP is a five item scale in Minneapolis, three in Wooster sample.

25 The HOUSESAT range implicit in the comparison is 20 versus 0.

26 the NEIGHSAT range implicit in the comparison is 5 versus 1.

27 The calculations of expected values of upkeep expenditure proceed as follows:

(a) $E(\text{UPKEEP\$}) = P(\text{UPKEEP?}=1)(\text{UPKEEP\$}|\text{UPKEEP}=1)$
$$=(C_1 + [B_i][X_i])\,(C_2 + [D_j][X_j])$$
$$i = 1, \ldots, n_i \qquad j = 1, \ldots, n_j$$

where C is a constant and $[B]$, $[D]$ are vectors of coefficients to be estimated from regression, and $[X]$ are vectors of explanatory variables.

To find the change in (a) associated with a change in a given variable X_k, one simply takes the partial derivative of (a) with respect to X_k.

(b) $\delta E \,/\, \delta X_k = (C_1 + [B_i][X_i])D_k + (C_2 + [D_j][X_j])B_k$

But the parenthetic terms just represent particular values of UPKEEP? and UPKEEP\$, respectively. So we can arbitrarily pick the mean value for these variables for the given sample, $\overline{\text{UPKEEP?}}$ and $\overline{\text{UPKEEP\$}}$, respectively, and substitute them into (b) yielding:

(c) $\delta E \,/\, \delta X_k = (\overline{\text{UPKEEP?}})D_k + (\overline{\text{UPKEEP\$}})B_k$

Now it is often the case in the present model that some other explanatory variable in the model, X_m, is itself a linear function of X_k:

(d) $X_m = C_m + [F_l][X_k] \quad l = 1, \ldots, k, \ldots, n_m$

In this case (c) becomes:

(e) $\delta F \,/\, \delta X_k = (\overline{\text{UPKEEP?}})(D_k + F_m F_k) + (\overline{\text{UPKEEP\$}})(B_k + F_m F_k)$

28 This estimate is obtained by first calculating a reduced-form equation of DEFECTS?, wherein all intervening variables have been solved in terms of their component exogenous variables. Next, the partial derivative of this reduced form is taken with respect to the given explanatory variable.

29 This pattern does not occur for STAGE1 and lower-education homeowners, however, because for them the path by satisfaction is voided; see table 6.6.

30 This, again, is undoubtedly due to the cross-sample difference in how the TENURE index was computed.

31 That is, when IDENTIFY and NIDENTIFY are at least equal to their respective sample
    means; otherwise, COHESION1 = 0.
32 The relationship between separate measures of individual and aggregate social interac-
    tion and the incidence of exterior home defects is much smaller and less frequently
    statistically significant than those cited above for expenditures. In lower-valued areas
    of both samples, IDENTIFY and NIDENTIFY are both (indirectly) associated with a somewhat
    higher incidence of DEFECTS? through their inverse relationship with VALUEX(LOW) (see
    tables 9.6, 9.8, and 9.10). Comparing extrema, those with maximal value of IDENTIFY
    have a .04 higher incidence of DEFECTS? (in both samples) than those with the minimal
    value; the comparable figure for NIDENTIFY is .06 in Wooster and .12 in Minneapolis.
    For STAGE2, 3, and 4 homeowners in Wooster, however, NIDENTIFY is inversely related
    to DEFECTS? because it is positively associated with VALUEEXP(LOW) and negatively asso-
    ciated with NEIGHEXP.
33 Calculated from figures 9.1 and 9.2 using respective sample means of UPKEEP$ as base.
34 The only exceptions are for STAGE2 in Wooster and FEMALE in Minneapolis, which show
    some indirect relationships between upkeep behavior and NINTEGRATE in low-valued
    areas.

10   Neighborhoods, Homeowners, and Housing Upkeep: Empirical Findings

1   Mean annual expected UPKEEP$ is $530 in Wooster, $1,772 in Minneapolis. Mean
    DEFECTS? is .045 in Wooster, .151 in Minneapolis.
2   The model is cross-sectional. Nevertheless, it is reasonable to employ it in this hypo-
    thetical intertemporal illustration. For purposes of those illustrations the parameters of
    the Minneapolis model are used.
3   A regression of owner-assessed property value on characteristics of the dwelling and
    neighborhood reveals that the presence of other dwellings on the block with exterior
    defects reduces aggregate values by over $2,500 in Minneapolis, on average (see chapter
    12).
4   See table 5.2. In real-world situations it is likely that homeowners' NEIGHEXP and
    VALUEEXP are also altered endogenously. Unfortunately, the expectations model of chap-
    ter 7 is not robust enough to yield a quantitative estimate of such. This effect is therefore
    omitted from the scenarios.
5   MNINCOME is a component of BLOCKQUAL (see table 5.2).
6   Via changing DILAP and AVEVALUE in BLOCKQUAL (see table 5.2). Under the assumptions
    above, the externality effect via AVEVALUE is four times larger than that via DILAP.
7   Three percentage points of this effect is due to the direct impact of MARRIED (see table
    9.7). Here, as elsewhere when DEFECTS? is a function of the homeowner characteristic
    being changed, the externality effect contributes only 14 percent to the overall change in
    DEFECTS?.
8   The five items making up IDENTIFY are: HELPFUL, FRIENDLY, SIMILAR, COMMON, AC-
    TIVITY (see table 5.3). If each component drops by one index point, IDENTIFY drops by
    1.389 in Wooster, 1.033 in Minneapolis. For these scenarios it is also helpful to refer to
    figures 9.1 and 9.2.
9   In Wooster the effect is even larger: 9 percent.
10 Assuming the altered homeowners began at the mean IDENTIFY and all others at the
    maximum IDENTIFY.

11 In Wooster the drop would be 26 percent.

12 Succession may be accompanied by changes in tenure as well. Chapter 13 provides evidence that a shift from owner to renter occupancy can also have deleterious effects on home upkeep.

13 Surprisingly, the prevalent attitude that integration will lower property values (Schuman et al. 1985) should not lead white homeowners in integrating areas to defer upkeep. On the contrary, in lower-value neighborhoods pessimism about capital gains appears to spawn compensatory, trend-bucking behavior.

14 This study offers no support for this "white flight" scenario, however, and other empirical evidence is mixed (see Wilson 1983).

15 Empirically there has been some limited support for the hypothesis that gentrification encourages original owners to rehabilitate their properties (see Clay 1979, and De-Giovanni 1984).

16 This is especially true if renter-occupancy is replaced by owner-occupancy in the gentrification process (see chapter 12).

11 Neighborhoods, Homeowners, and Housing Upkeep: Implications for Public Policy

1 Detailed regression results available from the author. All the component variables of BLOCKQUAL and TRACTQUAL are disaggregated for this hedonic regression.

2 From the perspective of a local public official there may be other justifications that are less valid from a broader social context. These might be propping up the property-tax base in the jurisdiction or encouraging homeowners with children to move into and remain in the jurisdiction.

3 Recall that the BLOCKQUAL variable is correlated with DEFECTS?, and that BLOCKQUAL is an index made up of various aspects of the socioeconomic status of residents plus the physical environment.

4 In other contexts it has been found that public intervention even abets pessimism; see Goetze and Colton (1980).

5 This is further supported by the finding that neighborhood quality expectations are unrelated to block-face conditions.

6 Detailed comparative data on sampled cohesive and noncohesive areas are available from the author.

7 By contrast, Hunter (1974, ch.3) finds that local solidarity sentiments are directly related to residents' occupational status, and related in a U-shaped fashion with age. Neither of these claims is supported by these data.

8 This is consistent with the theoretical position (chapter 3) that a homeowner's sense of marginal well-being gained from upkeep investment is affected by his or her predictions about the neighborhood as a future place to live.

9 This is another manifestation of a threshold effect in reinvestment, the importance of which is stressed by Taub, Taylor, and Dunham (1984). Note that the mechanism for this effect is much different from the one they posit, however.

10 The goal should not be to make loans even to individuals who are poor credit risks. Indeed, foreclosed quasi-abandoned homes can be a blighting influence on neighborhoods, as experience with lax VA/FHA-financed residences attests.

11 For a fuller discussion of the former proposition, see, e.g., HUD (1978), Galster (1982), and Schuman et al. (1985); for the latter, see Yinger et al. (1979), Darden (1986), and Yinger (forthcoming).

12   For recent evidence on the persistence of these illegal barriers, see Newburger (1984) and Yinger (forthcoming).
13   E.g., Cleveland Heights and Shaker Heights in the Cleveland SMSA, Oak Park in the Chicago SMSA, and University City in the St. Louis SMSA.

12   Directly Encouraging Neighborhood Reinvestment through Public Subsidies

1   For a description and analysis of some of these programs, see Ahlbrandt and Cunningham (1979), Goetze (1979), Clay (1979), Varady (1986).
2   There have been few rigorous analyses of the comparative benefits and costs of policies for subsidizing the rehabilitation of residential properties. The cost of these subsidies is easy to quantify, but the benefits are more difficult to assess. Typically, the measure of program productivity employed has been the number of dwellings rehabilitated per unit of expenditure (HUD 1984), or the total upkeep expenditures by owners of subsidized units (Schoenberg and Rosenbaum 1980, 62). Such conventional measures fail to consider, however, the degree to which rehabilitation may have been forthcoming from private sources, even in the absence of public subsidies, and positive externalities for neighbors proximate to the rehabilitated dwellings may have been generated.
3   If the matching grant is directed toward dwelling improvements that constitute upward conversion, the slope of transformation function $G\mathcal{J}$ gets steeper. The origin at $\mathcal{J}$ also shifts to the right to reflect the cost savings provided by the grant in attaining the minimum upgrade $\bar{A}_{UC}$. Qualitatively, the analysis proceeds in an analogous fashion to that described in the text.
4   If a 100 percent grant is devoted to maintenance expenditures, the effect in figure 12.1 is to shift up F vertically by the amount of the grant, with the slope of the maintenance transformation function remaining unaltered.
5   Given the presumed diminishing returns associated with maintaining an older dwelling versus the perfectly malleable capital associated with upward conversion (see chapter 3), it is likely that $G'\mathcal{J}'$ will dominate DF. In some rare cases it might be possible for the price $P_{\bar{A}_t}$ to be high for upward conversion compared to that for positive maintenance. Here it is conceptually possible for the latter strategy to continue to dominate the former, even if the former is fully subsidized by a grant. In such a case the homeowner continues to allocate personal expenditures at E and takes the grant as a lump-sum, in-kind transfer of $\bar{A}_t$. Thus in this special case there is neither replacement or stimulation of private investment by public grants.
6   It is arbitrary that I and E fall on the same indifference curve in figure 12.2.
7   Details of these six programs are available from the author. For a description of federal home rehabilitation programs, see Chung (1973), Struyk and Soldo (1980, ch.7), HUD (1984), and Varady (1986).
8   Data were not collected on exactly which grant or loan program the homeowner participated in, or the specific terms of the subsidy. From the size of the sampled grants awarded, however, it can be deduced that most of the grants received were outright subsidies earmarked for code violation corrections, not smaller matching grants for fix and paint.
9   Econometric tests were conducted to ascertain whether there was a significant degree of simultaneity between the grants and loans variables and the dependent variables of upkeep expenditure. Such might be the case if, e.g., unusually high expenditures observed in the early part of the sample period proxied for an (unmeasured) proclivity to

rehabilitate to an exceptional degree, which, in turn, also resulted in the homeowner's aggressively applying for rehabilitation subsidies. In such a circumstance the regression error terms would not be independent and the coefficients of the subsidy variables would be biased. The test proposed by Hausman (1978) indicates, however, that the OLS specification is not inappropriate here.

10   ($2.62 × $1,260 grant) − $1,260 grant.

11   $3,611 loan + $1,246 induced private spending, where $1,246 = .345 × $3,611.

12   $65 per home × 14 homes affected = $910. The average per-parcel expenditure for both grants and loans combined was $2,400.

13   These estimates are similar to those obtained in other research. Coefficients of hedonic index studies conducted for several cities (e.g., Butler 1980, Galster 1982) suggest that inadequate plumbing and heating or exterior dilapidation can reduce a single-family home's value by at least 20 percent and 10 percent respectively.

14   Obviously, certain repairs and improvements manifest higher value-enhancement to cost ratios than others; figures assumed here are for generic averages of repairs accomplished under the auspices of the Minneapolis programs. Note that the conventional belief that idiosyncratic, personalized home improvements need not necessarily translate into equivalent increments of value is inapplicable here; only basic repairs that typically involve correcting code violations are considered.

15   To the extent that information and capital markets are not perfectly efficient, the enhanced values tend to understate the true benefits.

16   Bartik (1986) has argued that tenants' benefits in improved areas must also be included, distinct from property-value changes. Given their possible psychological ties to the area, tenants may not choose to move out even if areal quality and associated rents increase via rehabilitation beyond the optimal quantity they would choose to consume. As a result, there is a real loss in well-being for them. On the other hand, if the prerehabilitation quality of the area is below their optimum, the quality increase can raise their welfare. Bartik shows that the sign and magnitude of these effects depend on renter preferences and initial neighborhood conditions. His simulations reveal that per-tenant losses up to $35 annually and gains of over $24 annually are possible. Unfortunately, in the present model there are insufficient data to estimate this "Bartik effect," so it is assumed to be nil.

17   Technically such social costs also include the human effort involved in policy formulation and administration.

18   Perhaps, even more narrowly, those funded only by local revenues.

19   Randall (1976) finds that new construction in Scotland generated a superior benefit-cost ratio to rehabilitation subsidies.

20   The double asterisks indicate negative-cost loans that earn more interest than the discount rate—a hypothetical possibility only.

21   Such bonds are assumed to represent risk-free investment opportunities.

22   This result is ironic, because the Minneapolis deferred-loan program embodied an incentive whereby if the owner did not sell the home and hence repay the loan within seven years after receiving the subsidy, only 50 percent of the principal needed to be repaid.

23   This is also relevant when a pool of funding has previously been earmarked for housing rehabilitation, but the allocation between grants and loans has not been established.

24   In which case the value assumed for M cancels out of (12.3), whatever it was assumed to be.

25   Because direct leveraging represents such a large fraction of total benefits for grants, the assumption of smaller indirect leveraging and externality effects works to favor grants

over loans. In all calculations a public sector time horizon of twenty years and $E_L = E_G$ is assumed.

26 Or below some minimal amount below which one would not bother making a loan.

27 This principle is analogous to the situation of a price-discriminating monopolist selling in two separate markets, and is formally proven in any intermediate microeconomics text.

28 The marginal net benefit of loan function is not defined for $S_L = 0$. But at $S_L = 1$ it takes the value $B_L - 1 + \Sigma P(t) / (1 + R)^t$. At high values of S_L the function approaches $B_L - 1$ asymptotically.

29 A fuller treatment of options for aiding the elderly in home upkeep is given by Struyk and Soldo (1980, ch.8).

30 The loans and grants supported by Ahlbrandt and Brophy (1975) are applied within the context of a Neighborhood Housing Services framework.

13 Indirectly Encouraging Neighborhood Reinvestment through Expanding Homeownership

1 Grigsby (1963, 236) asserts that one-third of the cross-tenure differences in maintenance expenditures can be traced to owner-occupancy *per se*, although he presents no evidence for this claim.

2 For a more complex specification of depreciation and maintenance, see Chinloy (1980) and Margolis (1981). For simplicity, no other upkeep strategies besides maintenance are considered here.

3 In fact, poorer initial conditions at the start of a period likely lead to a greater maintenance effort during the period, as specified in (13.5).

4 Lower marginal returns to M due to inferior production possibilities in multifamily buildings will probably result in lower M for owners, *ceteris paribus*.

5 It is unlikely that such major upgrading investments would have been undertaken during the tenure of the current renter-occupants. Thus, for comparability these are excluded from both owner-occupant and absentee-owner samples.

6 It is also impossible in the present study to identify the condition of the structure one year earlier (C_{t-1}), or the price of maintenance as perceived by owners. It is assumed in the latter case that the market prices of maintenance and repair materials and contract labor are equal across tenures.

7 As a further check on these estimates a LOGIT model was specified and tested, comparable to those employed for UPKEEP? and DEFECTS? in chapter 9. The LOGIT estimates confirm the estimates reported here. Detailed results are available from the author.

8 What may superficially be perceived as an inconsistency between comparative expenditures and problem incidences can readily be understood by realizing that the likely effect of the i and g functions is to make the expenditure per condition relationship nonlinear.

9 This assumption results in all those spending less than $100 (but more than zero) presumably spending $50, and those spending greater than $100 presumably spending $540.

10 This finding conflicts with the multiple-regression results reported by Ozanne and Struyk (1976, 73–78). Finer stratifications comparable to theirs could not be undertaken here due to the small sample size for renters.

11 This is consistent with Sweeney's (1974) theoretical argument for owner-occupant maintenance superiority.
12 This methodology assumes that the occupancy characteristics of current renter-occupants does not significantly differ from those of absentee-owners. The procedure more
accurately estimates what the average tenant would do if she or he were the owner-
occupant. A comparable methodology is employed by Ozanne and Struyk (1976, 74–
77), although they find only trivial cross-tenure differences between actual and predicted values.
    It would have been desirable to employ this methodology for a wider set of household
strata. Especially interesting would have been a consideration of elderly households.
Unfortunately, inadequate subsample sizes for renter-occupants of single-family dwellings precluded such tests.
13 See Struyk (1976, 1977) and Grigsby and Rosenberg (1975, ch. 12) for more on programs
to encourage homeownership. In 1980 Minneapolis had six distinct such programs,
ranging from homesteading, to rehabilitation-subsidy buy-backs, to low-interest mortgages, to new construction in-fill subsidies.
14 Of course, the empirical results here are cross-sectional comparisons of current owners
with renters. It does not necessarily follow that in an intertemporal comparison the same
differences would be produced from converting renters to owners. If, e.g., renters rent
because they dislike upkeep responsibilities, converting them into homeowners might
not substantially enhance the observed reinvestment levels. But there is limited empirical validity to this hypothetical case. Clearly, many rent due to financial constraints.
The Wooster survey asked renters if they "would like to own a house if they could."
Thirty-nine percent responded "yes." Most of the "no" responses were elderly people.
Thus, there is reason to believe that nonelderly renters would be susceptible to public-
policy incentives, and that they would reinvest like current homeowners after they
became homeowners. These conclusions are further supported by the evidence in
Grigsby and Rosenberg (1975), especially chapter 12.
15 There is no reason to believe that improved upkeep would transpire if only single-family
dwellings had their tenure switched. Indeed, both Schafer (1977) and Mayer (1981) find
upkeep in owner-occupied multifamily dwellings to be superior to that in absentee-
owned multifamily units.

14 Conclusion

1 For clarity the physical-demographic component of neighborhood is subdivided here.
2 For a revealing demonstration of inter-neighborhood dynamic responses that employs a
computer-simulation model, see Kain and Apgar (1985).
3 Another important illustration is the public sector's unwitting role in abetting central-city
neighborhood deterioration by building expressways and extending infrastructure into
the suburban hinterland (see Downs 1981). A complementary discussion of systemic
neighborhood dynamics and the mechanisms of neighborhood decline is found in
Grigsby, Baratz, Maclennan, and Galster (1987).
4 Although this issue has not been investigated here.
5 Assuming no net change in aggregate expectations.
6 In this regard an overall antipoverty strategy is also commended as a neighborhood
reinvestment policy.

References

Advisory Committee to the U.S. Commission on Civil Rights. (1979) *Insurance Redlining: Fact Not Fiction*. Washington: USGPO.

Ahlbrandt, Roger, and Paul Brophy. (1975) *Neighborhood Revitalization*. Lexington, MA: Heath/Lexington.

Ahlbrandt, Roger, and James Cunningham. (1979) *A New Public Policy for Neighborhood Preservation*. New York: Praeger.

Amemiya, Takeshi. (1981) "Qualitative Response Models: A Survey." *Journal of Economic Literature* 19 (Dec.):1483–1536.

Appleyard, Donald. (1979) "The Environment as a Social Symbol." *Journal of the American Planning Association* 45 (Apr.):143–53.

Artle, R., and P. Varaiya. (1978) "Life Cycle Consumption and Homeownership." *Journal of Economic Theory* 18 (June):38–58.

Asmus, Karl, and Harvey Iglarsh. (1975) "Dynamic Model of Private Incentives to Housing Maintenance: Comment." *Southern Economic Journal* 42 (Oct.):326–29.

Babbie, Earl. (1973) *Survey Research Methods*. Belmont, CA: Wadsworth.

Bartik, Timothy. (1986) "Neighborhood Revitalization Effects on Tenants and the Benefit-Cost Analysis of Government Neighborhood Programs." *Journal of Urban Economics* 19 (Mar.):234–48.

Birch, David, E. Brown, R. Coleman, D. DaLomba, W. Parsons, L. Sharpe, and S. Weber. (1979) *The Behavioral Foundations of Neighborhood Change*. Washington: HUD-PDR.

Black, Harold, and Robert Schweitzer. (1980) "Discrimination in the Lending Decision: Home Improvement Loans." *Journal of Bank Research* 11 (Aut.):184–86.

Boehm, Thomas. (1981) "Tenure Choice and Expected Mobility." *Journal of Urban Economics* 10 (Nov.):375–89.

Boehm, Thomas, and Keith Ihlanfeldt. (1986) "The Improvement Expenditures of Urban Homeowners." *American Real Estate and Urban Economics Association Journal* 14 (Spr.):48–60.

Bratt, Rachel. (1983) "People and Their Neighborhoods: Attitudes and Policy Implications." In *Neighborhood Policy and Planning*, edited by Phillip Clay and Robert Hollister, pp. 133–50. Lexington, MA: Heath/Lexington.

Brown, Lawrence, and Eric Moore. (1971) "The Intra-Urban Migration Process: A Perspective." In *Internal Structure of the City*, edited by Larry Bourne, pp. 200–209. Toronto: Oxford University Press.

Brueckner, Jan. (1983) "Property Value Maximization and Public Sector Efficiency." *Journal of Urban Economics* 14 (July):1–15.

Brueggeman, William, and Richard Peiser. (1979) "Housing Choice and Relative Tenure Prices." *Journal of Financial and Quantitative Analysis* 14 (Nov.):735–51.

Brummel, Arden. (1979) "A Model of Intraurban Mobility." *Economic Geography* 55 (Oct.):338–52.

Butler, F., et al. (1969) *Moving Behavior and Residential Choice*. National Cooperative Highway Research Program Report 81. Washington: Highway Research Board, National Academy of Sciences.

Butler, Richard. (1980) "Cross-Sectional Variation in the Hedonic Relationship for Urban Housing Markets." *Journal of Regional Science* 20 (Nov.):439–53.

Campbell, Angus. (1981) *The Sense of Well-Being in America*. New York: McGraw-Hill.

Chinloy, Peter. (1980) "The Effect of Maintenance Expenditures on the Measurement of Depreciation in Housing." *Journal of Urban Economics* 8 (July):86–107.

Chow, Gregory. (1960) "Tests of Equality between Sets of Coefficients in Two Linear Regressions." *Econometrica* 28 (July):591–605.

Chung, H. C. (1973) *The Economics of Residential Rehabilitation*. New York: Praeger.

Clark, A., and Z. Rivin. (1977) *Homesteading in Urban USA*. New York: Praeger.

Clark, W., and J. Huff. (1977) "Some Empirical Tests of Duration-of-Stay Effects in Intraurban Migration." *Environment and Planning A* 9 (Dec.):1857–74.

Clark, W., and Jun Onaka. (1983) "Life-Cycle and Housing Adjustment as Explanations of Residential Mobility." *Urban Studies* 20 (Feb.):45–57.

Clay, Phillip. (1979) *Neighborhood Revitalization*. Lexington, MA: Heath/Lexington.

Courant, Paul. (1978) "Racial Prejudice in a Search Model of the Housing Market." *Journal of Urban Economics* 5 (July):329–45.

Cronin, F. O. (1978) "Intra-Urban Household Mobility: The Search Process." Washington: The Urban Institute.

Darden, Joe. (1986) "The Significance of Race and Class in Residential Segregation." *Journal of Urban Affairs* 8 (Win.):49–56.

Davis, Otto, and Andrew Whinston. (1967) "The Economics of Urban Renewal." In *Urban Renewal*, edited by James Wilson, pp. 50–67. Cambridge: MIT Press.

DeGiovanni, Frank. (1984) "An Examination of Selected Consequences of Revitalization in Six U.S. Cities." *Urban Studies* 21 (Aug.):245–59.

DeLeeuw, Frank, and Raymond Struyk. (1975) *The Web of Urban Housing*. Washington, DC: Urban Institute.

Diamond, Douglas, and George Tolley, eds. (1982) *The Economics of Urban Amenities*. New York: Academic Press.

Dildine, Larry, and Fred Massey. (1974) "Dynamic Model of Private Incentives to Housing Maintenance." *Southern Economic Journal* 40 (Apr.):40–48.

Downs, Anthony. (1973) *Opening up the Suburbs*. New Haven: Yale University Press.

——. (1981) *Neighborhoods and Urban Development*. Washington: Brookings Institution.

Duncan, Greg, and Sandra Newman. (1975) "People as Planners: The Fulfillment of Residential Mobility Expectations." In *Five Thousand American Families*, vol. 3, edited by Greg Duncan and James Morgan, pp. 279–318. Ann Arbor: Institute for Survey Research, University of Michigan.

Fishbein, Martin, and Icek Ajzen. (1975) *Belief, Attitude, Intention and Behavior*. Reading, MA: Addison-Wesley.

Foote, Nelson, Janet Abu-Lughod, Mary Foley, Louis Winnick. (1960) *Housing Choices and Housing Constraints*. New York: McGraw-Hill.

Galster, George. (1979) "Interracial Differences in Housing Preferences." *Regional Science Perspectives* 9, no. 1:1–17.

——. (1980) *Consumers' Housing Satisfaction, Improvement Priorities, and Needs*. Columbus: Ohio State University Center for Real Estate Education and Research.

——. (1981) "A Neighborhood Interaction Model of Housing Maintenance and Quality Changes by Owner Occupants." *Regional Science Perspectives* 11, no. 2:29–48.

————. (1982) "Black and White Preferences for Neighborhood Racial Composition." *American Real Estate and Urban Economics Association Journal* 10 (Spr.):39–66.

————. (1983) "Empirical Evidence on Cross-Tenure Differences in Home Maintenance and Conditions." *Land Economics* 59 (Feb.):107–13.

————. (1986) "What Is Neighborhood?: An Externality-Space Approach." *International Journal of Urban and Regional Research* 10 (June):243–61.

Galster, George, and Garry Hesser. (1981) "Residential Satisfaction: Contextual and Compositional Correlates." *Environment and Behavior* 16 (Nov.):737–58.

Galster, George, John Pitkin, and Jerome Rothenberg. (1975) "A Model of Housing Market Behavior in a Sample of SMSA's in the 1960s: An Overview." Cambridge: Harvard-MIT Joint Center for Urban Studies.

Gans, Herbert. (1967) *The Levittowners*. New York: Random House.

Ginsberg, Ralph. (1983) *Offsite Effects: Community Development Strategies Evaluation*. Philadelphia: University of Pennsylvania Press.

Goetze, Rolf. (1976). *Building Neighborhood Confidence*. Cambridge, MA: Ballinger.

————. (1979) *Understanding Neighborhood Change*. Cambridge, MA: Ballinger.

Goetze, Rolf, and Kent Colton. (1980) "The Dynamics of Neighborhood." *Journal of the American Planning Association* 46 (Spr.):184–94.

Golledge, R. G. (1981) "Misconceptions, Misinterpretations and Misrepresentations of Behavioral Approaches to Human Geography." *Environment and Planning A* 13 (Nov.): 1325–44.

Goodman, J. L. (1976) "Housing Consumption Disequilibrium and Local Residential Mobility." *Environment and Planning* 8, no. 8:855–74.

Gordon, Raymond. (1975) *Interviewing: Strategy, Techniques, and Tactics*. Homewood, IL: Dorsey Press.

Granovetter, Mark. (1978) "Threshold Models of Collective Behavior." *American Journal of Sociology* 83 (May):1420–43.

Grigsby, William. (1963) *Housing Markets and Public Policy*. Philadelphia: University of Pennsylvania Press.

Grigsby, William, and Louis Rosenberg. (1975) *Urban Housing Policy*. New York: APS Publications.

Grigsby, William, and T. C. Corl. (1983) "Declining Neighborhoods: Problem or Opportunity?" *Annals of the AAPSS* 465 (Jan.):86–97.

Grigsby, William, Morton Baratz, Duncan Maclennan, and George Galster. (1987) *The Dynamics of Neighborhood Change and Decline*. London: Pergamon.

Haggerty, Lee. (1982) "Differential Social Contact in Urban Neighborhoods." *Sociological Quarterly* 23 (Sum.):359–72.

Hallman, Howard. (1984) *Neighborhoods: Their Place in Urban Life*. Beverly Hills, CA: Sage.

Hanushek, Eric, and John Quigley. (1978) "An Explicit Model of Intra-Metropolitan Mobility." *Land Economics* 54 (Nov.):411–29.

Hausman, Jerry. (1978) "Specification Tests in Econometrics." *Econometrica* 46 (Nov.): 1251–70.

Hollister, Robert, Deborah Auger, Adrian Walter, and Timothy Pattison. (1978) *Measuring Neighborhood Confidence*. Cambridge: MIT Dept. of Urban Studies and Planning.

Housing and Urban Development, Department of, United States. (1978) *The 1978 HUD Survey on the Quality of Community Life*. Washington: HUD-PDR-350.

————. (1984) *Rehabilitating Rental Housing: The Benefits and Costs of Alternative Approaches*. Washington: USGPO.

Hunter, Albert. (1974) *Symbolic Communities*. Chicago: University of Chicago Press.

————. (1979) "The Urban Neighborhood: Its Analytical and Social Contexts." *Urban Affairs Quarterly* 14 (Mar.):267–88.

Ingram, Gregory, and Yitzhak Oron. (1977) "Production of Housing Services from Existing Dwelling Units." In *Residential Location and Urban Housing Markets*, edited by Gregory Ingram, pp. 273–314. New York: NBER.

Johnson, Michael. (1981) "A Cash Flow Model of Rational Housing Tenure Choice." *American Real Estate and Urban Economics Association Journal* 9 (Spr.):1–17.

Johnston, J. (1972) *Econometric Methods*. 2d ed. New York: McGraw-Hill.

Jones, Colin. (1979) "Housing: The Element of Choice." *Urban Studies* 16 (June):197–204.

Kain, John, and John Quigley. (1970) "Measuring the Value of Housing Quality." *Journal of the American Statistical Association* 65 (June):532–48.

Kain, John, and John Quigley. (1975) *Housing Markets and Racial Discrimination*. New York: NBER.

Kain, John, and William Apgar. (1985) *Housing and Neighborhood Dynamics*. Cambridge: Harvard University Press.

Kau, James, and Donald Keenan. (1981) "On the Theory of Interest Rates, Consumer Durables, and the Demand for Housing." *Journal of Urban Economics* 10 (Sept.):183–200.

Keller, Suzanne. (1968) *The Urban Neighborhood*. New York: Random House.

King, A. Thomas. (1980) *Discrimination in Mortgage Lending*. New York: Graduate School of Business Administration, New York University.

Krumm, Ronald. (1980) "Neighborhood Amenities: An Economic Analysis." *Journal of Urban Economics* 7 (Mar.):208–24.

Lansing, John, Robert Marans, and Robert Zehner. (1970) *Planned Residential Environments*. Ann Arbor: Institute for Survey Research, University of Michigan.

Laska, Shirley, and Daphne Spain, eds. (1980) *Back to the City*. New York: Pergamon.

Leven, Charles, James Little, Hugh Nourse, and R. Reed. (1976) *Neighborhood Change: The Dynamics of Urban Decay*. New York: Praeger.

Listokin, David, and Stephan Casey. (1980) *Mortgage Lending and Race*. New Brunswick, NJ: Center for Urban Policy Research, Rutgers University.

Little, James. (1977) "The Dynamics of Neighborhood Change." In *A Decent Home and Environment*, ed. Donald Phares, pp. 63–78. Cambridge, MA: Ballinger.

Lynch, Kevin. (1960) *The Image of the City*. Cambridge: MIT Press.

MacRae, Duncan. (1982) "Urban Housing with Discrete Structures." *Journal of Urban Economics* 11 (Mar.):131–47.

Marcuse, Peter. (1971) "Social Indicators and Housing Policy." *Urban Affairs Quarterly* 7 (Dec.):193–217.

Margolis, Stephen. (1981) "Depreciation and the Maintenance of Houses." *Land Economics* 57 (Feb.):190–211.

Mark, Jonathan, Thomas Boehm, and Charles Leven. (1979) "A Probability Model for Analyzing Interneighborhood Mobility." In *The Economics of Neighborhood*, ed. David Segal, pp. 43–56. New York: Academic Press.

Mayer, Neil. (1981) "Rehabilitation Decisions in Rental Housing." *Journal of Urban Economics* 10 (July):76–94.

McConney, Mary. (1985) "An Empirical Look at Housing Rehabilitation as a Spatial Process." *Urban Studies* 22 (Feb.):39–48.

McDonald, John. (1979) *Economic Analysis of an Urban Housing Market*. New York: Academic Press.

McGuire, Chester. (1974) "The Depreciation of Housing." Ph.D. dissertation, University of Chicago.

McKelvey, Richard, and William Zavoina. (1975) "A Statistical Model for the Analysis of Ordinal Level Dependent Variables." *Journal of Mathematical Sociology* 4:103–20.

Mendelsohn, Robert. (1977) "Empirical Evidence on Home Improvements." *Journal of Urban Economics* 4 (Oct.):459–68.

Michelson, William. (1976) *Man and His Urban Environment*. Reading, MA: Addison-Wesley.

———. (1977) *Environmental Choice, Human Behavior, and Residential Satisfaction*. New York: Oxford University Press.

Minneapolis, City of. (1980) *State of the City, 1979*. Minneapolis: Office of Mayor/Planning Department.

———. (1981) *State of the City, 1980*. Minneapolis: Office of Mayor/Planning Department.

Minneapolis Housing and Redevelopment Authority. (1980) "Status Report," Housing Resource Department, MHRA, City of Minneapolis.

Moorhouse, John. (1972) "Optimal Housing Maintenance under Rent Control." *Southern Economic Journal* 39 (July):93–106.

Morris, Earl. (1976) *Conceptualization and Measurement of Consumer Satisfaction and Dissatisfaction*. Cambridge, MA: Marketing Science Institute.

Morris, Earl, Sue Crull, and Mary Winter. (1976) "Housing Norms, Housing Satisfaction and the Propensity to Move." *Journal of Marriage and the Family* 38 (May): 309–20.

Muth, Richard. (1969) *Cities and Housing*. Chicago: University of Chicago Press.

———. (1982) "A Numerical Model of Urban Housing Markets with Durable Structures." In *Research in Urban Economics*, vol. 2, edited by J. Vernon Henderson, pp. 91–129. Greenwich, CT: JAI Press.

Myers, Dowell. (1983) "Population Processes and Neighborhoods." In *Neighborhood Policy and Planning*, edited by Phillip Clay and Robert Hollister, pp. 113–32. Lexington, MA: Heath/Lexington.

———. (1984) "Turnover and Filtering of Postwar Single-Family Homes." *Journal of the American Planning Association* 50 (Sum.):352–58.

Newburger, Harriet. (1984) *Recent Evidence on Discrimination in Housing*. Washington: HUD/PDR.

Newman, Sandra, and Greg Duncan. (1979) "Residential Problems, Dissatisfaction and Mobility." *Journal of American Planning Association* 45 (Apr.):154–66.

Ojile, Michael. (1977) "Renewal Funds and Activity Analysis." Unpublished report, Planning Department, City of Minneapolis.

Olsen, Edgar. (1969) "A Competitive Theory of the Housing Market." *American Economic Review* 54 (Mar.):612–21.

Ozanne, Larry, and Raymond Struyk. (1976) *Housing from the Existing Stock*. Washington: Urban Institute.

Palen, J., and Bruce London. (1984) *Gentrification, Displacement, and Neighborhood Revitalization*. Albany: SUNY Press.

Peterson, George, Arthur Solomon, Hadi Madjid and William Apgar. (1973) *Property Taxes, Housing and the Cities*. Lexington, MA: Heath/Lexington.

Pindyck, Robert, and Daniel Rubinfeld. (1981) *Econometric Models and Economic Forecasts*. 2d ed. New York: McGraw-Hill.

Pines, David, and Yoram Weiss. (1976) "Land Improvement Projects and Land Values." *Journal of Urban Economics* 3 (Jan.):1–13.

Pitz, Gordon, and Scott Geller. (1976) "Revision of Opinion and Decision Times in an Information-Seeking Task." *Journal of Experimental Psychology* 83 (Mar.):400–405.

Porell, Frank. (1982a) "The Effects of Generalized Relocation Costs upon Intraurban Household Relocation." *Journal of Regional Science* 22 (Feb.):33–55.

———. (1982b) *Models of Intraurban Residential Relocation*. Boston: Kluwer-Nijhoff.

Public Affairs Counseling. (1975) *The Dynamics of Neighborhood Change.* San Francisco and Washington: PAC/HUD-PDR-108.

Quigley, John. (1979) "What Have We Learned about Urban Housing Markets?" In *Current Issues in Urban Economics,* edited by Peter Mieszkowski and Mahlon Straszheim, pp. 391–429. Baltimore: Johns Hopkins University Press.

Quigley, John, and Daniel Weinberg. (1977) "Intra-Urban Residential Mobility: A Review and Synthesis." *International Regional Science Review* 2 (Fall):41–66.

Quinn, Michael, Donald Elliott, Robert Mendelson, and Jeffrey Thomen. (1980) "Maintenance Effort and the Professional Landlord." *American Real Estate and Urban Economics Association Journal* 8 (Win.):345–69.

Rafter, David. (1985) "Implementing Housing Rehabilitation Programs." *Journal of Urban Affairs* 7 (Spr.):47–64.

Randall, J. N. (1976) "The Costs and Benefits of Improving Older Houses." *Urban Studies* 13 (Oct.):345–48.

Rapoport, A., and A. Chammah. (1965) *The Prisoner's Dilemma.* Ann Arbor: University of Michigan Press.

Roistacher, Elizabeth. (1974) "Residential Mobility." In *Five Thousand American Families,* vol. 2, edited by James Morgan, pp. 41–78. Ann Arbor: Institute for Survey Research, University of Michigan.

———. (1975) "Residential Mobility: Planners, Movers and Multiple Movers." In *Five Thousand American Families,* vol. 3, ed. Greg Duncan and James Morgan, pp. 259–78. Ann Arbor: Institute for Survey Research, University of Michigan.

Rothenberg, Jerome. (1967) *An Economic Evaluation of Urban Renewal.* Washington: Brookings Institution.

———. (1981) "Housing Investment, Housing Consumption and Tenure Choice." Paper presented at Urban Economics Conference, University of California at Santa Cruz (Oct.).

Ryker, Randy, Louis Pol, and Rebecca Guy. (1984) "Racial Discrimination as a Determinant of Home Improvement Loans." *Urban Studies* 21 (May):177–82.

Schafer, Robert. (1977) *Maintenance and Operating Behavior of Resident and Absentee Landlords.* Department of City Planning Discussion Paper DD77-10. Cambridge: Harvard University Press.

Schafer, Robert, and Helen Ladd. (1980) *Equal Credit Opportunity in Mortgage Lending.* Cambridge: MIT-Harvard Joint Center for Urban Studies.

Schoenberg, Sandra, and Patricia Rosenbaum. (1980) *Neighborhoods that Work.* New Brunswick, NJ: Rutgers University Press.

Schuman, Howard, Charlotte Steeh, and Lawrence Bobo. (1985) *Racial Attitudes in America.* Cambridge: Harvard University Press.

Seek, N. H. (1983) "Adjusting Housing Consumption: Improve or Move?" *Urban Studies* 20 (Nov.):455–69.

Segal, David, ed. (1979) *The Economics of Neighborhood.* New York: Academic Press.

Segal, David. (1980) "A Model to Forecast Neighborhood Change: The Example of New York City." Paper presented at Eastern Economics Association Meetings, Montreal (May).

Shear, William. (1983) "Urban Housing Rehabilitation and Move Decisions." *Southern Economic Journal* 49 (Apr.):1030–52.

Shear, William and Bruce Carpenter. (1982) *Housing Rehabilitation, Move Decisions and Neighborhood Change.* Washington: HUD-PDR-2604.

Smith, Richard. (1975) "Measuring Neighborhood Cohesion." *Human Ecology* 3, no. 3:143–60.

Smith, Wallace. (1970) *Housing: The Social and Economic Elements*. Berkeley: University of California Press.

Speare, Alden. (1970) "Homeownership, Life-Cycle Stage, and Residential Mobility." *Demography* 7 (Nov.):449–58.

———. (1974) "Residential Satisfaction as an Intervening Variable in Residential Mobility." *Demography* 11 (May):1973–88.

Speare, Alden, Sidney Goldstein, and William Frey. (1974) *Residential Mobility, Migration and Metropolitan Change*. Cambridge, MA: Ballinger.

Stegman, Michael. (1972) *Housing Investment in the Inner City: The Dynamics of Decay*. Cambridge, MA: MIT Press.

Sternlieb, George. (1966) *The Tenement Landlord*. New Brunswick, NJ: Rutgers University Press.

Sternlieb, George, and Robert Burchell. (1973) *Residential Abandonment*. New Brunswick, NJ: Rutgers University Press.

Stewart, James, and Thomas Hyclak. (1986) "Determinants of Household Expenditures for Additions, Alterations, Replacements, and Repairs to Owner-Occupied Residences." Unpublished paper, Department of Economics, Pennsylvania State University.

Strickland, Donald, and Dennis Judd. (1982) "Capital Investment in Neighborhoods: Theories which Inform National Urban Policy in the U.S." *Population Research and Policy Review* 1 (Jan.):59–78.

Struyk, Raymond. (1976) *Homeownership: The Economic Determinants*. Lexington, MA: Heath/Lexington.

———. (1977) *Should Government Encourage Homeownership?* Washington: Urban Institute.

Struyk, Raymond, and Beth Soldo. (1980) *Improving the Elderly's Housing*. Cambridge, MA: Ballinger.

Survey Research Center. (1969) *Interviewers' Manual*. Ann Arbor: Institute for Survey Research, University of Michigan.

Suttles, Gerald. (1972) *The Social Construction of Communities*. Chicago: University of Chicago Press.

Sweeney, James. (1974) "Housing Unit Maintenance and the Mode of Tenure." *Journal of Economic Theory* 8 (July):111–38.

Taggart, Robert. (1970) *Low Income Housing: A Critique of Federal Aid*. Baltimore: Johns Hopkins University Press.

Taub, Richard, D. Garth Taylor, and Jan Dunham. (1984) *Paths of Neighborhood Change*. Chicago: University of Chicago Press.

United States Bureau of the Census. (1972) *1970 Census of Population and Housing*. Washington: USGPO-PHC (2).

———. (1983) *1980 Census of Population and Housing; Census Tracts: Minneapolis*. Washington: USGPO.

Urban-Suburban Investment Group. (1977) *Redlining and Disinvestment as a Discriminatory Practice in Residential Mortgage Loans*. Chicago: University of Illinois at Chicago Circle, Center for Urban Studies.

Vandell, Kerry. (1981) "The Effects of Racial Composition on Neighborhood Succession." *Urban Studies* 18 (Oct.):315–33.

Varady, David. (1975) "Determinants of Mobility in an Inner City Community." *Regional Science Perspectives* 5:154–78.

———. (1982a) "Housing Satisfaction as an Intervening Variable in Explaining Residential Mobility Decisions." Paper presented at Regional Science Association Meetings, Pittsburgh (Nov.).

———. (1982b) "Indirect Benefits of Subsidized Housing Programs." *Journal of the American Planning Association* 48 (Aut.):432–40.

———. (1983) "Determinants of Residential Mobility Decisions." *Journal of the American Planning Association* 49 (Spr.):184–99.

———. (1984a) "Residential Mobility in the Urban Homesteading Demonstration Neighborhoods." *Journal of the American Planning Association* 50 (Sum.):346–51.

———. (1984b) "Neighborhood Confidence and Incumbent Upgrading." Paper presented at Association of Collegiate Schools of Planning Meetings, New York (Nov.).

———. (1986) *Neighborhood Upgrading: A Realistic Assessment.* Albany: SUNY Press.

Varady, David, and Sheila Rose. (1983) "Dynamics of Neighborhood Attitudinal Change." Paper presented at Urban Affairs Association Meetings, Flint, MI (Mar.).

Vaskowics, Laszlo, and Peter Franz. (1984) "Residential Areal Bonds in the Cities of West Germany." In *The Residential Areal Bond,* edited by P. Peachy, E. Bodzenta, and W. Mirowski, pp. 148–77. New York: Irvington Publishers.

Warren, Roland. (1978) *The Community in America.* Chicago: Rand McNally.

Warwick, Donald, and Charles Lininger. (1975) *The Sample Survey: Theory and Practice.* New York: McGraw-Hill.

Webber, Michael, Richard Symanski, and James Root. (1975) "Toward a Cognitive Spatial Theory." *Economic Geography* 51 (Apr.):100–116.

Weicher, John, and Thomas Thibodeau. (forthcoming) "Filtering and Housing Markets: An Empirical Analysis." *Journal of Urban Economics.*

Weinberg, Daniel, and Reilly Atkinson. (1979) "Place Attachment and the Decision to Search for Housing." *Growth and Change* 10 (Apr.):22–29.

Weinberg, Daniel, Joseph Friedman, and Steven Mayo. (1981) "Intraurban Residential Mobility: The Role of Transaction Costs, Market Imperfections and Household Disequilibrium." *Journal of Urban Economics* 9 (May):332–48.

Weisbrod, Glen, and Avis Vidal. (1981) "Housing Search Barriers for Low Income Renters." *Urban Affairs Quarterly* 16 (June):465–82.

Wheaton, William. (1977) "A Bid-Rent Approach to Housing Demand." *Journal of Urban Economics* 4 (Apr.):200–217.

Wilson, Thomas. (1983) "White Response to Neighborhood Racial Change." *Sociological Focus* 16 (Oct.):305–18.

Winger, Alan. (1973) "Some Internal Determinants of Upkeep Spending by Urban Homeowners." *Land Economics* 49 (Nov.):474–79.

Wurdock, Clarence. (1981) "Neighborhood Racial Transition." *Urban Affairs Quarterly* 17 (Sept.):75–89.

Yinger, John. (forthcoming) "The Racial Dimension of Urban Housing Markets in the 1980s." In *Changing Patterns of Racial Segregation in the 1980s,* ed. Gary Tobin. Beverly Hills, CA: Sage.

Yinger, John, George Galster, Barton Smith, and Fred Eggers. (1979) "The Status of Research into Racial Discrimination and Segregation in American Housing Markets." *HUD Occasional Papers* 6 (Dec.):55–175.

Zonn, Leo. (1979) "Housing and Urban Blacks: A Social Distance-Residential Distance View." *Annals of Regional Science* 13 (Mar.):55–65.

Zonn, Leo. (1980) "Information Flows in Black Residential Search Behavior." *Professional Geographer* 32 (Feb.):43–50.

Glossary of Names and Definitions of Variables

Homeowner Characteristics

EDUCATION   Years of educational attainment. Higher of household head or spouse or highest of multiple-headed household. Code: 7 if grade school; 10 if some high school; 11 if vocational training but no high school diploma; 12 if high school diploma; 13 if associate degree or post–high school vocational-technical training; 14 if some college but no degree; 16 if undergraduate college degree; 19 if graduate training

INCOME   Total $ income of all household members from all sources in year prior to survey, minus annual $ mortgage payments, multiplied by "transitory effect" adjustment factor. Adjustment factor depends on respondent's assessment of how previous year's income compared with normal household income over last five years. Code: 1.2 if "much lower than normal"; 1.1 if "somewhat lower than normal"; 1.0 if "about the same as normal"; .9 if "somewhat higher than normal"; .8 if "much higher than normal"

MARRIED   1 if married male–headed household; zero otherwise

FEMALE   1 if unmarried (single, widowed, divorced) female–headed household; zero otherwise

MULTI   1 if multiple-headed household or single male–headed household; zero otherwise

OCCUPANTS   Number of year-round residents occupying the dwelling, of all ages and regardless of relationship to household head

BLACK   1 if head of household is black; zero otherwise

STAGE1   1 if household in first stage of life cycle (head under age 45, no children in home); zero otherwise

STAGE2   1 if household in second stage of life cycle (head any age, youngest child in home under age 5); zero otherwise

STAGE3   1 if household in third stage of life cycle (head any age, youngest child in home aged 5–14); zero otherwise

STAGE4   1 if household in fourth stage of life cycle (head any age, youngest child in home over age 14); zero otherwise

STAGE5   1 if household in fifth stage of life cycle (head over age 45, no children at home)

NUMMOVES   Number of moves the household has made during the last five years

PRIORHOME   1 if previous home occupied by household was single-family detached dwelling; zero otherwise

EARLYHOME   1 if home in which respondent grew up was single-family detached dwelling; zero otherwise

LONGEVITY   Number of years household has lived in current dwelling

Dwelling Characteristics

BUILT60–69   1 if dwelling built 1960–69; zero otherwise
BUILT40–59   1 if dwelling built 1940–59; zero otherwise
BUILT20–39   1 if dwelling built 1920–39; zero otherwise
BUILTPRE-20   1 if dwelling built before 1920; zero otherwise
GARAGE   1 if dwelling has enclosed parking for one vehicle or more (either attached or unattached to house); zero otherwise
AIRCOND   1 if dwelling has air-conditioning for majority of rooms; zero otherwise
WOOD   1 if dominant exterior construction of dwelling is wood clapboard siding, zero otherwise
NOHEAT   1 if dwelling has no central heating, zero otherwise
ROOMS   Number of finished rooms in the dwelling, including any in basement or attic but excluding bathrooms
BATHRMS   Number of bathrooms in dwelling, including fractional. Code: 1 if full bathroom (must have flush toilet and bathtub or shower and sink with piped water); .5 if half-bath (must have flush toilet and either tub, shower, or sink)
YARD   Street frontage of lot on which dwelling located, in feet
ROOM/OCC   Number of rooms divided by number of occupants in dwelling
BATH/OCC   Number of bathrooms divided by number of occupants in dwelling
YARD/OCC   Lot front footage divided by number of occupants in dwelling

Physical Neighborhood Characteristics

DILAP   Percentage of dwellings having one or more of following exterior defects, as assessed by interviewer: broken or boarded-up windows; badly peeling paint; broken steps, railings or siding; sagging or holed roof with many missing shingles; sagging, settling or cracked foundation. Wooster: all dwellings in planning area; Minneapolis: owner-occupied dwellings on block face
AVEVALUE   Mean owner-assessed property value of owner-occupied dwellings. Wooster: planning area; Minneapolis: block face
AVEV   Mean property value of specified owner-occupied dwellings as defined by U.S. census. Minneapolis only: census tract
NONRESID   1 if interviewer assessed that nonresidential land uses present on block face; zero otherwise. Both Wooster and Minneapolis
DENSITY   Households per acre of residential land. Wooster only: planning area
COMHSHLD   Proportion of census tract devoted to commercial land uses. Minneapolis tracts only

Demographic Neighborhood Characteristics

PERBLACK   Percentage of black households. Wooster: all households in planning area; Minneapolis: owner-occupants on block face
PBLACK   Percentage of black households. Minneapolis only: all households in census tract
PEROWNER   Percentage of dwellings that are owner-occupied. Wooster only: planning area

POWNER   Percentage of dwellings specified owner-occupied. Minneapolis only: census tract

STABLE   Percentage of households living in current dwelling 10 or more years. Wooster: all households in planning area; Minneapolis: owner-occupants on block face

PERSTA   Percentage of households living in current dwelling 10 or more years. Minneapolis only: all households in census tract

MNINCOME   Mean income of households. Wooster: all households in planning area, 1974; Minneapolis: owner-occupants on block face, 1979

AVEINC   Mean income of households. Minneapolis only: all households in census tract, 1979

Social-Interactive Neighborhood Characteristics

KNOWNAME   Number of adults in half-dozen nearest households known by name by respondent: 4 if all; 3 if nearly all; 2 if half; 1 if just a few; 0 if none

CHATWITH   Respondent's frequency of talking with half-dozen nearest neighbors. Code: Wooster: 6 if every day; 5 if several times weekly; 4 if once a week; 3 if 2–3 times monthly; 2 if once a month; 1 if few times a year, rarely; 0 if never. Minneapolis: 7 if nearly every day; 6 if six times weekly; 5 if five times weekly; 4 if four times weekly; 3 if three times weekly; 2 if twice weekly; 1 if once a week; .25 if once a month; 0 if never

BILLINFO   Would respondent be willing to give out any information if a bill collector came around asking about a neighbor? Code: 4 if definitely would; 3 if probably would; 2 if probably would not; 1 if definitely would not

FRIENDLY   Respondent's description of neighborhood friendliness on five-point scale: 1 if unfriendly people . . . 5 if friendly people

HELPFUL   Respondent's description of neighborhood helpfulness on five-point scale: 1 if unhelpful neighbors . . . 5 if helpful neighbors

SIMILAR   Respondent's description of neighborhood similarity on five-point scale: 1 if people different from me . . . 5 if people stress activities with neighbors

COMMON   Respondent's description of neighborhood commonality on five-point scale: 1 if people have nothing in common . . . 5 if people have much in common

Indexes of Social-Interactive Dimension of Neighborhood

IDENTIFY   Index measuring the degree of homeowner identification with respondent-defined neighbors; see table 5.3 for details

INTEGRATE   Index measuring the degree of homeowner integration with respondent-defined neighbors; see table 5.3 for details

NIDENTIFY   Mean of IDENTIFY for neighborhood. Planning area in Wooster; block face in Minneapolis

NINTEGRATE   Mean of INTEGRATE for neighborhood. Planning area in Wooster; block face in Minneapolis

COHESION1   IDENTIFY × NIDENTIFY only if both terms are greater than the respective mean value for the sample; zero otherwise

COHESION2   INTEGRATE × NINTEGRATE only if both terms are greater than the respective mean value for the sample; zero otherwise

Public Policy Variables (*Minneapolis sample only*)

GRANT$ Annual average dollar value of public grants received by homeowner for property maintenance, repairs, or improvements during the past five years, if any (or for however long LONGEVITY, if less than five years)

LOAN$ Annual average dollar value of low-interest loans received by homeowners for property maintenance, repairs, or improvements during the past five years, if any (or for however long LONGEVITY, if less than five years)

QUALIFY 1 if homeowner lives in area officially designated as qualifying for CDBG and/or Urban Renewal, but such funds have not been allocated to area yet; zero otherwise

NOTQUALIFY 1 if homeowner lives in area that does not qualify for CDBG or Urban Renewal; zero otherwise

GRANT? 1 if any public grants received by homeowner for property maintenance, repairs, or improvements during past five years; zero otherwise

LOAN? 1 if any low-interest loans received by homeowner for property maintenance repairs or improvements during past five years; zero otherwise

Indexes of Physical-Demographic Dimension of Neighborhood

TENURE Index measuring the stability of tenure of neighborhood: % owner-occupants and those living in dwelling 10+ years in Wooster planning area; % living in dwelling 10+ years in Minneapolis block face; see table 5.2

AREAQUAL Index of "quality" of structures and residents in Wooster planning area; see table 5.2 for details

TRACTQUAL Index of "quality" of structures and residents in Minneapolis census tract; see table 5.2 for details

BLOCKQUAL Index of "quality" of structures and residents in Minneapolis block face; see table 5.2 for details

RACECOMP Index measuring the racial composition of neighborhood: % black households in Wooster; index of % of black households in tract and % of black homeowners on block face in Minneapolis; see table 5.2

RACECOMPB Index taking value of RACECOMP if respondent black; zero otherwise

RACECOMPW Index taking value of RACECOMP if respondent white; zero otherwise

Homeowner's Subjective Evaluations and Expectations

HOUSESAT Degree of satisfaction with dwelling. Code: 1 if very dissatisfied; 2 if dissatisfied; 3 if satisfied; 4 if very satisfied

NEIGHSAT Degree of satisfaction with neighborhood. Code: 1 if very dissatisfied; 2 if dissatisfied; 3 if satisfied; 4 if very satisfied

NEIGHEXP Index of expectations about neighborhood changes in next 1–2 years. Code: 1 if good changes; 2 if no changes, or good and bad cancel out; 3 if bad changes foreseen

VALUEEXP Index of expectations about neighborhood property value changes in next five years. Code: 1 if rise a great deal; 2 if rise somewhat; 3 if stay about same; 4 if fall somewhat; 5 if fall a great deal. In Wooster, categories 1 and 2 and categories 4 and 5 are combined.

NEIGHX(LOW) NEIGHEXP × (1 if area is of low quality; 0 if otherwise). "Area" in Wooster defined as planning area; in Minneapolis as block. "Low quality" defined as one standard deviation or more below mean property value of sample.

VALUEX(LOW) VALUEEXP × (1 if area is of low quality; 0 if otherwise). "Area" in Wooster defined as planning area; in Minneapolis as block. "Low quality" defined as one standard deviation or more below mean property value of sample.

ALIENATED Index of alienation, scaled from minimum of 4 to maximum of 16; composite of responses to four items: (a) "You sometimes can't help wondering whether anything is worthwhile anymore." (b) "It's hardly fair to bring a child into the world with the way things look for the future." (c) "Most public officials are not really interested in the problems of the average person." (d) "Most people don't really care what happens to the next person." Code for responses to each item: 1 if strongly disagree; 2 if disagree; 3 if agree; 4 if strongly agree

Homeowner's Mobility Plans

STAY0–2 1 if plans to stay in neighborhood 2 years or less; zero otherwise

STAY3–10 1 if plans to stay in neighborhood 3–10 years; zero otherwise

STAY10+ 1 if plans to stay in neighborhood 10 or more years; zero otherwise

STAYPERM 1 if plans to stay in neighborhood permanently or until death; zero otherwise

Homeowner's Housing Upkeep Investments

UPKEEP? 1 if homeowner made expenditures on home and yard maintenance or repairs during previous year, and/or if homeowner made improvements or additions to dwelling or replacements of plumbing, heating or electrical systems during previous five years; zero otherwise

UPKEEP$ Expenditures on interior and exterior painting or wall papering, yard or drive maintenance, interior and exterior normal repairs, repairs (not replacement) of plumbing or heating equipment during previous year, plus prorated annual expenditures on replacement (not repair) of plumbing, heating, or electrical equipment, interior remodeling, structural additions, improvements or additions to mechanical systems, insulation, roof, etc. Prorate is to divide by 5 if LONGEVITY equals more than 5, or divide by LONGEVITY otherwise

DEFECTS? 1 if interviewer assesses dwelling as having one or more residential defects: broken or boarded-up windows; trash or litter on premises; badly peeling exterior paint; broken steps, railing, or siding; sagging or missing shingles on roof; sagging or cracked foundation. Zero otherwise

Other Adjustments

CONTRACT 1 if homeowner hired worker(s) to perform upkeep activities; zero otherwise. Minneapolis only

Index